Spreadsheet Implementation Technology

Peter Sestoft

Spreadsheet Implementation Technology

Basics and Extensions

The MIT Press
Cambridge, Massachusetts
London, England

MIT Press books may be purchased at special quantity discounts for business or sales promotional use. For information, please email special_sales@mitpress.mit.edu.

This book was set in New Century Schoolbook by the author using LaTeX.

Printed and bound in the United States of America.

Library of Congress Cataloging-in-Publication Data

Sestoft, Peter.
Spreadsheet implementation technology : basics and extensions / Peter Sestoft.
    p.   cm.
Includes bibliographic references and index.
ISBN 978-0-262-52664-7 (pbk. : alk. paper)
1. Electronic spreadsheets—Computer programs. 2. Functional programming (Computer science) 3. Object-oriented methods.   I. Title.
HF5548.2.S43724   2014
005.54—dc23
2014006940

10 9 8 7 6 5 4 3 2 1

Contents

Preface

Spreadsheet programs are used daily by millions of people for tasks ranging from neatly organizing a list of addresses, to analysis of biological data sets, to complex economical simulations. Spreadsheet programs are easy to learn and convenient to use because they have a clear visual data model (tables) and a simple, efficient underlying computation model (functional and side effect free). It has been estimated that by 2012 there would be at least 13 million "end-user programmers" in the United States, chiefly using spreadsheets to build non-trivial computational models [135, section 4.3].

Spreadsheet programs are usually not held in high regard by professional software developers [30]. However, their implementation involves a large number of non-trivial design considerations and space-time tradeoffs. Moreover, the basic spreadsheet model can be extended, improved, or otherwise experimented with in many ways, both to test new technology and to provide new functionality in a context that could be helpful to a very large number of users.

Yet there does not seem to be a coherently designed, reasonably efficient open source spreadsheet implementation that is a suitable platform for experiments. Existing open source spreadsheet implementations such as Gnumeric and OpenOffice Calc are rather complex, they are usually written in unmanaged languages such as C and C++, and the documentation of their internals is sparse. Spreadsheet implementations written for pedagogical reasons abound but often fail to scale to realistic problem sizes. Commercial spreadsheet implementations such as Microsoft Excel neither expose their internals through their source code nor through adequate documentation of data representations and functions.

Goals of this book The purpose of this book is to enable others to make experiments with innovative spreadsheet functionality and with new ways to implement such functionality. Therefore, we have attempted to collect in one place a considerable body of knowledge about spreadsheet implementation.

To our knowledge neither the challenges of efficient spreadsheet implementation nor possible solutions to them are systematically presented in the existing scientific literature. There are many patents on spreadsheet implementation, but they offer a very fragmented picture. Most patents do not describe design alternatives, and many also neglect to describe relevant academic work on which they are based.

This book is an attempt to provide a more coherent picture by gleaning information from experience with existing spreadsheet implementations, from our own implementation Corecalc, from the scientific literature, and from patents and patent applications. For commercial software, this necessarily involves some guesswork, but we have not resorted to any form of reverse engineering.

Moreover, we present Funcalc, which extends Corecalc with an implementation of user-defined functions, expressed solely using standard spreadsheet concepts such as cells, formulas, and references, requiring no external languages such as VBA, Python, or Java. This work is inspired by the ideas of Peyton-Jones and others [120], but here we emphasize performance because libraries of user-defined functions will not replace built-in functions in practice unless they are equally fast.

Technologically, Funcalc uses run-time code generation to obtain good performance while preserving full spreadsheet interactivity. This approach exploits the highly optimizing just-in-time compilers of modern managed software platforms while minimizing the amount of engineering and software maintenance required on our part.

Contents   The book comprises the following parts:

- Chapter 1 summarizes the spreadsheet computation model and the most important challenges for efficient recalculation. This includes a survey of scholarly works, spreadsheet implementations, and some patents.

- Chapter 2 describes Corecalc, a core implementation of essential spreadsheet functionality for making practical experiments, chapter 3 discusses alternatives to some of the design decisions made in Corecalc, and chapters 4 and 5 investigate data structures to support minimal recalculation.

- Chapter 6 introduces and motivates Funcalc, an extension of Corecalc with compiled sheet-defined functions, which permits users to define their own functions without extraneous programming languages and without any loss of efficiency compared to built-in functions. Chapters 7 through 9 describe the Funcalc implementation and possible design variations and extensions.

- Chapter 10 shows how partial evaluation, or automatic function specialization, fits particularly well with the interactive and side effect-free spreadsheet programming model.

- Chapter 11 contains a user manual for the Funcalc implementation.

The implementations of Corecalc and Funcalc are available in source form under a liberal license and are written in C# using only managed code.

Goals of the Corecalc implementation   The purpose of the Corecalc implementation described in chapters 2 through 4 of this book is to provide a source code platform for experiments with spreadsheet implementation, presenting also the underlying design ideas and considerations. The Corecalc implementation is written in C# and provides all essential spreadsheet functionality. The implementation is small and simple enough to allow experiments with design decisions and extensions, yet complete and efficient enough to benchmark against real spreadsheet programs such as Microsoft Excel, Gnumeric, and OpenOffice Calc.

Goals of the Funcalc implementation   The purpose of the Funcalc implementation described in chapters 6 through 9 is to demonstrate that sheet-defined functions can be both convenient and fast, while retaining the highly interactive spreadsheet work mode, and hence empower spreadsheet end users. The Funcalc implementation is an extension of Corecalc.

Pedagogical side benefits   A realistic spreadsheet implementation draws on and illustrates a range of software technologies and computer science subjects. In this book we will encounter "asides"—sections that briefly introduce the following subjects:

- The formal description of the semantics, or meaning, of formula evaluation and spreadsheet recalculation (section 1.8).

- The representation of formulas as abstract syntax, and the conversion of concrete syntax (text) into abstract syntax, using a simple lexer and parser generator (section 2.2.1).

- Interpretation, or evaluation, of formula abstract syntax (section 2.7).

- Concepts of object-oriented programming (section 2.1.2) and functional programming (sections 2.3 and 4.2.3).

- The representation of binary floating-point numbers according to the IEEE-754 standard [81] (section 2.8.1).

- A space- and time-efficient data structure for representing large sparse arrays (section 2.16), and the features of current computer hardware that contribute to the efficiency of this data structure.

- The Common Intermediate Language (CIL) bytecode used in the Microsoft .NET platform (sections 7.5 and 7.7).

- Compiler technology, how to get from formula abstract syntax to a list of bytecode instructions (chapters 7 and 8).

- The notion of tail call for executing certain recursive function calls in constant space (section 8.3.2).

- The concept of program specialization or partial evaluation [85], as applied to sheet-defined functions (section 10.1).

When necessary, we will briefly introduce such prerequisites and also provide references to further reading on these subjects.

Availability and license   The complete implementation, including documentation, is available in binary and source form from the IT University of Copenhagen:

http://www.itu.dk/people/sestoft/funcalc/

The Corecalc implementation is copyrighted by the authors and distributed under an MIT-style license:

> Copyright © 2006-2014 Peter Sestoft and others
>
> Permission is hereby granted, free of charge, to any person obtaining a copy of this software and associated documentation files (the "Software"), to deal in the Software without restriction, including without limitation the rights to use, copy, modify, merge, publish, distribute, sublicense, and/or sell copies of the Software, and to permit persons to whom the Software is furnished to do so, subject to the following conditions:
>
> The above copyright notice and this permission notice shall be included in all copies or substantial portions of the Software.
>
> THE SOFTWARE IS PROVIDED "AS IS", WITHOUT WARRANTY OF ANY KIND, EXPRESS OR IMPLIED, INCLUDING BUT NOT LIMITED TO THE WARRANTIES OF MERCHANTABILITY, FITNESS FOR A PARTICULAR PURPOSE AND NONINFRINGEMENT. IN NO EVENT SHALL THE AUTHORS OR COPYRIGHT HOLDERS BE LIABLE FOR ANY CLAIM, DAMAGES OR OTHER LIABILITY, WHETHER IN AN ACTION OF CONTRACT, TORT OR OTHERWISE, ARISING FROM, OUT OF OR IN CONNECTION WITH THE SOFTWARE OR THE USE OR OTHER DEALINGS IN THE SOFTWARE.

This means that you can use and modify the Corecalc and Funcalc software for any purpose, including commerce, without a license fee, but the copyright notice must remain in place, and you cannot blame us for any consequences of using or abusing the software. In particular, we accept no responsibility in case the commercial exploitation of an idea presented in this book is construed to violate one or more patents.

Also, all trademarks belong to their owners.

Acknowledgments   This text began to take shape, and much new work on Funcalc was done, during a visit to Greg Morrisett's group at Harvard University in March–July 2009 in a splendid corner office across from the Museum of Natural History. Some of the chapters describing Corecalc are based on a previous technical report [137], but we have revised them considerably to reflect the development of Funcalc.

The original impetus to look at spreadsheet technology came from Simon Peyton Jones and Margaret Burnett during a visit to Microsoft Research, Cambridge, UK, in 2001, and from their 2003 paper with Alan Blackwell [120].

Thomas S. Iversen investigated the use of run-time code generation for speeding up spreadsheet calculations in his 2006 MSc thesis project [84], jointly supervised with Torben Mogensen (DIKU, University of Copenhagen). Parts of this work are summarized in [137, chapter 5]. Thomas also restructured the core code base and added functionality to read XMLSS files exported from Microsoft Excel.

Daniel S. Cortes and Morten W. Hansen investigated how to design and implement sheet-defined functions, thus allowing spreadsheet users to define their own functions using well-known spreadsheet concepts. This work was done in their 2006 MSc thesis project [37].

Quan Vi Tran and Phong Ha investigated an alternative implementation of function sheets, using the infrastructure provided by Microsoft Excel. This work was done in their 2006 MSc thesis project [72].

Morten Poulsen and Poul Serek implemented and experimented with the extended support graph construction in sections 5.1 through 5.4 [122]. Subsequently, they built the first compiler implementation of sheet-defined functions, based on my early versions of the design laid out in chapters 6 to 8.

Several groups of students have investigated distributed collaborative spreadsheets based on the Corecalc platform, in particular Vincens Riber Mink and Daniel Schiermer [104]. Nader Salas furthermore considered full traceability [134].

Other IT University students, including Jacob Atzen, Claus Skoubølling Jørgensen, Jens Lind, Poul Brønnum, Jens Hamann, Hui Xu, Mainul Liton, Linas Patapavicius, Rasmus Nielsen, Jens Zeilund Sørensen, Hildur Uffe Flemberg, Martin Jeanty Larsen, Jonas Druedahl Rask, and Simon Eikeland Timmermann, investigated other parts of the spreadsheet design space and provided valuable insights, comments, and corrections to this book.

Michael Reichhardt Hansen and the publisher's anonymous reviewers provided many valuable comments and suggestions, which led to significant improvements of the presentation.

It was a great pleasure to work with Ada Brunstein, Marie Lufkin Lee, Marc Lowenthal, and Virginia Crossman at MIT Press during the book's somewhat protracted gestation.

Naming Conventions

Name	Meaning	Type	Page
act	void delegate	Action⟨T⟩	
ae	adjusted expression	Adjusted⟨Expr⟩	68
arr	array value	ArrayValue	48
c	column index	int	
ca	cell address, absolute	CellAddr	51
ccar	cell or cell area reference	CellRef, CellArea	114
cell	cell	Cell	39
col	column number, zero-based	int	
cols	column count	int	
deltaCol	column increment	int	
deltaRow	row increment	int	
dlg	non-void delegate	Func⟨T⟩	54
e	expression in formula	Expr	40
es	expression array	Expr[]	
fca	full cell address, absolute	FullCellAddr	
fv	function value, closure	FunctionValue	201
lr	lower right corner of area	RARef	49
r	row index	int	
raref	relative/absolute reference	RARef	49
row	row number, zero-based	int	
rows	row count	int	
sheet	sheet	Sheet	38
ul	upper left corner of area	RARef	49
v	value	Value	44
vs	value array	Value[]	
workbook	workbook	Workbook	36

Chapter 1

What Is a Spreadsheet

To answer the question "What is a spreadsheet?", one may point to Microsoft Excel, OpenOffice Calc, or Gnumeric. However, that would provide poor guidance for designing variations and novel extensions to the spreadsheet concept, as in part II of this book. An understanding of spreadsheet concepts should leave open the possibility of designing such variations and extensions, yet those variations and extensions should behave "as expected" by experienced spreadsheet users—an idea that is known as the principle of least astonishment.

1.1 History

The first spreadsheet program in the modern sense was VisiCalc, developed by Dan Bricklin and Bob Frankston in 1979 for the Apple II computer [21, 63, 164] and [22, chapter 12]. A version for MS-DOS on the IBM PC was released in 1981; the size of the executable was a modest 27 KB.

Many different spreadsheet programs followed, including SuperCalc, Lotus 1-2-3 whose first version was 85 KB [132], PlanPerfect, QuattroPro, and many more. By now the dominating spreadsheet program is Microsoft Excel [102], whose executable (version 2013) weighs in at 19,917 KB. Several open source spreadsheet programs exist, including Gnumeric [66] and OpenOffice Calc [115]. Moreover, there are multiple online collaborative spreadsheet programs running in browsers, such as Google Docs (part of Google Drive) [68]. See also the encyclopedia paper [1], the introduction to Felienne Hermans' PhD thesis [76], or Wikipedia's entry on spreadsheets [163].

1.2 Basic concepts

All spreadsheet programs have the same visual model: a two-dimensional grid of cells. Columns are labeled with letters A, B, ..., Z, AA, ..., rows are labeled with

numbers 1, 2, ..., cells are addressed by row and column: A1, A2, ..., B1, B2, ...,
and rectangular cell areas by their corner coordinates, such as B2:C4. A cell can
contain a number, a text, or a formula. A formula can involve constants, arithmetic
operators such as (*), functions such as SUM(...), and, most importantly, references to other cells such as C2 or to cell areas such as D2:D4. Also, spreadsheet
programs perform automatic recalculation: whenever a user edits the contents of
a cell, all cells that directly or transitively depend on that cell will be recalculated
automatically.

Figure 1.1 shows an example spreadsheet, summarizing the grades given in an
exam. Column A lists the possible grades $-3, 00, 02, 4, 7, 10, 12$; they correspond to
the F, FX, E, D, C, B, and A grades on the European ECTS scale. Column B shows
the number of times each grade was awarded in this particular exam, and column C
computes the product of the grade and number of times awarded. Cell B9 computes
the total number of grades awarded (the sum of column B), cell C9 computes the sum
of the products (the sum of column C), and cell C11 computes the average grade (the
ratio C9/B9). Column D computes what percentage each grade constitutes of the
total number of grades. Figure 1.2 shows the formulas used in these computations.

◇	A	B	C	D
1	Grade	Count	Product	Count %
2	-3	1	-3	1.7
3	0	6	0	10.3
4	2	5	10	8.6
5	4	9	36	15.5
6	7	19	133	32.8
7	10	14	140	24.1
8	12	4	48	6.9
9	Sum		58	364
10				
11		Average	6.3	
12				

Figure 1.1: Spreadsheet window summarizing grades given in an exam. Column
A hold the grades, B the number of times each grade was given, C computes their
product, and D computes the percentage distribution of the grades. Cell C11 computes the average grade.

Modern spreadsheet programs have one further essential feature in common. A
reference in a formula can be *relative* such as C2, or *absolute* such as $B$5, or a
mixture such as B$5, which is row-absolute but column-relative.

This distinction matters when the reference occurs in a formula that is copied
from one cell to another. In that case, an absolute reference remains unchanged,
whereas a relative reference gets adjusted by the distance (number of columns and
rows) from the original cell to the cell receiving the copy. For instance, a row-
absolute and column-relative reference such as B$5 will keep referring to the same
row but will have its column adjusted when copied. The adjustment of relative references works also when copying a formula from one cell to an entire cell area: each
copy of the formula gets adjusted according to its goal cell. Interestingly, the original VisiCalc program did not distinguish between relative and absolute references

in formulas; instead one had to indicate which references to adjust (relative) and which not to adjust (absolute) at each formula copy operation.

Figure 1.2 shows the formulas behind the sheet from figure 1.1. The formulas in C3:D8 are copies of that in C2, with the row numbers automatically adjusted from 2 to 3, 4, and so on. The formula in C9 is a copy of that in B9, with the column automatically adjusted from B to C in the cell area reference. Finally, the formulas in D3:D8 are copies of the formula =B2/$B$9*100 in D2; note how the relative row number 2 in B2 gets adjusted whereas the absolute row number 9 in $B$9 does not.

◇	A	B	C	D
1	Grade	Count	Product	Count %
2	-3	1	=A2*B2	=B2/$B$9*100
3	0	6	=A3*B3	=B3/$B$9*100
4	2	5	=A4*B4	=B4/$B$9*100
5	4	9	=A5*B5	=B5/$B$9*100
6	7	19	=A6*B6	=B6/$B$9*100
7	10	14	=A7*B7	=B7/$B$9*100
8	12	4	=A8*B8	=B8/$B$9*100
9	Sum	=SUM(B2:B8)	=SUM(C2:C8)	
10				
11		Average	=C9/B9	
12				

Figure 1.2: The formulas behind the spreadsheet in figure 1.1.

So far, we have viewed a spreadsheet as a rectangular grid of cells. An equally valid view is that a spreadsheet is a graph whose nodes are cells and whose edges (arrows) are the dependencies between cells (see figure 1.3). The two views correspond roughly to what is called the physical and logical views by Isakowitz [83]. It is notable how messy the graph (with explicit dependencies between cells) looks compared with the rectangular layout with its implicit cell dependencies.

1.3   Cell reference formats

Usually, cell references and cell area references are entered and displayed in the *A1 format* shown above, consisting of a column and a row indication. References are relative by default, and an absolute column or row is indicated by the dollar ($) prefix. The A1 cell reference format originates in VisiCalc [21].

Microsoft's Multiplan spreadsheet program (1982) used a different format, called the *R1C1 format*, in which the row number is shown followed by the column number (so the opposite of the A1 format). References are numeric for both rows and columns, and absolute by default, with relative references indicated by an offset in square brackets. When the offset is zero it is left out, so RC means "this cell". The R1C1 format was used also in Piersol's 1986 spreadsheet implementation [121].

The R1C1 format is interesting because it is used in Excel's XML Spreadsheet 2003 (XMLSS) export format, and because Excel and Gnumeric (but apparently not OpenOffice Calc) can optionally display formulas in R1C1 format. Also, it is close to the internal format of our implementation Corecalc.

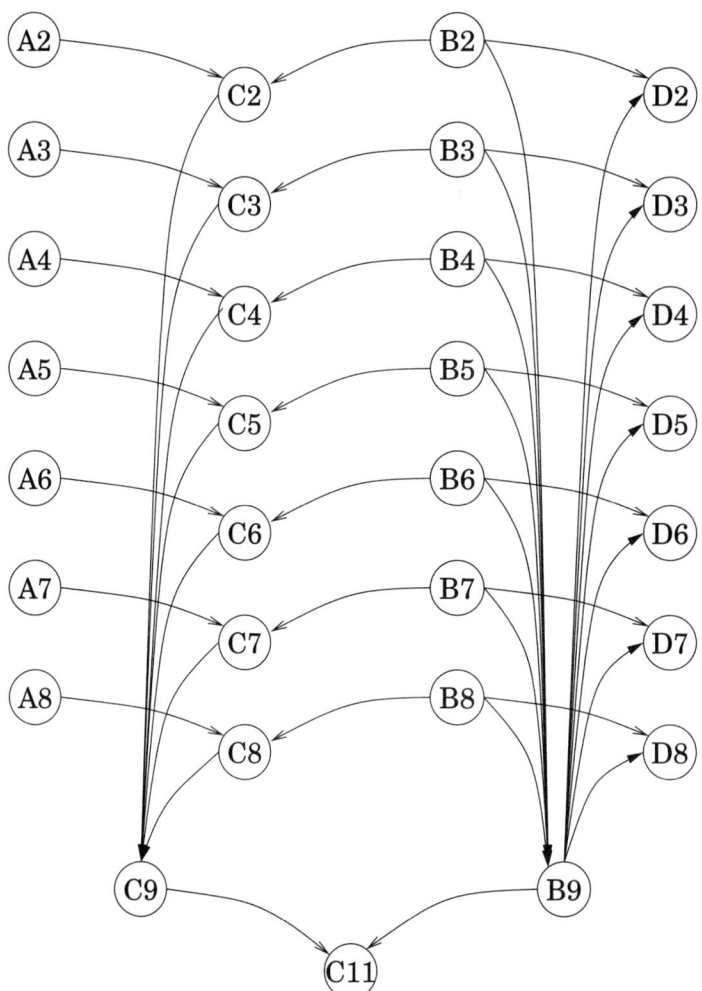

Figure 1.3: A graph-oriented view of the spreadsheet in figures 1.1 and 1.2.

The main virtue of R1C1 format is that it is invariant under the adjustment of relative cell references implied by copying of a formula. Figure 1.4 compares the two reference formats.

A1 format	R1C1 format	Meaning
A1	R[-1]C[-1]	Relative; previous row, previous column
A2	RC[-1]	Relative; this row, previous column
B1	R[-1]C	Relative; previous row, this column
B2	RC	Relative; this cell
C3	R[+1]C[+1]	Relative; next row, next column
$A$1	R1C1	Absolute; row 1, column 1 (A)
$A$2	R2C1	Absolute; row 2, column 1 (A)
$B$1	R1C2	Absolute; row 1, column 2 (B)
$B$2	R2C2	Absolute; row 2, column 2 (B)
$C$3	R3C3	Absolute; row 3, column 3 (C)
$A1	R[-1]C1	Relative row (previous); absolute column 1 (A)

Figure 1.4: References from cell B2 shown in A1 format and in R1C1 format.

1.4   Formulas, functions, and arrays

As already shown, a formula in a cell is an expression that may contain references to other cells, standard arithmetic operators such as (+), and calls to functions such as SUM. Most spreadsheet programs implement standard mathematical functions such as EXP, LOG, and SIN; statistical functions such as MEDIAN and probability distributions; functions to generate pseudo-random numbers such as RAND; functions to manipulate times and dates such as NOW and TODAY; financial functions such as "present value"; a conditional function IF; array functions (see below); and much more.

Some functions take arguments that may be a cell area reference, or range, such as D2:D4, which denotes the three cells D2, D3, and D4. In general an area reference consists of two cell references, here D2 and D4, giving two corners of a rectangular area of a sheet. The cell references giving the two corners may be any combination of relative, absolute, or mixed relative/absolute. For instance, one may enter the formula =SUM(A$1:A1) in cell B1 and copy it to cell B2 where it becomes =SUM(A$1:A2), to cell B3 where it becomes =SUM(A$1:A3), and so on, as shown in figure 1.5. The effect is that column B computes the partial sums of the numbers in column A. Moreover, since the corner references were column relative, copying column B's formulas to column C would make column C compute the partial sums of column B.

Some built-in functions, called array functions, return an entire array (or matrix) of values rather than a number or a text string. Such functions include TRANSPOSE, which transposes a cell area, and MMULT, which computes matrix multiplication.

	A	B
1	0.5	=SUM(A$1:A1)
2	=A1*1.00001	=SUM(A$1:A2)
3	=A2*1.00001	=SUM(A$1:A3)
...	...	...
12288	=A12287*1.00001	=SUM(A$1:A12288)

Figure 1.5: Adjustment of cell area references when copying a formula.

The array result must then be distributed over a rectangular cell area of the same shape, so that each cell in the area receives one component (one atomic value). In Excel, Gnumeric, and OpenOffice Calc, this is achieved by entering the formula as a so-called *array formula*. First one marks the *display area*, that is, the cell area that should receive the values, then one enters the formula in the formula bar, and finally one types Ctrl+Shift+Enter instead of just Enter to complete the formula entry. This holds for Excel on Windows; for MacOS versions of Excel, use Cmd+Enter. The resulting formula is shown in curly braces, like {=TRANSPOSE(A1:B3)}, in every cell of the display area, although each cell contains only one component of the result. See figure 1.6 for an example.

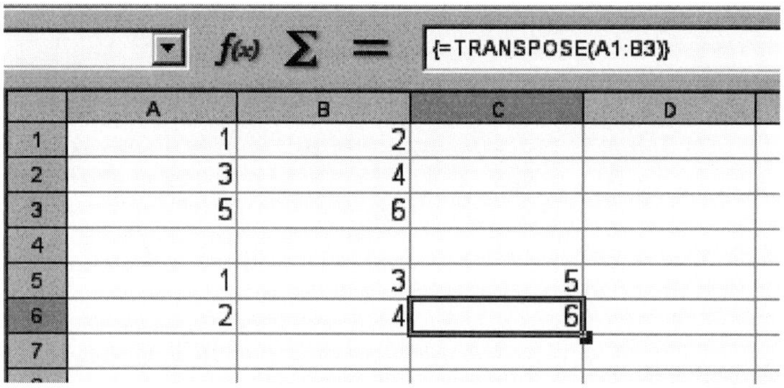

Figure 1.6: The array formula {=TRANSPOSE(A1:B3)} in result area A5:C6.

Finally, modern spreadsheet programs allow the user to define multiple related sheets, bundled in a so-called *workbook*. A cell reference can optionally refer to a cell on another sheet in the same workbook using the notation Sheet2!A$1 in Excel and Gnumeric and Sheet2.A$1 in OpenOffice Calc. Similarly, cell area references can be qualified with the sheet name, as in Sheet2!A$1:A1. Naturally, the two corners of a cell area must lie within the same sheet.

The Corecalc spreadsheet implementation described in part I of this book supports all the functionality described above, including built-in functions and array formulas.

1.5   Other spreadsheet features

Most modern spreadsheet programs furthermore provide business graphics (bar charts, pie charts, scatterplots), pivot tables, database access, spell checkers, and a large number of other useful and impressive features. Microsoft Excel'97 even contained a flight simulator, which was activated as follows: open a new workbook; press F5; enter X97:L97 and press Enter; press Tab; press Ctrl+Shift; click the Chart Wizard button. Such features shall not concern us here.

1.6   Dependency, support, and cycles

Clearly, a central concept is the dependency of one cell on the value of another. When cell C2 contains the formula =A2*B2, as in figure 1.2, we say that C2 *directly depends on* cells A2 and B2, and cells A2 and B2 *directly support* cell C2. Some spreadsheet programs, notably Excel and OpenOffice Calc, can display the dependencies using a feature called *formula audit*. For instance, figure 1.7 shows which cells directly or indirectly depend on B2. This visualization simply combines part of the graphical view in figure 1.3 with the usual spreadsheet grid view.

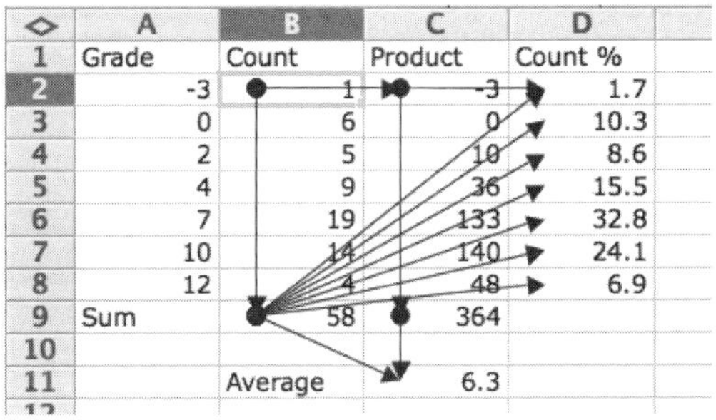

Figure 1.7: The direct and indirect dependencies on cell B2 in the sheet from figures 1.1 and 1.2.

A cell may directly depend on any number of other cells. For instance, cell C11 in figure 1.7 directly depends on B9 and C9. Similarly, a cell may directly support any number of other cells: cell B9 directly supports C11 and the cells in range D2:D8.

More precisely, C11 both *statically* and *dynamically* depends on B9 and C9. By static dependency we mean that the formula text in C11 refers to cells B9 and C9, and by dynamic dependency we mean that calculating the value of C11 requires calculating the values of those cells.

A static dependency may or may not cause a dynamic dependency; it is an approximation of dynamic dependency. For instance, a cell containing the formula =IF(G1<>0, G2, G3) statically depends on G1, G2, and G3, but in any given recalculation dynamically depends only on G1 and G2, or on G1 and G3, depending on G1 being non-zero or zero. This is because IF is a non-strict function (see section 1.7.4).

A cell *transitively depends on* another cell (possibly itself) if there is a non-empty chain of direct dependencies from the former to the latter. For instance, cell C11 indirectly depends on B2, through B9 (and also through C2 and C9). The notion of *transitive support* is defined similarly. For instance, cell B2 transitively supports C2, D2, B9, C9, C11, and the cells in range D2:D8—the latter because B9 supports them.

If a cell statically transitively depends on itself, then there is a *static cycle* in the workbook; and if a cell dynamically transitively depends on itself, then there is a *dynamic cycle*. Sections 1.7.6 and 4.4 have more to say about cycles.

1.7   Recalculation

When the contents of a cell are changed by editing it, all cells supported by that cell, whether in the same sheet or another sheet in the workbook, must be recalculated. The purpose is to implement level 3 liveness, that is, the automatic and consistent recalculation and redisplay of results whenever the user has edited some data [152]. Such edits happen relatively frequently, although hardly more than once a second when performed by a human.

1.7.1   Recalculation order

Recalculation should be *completed* in dependency order: if cell B2 depends on cell A1, then the evaluation of A1 should be completed before the evaluation of B2 is completed. However, recalculation can be *initiated* in bottom-up or top-down order.

In *bottom-up* order, recalculation starts with cells that do not depend on any other cells and always proceeds with cells that depend only on cells already computed.

In *top-down* order, recalculation may start with any cell. When the value of an as yet uncomputed cell is needed, that cell is computed, and when that computation is completed, the computation of the original cell is resumed. The subcomputation may recursively lead to further subcomputations but will terminate unless there is a dynamic cyclic dependency. The Corecalc implementation uses a mixture of top-down and bottom-up recalculation (see sections 2.12 and 4.3).

1.7.2   Requirements on recalculation

The design of the recalculation mechanism is central to the efficiency and reliability of a spreadsheet implementation, and the design space turns out to be large. First let us consider the requirements on a recalculation after a user has edited a single cell, since this is the most frequent scenario:

- Recalculation should ensure *consistency* of cell values and formulas. After a recalculation, the value of a cell is consistent with the cell's formula and the values of the cells to which the formula refers. In other words, if the formula contains no calls to volatile functions, then reevaluating (only) the formula would give the same value. Similarly, if the formula does contain calls to volatile functions, then there must be plausible values of those volatile functions that would result in the cell's value. This requirement is formalized in section 1.8.

In practice, Excel sometimes violates the consistency requirement (see discussion in example 6.26).

- Recalculation should be efficient in time and space. Preferably, it should avoid recalculating a cell formula that does not contain calls to volatile functions and whose precedent cells' values have not changed since the last recalculation. The consistency principle means that such evaluation (or not) is not observable, and hence is harmless, but it is reasonable to expect that a good recalculation mechanism takes time linear in the size of formulas in those cells supported by the cells that have changed. Also, it is preferable for supporting data structures to require space that is at most linear in the total size of formulas in the workbook (see section 1.7.3).

  For the same reasons of efficiency, recalculation should preferably avoid evaluating unused arguments of IF(e1, e2, e3) and other non-strict functions (see section 1.7.4). When we introduce sheet-defined functions in part II of the book, it becomes essential to avoid evaluating such unused arguments to ensure termination of recursively defined functions.

- Every recalculation should evaluate RAND() and other volatile functions (see section 1.7.5).

- The spreadsheet implementation can freely choose the recalculation order in two senses: the order in which cell values are calculated and updated is unspecified, and the order of subexpression evaluation is unspecified. For instance, the result of NOW()-NOW() may be negative, zero, or positive.

- Recalculation should accurately detect dynamic cycles (see section 1.7.6).

These requirements still leave considerable latitude for a recalculation mechanism: cells may be evaluated in parallel (provided they do not depend on each other), a cell may not be evaluated at all (provided no displayed cell depends on it, directly or indirectly), a cell may be evaluated multiple times, and so on, so long as the final result is consistent.

1.7.3   Efficient recalculation

One way to ensure that recalculation takes time at most linear in the total size of formulas is to make sure that each formula and each array formula is evaluated at most once in every recalculation. This is rather easy to ensure: visit every active cell and evaluate its formula if not already evaluated, recursively evaluating any cells it depends on. This simple mechanism, described in section 2.12, evaluates every formula exactly once in each recalculation, using extra space (for the recursion stack) that is at most linear in the total size of formulas.

It is possible but surprisingly complicated to do better than this. We show how in sections 3.3 and 4.3.

1.7.4   Non-strict functions

Most built-in functions in spreadsheet programs are strict: they require all their arguments to be evaluated before they are called. But the function IF(e1, e2, e3) is *non-strict*, as it evaluates at most one of e2 and e3. For instance, the function call IF(A2<>0, 1/A2, 1) evaluates its second operand 1/A2 only if the value of A2 is different from zero.

It is straightforward to implement non-strict functions: simply postpone argument evaluation until it is clear that the argument is needed. However, the existence of non-strict functions means that a static cyclic dependency may turn out to be harmless, and it complicates the use of topological sorting to determine a safe recalculation order (see section 3.3.3).

1.7.5   Volatile functions

Some functions are *volatile*. Although they take no arguments, different calls typically produce different values. The most common volatile functions are NOW(), which returns the current time, and RAND(), which returns a random number between 0 and 1. A formula whose result depends on a volatile function must be evaluated once in each recalculation. For instance, a cell containing =IF(RAND()>0.5, 11, 22) will be evaluated in every recalculation and may or may not produce a new value each time. However, in IF(RAND()>0.5, NOW(), 10), if the condition happens to evaluate to false, then the call to NOW() may not be evaluated.

Volatile functions are easy to implement, but a spreadsheet implementation must keep track of which cells contain calls to volatile functions (see sections 3.3.1 and 3.3.2).

1.7.6   Dependency cycles

If a cell dynamically depends on itself in a recalculation, then this will be discovered and reported, regardless of whether there exists a value of the cell that would satisfy the consistency principle. For instance, if cell B1 contains the formula =2/B1, then even though recalculation could put B1 equal to $\sqrt{2}$ or $-\sqrt{2}$ and thereby achieve the required consistency, it should instead report a cyclic dependency. Thus, a spreadsheet implementation should not be expected to compute numerical solutions or fixed points through the use of cyclic dependencies. (This view is not universally held. It seems to be a common, although risky, practice in some financial models to define equation systems by cyclic dependencies and then recalculating the spreadsheet until the results have converged.)

The existence of non-strict functions has implications for the presence or absence of cycles. Assume that cell A1 contains the formula `IF(A2<>0, A1, 1)`. Then it would seem that there is a cyclic dependency of A1 on A1, but that is the case only if A2 is non-zero—only those arguments of an `IF`-function that actually get evaluated can introduce a cycle.

Both Excel and OpenOffice Calc take that approach and report a cyclic dependency involving the argument of a non-strict functions only if the argument actually needs to be evaluated. Strangely, Gnumeric does not appear to detect and report cycles at all, whether involving non-strict functions or not.

1.7.7   Spreadsheets are dynamically typed

Spreadsheet programs distinguish among several types of data, such as numbers, text strings, logical values (Booleans), and arrays. However, this distinction is made dynamically, in the style of Scheme [145], rather than statically, in the style of Haskell [74] or Standard ML [103].

For instance, the formula `=TRANSPOSE(IF(A1>0, B1:C2, 17))` is perfectly OK so long as A1>0 is true, so that the argument to `TRANSPOSE` is an array-shaped cell area, but evaluates to an array of `ArgType` error values if A1>0 is false.

Similarly, it is fine for cell D1 to contain the formula `=IF(A1>0, 42, D1)` so long as A1>0 is true, but if A1>0 is false, then there is a cyclic dependency in the sheet evaluation.

Because of dynamic typing, a spreadsheet implementation must in general wrap numbers and other values as objects so that it can distinguish them at run-time (see section 2.8).

1.7.8   Error values must be propagated

Because spreadsheet formulas, like languages such as Lisp, Javascript, and Ruby, are dynamically typed, the evaluation of an expression may fail due to giving the wrong number of arguments to a function, due to the wrong type of argument, and for many other reasons.

Two points are worth noting. First, such failures of evaluation should be tolerated because they are likely to arise during editing of a spreadsheet model. Therefore, a failure should not crash the spreadsheet program by throwing an exception, say. Second, there may be hundreds of such failed evaluations in a single recalculation (e.g., during major edits to a spreadsheet model), and such failures should not open hundreds of warning dialogs or similar.

Therefore, spreadsheet programs simply let a failed evaluation produce a distinguished kind of value—an error value. Further computations must propagate such an error value so that it can be easily traced back to its original cause. For example, applying the mathematical logarithm function to a string as in `LOG("zwei")` should produce an ArgType error value, and further computation must propagate this error. Hence, `10+LOG("zwei")` must produce ArgType error as well, and so must comparisons such as `10+LOG("zwei") < A1` and conditional expressions such as IF(10+LOG("zwei") < A1, 22, 33). Applying the logarithm to a negative number as in LOG(-3) must produce a NumError error value and so must any more complex expression that depends on this function call.

Thus, if a subexpression of a formula evaluates to an error value, then this error value will be propagated as the result of the formula. If multiple subexpressions evaluate to error values, then one of them will be propagated as the result of the formula. This is similar to exception propagation in an imperative language whose evaluation order is indeterminate. In particular, if *e1* evaluates to an error in IF(e1, e2, e3), then the entire *IF*-expression evaluates to that error.

1.7.9   Spreadsheets are functional programs

The recalculation mechanism of a spreadsheet program is in a sense dual to that of lazy functional languages such as Haskell [74]. In a lazy functional language, an intermediate expression is evaluated only when there is a demand for it, and its value is then cached so that subsequent demands will use that value.

In a spreadsheet, a formula in a cell is (re)calculated only when some cell on which it depends has been recalculated, and its value is then cached so that all cells dependent on it will use that value.

So calculation in a lazy functional language is driven by *demand for output*, whereas (re)calculation in a spreadsheet typically is driven by *availability of input*. These evaluation strategies may be characterized as "backwards flow of demand" versus "forwards flow of data".

The absence of assignment, destructive update, and proper recursive definitions implies that there are no data structure cycles in spreadsheets. All cyclic dependencies are computational and detected by the recalculation mechanism.

Some researchers have proposed spreadsheet programs that are lazy also in the above sense of evaluation being driven by demand for output; see Nuñez [113] and Du and Wadge [48], who call this *eductive evaluation*.

1.8   Aside: Formal semantics of spreadsheets

Here we give a simple formal semantics of spreadsheet recalculation, relating this semantics to the informal discussion in the preceding section. None of the immediately following chapters depends on this formalization so it may be skipped without much loss of context.

Rather than showing *how* recalculation should work by giving a somewhat algorithmic description in the form of a denotational or operational semantics [112], we specify *what* a recalculation should achieve, namely, consistency between the values calculated for each formula cell.

Such consistency can be specified by giving a semantics for the evaluation of individual cell formulas only, rather than for recalculation of the whole sheet or workbook. In this way, we avoid overspecifying the recalculation process, leaving it unspecified in which order cells are updated, whether cells are recalculated sequentially or in parallel, whether the value of a cell needs to be calculated at all (in case no cell that it depends on has changed), or whether it may be calculated more than once (say, in a speculative parallel computation) during a single recalculation.

We believe that the semantics given in this section reflects actual spreadsheet implementation, but to avoid notational and conceptual clutter, we make some simplifications:

- The only types of values are Number and Error, not strings and arrays. Numbers suffice to represent also the logical values false (zero) and true (any non-zero number).

- We consider only a single sheet, not multi-sheet workbooks.

- Infix arithmetic operations such as B2+7 and comparisons B2<10 will be represented as prefix function calls such as +(B2,7) and <(B2,10).

- We consider only cell references such as B2, not area references such as B2:C4. Also, note that the distinction between relative (B2) and absolute ($B$2) references does not matter when evaluating a formula, only when copying it.

- Functions propagate errors from all their arguments, except $IF(e_1, e_2, e_3)$, which propagates errors only from the condition e_1 and from the single branch (e_2 or e_3) that gets evaluated.

- The only volatile function is RAND().

- A constant cell, such as 7, will be represented by a constant formula =7.

The semantics presented here is easily extended to other types of values, multi-sheet workbooks, cell area references (ranges), other non-strict functions than IF, other volatile functions than RAND(), and a distinction between constant cells (that never need to be evaluated) and formula cells (that may need to be evaluated). However, that would just increase notational clutter without giving much new insight.

The simplified formulas used in this section are described in figure 1.8.

$$
\begin{array}{lll}
e & ::= & \texttt{n} & \text{number constant} \\
& | & \texttt{ca} & \text{cell reference} \\
& | & \texttt{IF}(e_1, e_2, e_3) & \text{conditional expression} \\
& | & \texttt{RAND}() & \text{volatile function} \\
& | & \texttt{F}(e_1, \ldots, e_n) & \text{function call}
\end{array}
$$

Figure 1.8: Syntax of the simplified formula language.

1.8.1   Semantic sets and functions

To describe the evaluation of formulas, we use the semantic sets and functions defined in figure 1.9. These are sometimes called semantic domains, but here they are ordinary sets and partial functions. For instance, $Value = Number + Error$ is the set of values, where a value v is either a proper number such as 0.42 in set $Number$ or an error such as #DIV/0! in set $Error$. The set $Addr$ contains cell addresses ca such as B2.

To describe the formulas of a worksheet, we use a map $\phi : Addr \rightarrow Expr$ so that when $ca \in Addr$ is a cell address, $\phi(ca)$ is the formula in cell ca. If cell ca is blank, then $\phi(ca)$ is undefined. The domain of ϕ is $dom(\phi) = \{\ ca \mid \phi(ca)\ \text{is defined}\ \}$, the set of cell addresses that have a formula, that is, the set of non-blank cells. The ϕ function is not affected by recalculation, only by editing the sheet.

The result of a recalculation is modeled by function $\sigma : Addr \rightarrow Value$, where $\sigma(ca)$ is the computed value in cell ca. The σ function gets updated by each recalculation (see section 1.8.3).

$$
\begin{array}{rcll}
n & \in & Number & = \quad \{\ \text{proper numbers}\ \} \\
  &   & Error & = \quad \{\ \text{\#DIV/0!, \#CYCLE!}\ \} \\
ca & \in & Addr & = \quad \{\ \text{cell addresses}\ \} \\
v & \in & Value & = \quad Number + Error \\
e & \in & Expr   & = \quad \{\ \text{formulas, see figure 1.8}\ \} \\
\phi & &   & \in \quad Addr \rightarrow Expr \\
\sigma & &   & \in \quad Addr \rightarrow Value \\
\end{array}
$$

Figure 1.9: Sets and maps used in the spreadsheet semantics: $Number$ is the set of proper floating-point numbers, excluding NaNs and infinities (section 2.8.1); $Error$ is the set of error values; $Addr$ the set of cell addresses; $Value$ the set of values (either number or error); and $Expr$ the set of formulas.

1.8.2   Semantics of formula evaluation

The semantics for formulas is given as a natural semantics [87], a variant of operational semantics [112], using inference rules that involve big-step evaluation judgments. An evaluation judgment has the form $\sigma \vdash e \Downarrow v$, which says: When σ describes the calculated values of all cells, then formula e may evaluate to value v. Note that v may be a number value or an error value.

To understand inference rules, consider this rule:

$$\frac{\sigma \vdash e_i \Downarrow v_i \in Error}{\sigma \vdash \text{F}(e_1,\ldots,e_n) \Downarrow v_i} \ (e5e)$$

This inference rule consists of a premise above the line and a conclusion below the line. The conclusion concerns the value of a function call expression $\text{F}(e_1,\ldots,e_n)$, and the premise concerns the value of one of the call's argument expressions e_i. The rule can be read as follows: If there is some argument expression e_i that may evaluate to an error value v_i, then the function call may evaluate to the error value v_i also. That is, the rule describes the propagation of errors from argument to result in a function call. If multiple arguments e_i and e_j may evaluate to different error values v_i and v_j, then the rule does not specify which error will be propagated to the call's result.

For another example, consider this rule, also for a function call $F(e_1, \ldots, e_n)$ with n arguments:

$$\frac{\sigma \vdash e_1 \Downarrow v_1 \notin Error \quad \ldots \quad \sigma \vdash e_n \Downarrow v_n \notin Error}{\sigma \vdash F(e_1, \ldots, e_n) \Downarrow f(v_1, \ldots, v_n)} \ (e5v)$$

This rule has n premises and can be read as follows: If all argument expressions $e_1, \ldots, e_n$ may evaluate to non-error values $v_1, \ldots, v_n$, then the value of the function call is obtained by applying the actual function f to these values, as in $f(v_1, \ldots, v_n)$.

The "may" is important because, in general, an expression may evaluate to multiple different values. For instance, RAND() may evaluate to any number between 0.0 (included) and 1.0 (excluded). Hence, 7+1/RAND() may evaluate to some number greater than $7 + 1$ or to the error #DIV/0! in case RAND() produces 0.0.

The complete set of inference rules that describe when a formula evaluation judgment $\sigma \vdash e \Downarrow v$ holds are given in figure 1.10. Note that there are five groups of rules (e1), (e2x), (e3x), (4), (e5x), each corresponding to one of the five kinds of formulas in figure 1.8. Also, the formula fragments that appear in the premises are always smaller than the formula that appears in the conclusion. Hence, one can make a conclusion about a given formula through a finite number of rule applications.

The formula evaluation rules in figure 1.10 may be explained as follows:

- Rule (e1) says that a number constant n evaluates to that constant's value.

- Rule (e2b) says that a reference ca to a blank cell, that is, one for which $\sigma(ca)$ is not defined, gives value 0.0.

- Rule (e2v) says that a reference ca to a non-blank cell evaluates to the value $\sigma(ca)$ calculated for that cell. This value may be a number or an error.

- Rule (e3e) says that the expression $IF(e_1, e_2, e_3)$ may evaluate to error v_1 if the condition e_1 may evaluate to error v_1.

- Rule (e3f) says that $IF(e_1, e_2, e_3)$ may evaluate to value v provided the condition e_1 may evaluate to the non-error number zero and the "false branch" e_3 may evaluate to v.

- Rule (e3t) says that $IF(e_1, e_2, e_3)$ may evaluate to value v provided the condition e_1 may evaluate to some non-error non-zero number v_1 and the "true branch" e_2 may evaluate to v.

$$\frac{}{\sigma \vdash \mathbf{n} \Downarrow n} \ (e1)$$

$$\frac{ca \notin dom(\sigma)}{\sigma \vdash \mathbf{ca} \Downarrow 0.0} \ (e2b)$$

$$\frac{ca \in dom(\sigma) \qquad \sigma(ca) = v}{\sigma \vdash \mathbf{ca} \Downarrow v} \ (e2v)$$

$$\frac{\sigma \vdash e_1 \Downarrow v_1 \in Error}{\sigma \vdash \mathtt{IF}(e_1, e_2, e_3) \Downarrow v_1} \ (e3e)$$

$$\frac{\sigma \vdash e_1 \Downarrow 0.0 \in Number \qquad \sigma \vdash e_3 \Downarrow v}{\sigma \vdash \mathtt{IF}(e_1, e_2, e_3) \Downarrow v} \ (e3f)$$

$$\frac{\sigma \vdash e_1 \Downarrow v_1 \in Number \qquad v_1 \neq 0.0 \qquad \sigma \vdash e_2 \Downarrow v}{\sigma \vdash \mathtt{IF}(e_1, e_2, e_3) \Downarrow v} \ (e3t)$$

$$\frac{0.0 \leq v < 1.0}{\sigma \vdash \mathtt{RAND}() \Downarrow v} \ (e4)$$

$$\frac{\sigma \vdash e_i \Downarrow v_i \in Error}{\sigma \vdash \mathtt{F}(e_1, \ldots, e_n) \Downarrow v_i} \ (e5e)$$

$$\frac{\sigma \vdash e_1 \Downarrow v_1 \notin Error \qquad \ldots \qquad \sigma \vdash e_n \Downarrow v_n \notin Error}{\sigma \vdash \mathtt{F}(e_1, \ldots, e_n) \Downarrow f(v_1, \ldots, v_n)} \ (e5v)$$

Figure 1.10: Evaluation rules for simplified spreadsheet formulas.

- Rule (e4) says that function call RAND() may evaluate to any (non-error) number v greater than or equal to zero and less than one. Hence, this rule models non-deterministic choice. It allows any formula that involves a call to RAND() to be evaluated in a recalculation. However, it does not *require* such reevaluation as in section 1.7.5, nor does it require RAND() to produce a different number every time it is called. Such a requirement would not make sense; by definition, a random number generator is permitted to return whatever result it wants. So according to this operational semantics, RAND() might consistently return 0.42 whenever it is called, although that would be rather disappointing and useless.

- Rule (e5e) says that a call $F(e_1,\ldots,e_n)$ to a function F may evaluate to error v_i if one of its arguments e_1 may evaluate to error v_i. Note that if more than one argument may evaluate to an error, then the function call may evaluate to any of these. Hence, the semantics does not prescribe an evaluation order for arguments, such as a left to right or right to left.

- Rule (e5v) says that a call $F(e_1,\ldots,e_n)$ to a function F may evaluate to value v if each argument e_i may evaluate to non-error value v_i, and applying the actual function f to arguments $(v_1,\ldots,v_n)$ produces value v. The final result v may be a number such as 5, for instance, if the call is $+(2,3)$; or it may be an error such as #DIV/0!, for instance, if the call is /(1.0, 0.0).

1.8.3   Semantics of recalculation

Now that we know how to evaluate a formula, given values of all cells in the worksheet, we can describe the semantics of a recalculation. A recalculation must find a value for every non-blank cell ca in the sheet, and that value $\sigma(ca)$ must agree with the formula $\phi(ca)$ held in that cell. These are the central consistency requirements on a recalculation, informally stated in section 1.7.2 and formally described in figure 1.11. These requirements leave it completely unspecified how the recalculation works, whether it recalculates all or only some cells, whether it does so sequentially or in parallel, whether it guesses the values or computes them, and so on. This underspecification is essential to permit a range of implementation strategies and optimizations.

$$
\begin{array}{ll}
(1) & dom(\sigma) = dom(\phi) \\
(2) & \forall ca \in dom(\phi).\sigma \vdash \phi(ca) \Downarrow \sigma(ca)
\end{array}
$$

Figure 1.11: The consistency requirements on a recalculation. Requirement (1) says that a recalculation must find a value $\sigma(ca)$, possibly an error, for every non-blank cell ca. Requirement (2) says that the computed value $\sigma(ca)$ must agree with the cell's formula $\phi(ca)$.

1.8.4   Properties of the semantics

We believe the semantics given by the formula evaluation rules (figure 1.10) and
the consistency requirements on recalculation (figure 1.11) faithfully models actual
spreadsheet implementations such as Microsoft Excel, OpenOffice Calc, Gnumeric,
and Corecalc as described in this book. In particular:

- It prescribes that all references to a non-blank cell $ca \in dom(\sigma)$ produce the
  same value. This may be an error value.

- It prescribes that a reference to a blank cell $ca \notin dom(\sigma)$ produces the non-
  error value 0.0.

- It prescribes error propagation from arguments to results, as informally required in section 1.7.8, thanks to rules (e3e) and (e5e).

- It prescribes non-propagation of errors from the unevaluated branch of an IF-
  expressions, as informally required in section 1.7.4, thanks to rules (e3f) and
  (e3t).

- Even though neither the formula semantics in figure 1.10 nor the consistency
  requirements in figure 1.11 mention cyclic dependencies, the semantics does
  provide a useful model of recalculation in the presence of one or more cyclic
  dependencies (see section 1.8.5).

- It seems that the semantics can be extended to account for functions such
  as INDIRECT, COUNTIF, and SUMIF that interpret strings as formulas or cell
  references (see section 1.8.6).

1.8.5   Formal semantics of cyclic dependencies

If a sheet has a cyclic dependency, then it may be impossible for recalculation to find
non-error values for the cells involved in the cycle. For instance, if cell B2 contains
the formula =B2+1, then there is no proper (finite and non-NaN) number value
$y = \sigma(\text{B2}) \in Number$ such that $y = y + 1$. Due to requirement (1) from figure 1.11,
recalculation must find *some* value for that cell.

   The recalculation process can satisfy the requirements simply by giving cell B2
an error value such as #CYCLE!. In that case, the formula semantics rule (e5e) will
ensure that the formula B2+1, or +(B2,1), evaluates to error #CYCLE! too, hence
fulfilling requirement (2) on recalculation consistency. In fact, any error value will
satisfy requirement (2), but #CYCLE! is the most sensible error to choose. This
would implement the informal requirement from section 1.7.6 to discover dynamic
dependency cycles.

   Note that recalculation cannot gratuitously produce error values in the absence
of cyclic dependencies. If cell B2 contains the formula =41+1, then by requirement
(2) the result $\sigma(\text{B2})$ must be 42, not an error. More generally, if cell ca depends
only on cells that have no cyclic dependencies, if no function called from those cells'

formulas produces a #CYCLE! error, and if the spreadsheet is finite, then cell $\sigma(ca)$ cannot be #CYCLE!. This can be proved by induction on the depth of dependencies.

On a more speculative note, some cyclic dependencies might conceivably have non-error solutions. For instance, if cell B2 contains the formula =5+B2/2, then a particularly clever recalculation mechanism may find the value $\sigma(B2) = 10.0$ for B2, satisfying requirement (2). None of the standard spreadsheet implementations does that, reporting instead a cyclic dependency. However, they typically report the cycle not through an error value but through a dialog box, a status flag, or a marker in the affected cell itself. This allows spreadsheet users to perform multiple recalculations to see whether the computed value converges. However, this practice is dangerous, as the spreadsheet may never reach the consistency one usually expects, and which is embodied in our consistency requirement (2) in figure 1.11. Strange conclusions—within finance, science, or engineering—may be drawn from such circular spreadsheets.

1.8.6   The semantics of reflective functions

Spreadsheet implementations provide a few built-in functions that interpret strings as formulas or cell references, such as INDIRECT("B2"), which evaluates to the value of cell B2, and COUNTIF(A5:A9, "< 10"), which counts the number of values in A5:A9 that are less than 10. Moreover, the string argument may be computed from other data, as in COUNTIF(A5:A9, "<" & B2), which counts the number of values in A5:A9 that are smaller than the value in cell B2.

Another example is INDIRECT("B"&FLOOR(1+500*RAND(),1)), which refers to a random cell among B1:B500 depending on the outcome of RAND().

What is unusual about such "reflective" functions is that their evaluation may refer to cells and ranges that are not explicitly given as arguments.

Nevertheless, it seems that the formula semantics can be extended to account for reflective functions simply by passing σ as an additional argument to the underlying function. For instance, the meaning of INDIRECT(e_1) can be described like this:

$$\frac{\sigma \vdash e_1 \Downarrow v_1 \notin Error}{\sigma \vdash \text{INDIRECT}(e_1) \Downarrow indirect(\sigma, v_1)}$$

The underlying *indirect* function must check that v_1 is a string and has the correct format for a cell reference ca and then look up and return $\sigma(ca)$, or else return an error. The same treatment should work for COUNTIF, SUMIF, and related functions.

1.9   Related work

Despite some non-trivial implementation design issues, the technical literature on spreadsheet implementation is relatively sparse, as opposed to the trade literature consisting of spreadsheet manuals, handbooks, and guidelines. There is also a considerable scholarly literature on ergonomic and cognitive aspects of spreadsheet use

[83], risks and mistakes in spreadsheet use, and techniques to avoid them [126]. The European Spreadsheet Risks Interest Group (EuSpRiG) [53] holds an annual conference on the topic. The EUSES consortium (for *End Users Shaping Effective Software*) has published many papers on how to mitigate spreadsheet risks [54] as well as the *EUSES Spreadsheet Corpus* [58] that enables empirical investigation of real-world spreadsheets. Ray Panko maintains a website on spreadsheet error research [118], and a spreadsheet analytics company maintains a comprehensive bibliography on spreadsheet errors and testing techniques [80].

More recently, Felienne Hermans and others have started applying general software engineering concepts, principles, and tools to the development of spreadsheet models [76].

However, our main interest here is spreadsheet implementation and variations and extensions on the spreadsheet concept. Literature in that area includes Piersol's 1986 paper [121] on implementing a spreadsheet in Smalltalk. On the topic of recalculation, the paper hints that at first, an idea similar to update event listeners (section 3.3.1) was attempted but was given up in favor of another mechanism that more resembles that implemented by Corecalc, described in section 2.12.

De Hoon's 1995 MSc thesis [41] and related papers [42] describe a rather comprehensive spreadsheet implementation in the lazy functional language Clean. The resulting spreadsheet is somewhat non-standard, as it uses the Clean language for cell formulas, allows the user to define further functions in that language, and supports symbolic computation on formulas. Other papers on extended spreadsheet paradigms in functional languages include Davie and Hammond's Functional Hypersheets [40] and Lisper and Malmström's Haxcel interface to Haskell [93].

Nuñez's remarkable 2000 MSc thesis [113] presents an extended spreadsheet system called ViSSh (Visualization Spreadsheet). The system is based on three ideas. First, as in Piersol's system, there is a rich variety of types of cell contents, such as graphical components; second, the functional language Scheme is used for writing formulas, and there is no distinction between values and functions; and third, the system uses lazy evaluation so recalculation is performed only when it has an impact on observable output. Among other things, these generalizations enable a spreadsheet formula to "call" another sheet as a function. The implementation seems to maintain both an explicit dependency graph (for each cell, a set of the cells that it refers to) and an explicit support graph (for each cell, a set of the cells that refer to it). Such explicit representations can be very memory-consuming when there are multiple copies of formulas with cell area arguments, as discussed in section 3.3.2. Chapters 4 and 5 describe more compact symbolic representations.

Jocelyn Paine describes how to generate a VBA (Visual Basic for Applications) function from Excel formulas [117]. This work is inspired by [120] but unfortunately seems somewhat incomplete. For instance, it appears not to handle Excel's IF function, which indeed requires special treatment and in particular if recursion is allowed (see chapter 9).

Wang and Ambler developed an experimental spreadsheet program called Formulate [161]. Region arguments are used instead of the usual relative/absolute cell references, and functions are applied based on the shape of their region arguments.

The Formulate implementation does not appear to be publicly available.

Burnett et al. developed Forms/3 [28], which contains several generalizations of the spreadsheet paradigm. New abstraction mechanisms are added, and the evaluation mechanism is extended to react not only to user edits but also to external events such as time passing or new data arriving asynchronously on a stream. Forms/3 is implemented in Liquid Common Lisp and is available (for non-commercial use) in binary form for the Sun Solaris and HP-UX operating systems, but it does not appear to be available in source form.

A MITRE technical report [61] by Francoeur presents a recalculation engine, called ExcelComp, in Java for Excel spreadsheets. The engine has an interpreted mode and a compiled mode. The approach requires that the spreadsheet does not contain any static cyclic dependencies, and it is not clear that it handles volatile functions (section 1.7.5). There is no discussion of the size of the dependency graph or techniques for representing it compactly. The ExcelComp implementation is not available to the public [62].

Yoder and Cohn have written a whole series of papers on spreadsheets, data-flow computation, and parallel execution. Topics include the relation among spreadsheet computation, demand-driven (eductive, lazy) and data-driven (eager) evaluation, parallel evaluation, and generalized indexing notations [168], as well as the design of a spreadsheet language Mini-SP with array values and recursion (not unlike Corecalc) and a case study solving several non-trivial computation problems [169]. They also present a Generalized Spreadsheet Model in which cell formulas can be Scheme expressions, including functions, and an explicit "dependency graph" (actually a support graph as defined in section 3.3.2 and chapter 4) is used to perform minimal recalculation and schedule parallel execution [167, 170].

Clack and Braine present a spreadsheet paradigm that includes features from functional programming, such as higher-order functions, as well as features from object-oriented programming, such as virtual methods and dynamic dispatch [34].

None of the investigated implementations appears to use the sharing-preserving formula representation of Corecalc.

In addition to Yoder and Cohn's papers mentioned above, there are a few other papers on parallelization of spreadsheet computations. For instance, Wack [159] investigates how the dependency graph can be used to schedule parallel computation.

Lew and Halverson [90] proposed creating field-programmable custom hardware for spreadsheet evaluation. Custom circuitry realizing a particular spreadsheet's formula would be generated at run-time by configuring an FPGA (field-programmable gate array) chip attached to a desktop computer. This can be thought of as run-time hardware generation, an extreme form of run-time code generation. In addition, it should be possible to perform computations in parallel; spreadsheets lend themselves well to parallelization because of a fairly static dependency structure.

A paper by Stadelmann [147] describes a spreadsheet paradigm that uses equational constraints (as in constraint logic programming) instead of unidirectional formulas. Some patents (numbers 11 and 16) propose a similar idea. This seriously changes the recalculation machinery needed; Stadelmann used Wolfram's Mathematica [166] tool to compute solutions.

A spreadsheet paradigm that computes with intervals, or even interval constraints, is proposed by Hyvönen and de Pascale [43, 78, 79].

The interval computation approach was used in the PhD thesis [11] of Ayalew as a tool for testing spreadsheets. A user can create a "shadow" sheet with interval formulas that specify the expected values of the real sheet's formulas.

Burnett and her group have developed methods for spreadsheet testing, in particular the Wysiwyt or "What You See Is What You Test" approach [29, 127, 128, 129, 57] within the EUSES consortium [144]. This work is also the subject of patents 9 and 10, listed in appendix B.

The research group *SpreadSheets as a Programming Paradigm* (SSaaPP) [9] at the University of Minho investigates extensions of the spreadsheet paradigm and spreadsheet use, such as their interaction with relational databases [39] and model-driven spreadsheet engineering [38].

Gulwani and others [71] have investigated how to synthesize spreadsheet functions or formulas from a small set of examples of the transformations desired.

Several researchers have recently proposed various forms of type systems for spreadsheets, usually to support units of measurements so that one can prevent accidental addition of dollars and yen or of inches and kilograms. Some notable contributions include Erwig and Burnett [51], Ahmad and others [6], Antoniu and others [8], Coblenz [35], Abraham and Erwig [2, 4, 5], Chambers [31], and Cheng and Rival [33].

1.10   Online resources and implementations

The company Decision Models sells advice on how to improve recalculation times for Excel spreadsheets, and in that connection it provides useful technical information about Excel's implementation (see section 3.3.5) on its website [45]. Charles Williams maintains an interesting blog *Excel and UDF Performance Stuff* with technical information about Excel and advice on its efficient use [165].

There are quite a few open source spreadsheet implementations in addition to the modern comprehensive implementations Gnumeric [66] and OpenOffice Calc [115], already mentioned. A Unix classic is `sc`, originally written by James Gosling and now maintained by Chuck Martin [97], and the several descendants of `sc` such as `xspread`, `slsc`, and `ss`. The user interface of `sc` is text-based, reminiscent of VisiCalc, SuperCalc, and other MS DOS era spreadsheet programs.

A comprehensive and free spreadsheet program is Abykus [143] by Brad Smith. This program is not open source and presents a number of generalizations and deviations relative to the mainstream (Excel, OpenOffice Calc, and Gnumeric).

One managed code open source spreadsheet program is Vincent Granet's XXL [70], written in STk, a version of Tk based on the Scheme programming language. Another one, currently less developed, is Einar Pehrson's CleanSheets [119], which is written in Java. Martin Manns' Pyspread uses Python code for cell formulas [95]. More spreadsheet programs—historical, commercial, or open source—are listed on Chris Browne's spreadsheet website [23], with historical notes connecting them. Another source of useful information is the list of frequently asked questions [136] from the Usenet newsgroup `comp.apps.spreadsheets`, although the last update was in June 2002. The newsgroup itself [155] seems to be devoted mainly to spreadsheet application and does not appear to receive much traffic.

There are a number of commercial closed source managed code implementations of Excel-compatible spreadsheet recalculation engines, graphical components, and report generators. Two such implementations are SpreadsheetGear for .NET [146] and the seemingly defunct Formula One for Java [124]. The lead developer for both is (or was) Joe Erickson. Two other implementations are KDCalc [82] from Knowledge Dynamics Inc. and SpreadsheetConverter by Framtidsforum AB [60]. Such implementations are typically used to implement spreadsheet logic on servers without the need to manually reimplement formulas and so on in Java, C#, or other programming languages.

Spreadsheet implementation is frequently used to illustrate the use of a programming language or software engineering techniques. For instance, that was the original goal of the above-mentioned XXL spreadsheet program. A very early example is the MicroCalc spreadsheet program distributed in source form with Borland Turbo Pascal 1.0 (November 1983), still available at Borland's "Antique Software" site [20]. Another example is the spreadsheet chapter in John English's Ada95 book [50, chapter 18]; however, this is clearly not designed with efficiency in mind.

1.11   Spreadsheet implementation patents

The dearth of technical and scientific literature on spreadsheet implementation is made up for by the great number of patents and patent applications. Searches for such documents can be performed at the European Patent Office's Espacenet [114], the US Patents and Trademarks Office [154], or Google Patents [69]. As of June 2013, there were 611 granted US patents in which the word "spreadsheet" appears in the title or abstract and many more patent applications. Appendix B lists several patents and patent applications that appear to be concerned with the *implementation* rather than the *use* of spreadsheets. A separate technical report [140] lists many more spreadsheet implementation patents.

Some patents of interest are:

- Harris and Bastian at WordPerfect Corporation have a patent, number 17 in appendix B, on a method for "optimal recalculation", further discussed in section 3.3.7.

- Roger Schlafly has two patents, numbers 13 and 15 in appendix B, that describe run-time compilation of spreadsheet formulas to x86 code. A distinguishing feature is the clever use of the math coprocessor and the then relatively new IEEE 754 binary floating-point number representation, and especially its NaN (not-a-number) values, to achieve very fast formula evaluation (see section 2.8.1).

- Bruce Jones and others at Microsoft have a patent, number 3 in appendix B, on multiprocessor recalculation of spreadsheet formulas. It includes a description of the uniprocessor recalculation model that agrees with that given by La Penna [88], summarized in section 3.3.5.

In fact, in one of the very first software patent controversies, several major spreadsheet implementors were sued in 1989 for infringing on US Patent No. 4398249, filed by Rene K. Pardo and Remy Landau in 1970 and granted in 1983 [86]; it is number 18 in appendix B. The patent basically describes an application of topological sorting and appears to contain no technological innovation. The United States Court of Appeals for the Federal Circuit in 1996 upheld the District Court's ruling that the patent is unenforceable [153].

Of particular relevance to Funcalc, described in part II of this book, are the surprisingly many patents and patent applications that claim to have invented compilation of spreadsheet models to more traditional kinds of code, similar to the compiled-mode version of Francoeur's implementation [61] mentioned above:

- Schlafly's patents (numbers 13 and 15 in appendix B) describe compilation of individual formulas to x86 machine code.

- Khosrowshahi and Woloshin's patent (number 8) describes compilation of a spreadsheet model with designated input and output cells to code in a procedural programming language.

- Rank and Pampuch's patent (number 2) describes the idea, but few technical details, of cross-compilation of spreadsheet formulas for space-conserving execution on small-memory mobile devices. This involves, for instance, leaving out unused library functions.

- Rubin and Smialek have a series of patents (including number 1) that describe a spreadsheet recalculation engine, as well as the compilation of individual formulas to source code in Java and other languages. It does not seem to handle non-strict functions such as IF specially, and thus hardly is faithful to Excel or OpenOffice Calc semantics. Probably the system described is the commercial tool KDCalc [82], which allows Excel workbooks to be compiled to web applications and more.

- Waldau's patent application (number 7) describes cross-compilation to another platform, such as a mobile phone or web service. This is a technically substantial patent with references to relevant prior art, such as Schlafly's patents. It describes compilation to dynamically typed and statically typed languages (JavaScript and Java), and how to present the generated code as a WML service, say. Probably the technology described by this application is that used in the SpreadsheetConverter product [60].

- Tanenbaum's patent applications (number 5 and 6) describe compilation of a spreadsheet model with designated input and output cells to C source code.

Part I

Corecalc and Interpretation

Chapter 2

Corecalc Implementation

This chapter describes the Corecalc spreadsheet core implementation, focusing on concepts and their software implementation. Hopefully this will be useful to people who want to modify or extend the Corecalc implementation or who want to create their own spreadsheet implementations.

After defining basic spreadsheet concepts (section 2.1), we consider the grammar of cell contents and how to parse it (section 2.2) and the object-oriented representation of workbooks, sheets, and cells (sections 2.4 through 2.6). Then we consider the representation and evaluation of formula expressions (section 2.7), the resulting run-time values (section 2.8), the representation of cell references and how to perform a simple recalculation (sections 2.9 through 2.13), how to define built-in functions and operators (section 2.14), and how to neatly display formulas that use them (section 2.15). We also develop a space- and time-efficient representation of large sparse sheets (section 2.16). All these sections together describe machinery used for efficient recalculation in a core spreadsheet implementation.

Finally, we consider edit operations that a user may perform on a spreadsheet, such as copying (copy-and-paste) and moving (cut-and-paste) of cells and insertion and deletion of rows and columns. Such bulk edit operations have nothing to do with efficient recalculation but must update cell references in formulas. Sections 2.17 through 2.20 describe such reference updates and their implementation.

Following this chapter, chapter 3 presents additional alternatives to some Corecalc implementation decisions. Chapters 4 and 5 consider which cells must be recalculated when a particular cell is changed and present two ways to explicitly store and maintain this information.

2.1   Workbooks, sheets, cells, formulas, and values

Whereas chapter 1 gave an informal summary of spreadsheet concepts such as workbook, sheet, cell, and formula, this section gives more precise definitions in the context of Corecalc.

2.1.1   Spreadsheet concepts in Corecalc

We first define main Corecalc concepts in the and-or style of Landin and Burge [26]. In the next subsection, we relate them to an object-oriented implementation as summarized in figure 2.1 using UML notation.

- A *workbook* of class Workbook (section 2.4) consists of a collection of sheets.

- A *sheet* of class Sheet (section 2.5) is a rectangular array, each of whose elements may contain null or a cell.

- A non-null *cell* of abstract class Cell (section 2.6) may be

  - a constant, which is either a floating-point number of class NumberCell, a constant text string of class TextCell, or a blank cell of class BlankCell
  - or a formula of class Formula
  - or an array formula of class ArrayFormula.

  A cell could also specify the formatting of contents, data validation criteria, background color, and other attributes, but currently it does not.

- A *formula* of class Formula (section 2.6) consists of

  - a non-null expression of class Expr to produce the cell's value
  - and a cached value of class Value
  - and a workbook reference of class Workbook
  - and a `state` field of type CellState.

- An *array formula* of class ArrayFormula (section 2.6) consists of

  - a non-null cached array formula of class CachedArrayFormula
  - and a cell address of struct type CellAddr.

- A *cached array formula* of class CachedArrayFormula (section 2.6) consists of

  - a formula of class Formula
  - and the address, as a pair (c, r), at which that formula was entered
  - and the corners (`ulCa`, `lrCa`) of the rectangle of cells sharing the formula.

- An *expression* of abstract class Expr (section 2.7) may be

  - a floating-point constant of class NumberConst
  - or a constant text string of class TextConst
  - or a static error of class Error

- – or a cell reference of class CellRef, consisting of a sheet and a single relative/absolute reference
- – or an area reference of class CellArea, consisting of a sheet and two relative/absolute references
- – or a call of a function or operator, of class FunCall.

- A *value* of abstract class Value (section 2.8) is produced by evaluation of an expression. A value may be

  - – a floating-point number of class NumberValue
  - – or a text string of class TextValue
  - – or an error value of class ErrorValue
  - – or an array value of class ArrayValue
  - – or an external object reference encapsulated as an ObjectValue, used for results of external functions (section 8.7.2)
  - – or a function value of class FunctionValue, used to implement higher-order sheet-defined functions (sections 2.8.5 and 8.4.1).

- An *atomic value* is a NumberValue or a TextValue.

- An *array value* of abstract class ArrayValue (section 2.8.4) may be

  - – an *explicit array* of class ArrayExplicit, which is a window onto a rectangular array of Values, some of which may be null
  - – or an *array view* of class ArrayView, which is a window onto a sheet
  - – or an *array double matrix* of class ArrayDouble, which is a matrix of floating-point numbers.

- A *raref* or relative/absolute reference of class RARef (section 2.9) is a four-tuple (`colAbs`, `col`, `rowAbs`, `row`) used to represent cell references `A1`, `$A$1`, `$A1`, `A$1`, and area references `A1:$B2` and so on in formulas. If the `colAbs` field is true, then the column reference `col` is absolute (`$`), otherwise relative (non-`$`); and similarly for rows.

- A *cell address* of struct type CellAddr (section 2.11) is the absolute, zero-based location (*col*, *row*) of a cell in a sheet.

- A *function* of class Function (section 2.14) represents a built-in function such as `SIN` or a built-in operator such as (+).

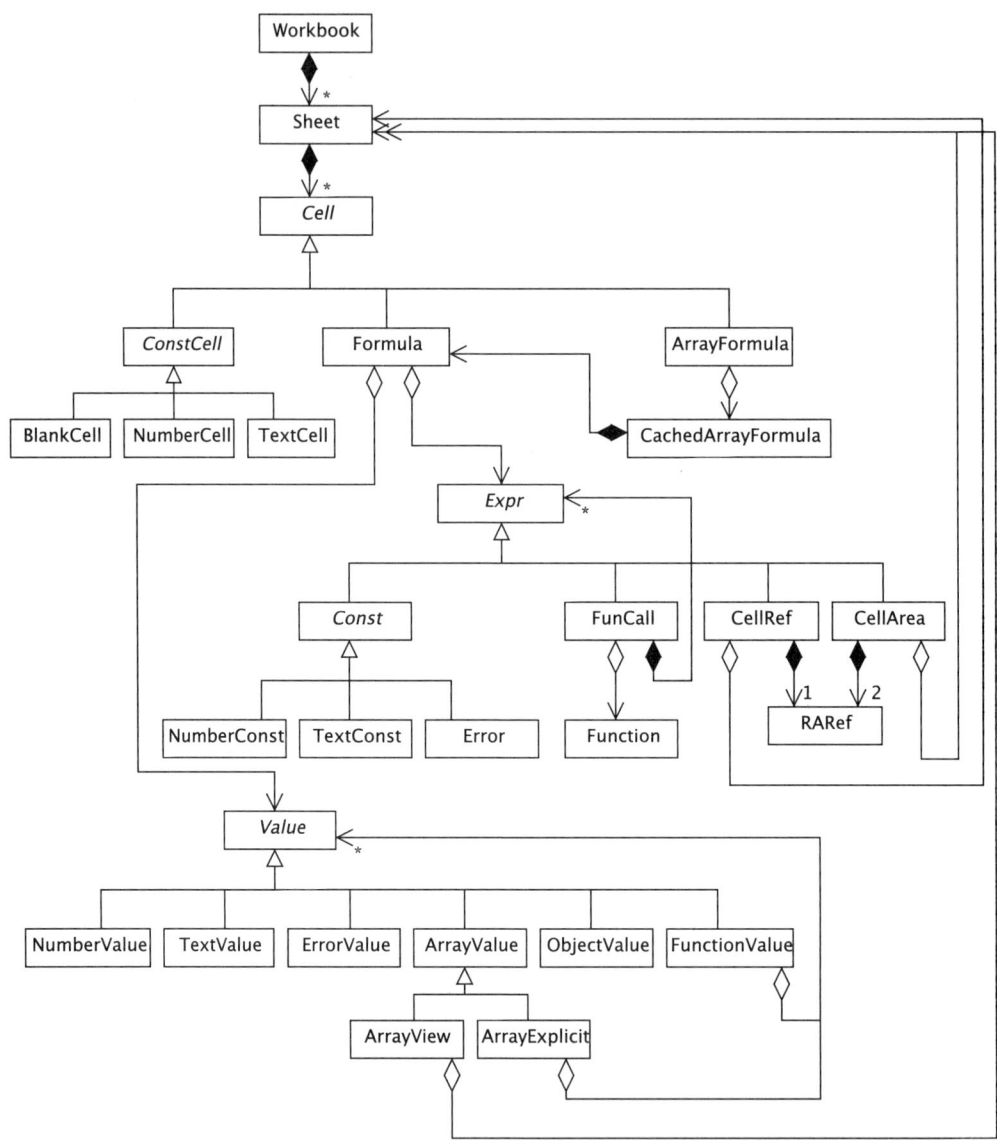

Figure 2.1: The classes supporting interpretive evaluation in Corecalc and Funcalc. A triangular arrow denotes inheritance, with the arrow pointing at the base class; an arrow originating in an open rhombus denotes aggregation; and an arrow originating in a solid rhombus denotes composition (see section 2.1.2).

2.1.2 Aside: Object-oriented software

A spreadsheet implementation manipulates and evaluates spreadsheet formulas and is an example of a program that processes other programs, just like a compiler. Hence, these "other programs", for instance, spreadsheet formulas, must be represented as data. Although an expression such as `23 + SIN(A1)` can be considered a string of characters "2", "3", " ", "+", and so on, it is impractical to manipulate an expression that is represented simply as a string.

Corecalc is written in C#, a class-based, object-oriented programming language, so inside Corecalc, an expression is represented by several objects, each corresponding to part of the expression. In general, class-based, object-oriented software consists of a number of class definitions, where each class contains fields (that hold data, such as references to other objects) and methods (that define behavior or computation). During execution, the software creates multiple objects, or instances, from each class. Each object instance x has its own copy of the class's fields, and a call `x.m()` to a method on instance x will work on x's copy of the fields.

For instance, Corecalc defines a class CellRef, and each object instance of CellRef represents a cell reference such as A1. Likewise, there is a class FunCall, where each object instance of FunCall represents the application of a function, such as `SIN`, to argument expressions, each of which is represented by an object that is an instance of a suitable class.

Concretely, the expression `23 + SIN(A1)` will be represented by a Number-Const object representing 23, a CellRef object representing the A1 reference, a Fun-Call object representing the application of function `SIN` to the A1 reference, and a FunCall object representing the application of the + operator to 23 and the `SIN` function call, as illustrated in figure 2.2.

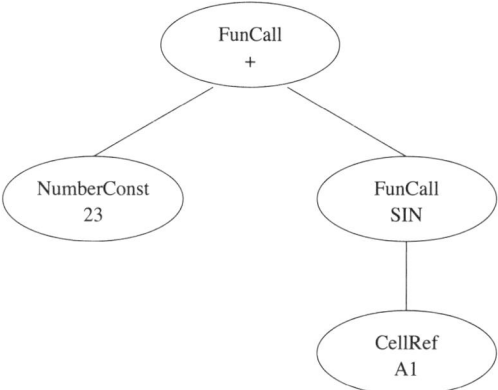

Figure 2.2: Internal representation, or abstract syntax, for the expression `23 + SIN(A1)`. There is one object of class NumberConst, one object of class CellRef, and two objects of class FunCall. Each FunCall object has a field that refers to the function's argument expressions, which are themselves objects; the `SIN` FunCall instance has one argument, the + FunCall instance has two arguments.

The classes in object-oriented software may be related in several ways, all illustrated in figure 2.1. First, *inheritance* is indicated by a triangular arrow that points from the inheriting class to its base class or superclass. For instance, class NumberValue inherits from abstract class Value; this means that a NumberValue is a special case of a Value, and any operation that is meaningful for a value (such as printing it) is meaningful for a number value also. The classes inheriting from Value form a class hierarchy, which says that a Value may be either a NumberValue or a TextValue or ...; hence, the diagram reflects exactly the written definition of a value, with cases separated by "or" in section 2.1.1. In figure 2.1, there are three notable class hierarchies, rooted at the abstract classes Cell, Expr, and Value.

Second, *aggregation* is shown by an arrow originating in an open rhombus. An object of the class at the rhombus end has a reference to an object of the class at the other end; an asterisk on the arrow means zero or more references. For instance, a Formula object has a reference to a Value object and a reference to an Expr object, namely, the formula's expression and its cached value, just as in the written definition of formula on page 28. With aggregation, multiple Formula objects may refer to the same Value object because multiple formulas may cache the same value.

Third, *composition* is shown by an arrow originating in a solid rhombus. An object of the class at the rhombus end has a reference to an object of the class at the other end, just as in aggregation, but with composition there can only be one reference to the referred-to object: the object at the solid rhombus end "owns" the referred-to object. For instance, a Workbook object may refer to multiple Sheet objects, but each Sheet object is referred to by only one Workbook object: the same sheet cannot belong to multiple workbooks.

The combination of inheritance and either aggregation or composition is an example of the composite pattern, an object-oriented design pattern [64]. For instance, in figure 2.1, class FunCall is a subclass of Expr (inheritance), and a FunCall object can hold zero or more unique references to Expr objects (composition). This means that one can build an expression tree through the use of FunCall objects, as illustrated in figure 2.2. Similarly, the FunctionValue, ArrayView, and ArrayExplicit classes are subclasses of Value (inheritance), and objects of these classes can hold references to Value objects (aggregation). This means that one can build a value graph through the use of FunctionValue, ArrayView, and ArrayExplicit objects.

Which classes and inheritance relationships are relevant depends on their use. For instance, in the compiled implementation of sheet-defined functions explained in chapters 7 and 8, it is useful to represent expressions by a more elaborate class hierarchy, as shown by figure 7.3, which has more than 30 classes, compared with just 8 expression-related classes in figure 2.1.

Aggregation and composition correspond to the definitions of formula, array formula, and so on, with cases separated by "and" in section 2.1.1. Thus, although figure 2.1 and section 2.1.1 look very different, they are simply different presentations of the same set of concepts.

2.2   Syntax and parsing

The contents of a spreadsheet cell are entered as a string but must be converted to an internal representation before they can be evaluated. This section outlines the conversion and also presents the syntax (grammar) that Corecalc formulas must adhere to.

2.2.1   Aside: Scanning, parsing, and abstract syntax

As described above, inside Corecalc, a formula is represented by several objects. However, when a user enters a formula or when a spreadsheet is loaded from a file, a formula is represented as a string of characters. Hence, the formula needs to be converted from the string representation, called concrete syntax, to the internal object representation, called abstract syntax. This conversion is performed by the processes of scanning and parsing, as illustrated in figure 2.3.

Figure 2.3: Scanning converts a string of characters into a sequence of tokens, and parsing further converts it into an abstract syntax tree, such as that in figure 2.2.

- Scanning converts the string representation of an expression into a stream of tokens. For instance, the string "`23 + SIN(B1)`" consists of the tokens `23`, `+`, `SIN`, `(`, `B1`, and `)`. Note that each coherent part of the string, such as `23` and `SIN`, is kept together as a token, and extra spaces are not represented by tokens.

- Parsing converts the sequence of tokens into an abstract syntax tree, represented by objects. In the example "`23 + SIN(B1)`", the object representation will be exactly as already shown in figure 2.2. Note that parentheses are not represented in the abstract syntax; instead, the tree structure shows which subexpressions belong together.

In short, scanning concerns the local structure of an expression or a program, and parsing concerns its global structure, such as the nesting and matching of parentheses. Scanning is also called lexing (and tokens are also called lexemes) because it concerns the formation of words.

Scanner and parser programs may be written by hand but are often generated automatically by tools such as the classical `lex` and `yacc` from the mid-1970s [7]. A scanner generator takes as input a scanner specification, which describes each possible token by a regular expression such as `digit { digit }` for an integer token. A parser generator takes as input a parser specification, which describes the legal forms of an expression or a program by a context-free grammar as shown in figure 2.4. The full parser specification (not shown) would also describe how to build the abstract syntax for each form of expression. The Corecalc scanner and parser were generated by the CoCo/R tool [106] (see section 2.2.3).

There is a rich literature on scanning and parsing, regular expressions, and various classes of grammars, going back to the late 1950s. For references, see [7].

2.2.2 Corecalc cell contents syntax

The legal contents of a non-blank cell in Corecalc is similar to that of a non-blank cell in Excel, Gnumeric, or OpenOffice Calc. The grammar in figure 2.4 describes cell contents by the non-terminal `CellContents`, which says that it must be a number, a quoted text, a string, or a formula, where a formula is an equals sign "=" followed by an expression. An expression, described by non-terminal `Expr`, either consists of an infix operator applied to other expressions or is a cell reference, an area reference, a number, a string, an expression in parentheses, or a function call.

```
Expr ::=                           Raref ::=
    Expr == Expr                       Column Row
  | Expr <> Expr                     | $ Column Row
  | Expr < Expr                      | Column $ Row
  | Expr <= Expr                     | $ Column $ Row
  | Expr > Expr                      | R Offset C Offset
  | Expr >= Expr
  | Expr & Expr                    Offset ::=
  | Expr + Expr                        <empty>
  | Expr - Expr                      | Uint
  | Expr * Expr                      | [ Int ]
  | Expr / Expr
  | Expr ^ Expr                    Call ::=
  | Raref                              Name ( Exprs )
  | Raref : Raref
  | Sheetref                       Exprs ::=
  | Number                             Expr
  | " String "                       | Expr , Exprs
  | ( Expr )
  | Call                           CellContents ::=
                                       Number
Sheetref ::=                         | ' String
    Name ! Raref                     | " String "
  | Name ! Raref : Raref             | = Expr
```

Figure 2.4: The syntax of Corecalc cell contents is described by non-terminal `CellContents`. Token `Number` is a floating-point constant; `String` is a sequence of characters; `Name` is a legal function or sheet name; `Column` is a column name A, B, ...; `Row` is a row number 1, 2, ...; `Uint` is a non-negative integer; and `Int` is an integer.

As in Excel and OpenOffice Calc, an array formula has no special syntax but is written as an ordinary formula. In Corecalc it is distinguished not by the special final incantation Ctrl+Shift+Enter but simply by being entered after the selection of a whole target cell area rather than a single target cell.

The Corecalc grammar does not permit ranges to specify multiple sheets, although this is permitted in Excel with notation such as SUM(Sheet1:Sheet12!B2) and in OpenOffice Calc with notation such as SUM(Sheet1.B2:Sheet12.B2). It would be quite easy to permit this. Also, Corecalc does not permit full-column references such as SUM(B:B), although they are permitted in Excel.

2.2.3   Formula parsing

We have rewritten the above grammar to produce a scanner and parser specification for the CoCo/R tool [106]; the rewritten specification is in file Spreadsheet.ATG. CoCo/R is a relatively simple tool that generates so-called recursive descent parsers, so the grammar rewrite is necessary to give operators the correct associativity and precedence while avoiding left recursive grammar productions. All operators are left associative, even the exponentiation operator (^), just as in Excel and OpenOffice Calc. The resulting parser builds and returns the abstract syntax tree as a Cell object. The following problems must be considered:

- When parsing a formula, we must know the workbook that contains it and the cell address at which it was entered. Otherwise we cannot resolve relative cell and area references, and sheet-absolute ones, to our abstract syntax.

- The CoCo/R scanner apparently does not support the definition of overlapping token classes, such as an identifier ([a-zA-Z][a-zA-Z0-9]*) and a column name ([a-zA-Z]+). This complicates the notation for calls to functions, such as LOG10, whose name looks like a cell reference. This was not a problem in Excel 2003, in which the last column name was IV.

2.2.4   Interning of cell contents

Corecalc can read XML Spreadsheet 2003 (XMLSS file format) files with suffix .xml as exported from Excel, a workbook format in which formulas are stored as text using the R1C1 cell reference format (section 1.3). An XMLSS file is read using the XmlReader class from the .NET class library, and individual cell contents are parsed using the CoCo/R-based parser described in section 2.2.3.

To conserve memory and speed up loading of spreadsheets, cell contents are "interned" by maintaining a dictionary that maps the text representation of a cell's contents to the abstract syntax tree representation created by the parser. For instance, if some cell contains the formula =SUM($A$1:$A$9), then the interning dictionary will map the string "=SUM($A$1:$A$9)" to the formula's abstract syntax tree of type Cell (section 2.6). If the same formula string is encountered again in another cell, then the abstract syntax tree is reused for that cell. This saves both parsing and allocation of the abstract syntax tree.

Since the R1C1 reference format is copy-invariant (section 1.3), this means that all cells in the workbook that were created by copying some other cell (or that could have been created that way) will be represented only once as an abstract syntax tree in memory.

2.3 Aside: Functional concept modeling

Yet a third way to represent the same concepts as figure 2.1 and section 2.1.1 would be to use functional-style type declarations. If Corecalc had been implemented in the F# functional language, then we might have defined the same concepts using the type declarations shown in figure 2.5.

The type notation `sheet list` means "list of sheets". Likewise, `cell option` means "either a cell or nothing", and `t [,]` means "two-dimensional array each of whose elements has type `t`", so `cell option [,]` means "two-dimensional array each of whose elements is a `cell` or nothing".

In functional programming, the "or" definitions in section 2.1.1 become type definitions with alternatives separated by a vertical bar "`|`"; compare, for instance, type `value` in the figure with the definition of *value* on page 29.

The "and" definitions become record types, as in type `formula`:

```
{ e: expr; cached: value option; wb: workbook; state: cellstate }
```

This record has four components called `e`, `cached`, `wb`, and `state`, as prescribed in the definition of a formula on page 28.

One possible disadvantage of the functional type declarations in figure 2.5 is that they are too concrete. For instance, a `sheet` is defined as a two-dimensional array of cells. While this is conceptually correct, it is too naïve for representing very large sparse sheets. The somewhat more abstract object-oriented class diagram in figure 2.1 allows for more sophisticated sheet implementations (see section 2.16).

2.4 Workbooks and sheets

A workbook of class Workbook contains zero or more sheets, organized as a list of non-null Sheet references, where no two references refer to the same Sheet object.

Notable methods on class Workbook include:

- `void` **AddSheet** `(Sheet sheet)` adds `sheet` at the end of the workbook.

- `Sheet` **this**`[String name]` returns the named sheet.

- `void Recalculate()` initiates a recalculation of all changed and volatile cells, and all cells transitively dependent on these, in all sheets of the workbook (see section 4.3.1).

- `void RecalculateFull()` initiates a full recalculation of all active cells in all sheets of the workbook (see section 4.3.1).

```
type workbook = sheet list
and sheet = cell option [,]
and cell =
    | NumberCell of double
    | TextCell of string
    | BlankCell
    | Formula of formula
    | ArrayFormula of arrayformula
and formula =
    { e: expr; cached: value option; wb: workbook; state: cellstate }
and arrayformula =
    { caf: cachedarrayformula; ca: celladdr }
and cachedarrayformula =
    { f: formula; c: int; r: int; ulCa: celladdr; lrCa: celladdr }
and expr =
    | NumberConst of double
    | TextConst of string
    | Error of error
    | CellRef of sheet * raref
    | CellArea of sheet * raref * raref
    | FunCall of func * expr list
and value =
    | NumberValue of double
    | TextValue of string
    | ErrorValue of errorvalue
    | ArrayValue of arrayvalue
    | ObjectValue of objectvalue
    | FunctionValue of sdf * value list
and arrayvalue =
    | ArrayExplicit of value [,]
    | ArrayView of sheet * celladdr * celladdr
    | ArrayDouble of double [,]

type raref =
    { colAbs: bool; col: int; rowAbs: bool; row: int }
type celladdr = int * int
type cellstate = Dirty | Computing | Uptodate
```

Figure 2.5: Hypothetical F# type declarations, representing the same concepts as the class diagram in figure 2.1 and the definitions on section 2.1.1. Note in particular the structural similarity to the latter. For brevity, some types (`func`, `error`, etc.) are not shown.

- void `RecalculateFullRebuild()` initiates a full recalculation but first rebuilds the support graph (see section 4.2.9).

2.5   Sheets

A Sheet contains a rectangular array of cells (think of it as having type Cell[,]), each element of which may be null, representing a blank cell, or non-null, representing an active cell. No two cell references from the same sheet or from different sheets can refer to the same Cell object.

Notable methods on class Sheet include:

- Cell **InsertCell**(String text, CellAddr ca) parses text to obtain an abstract syntax tree of type Cell, stores that at position ca in the sheet, and returns it.

- void **SetArrayFormula**(Cell cell, int col, int row, CellAddr ulCa, CellAddr lrCa) creates a CachedArrayFormula from cell, which must be a Formula at position col, row, and stores ArrayFormula objects in the cells in the area with corners ulCa and lrCa, all sharing the same CachedArrayFormula.

- void **InsertRowCols**(int R, int N, bool doRows) inserts N new rows (or columns) before row (or column) R >= 0 in this sheet, and adjusts all referring formulas in this sheet and other sheets by calling InsertRowCols on active cells. Performs row insertion if doRows is true, otherwise column insertion; supports both cases to avoid code duplication (see section 2.19).

- void **MoveCell**(int fromCol, int fromRow, int col, int row) moves the cell contents in cell (fromCol,fromRow) to cell (col, row).

- void **PasteCell**(Cell cell, CellAddr ca, int cols, int rows) pastes or copies cell, which must be a formula or constant, to the cell area that has upper left-hand corner (ca.col, ca.row) and cols columns and rows rows. If cell is a formula, all the resulting Formula objects will be distinct but will share the same underlying Expr object.

- void **PasteCell**(Cell cell, CellAddr ca) pastes or copies cell, which must be a formula or constant, to the cell address ca. If cell is a formula, then the new cell has its own Formula object, but it shares cell's underlying Expr object.

- void **RecalculateFull**() initiates a full recalculation of all active cells in the sheet.

- void **Reset**() calls Reset() on every active cell in the sheet.

- void **ShowAll**(Shower show) calls the passed method show on every active cell in the sheet, passing its column, row, and value.

- `String` **`Show`**`(int col, int row)` returns a string representing the Cell contents at position (`col`,`row`).

- `String` **`ShowValue`**`(int col, int row)` returns a string representing the value (if any) in the cell at position (`col`,`row`).

- `Cell` **`this`**`[int col, int row]` gets or sets the cell at position (`col`,`row`) in the sheet.

- `Cell` **`this`**`[CellAddr ca]` gets or sets the cell at position in the sheet.

2.6   Cells, formulas, and array formulas

A cell in a sheet may contain an object of abstract type Cell, which has concrete subclasses BlankCell, NumberCell, TextCell, Formula, and ArrayFormula (see figure 2.1).

Abstract class Cell has the following significant methods:

- `Value` **`Eval`**`(Sheet sheet, int col, int row)` evaluates the cell's contents, and all cells that it depends on, and marks the cell up to date, unless already up to date; then returns the cell's value.

- `void` **`InsertRowCols`**`(Dictionary<Expr,Adjusted<Expr>> adjusted, Sheet mod, bool thisSheet, int R, int N, int r, bool doRows)` adjusts the formula in this cell, originally in row (or column) r, after insertion of N new rows (or columns) before row (or column) R `>= 0`. Performs row insertion if `doRows` is true; otherwise performs column insertion (see section 2.19).

- `Cell` **`MoveContents`**`(int deltaCol, int deltaRow)` returns a new cell object, resulting from moving the given cell by (`deltaCol`, `deltaRow`).

- `static Cell` **`Parse`**`(String text, Workbook workbook, int col, int row)` parses `text` to an abstract syntax tree of type Cell, assuming the cell's position is (`col`, `row`).

- `void` **`ResetCellState`**`()` resets the cell's `state` flag, if any, to Dirty (see section 2.12).

- `String` **`Show`**`(int col, int row, Format fo)` shows the cell's contents (nothing, constant, formula, array formula).

- `String` **`ShowValue`**`(Sheet sheet, int col, int row)` returns a string displaying the cell's value, if necessary computing it first.

A floating-point constant is represented by a NumberCell object, and a text constant is represented by a TextCell object. A blank cell is usually represented by a null reference, but if the blank cell is referred to by some other cell, its support set (section 4.2) will be non-empty and must be stored somewhere, so a BlankCell object is created for that purpose.

An ordinary number- or text-valued formula is represented by a Formula object and is basically an expression together with machinery for caching its value, once computed. Thus, a formula contains a non-null expression of class Expr, a cached value of class Value, a cell state field to control recalculation (see section 2.12), and a reference to the containing workbook. The latter serves to resolve absolute sheet references within the expression.

Whereas a given Formula object shall not be reachable from multiple distinct Cell[,] elements, an Expr object may well be reachable from many distinct Formula objects. In fact, it is a design objective of Corecalc to achieve such sharing of Expr objects (see section 2.9).

An array formula computes an array value, that is, a rectangular array of values. This result must be distributed over a rectangular cell area of the same shape as the array value, so that each cell in the area receives one component (one ordinary value) from the array value, just as in Excel and OpenOffice Calc. An ArrayFormula is a cell entry that represents one cell's component of the array. Hence, an ArrayFormula object in a sheet cell contains two things: a non-null reference to a CachedArrayFormula object shared among all cells in the cell area, and that particular sheet cell's (col, row) location within the cell area. The shared CachedArrayFormula contains a Formula, whose expression must evaluate to an ArrayValue, as well as an indication of the cell area's location within the sheet.

The evaluation of one cell in the array formula's cell area will evaluate the underlying shared Formula once and cache its value (which must be of type ArrayValue) for use by all cells in the cell area.

2.7   Evaluation of expressions

The abstract class Expr has concrete subclasses NumberConst, TextConst, Error, CellRef, CellArea, and FunCall (see figure 2.1). Expressions can be nested and are used to construct formulas; whereas a formula caches its value, an expression does not.

Class Expr has the following abstract methods:

- Value **Eval**(Sheet sheet, int col, int row) evaluates the expression at cell address sheet[col, row], where sheet must be non-null, and returns the result.

- Expr **Move**(int deltaCol, int deltaRow) returns a new Expr in which relative cell references have been updated as if the containing cell were moved, not copied, by deltaCol columns and deltaRow rows (see section 2.18).

- Adjusted<Expr> **InsertRowCols**(Sheet modSheet, bool thisSheet, int R, int N, int r, bool doRows) returns an expression, originally in row (or column) r, adjusting its references after insertion of N new rows (or columns) before row (or column) R >= 0. Performs row insertion if doRows is true; otherwise performs column insertion (see section 2.19).

- String **Show**(int col, int row, int ctxpre, Format fo) returns a string resulting from prettyprinting the expression in a "fixity" context ctxpre that describes the precedence of the enclosing operator, and with formatting options fo (see section 2.15).

2.7.1   Number constant expressions

A NumberConst represents a floating-point constant such as 3.14 in a formula. A NumberConst object encapsulates the number, represented as a NumberValue (section 2.8); its Eval method returns that value:

```
class NumberConst : Const {
  private readonly NumberValue value;
  public NumberConst(double d) {
    value = new NumberValue(d);
  }
  public override Value Eval(Sheet sheet, int col, int row) {
    return value;
  }
  public override String Show(int col, int row, int ctxpre,
                              Format fo)
  {
    return value.ToString();
  }
}
```

2.7.2   Text constant expressions

A TextConst represents a text constant such as "foo" in a formula and is very similar to a NumberConst, except in the way the constant is displayed:

```
class TextConst : Const {
  public readonly TextValue value;
  public TextConst(String s) {
    value = TextValue.MakeInterned(s);
  }
  public override Value Eval(Sheet sheet, int col, int row) {
    return value;
  }
  public override String Show(int col, int row, int ctxpre,
                              Formats fo)
  {
    return "\"" + value + "\"";
  }
}
```

Since a given text constant (such as `"June"`) may appear many times in a workbook, an effort is made to store the underlying TextValue only once, by "interning", as shown in the TextConst constructor.

2.7.3   Error constant expressions

An Error constant expression may arise from an editing operation. For instance, a cell reference such as `B2` will be replaced by the error constant `#REF!` in case column B or row 2 gets deleted (see section 2.20).

2.7.4   Cell reference expressions

A CellRef represents a cell reference such as `$B7`; it consists of a RARef (section 2.9) and, if the cell reference is sheet-absolute, a sheet reference. A cell reference is evaluated relative to a given sheet, column, and row. Its evaluation involves computing the referred-to cell address `ca` and evaluating the formula in that cell.

```
class CellRef : Expr {
  private readonly RARef raref;
  private readonly Sheet sheet;    // non-null if sheet-absolute
  public override Value Eval(Sheet sheet, int col, int row) {
    CellAddr ca = raref.Addr(col, row);
    Cell cell = (this.sheet ?? sheet)[ca];
    return cell == null ? null : cell.Eval(sheet, ca.col, ca.row);
  }
  public override String Show(int col, int row, int ctxpre,
                             Format fo)
  {
    String s = raref.Show(col, row, fo);
    return sheet==null ? s : sheet.Name + "!" + s;
  }
}
```

The C# expression `(this.sheet ?? sheet)` evaluates to `this.sheet` if it is non-null (when the cell reference in sheet-relative) and otherwise to `sheet` (when the cell reference is sheet-absolute).

2.7.5   Cell area reference expressions

A CellArea represents a cell area reference such as `$B7:B52` in a formula. It consists of two RARefs (section 2.9) giving the area's corner cells and, if the cell area reference is sheet-absolute, a sheet reference. A cell area is evaluated, by `Eval`, relative to a given sheet, column, and row, by finding the cell addresses of the upper left corner `ulCa` and lower right corner `lrCa` of the referred-to cell area, and creating an ArrayView (section 2.8) of the cell area. Then every non-blank cell in the view is evaluated by calling the indexer `view[c,r]` to detect attempts to create a cyclic view, and finally the view is returned:

```
class CellArea : Expr {
  private readonly RARef ul, lr;   // upper left, lower right
  private readonly Sheet sheet;     // non-null if sheet-absolute
  public override Value Eval(Sheet sheet, int col, int row) {
    CellAddr ulCa = ul.Addr(col, row), lrCa = lr.Addr(col, row);
    ArrayView view = ArrayView.Make(ulCa, lrCa, this.sheet ?? sheet);
    for (int c = 0; c < view.Cols; c++)
      for (int r = 0; r < view.Rows; r++) {
        Value ignore = view[c, r];
      }
    return view;
  }
  public override String Show(int col, int row, int ctxpre,
                              Format fo)
  {
    String s = ul.Show(col, row, fo) + ":" + lr.Show(col, row, fo);
    return sheet==null ? s : sheet.Name + "!" + s;
  }
  ...
}
```

2.7.6 Function call and operator expressions

A FunCall represents a function call such as `SIN(B7)`, or an infix operator application such as `A1+B6`, in a formula. It consists of a Function object representing the function to call and a non-null array of non-null argument expressions. A function call is evaluated relative to a given sheet, column, and row by invoking the function's `applier` (section 2.14) on the argument expressions and sheet, column, and row. The argument expressions are passed unevaluated to cater for non-strict functions such as `IF`. The `Show` function displays the function call in prefix or infix notation as appropriate (see section 2.15). Section 2.14 describes the function call machinery in more detail.

```
class FunCall : Expr {
  private readonly Function function;   // Non-null
  private readonly Expr[] es;            // Non-null, elts non-null
  public override Value Eval(Sheet sheet, int col, int row) {
    return function.applier(sheet, es, col, row);
  }
  public override String Show(int col, int row, int ctxpre,
                              Format fo)
  {
    StringBuilder sb = new StringBuilder();
    int pre = function.fixity;
    if (pre == 0) { // Not operator
      ... show as F(arg1, ..., argN) ...
    } else { // Operator; es.Length must 1 or 2
      ... show as arg1+arg2 or similar ...
```

```
    }
    return sb.ToString();
  }
  ...
}
```

2.8   Run-time values

The abstract class Value has subclasses NumberValue, TextValue, ErrorValue, ArrayValue, ObjectValue, and FunctionValue as shown in figure 2.1. This means that values, including numbers, are wrapped as objects at run-time, which incurs a cost in time and memory.

A NumberValue represents a floating-point number or a logical value (see section 2.8.2). A TextValue represents a text string and has a public readonly field `value` containing that string. An ErrorValue represents the result of an illegal operation (there are no exceptions in spreadsheets) and has a public readonly field `msg` of type String holding a description of the error (see section 2.8.3). An ArrayValue represents the value of a cell area expression or the result of an array formula, as described in section 2.8.4.

A Value has a method `Apply` that applies a delegate `act` to components of the value, useful for implementing `SUM` and other aggregate functions:

```
public abstract class Value {
  public virtual void Apply(Action<Value> act) {
    act(this);
  }
}
```

Here the .NET `Action<T>` delegate type represents a `void` function that takes an argument of type `T`. The only non-trivial override of `Apply` is on array values (see section 2.8.4).

2.8.1   Aside: Representation of floating-point numbers

Modern computers represent floating-point numbers such as 3.14159 or $-6.02 \cdot 10^{23}$ according to the IEEE 754-2008 standard for binary floating-point arithmetic [81], designed chiefly by William Kahan [142]. In particular, a number of type `double` in C# or Java is represented as a 64-bit binary floating-point number, and arithmetic operations (such as +) and mathematical functions (such as `Math.Sqrt`) must follow this standard.

A 64-bit floating-point number has three components: a 1-bit sign s, an 11-bit biased exponent e, and 52 fractional significand bits f, like this:

```
s eeeeeeeeeee fffffffffffffffffffffffffffffffffffffffffffffffffffff
```

Such a `double` number can be of one of several different kinds:

Kind	s	eeeeeeeeee	f...	Purpose
Normal		00000000001 to 11111111110		Usual numbers
Plus zero	0	00000000000	0...0	Plus zero
Minus zero	1	00000000000	0...0	Minus zero
Denormal		00000000000	non-0	Underflow
Plus infinity	0	11111111111	0...0	Overflow
Minus infinity	1	11111111111	0...0	Overflow
NaN		11111111111	1f...	Errors

The value represented by a 64-bit normal number:

```
s eeeeeeeeee ffffffffffffffffffffffffffffffffffffffffffffffffffff
```

is computed as follows:

$$s \cdot 2^{p-1023} \cdot m$$

where $s = +1$ or $s = -1$ according as the s-bit is 0 or 1; where p is the value of eeeeeeeeee when interpreted as an unsigned binary integer; and where m is the value of 1.fff...fff when interpreted as an unsigned binary fraction with a single 1 before the binary point and the 52 fff...fff bits after the binary point. Note that the 64 bits actually stored contain only the fractional part fff...fff of the binary number 1.fff...fff.

The following holds for normal numbers. There are 2^{52} or roughly $4 \cdot 10^{15}$ different m values, corresponding to 15–16 decimal digits of precision. Since the largest normal p value is 2046, the largest representable normal magnitude is $2^{2046-1023} \cdot 2 = 2^{1024}$ or roughly $1.8 \cdot 10^{308}$. Similarly, the smallest representable normal magnitude is $2^{1-1023} \cdot 1 = 2^{-1022}$ or roughly $2.2 \cdot 10^{-308}$, but denormal numbers can represent even smaller magnitudes, although with lower precision.

Here are some examples of normal numbers, zeroes, denormal numbers, infinities, and NaNs:

```
s eeeeeeeeee ffffffffffffffffffffffffffffffffffffffffffffffffffff
0 01111111111 0000000000000000000000000000000000000000000000000000 = 1.0
0 01111111110 0000000000000000000000000000000000000000000000000000 = 0.5
1 10000000101 1101101010000000000000000000000000000000000000000000 = -118.625
0 01111111110 1111111111111111111111111111111111111111111111111111 = 0.999...9
0 01111111011 1001100110011001100110011001100110011001100110011010 = 0.1
0 00000000000 0000000000000000000000000000000000000000000000000000 = 0.0
1 00000000000 0000000000000000000000000000000000000000000000000000 = -0.0
0 00000000000 0001000000000000000000000000000000000000000000000000 = 1.39E-309
0 11111111111 0000000000000000000000000000000000000000000000000000 = +Infinity
1 11111111111 0000000000000000000000000000000000000000000000000000 = -Infinity
s 11111111111 1000000000000000000000000000000000000000000000000000 = NaN
s 11111111111 1000000000000000000000000000000000000000000000000001 = another NaN
```

We shall say that a number is *proper* if it is normal, denormal, or a zero; these are our "usual" numbers. We have both positive and negative zero, but these are indistinguishable by comparisons, and so the difference is visible only in very special cases. A denormal number is used to handle underflow and is different from a normal number chiefly in having less precision. Infinities are used to represent overflow and the results of operations such as `1.0/0.0` and `Math.Log(0.0)`.

A NaN is a special value that means "not a number". It is used to represent errors, such as the result of `Math.Sqrt(-1.0)`. Three properties make NaNs particularly interesting for our spreadsheet implementation. First, a NaN can be distinguished from proper numbers and infinities. Second, there are 2^{51}, or more than 10^{15}, different NaN values because only the first f-bit of a NaN is fixed: it must be 1 to distinguish NaNs from infinities. The remaining 51 f-bits are the NaN's *payload* bits, which we can set as we like, and hence use to distinguish different errors. Third, all arithmetic operations are required to preserve NaN operands and the payload bits, so we get error propagation for free. For instance, if d is a NaN, then `Math.Sqrt(6.1*d+7.5)` must be a NaN with the same payload. If both d1 and d2 are NaNs, then d1+d2 must be a NaN with the same payload as one of d1 and d2; which one is unspecified. This will be especially useful for efficient implementation of sheet-defined functions (see chapter 6, where example 6.1 illustrates the code simplicity and speed that can be achieved).

For further information about the IEEE binary floating-point representation and its subtleties, see the standard document itself [81], Goldberg's survey [67], or documents from William Kahan's homepage at Berkeley.

2.8.2   Number values and error values

A NumberValue represents a double-precision floating-point number or a logical value (0.0 meaning false, all other non-NaN numbers meaning true) and has a public readonly field `value` containing that number. When converting values to doubles and vice versa, we shall exploit the binary floating-point representation described in section 2.8.1. In particular, we shall rely on the hardware treatment of NaNs: use NaNs to represent errors, use the 51 payload bits of a NaN to distinguish different errors, and rely on arithmetic operators and mathematical functions to propagate not only a NaN argument but also its payload bits.

When converting a value to a double, we convert a NumberValue to a (non-NaN) double, convert an ErrorValue to the appropriate NaN, and convert everything else to the ArgType error value using method `Value.ToDoubleOrNan`:

```
public static double Value.ToDoubleOrNan(Value v) {
  if (v is NumberValue)
    return (v as NumberValue).value;
  else if (v is ErrorValue)
    return (v as ErrorValue).ErrorNan;
  else
    return ErrorValue.argTypeError.ErrorNan;
}
```

Conversely, when converting a double to a value, we convert a NaN to the corresponding ErrorValue, and convert a proper double to a NumberValue, where the

frequently used NumberValues representing 0.0 and 1.0 are preallocated static fields
in class NumberValue:

```
public static Value NumberValue.Make(double d) {
  if (double.IsNaN(d))
    return ErrorValue.FromNan(d);
  else if (d == 0)
    return ZERO;
  else if (d == 1)
    return ONE;
  else
    return new NumberValue(d);
}
```

This ensures that the double contained in a NumberValue is never a NaN.

2.8.3   Error values

To represent error values as NaN payload bits, we allocate and cache all ErrorValue
objects in a static global array. Then we can represent an error value by its index
into that array or by the NaN whose 51-bit payload is the signed encoding of that
index. Some of the preallocated errors are shown in figure 2.6. It is important that
the #NUM! error is at index 0 because the .NET System.Math functions produce
NaN values with payload zero. Custom error values can be created using the built-
in function ERR("MyError"). To prevent a spreadsheet from overflowing the global
value error table, the argument to the ERR function must be a text constant.

Index	Error value	Example cause
0	#NUM!	SQRT(-1)
1	#ERR: ArgCount	SQRT()
2	#ERR: ArgType	SQRT("four")
3	#NAME?	SQTR(4)
4	#REF!	Reference to cell that was deleted
5	#VALUE!	Selector in CHOOSE out of range
6	#NA	MATCH(-7,A1:A5 when A1 > -7
7	#ERR: Too many arguments	Call has too many arguments

Figure 2.6: Some preallocated values in the global error value table.

Class ErrorValue provides methods for converting a NaN to an ErrorValue and
vice versa. Method MakeNan(i) returns the NaN whose payload bits are the bits
from two-complement integer i. If d is a NaN, then method FromNan(d) returns
the error value represented by its NaN payload bits. If v is an ErrorValue, then
property v.ErrorNaN returns the NaN representing v.

2.8.4   Array values

An ArrayValue represents a rectangular structure of values and is either an *explicit array* of class ArrayExplicit, an *array view* of class ArrayView, or an *array double matrix* of class ArrayDouble. An array element value may itself be an array, so array values may be nested, unlike in Excel or OpenOffice Calc, but the nesting cannot be cyclic. An array may have null elements that do not hold values, corresponding to a blank cell in a sheet. An array of size 1x1 is distinct from an atomic value.

An explicit array consists of a two-dimensional array Value[,] of values, together with a pair (ulCa, lrCa) of cell addresses that defines a window on that underlying two-dimensional array. An explicit array is typically the result of functions such as TRANSPOSE or TABULATE (section 11.5) that must create a new array value. The window onto the underlying array allows for efficient implementation of the SLICE function (section 11.5), which simply creates a (smaller) window onto the underlying two-dimensional Value[,] array without copying it. The underlying array and the window may have zero columns, zero rows, or both. This is in contrast to a cell area reference such as B2:A1, which always denotes a non-empty cell area.

An *array view* consists of a sheet together with a pair (ulCa, lrCa) of cell addresses that defines a window on that underlying sheet. An array view is typically the result of a cell area expression such as A1:D50 or Data!A1:D50 that creates a view onto an existing sheet, or of applying the SLICE function to another array view. Array views allow for efficient evaluation of function applications such as SUM(A1:D50) without allocation of a large intermediate data structure. The window may have zero columns, zero rows, or both.

An *array double matrix* consists of a two-dimensional array (type double[,]) of floating-point numbers. This is intended for representation of the arguments and results of (external) linear algebra operations. When the result of a linear algebra function is passed to another such function, it is wasteful to wrap the floating-point numbers in NumberValue objects. Also, numeric libraries typically assume the indexing order [row,column], so we use that order for the inner double[,] array too, although it is the opposite of the external interface of array views.

Regardless of representation, an ArrayValue has an indexer this[col,row] that (evaluates and) accesses the array value's element at (col,row), relative to the window determined by ulCa. It also has an Apply method override that recursively applies the delegate act to each non-null element:

```
public abstract Value this[int col, int row] { get; }

public override void Apply(Action<Value> act) {
  for (int c = 0; c < Cols; c++) {
    for (int r = 0; r < Rows; r++) {
      Value v = this[c, r];
      if (v != null) // Only non-blank cells contribute
        if (v is ArrayValue)
          (v as ArrayValue).Apply(act);
        else
```

```
                act(v);
            }
        }
    }
```

2.8.5   Function values

A function value, or closure, is a partially applied sheet-defined function defined in the Funcalc extension of Corecalc and is represented by class FunctionValue. It consists of the index of a sheet-defined function and an array holding zero or more argument values for that function. For more information, see section 8.4.

2.9   Representation of cell references

Cell references should be represented so that they, and the expressions in which they appear, can be notionally "copied" without change. It is common for a spreadsheet formula to be entered in one cell and then copied to many (even thousands) of other cells. Sharing the same expression object among all those cells would give considerable space savings.

Hence, in Corecalc cell references and cell area references, we store absolute ($) references as absolute zero-based cell addresses and relative (non-$) references as positive, zero, or negative offsets relative to the address of the cell containing the formula. Concretely, Corecalc uses a class RARef, short for relative/absolute reference, to represent references in formulas:

```
public sealed class RARef {
    public readonly bool colAbs, rowAbs;   // True=abs, False=rel
    public readonly int colRef, rowRef;
    ...
    public CellAddr Addr(int col, int row) {
        return new CellAddr(this, col, row);
    }
    public String Show(int col, int row, Format fo) {
        if (fo.RcFormat)
            return "R" + RelAbsFormat(rowAbs, rowRef)
                + "C" + RelAbsFormat(colAbs, colRef);
        else { // A1 format
            CellAddr ca = new CellAddr(this, col, row);
            return (colAbs ? "$" : "") + CellAddr.ColumnName(ca.col)
                + (rowAbs ? "$" : "") + (ca.row+1);
        }
    }
}
```

A RARef is somewhat similar to the R1C1 reference format (section 1.3), but since we put the column number first and use zero-based numbering, a natural name for our format would be the *C0R0 format*. We chose to use C0R0 format for three reasons. First, it is obviously easier to process internally in the implementation than the external A1 format that a spreadsheet user sees. Second, the C0R0 format puts the column first and the row second, like the A1 format, which makes the mental conversion easier; this is unlike the R1C1 format used internally in Excel files, for instance. Third, most modern programming languages, including C#, have zero-based array indexing, so using the C0R0 format avoids the mental and computational off-by-one errors that the R1C1 format would most likely cause.

Figure 2.7 shows the four basic forms of a C0R0 format reference. As a consequence of this representation, an expression must be interpreted relative to the address of the containing cell when evaluating or displaying the expression. This adds a little extra run-time cost.

C0R0 format	Meaning
CcRr	Absolute reference to cell (c, r) where $0 \leq c, r$
CcR[r]	Absolute column c, relative row offset r
C[c]Rr	Relative column offset c, absolute row r
C[c]R[r]	Relative column offset c, relative row offset r

Figure 2.7: The four basic forms of C0R0 references.

We shall use the term *virtual copy* to denote a reference from a formula cell to a shared expression instance in this representation.

When an expression is moved (not copied) from one cell to another, its relative references must be updated and hence the abstract syntax tree must be duplicated (see section 2.18). But moving a formula does not increase the number of formulas, whereas copying may enormously increase the number of formulas, so it is more important to preserve and share the formula representation when copying the formula than when moving it.

Also, when rows or columns are inserted or deleted, both relative and absolute references may have to be adjusted in a way that preserves as much sharing of virtual copies as possible (see section 2.19).

2.10   Sheet-absolute and sheet-relative references

A cell reference `Sheet1!B7` or an area reference `Sheet1!B7:D9` may refer to another sheet than the one containing the enclosing formula. This is implemented by adding a `sheet` field to CellRef and CellArea. If the `sheet` field is non-null, then the reference is sheet-absolute and refers to a cell in that sheet. If the field is null, then the reference is sheet-relative and refers to a cell in the current sheet (the one containing the enclosing formula), that is, the sheet argument passed to the `Eval` method.

The `sheet` reference (or the absence of it) is preserved when copying or moving the CellRef or AreaRef from one sheet to another. Sheet-absolute references remain sheet-absolute, and sheet-relative references become references to the new sheet to which the enclosing formula gets copied.

The adjustment of column and row references is the same regardless of whether the reference is sheet-absolute or sheet-relative. Namely, a column-relative or row-relative but sheet-absolute reference presumably refers to a sheet that has a similar structure to the present one. We observe that OpenOffice Calc makes an additional distinction between sheet-relative and sheet-absolute references. A reference of the form `Sheet17.A1` is adjusted to `Sheet18.A1` if the formula is copied from Sheet1 to Sheet2. Excel does not support such sheet adjustment.

2.11   Cell addresses

A CellAddr represents an absolute cell address in a sheet as a pair of a zero-based column number and a zero-based row number. This is in contrast to a RARef (section 2.9), which represents cell references and cell area references in formulas. Given the column and row number of a RARef occurrence, the CellAddr constructor computes the absolute cell address that the RARef refers to:

```
public struct CellAddr {
  public readonly int col, row;
  public CellAddr(RARef cr, int col, int row) {
    this.col = cr.colAbs ? cr.colRef : cr.colRef + col;
    this.row = cr.rowAbs ? cr.rowRef : cr.rowRef + row;
  }
  public override String ToString() {
    return ColumnName(col) + (row+1);
  }
  ...
}
```

2.12   Simple recalculation

The value of a cell may depend on the values of other cells. Whenever any cell changes, the value of all dependent cells must be recalculated in some order that respects the dependencies (unless a cyclic dynamic dependency makes this impossible).

In the simplest reasonable scheme, a full recalculation of a workbook may be performed by recalculating all its sheets in some order and recalculating each sheet by reevaluating all its formula cells in some order, respecting dependencies. This approach will often reevaluate cells that depend only on cells whose values have not changed, to no avail. Section 4.3 describes a more sophisticated mechanism for minimal recalculation actually used in Corecalc. That mechanism reevaluates only those formula cells that depend on changed cells but requires an explicit representation of the dependencies between cells, the support graph (see chapter 4).

As a warm-up, we therefore describe a simpler mechanism that requires no explicit representation of these cell dependencies.

Regardless of the recalculation mechanism, a formula cell caches its value to make the run-time complexity linear in the number of non-blank cells.

To support recalculation and caching, each formula has a `state` field of enumeration type CellState. The possible states are Dirty (the cell's value cache is invalid), Computing (the cell value is currently being computed), and Uptodate (the cell's value cache is valid). There is also a state Enqueued, used only later in section 4.3.

At the beginning of a full recalculation, the state of every non-blank cell is set to Dirty. Each formula cell is then evaluated as follows:

1. If `state` is Uptodate, then return the cached value.

2. Else, if `state` is Computing, then the cell depends on itself; stop and report a cyclic dependency involving this cell.

3. Else, set `state` to Computing and evaluate the cell's expression. This will cause referred-to cells to be recomputed (and may ultimately reveal a cyclic dependency).

4. If the evaluation succeeds, save the result value in the cache, set `state` to Uptodate, and return the value.

The implementation of the `Eval` method in class Formula closely follows this recipe, evaluating the formula's expression e if the formula cell is dirty and setting the formula cell's value cache v afterward:

```
public override Value Eval(Sheet sheet, int col, int row) {
  switch (state) {
    case CellState.Uptodate:
      break;
    case CellState.Computing:
      FullCellAddr culprit = new FullCellAddr(sheet, col, row);
      String msg = String.Format("CYCLE in cell {0} formula {1}",
                                 culprit, Show(col, row, format));
      throw new CyclicException(msg, culprit);
    case CellState.Dirty:
      state = CellState.Computing;
      v = e.Eval(sheet, col, row);
      state = CellState.Uptodate;
      break;
  }
  return v;
}
```

Hence, all formulas are eventually recomputed, and when necessary they are recomputed in dependency order by simple recursive calls. This may cause deep recursion if there are long dependency chains and an unfortunate order of visits is chosen.

(This could be fixed as follows: If the recalculation depth exceeds some threshold, an approximate topological sort in dependency order might be performed and cells may be recomputed in that order. But that would lose the simplicity of the above scheme.)

One may represent the cell states by two boolean flags `visited` and `uptodate`, so that Dirty is `!visited` and `!uptodate`; Computing is `visited` and `!uptodate`; and Uptodate is `uptodate`. Then one can use a trick—let the meaning of true and false alternate—to avoid the costly resetting of each cell's state at the beginning of a full recalculation [137, section 2.11]. However, with minimal recalculation as described in section 4.3, this is neither quite as important for performance nor as easy to implement, so we shall not use that trick here.

Another possibility is to replace the cell state by (hash-based) sets of cells during recalculation, one set of the Visited cells and one set of the Uptodate ones; a cell is Dirty if it is in neither of these. Then one can reset all cells to Dirty very easily: simply discard the current Visited and Uptodate sets and replace them by empty sets. It is doubtful whether this is fast in practice, however, because it may require two set lookups (rather than a test of a enum type variable) to determine the state of a cell, and it may create much work for the garbage collector.

2.13   Cyclic references

The value of a cell may depend on the value of other cells and may directly or indirectly depend on itself. The purpose of the Computing state of a formula cell is to allow the recalculation mechanism to discover such dependencies, stop recalculation, and report the discovery of a cycle.

2.14   Built-in functions

Corecalc built-in functions include mathematical functions (SIN), cell area functions (SUM), array-valued functions (TRANSPOSE), non-strict conditional functions (IF), and volatile functions (RAND). Built-in operators include the usual arithmetic operators, such as +, −, *, and /.

Built-in functions and built-in operators are represented internally by objects of class Function:

```
public class Function {
  public readonly String name;
  public Applier Applier { get; private set; }
  public readonly int fixity;
  public bool IsPlaceHolder { get; private set; }
  private bool isVolatile;
  private static readonly IDictionary<String, Function> table;
  ...
}
```

The Function class uses a hash dictionary `table` to map a function name such as `"SIN"` or an operator name such as `"+"` to a Function object.

The most important component of a Function object is a delegate `applier` of type Applier. This delegate takes as argument a sheet reference, an array of argument expressions, and column and row numbers:

```
delegate Value Applier(Sheet sheet, Expr[] es, int col, int row);
```

Evaluation of a function call or operator application simply passes the argument expressions to the function's Applier delegate as shown in section 2.7.6. A family of auxiliary methods called `MakeFunction` can be used to create the Applier delegate for a strict function from a delegate representing the function; another family called `MakeNumberFunction` creates Appliers from delegates of return type `double`. We use the standard .NET generic delegate types to represent non-`void` functions:

```
public delegate R Func<R>();
public delegate R Func<A1,R>(A1 x1);
public delegate R Func<A1,A2,R>(A1 x1, A2 x2);
... and so on ...
```

2.14.1 Strict one-argument functions

Most functions are *strict*, that is, their arguments must be fully evaluated before the function is called. The applier for a strict function evaluates the argument expressions as if at cell `sheet[col,row]` and applies the function to the resulting argument values, each of type Value.

An applier for a strict unary function `dlg` from `double` to `double`, such as `SIN()`, can be manufactured like this:

```
private static Applier MakeNumberFunction(Func<double, double> dlg){
  return
    delegate(Sheet sheet, Expr[] es, int col, int row) {
      if (es.Length == 1) {
        Value v0 = es[0].Eval(sheet, col, row);
        return NumberValue.Make(dlg(Value.ToDoubleOrNan(v0)));
      } else
        return ErrorValue.argCountError;
    };
}
```

As can be seen above, the Applier checks that exactly one argument is supplied, evaluates it, attempts to extract a double (possibly a NaN representing an error value) from the result, applies the given delegate `dlg` to the `double`, creates a NumberValue from the result, and returns it. Due to the IEEE arithmetics requirement that NaN payload must be preserved (section 2.8.1), if `v0` is an error, then the result will be that same error.

This way new functions can easily be defined:

```
new Function("SIN",  MakeNumberFunction(Math.Sin));
new Function("SQRT", MakeNumberFunction(Math.Sqrt));
new Function("TAN",  MakeNumberFunction(Math.Tan));
```

2.14.2   Other strict functions

There are similar overloads of the `MakeNumberFunction` method for defining strict `double`-valued and `bool`-valued functions:

```
static Applier MakeNumberFunction(Func<double> dlg)
static Applier MakeNumberFunction(Func<double, double> dlg)
static Applier MakePredicate(Func<double, double, bool> dlg)
```

The `Func<double>` overload is used to define argument-less functions such as `RAND()` and `NOW()` (see section 2.14.3). The `Func<double,double,double>` overload is used to define arithmetic operators; for instance:

```
new Function("^", 8, MakeNumberFunction(ExcelPow));
new Function("*", 7, MakeNumberFunction((x, y) => x * y));
new Function("/", 7, MakeNumberFunction((x, y) => x / y));
new Function("+", 6, MakeNumberFunction((x, y) => x + y ));
```

An integer argument such as 6, 7, and 8 is used to indicate that the operator must be printed infix between its operands and in addition specifies its precedence (see section 2.15).

The `MakePredicate` method is used to define comparison operators; for instance:

```
new Function(">", 5, MakePredicate((x, y) => x > y));
new Function("=", 4, MakePredicate((x, y) => x == y));
```

Further overloads of `MakeNumberFunction` are used to define variable-argument but `double`-valued functions such as `SUM` and `AVERAGE` in section 2.14.4. Further overloads of the `MakeFunction` methods are used to define one-argument but array-valued functions such as `TRANSPOSE` in section 2.14.5 and other more general functions such as `MAP` (see section 11.5); for instance:

```
static Applier MakeNumberFunction(Func<Value[], double> dlg) { ... }
static Applier MakeFunction(Func<Value, Value> dlg) { ... }
static Applier MakeFunction(Func<Value[], Value> dlg) { ... }
```

2.14.3   Volatile functions

A volatile function is implemented just like any other function. For instance, the `RAND()` function can be implemented like this, where method `ExcelRand` simply calls `rnd.NextDouble` on a static field `rnd` of type System.Random:

```
new Function("RAND", MakeNumberFunction(ExcelRand), isVolatile:true)
```

where the `ExcelRand` method uses a .NET Math.Random object `random` to get a pseudo-random number between 0 and 1:

```
public static double ExcelRand() { return random.NextDouble(); }
```

The `NOW()` function, which as in Excel returns the number of fractional days since the beginning of the base date 30 December 1899, can be defined as follows:

```
new Function("NOW", MakeNumberFunction(ExcelNow), isVolatile: true);
```

The `ExcelNow` method reads the current time (in 100 nanosecond ticks) from the .NET DataTime class and converts it to a number of fractional days:

```
public static double ExcelNow() {
   return NumberValue.DoubleFromDateTimeTicks(DateTime.Now.Ticks);
}
```

The conversion is done by method `DoubleFromDateTimeTicks` in class Number-Value, using appropriate definitions of the constants `basedate` and `daysPerTick`:

```
static readonly long basedate = new DateTime(1899, 12, 30).Ticks;
static readonly double daysPerTick = 100E-9 / 60 / 60 / 24;

public static double DoubleFromDateTimeTicks(long ticks) {
   return (ticks - basedate) * daysPerTick;
}
```

The most notable aspect of volatile functions is that they cause complications in the design of the recalculation mechanism (see sections 3.3 and 4.3).

2.14.4   Functions with multiple arguments

Functions such as SUM, AVERAGE, MIN, and MAX take multiple arguments, some of which may be simple numbers, cell references, cell areas, or array values, as in SUM(A1:B4, 8) or SUM(MMULT(A1:B2, C1:D2)). These are evaluated by applying a suitable action to all arguments, and recursively to the elements of array values, using the `Apply` method on class Value (see section 2.8):

```
public static double Sum(Value[] vs) {
   double S = 0.0;
   foreach (Value outerV in vs)
     outerV.Apply(delegate(Value v)
     {
       S += NumberValue.ToDoubleOrNan(v);
     });
   return S;
}
```

The propagation of NaNs from argument to result in +=, described in section 2.8.1, ensures that if any argument to SUM is an error value, then the result will be that error value; and if any argument is not a NumberValue, then the result will be an ArgType error value.

In actual fact, to avoid loss of significant digits when adding many numbers of different magnitude, we use William Kahan's summation formula [67], so the implementation of SUM looks a little more mysterious:

```
public static double Sum(Value[] vs) {
  double S = 0.0, C = 0.0;
  foreach (Value outerV in vs)
    outerV.Apply(delegate(Value v)
    {
      double Y = NumberValue.ToDoubleOrNan(v) - C, T = S + Y;
      C = (T - S) - Y;
      S = T;
    });
  return S;
}
```

The rounding error introduced by the Kahan summation formula is dramatically smaller than that of the naive summation algorithm [67, Theorem 8]. The cost of three additional floating-point subtractions per addition is negligible compared with the costs of unwrapping number values and so on. We use the Kahan summation formulation also in the implementation of AVERAGE.

The above implementation of SUM is quite efficient even when applied to a large cell area on a sheet, as in SUM(A1:A10000), because the expression A1:A10000 evaluates to an array view of the sheet, not to a large explicit array value that must be allocated. Measurements made by Thomas Iversen [84] [137, section 5.2.2] show that avoiding the array allocation brings a four-fold speedup, so that the above implementation is only 3.4 times slower than Excel.

2.14.5   Functions with array-valued results

Some built-in functions produce an array value as result. This is the case in particular for functions used in array formulas: matrix transposition (TRANSPOSE), matrix multiplication (MMULT), linear regression (LINEST), and so on. The result of such a function is an explicit array value (section 2.8.4), which contains a two-dimensional array Value[,] of values.

For instance, function TRANSPOSE takes as argument one expression that evaluates to an ArrayValue argument with size $(cols', rows')$. The result is a new ArrayExplicit value whose underlying value array sheet has size $(cols, rows)$ with $cols = rows'$ and $rows = cols'$. Element $[c, r]$ of the result array contains the value of element $[r, c]$ the given argument array:

```
public static Value Transpose(Value v0) {
  if (v0 is ErrorValue) return v0;
  ArrayValue v0arr = v0 as ArrayValue;
  if (v0arr != null) {
    int cols = v0arr.Rows, rows = v0arr.Cols;
    Value[,] result = new Value[cols, rows];
    for (int c = 0; c < cols; c++)
      for (int r = 0; r < rows; r++)
        result[c, r] = v0arr[r, c];
    return new ArrayExplicit(result);
  } else
    return ErrorValue.argTypeError;
}
```

2.14.6 Non-strict functions

For a non-strict function, the Applier delegate is not created by a `MakeFunction` method but written outright. For instance, the three-argument function `IF` is defined like this:

```
new Function("IF",
    delegate(Sheet sheet, Expr[] es, int col, int row) {
      if (es.Length == 3) {
        Value v0 = es[0].Eval(sheet, col, row);
        NumberValue n0 = v0 as NumberValue;
        if (n0 != null && !Double.IsInfinity(n0.value)
                       && !Double.IsNaN(n0.value))
          if (n0.value != 0)
            return es[1].Eval(sheet, col, row);
          else
            return es[2].Eval(sheet, col, row);
        else if (v0 is ErrorValue)
          return v0;
        else
          return ErrorValue.argTypeErrorValue;
      } else
        return ErrorValue.argCountErrorValue;
    });
```

There must be three argument expressions in `es`. The first one must be non-null and is evaluated to obtain a NumberValue. If the `double` contained in that value is non-zero and non-NaN, then the second argument is evaluated by calling its `Eval` method; else the third argument is evaluated by calling its `Eval` method.

2.15 Prettyprinting formulas

To show operators properly in infix form and without excess parentheses, we store with every Function (section 2.14) an integer denoting its fixity and precedence. A *fixity* of 0 means that the function is not an infix operator, positive means infix left associative operator, and higher value means higher precedence (stronger binding). We could take negative to mean right associative and indicate precedence by the absolute value, but that does not seem to be needed in spreadsheet formulas. Even the exponentiation operator (^) is left associative in Excel and OpenOffice Calc. In Gnumeric, it is right associative as is conventional in programming languages.

Then we add a parameter `ctxpre` to the `Show` method of the Expr class to indicate the context's precedence. When the function to be printed is an infix with precedence less than `ctxpre`, we must enclose it in parentheses; otherwise there is no need for parentheses. Applications of functions that are not infix are printed as `F(e1, ..., en)`. Function arguments and top-level expressions have a `ctxpre` of zero. To prettyprint `(1-2)-3` without parentheses and `1-(2-3)` with parentheses, the prettyprinter distinguishes left-hand operands from right-hand operands by increasing the `ctxpre` of right-hand operands by one.

Another parameter to the `Show` method, of type Formats, controls other aspects of the display of formulas, such as whether references are shown in A1 or R1C1 format.

2.16   Sheet representation

Until now, we have thought of a sheet as a two-dimensional array of cells. Because a sheet may be very large and sparse, having few non-blank cells, it may be wasteful to represent it by a dense two-dimensional array Cell[,] of cell references.

Program	Columns	Rows	Cells
Excel 2003	255	65 536	16 777 216
Excel 2013	16 384	1 048 576	17 179 869 184
LibreOffice	1 024	1 048 576	1 073 741 824
OpenOffice Calc 4	1 024	1 048 576	1 073 741 824
Gnumeric	8 192	65 536	536 870 912
Corecalc (see below)	65 536	1 048 576	68 719 476 736

Figure 2.8: Maximal sheet sizes for some spreadsheet programs.

Figure 2.8 shows the sheet sizes permitted by some current (2014) spreadsheet programs. Clearly, the cells of a maximal Excel 2013 sheet must be mostly blank since just representing the 17 billion null pointers would require 137 GB of memory on a 64-bit architecture. We would like to be able to represent such large sparse sheets also in Corecalc and Funcalc.

2.16.1   The QT4 simplified quadtree

To represent large sparse sheets, we use a kind of simplified quadtree [56], which is a recursive subdivision of an array. This data structure, which we call QT4, is a four-level array representation that can hold 2^{16} = 65 536 columns and 2^{20} = 1 048 576 rows, thus exceeding the capabilities of current versions of MS Excel, Open Office, LibreOffice, and Gnumeric, as shown in figure 2.8. We divide a sheet into level-3 (basic) tiles of 2^4 = 16 columns and 2^5 = 32 rows each, thus reflecting that a sheet typically displays more rows than columns. Then we recursively group $16 \cdot 32$ level-3 tiles into one level-2 tile, and so on, to four levels; the topmost tile is at level 0. A blank or unpopulated level-3 tile is not allocated but simply represented by a null reference in a level-2 tile and so on for all levels. This can represent a total of $2^{4 \cdot 4}$ = 65 536 columns and $2^{4 \cdot 5}$ = 1 048 576 rows. Each tile holds $16 \cdot 32$ = 512 array references or cell references, which requires 4 KB of memory on a 64-bit architecture. The modest tile size is chosen because we expect it to work well with current memory management technology.

This idea is sketched in figure 2.9, although with only three levels of tiles, each having only 4 columns and 2 rows, for a total of $2^{3 \cdot 2}$ = 64 columns and $2^{3 \cdot 1}$ = 8 rows.

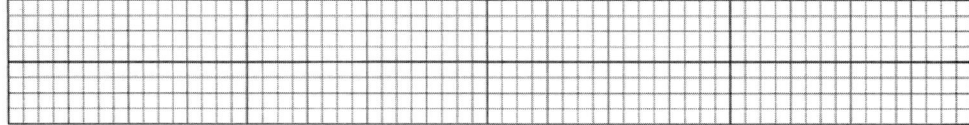

Figure 2.9: Simplified QT4 with only three levels of tiles, each having 4 columns and 2 rows. The level-0 tile (the entire figure) is divided into 8 level-1 tiles (heavy solid borders), each of which is divided into 8 level-2 tiles (fine solid borders), each of which is divided into 8 cells (fine dashed borders).

A read from an unallocated (null) tile gives a blank Cell (null). A write to an unallocated (null) tile must allocate the tile. A tile all of whose cells are empty is represented by null. The representation is sparse because we do not need to allocate a tile all of whose elements are null, whether it represents blank cells or absent lower-level tiles.

2.16.2   Space consumption of the QT4 representation

We define the basic parameters of the QT4 representation as compile-time integer constants, and we preallocate the level-0 tile of a sheet to slightly simplify the access code:

```
private const int
    LOGW = 4, W = 1 << LOGW, MW = W - 1, SIZEW = 1 << (4 * LOGW),
    LOGH = 5, H = 1 << LOGH, MH = H - 1, SIZEH = 1 << (4 * LOGH);
private readonly Cell[][][][] tile0 = new Cell[W * H][][][];
```

The constants LOGW and LOGH determine the tile size (W = 16 columns by H = 32 rows), as well as the maximal size of a sheet (SIZEW = 65 536 columns by SIZEH = 1 048 576 rows). The smaller 4 by 2 tiles in figure 2.9 would correspond to LOGW = 2 and LOGH = 1.

This representation is quite space efficient, both in total memory consumed and number of objects allocated. For instance, a blank sheet is represented by a single all-null level-0 tile, thus requiring 4 KB of storage (on a 64-bit architecture) and a single object (the tile) in heap memory.

A sheet that contains a single non-blank cell will require one level-3, one level-2, one level-1, and one level-0 tile, for a total allocation of 16 KB in 4 memory objects.

A fully populated "typical" sheet, comprising 64 columns by 320 rows, will require 40 level-3 tiles, one level-2 tile, one level-1 tile, and one level-0 tile, for a total allocation of 43 objects and 176 KB, in addition to the cell objects themselves. This is a space overhead of only 7.5% relative to a non-scalable, two-dimensional array representation; and this overhead may vanish (or be negative) if there are sizable blocks of blank cells within the sheet.

A fully populated maximal Excel 2003 sheet (256 columns by 65 536 rows, or 4 million cells) can be represented using $16 \cdot 2\,048 = 32\,768$ level-3 tiles, $1 \cdot 64 = 64$ level-2 tiles, $1 \cdot 2 = 2$ level-1 tiles, and 1 level-0 tile, for a total of 32 835 tiles (memory objects) or 131 340 KB, in addition to the cell objects themselves. This causes a space overhead of 0.2% compared to a flat two-dimensional array of size $256 \cdot 65\,536$.

An extremely sparse maximal sheet may have four non-blank cells, one in each corner, with the remaining 68 719 476 732 cells in the rectangle spanned by the corners being blank (null). Such a sheet can be represented using four level-3 tiles, four level-2 tiles, four level-1 tiles, and one level-0 tile, for a total of 13 objects and 52 KB of memory.

2.16.3   Implementation of QT4 indexing

Since a tile's column and row counts are powers of two, all index calculations can be implemented as integer shifts and bitwise operations, as shown below. For instance, in binary, the mask MW equals 0...01111 with LOGW 1-bits, so the remainder c%W, needed for the tilewise column index, can be computed as c&MW using only bitwise operations; and similarly for MH and H, of course. For speed, we represent each two-dimensional tile by a one-dimensional array and perform index calculations by the shift <<LOGH (instead of multiplication) and bitwise "or" (instead of addition). This also avoids one implicit null check, one array bounds check, and one memory access for each of the four tile accesses required for a cell access.

The complete code for indexing into the QT4 data structure is defined on the sheet representation class SheetRep and looks like this:

```
public Cell this[int c, int r] {
  get {
    if (c < 0 || SIZEW <= c || r < 0 || SIZEH <= r)
      return null;
    Cell[][][] tile1 =
      tile0[(((c>>(3*LOGW))&MW)<<LOGH)|((r>>(3*LOGH))&MH)];
    if (tile1 == null)
      return null;
    Cell[][] tile2 =
      tile1[(((c>>(2*LOGW))&MW)<<LOGH)|((r>>(2*LOGH))&MH)];
    if (tile2 == null)
      return null;
    Cell[] tile3 =
      tile2[(((c>>(1*LOGW))&MW)<<LOGH)|((r>>(1*LOGH))&MH)];
    if (tile3 == null)
      return null;
    return tile3[((c&MW)<<LOGH)|(r&MH)];
  }
}
```

2.16.4   Time consumption of QT4 operations

The representation turns out to be surprisingly fast. We see from the code that reading a non-blank cell requires 10 shift operations (by constant offsets), eight bitwise and-operations (by a constant bit pattern), four bitwise or-operations, three explicit null-checks, and four one-dimensional array accesses (each with an implicit null-check and bounds check). While these roughly 35 simple operations incur some run-time overhead, maybe 10–15 ns on a current 2.67 GHz processor, the real source of run-time overhead will be the four memory accesses if they cause cache misses.

In general, these costs are likely to be dwarfed by other costs when evaluating spreadsheet formulas. Experiments with the Funcalc implementation show that the cost of evaluating an access to an ordinary sheet cell is roughly 31 ns regardless of whether we use the QT4 implementation or a two-dimensional .NET array of Cell references. Also, the representation has no discernible effect on recalculation times. In conclusion, QT4 is sufficiently fast and memory efficient, and highly scalable.

To further understand the performance of the QT4 representation, also outside spreadsheet applications, we compared read access times for QT4 with those of a large (10 000 by 10 000) fully populated two-dimensional array on three different element access patterns: memory-friendly sequential, memory-hostile sequential, and random access (see figure 2.10).

First, comparing QT4 and two-dimensional arrays, we see that QT4 read access may be slower by a factor of around 5, but it may also be faster! Rather unexpectedly, in the case of memory-hostile access order, the complicated-looking code above is faster than the simple C# expression `arr[c,r]`. This is probably due to better memory locality in the small QT4 tiles and to cache misses and memory latency in the two-dimensional array. In fact, the Intel CPU Performance Counters can be

	2D array	QT4	Ratio
Memory-friendly	2.1	11.1	5.40
Memory-hostile	19.1	15.8	0.83
Random access	53.4	275.1	5.15

Figure 2.10: Time (ns) per read access for two-dimensional arrays and for QT4, and for three access patterns. Results for .NET 4.5 and Intel Core 2 Duo 2.66 GHz; Intel Xeon and Intel i7 are similar.

used to demonstrate that our tiles are small enough to benefit from the instruction pointer-based level-1 cache prefetcher [47], whereas the rows (and columns) of the 10 000 by 10 000 array are too large to so benefit. Also note that even though QT4 memory-friendly access is five times slower than plain array access, the absolute overhead is small, approximately 9 ns per access on a 2.66 GHz machine.

Next, comparing memory-friendly sequential access (which exploits the memory and cache structure well) with memory-hostile access (which does not), we see that for two-dimensional arrays the former is *much* faster than the latter, by a factor of 9.3. This phenomenon is well known to people writing scientific software. For QT4, this factor is only 1.4: it is more oblivious to which sequential access order is used.

Finally, for random element accesses, we see that QT4 is slower than two-dimensional arrays by a factor of 5.15. This is unsurprising because a truly random access in a very large QT4 structure is likely to cause a cache miss on all three lower levels of tiles, thus incurring at least three times the cost of a cache miss in the two-dimensional array. We also see that for two-dimensional arrays, random access is much slower than both kinds of sequential access; it is less clear why this is so.

These considerations and experiments show that the QT4 data structure is well suited for representation of large and sparse sheets, being efficient in space and time, and fairly oblivious to traversal order (column-wise or row-wise).

2.17   Copying formulas

The copying of formulas from one cell to one or more other cells is implemented using the Windows clipboard, which uses "Object Linking and Embedding" (OLE). For this reason, the application must run in a so-called "single-threaded apartment", which means that the application's `Main` method must have the STAThread attribute.

The clipboard can hold multiple formats at the same time, so to ease exchange with other applications, we copy to the clipboard a text representation of the cell contents, as well as the Corecalc internal description of the cell. The internal representation of the cell is simply the name of the sheet from which it is copied and the cell address at which it occurs. This can lead to surprises if that particular sheet cell is edited before one pastes from the clipboard.

A seemingly more robust alternative would be to transfer the actual cell object via the clipboard by serialization (thus requiring all cell, formula, and expression classes to have the Serializable attribute). However, that would lose sharing of expression abstract syntax, and in general causes mysterious problems, possibly because built-in functions use delegate objects that are not correctly deserialized.

2.18   Moving formulas

Thanks to the internal representation of references, the cell references and cell area references in a formula need not be updated when the formula is *copied* from one cell to one or more other cells. However, when a formula is *moved* from one cell to another cell by "cutting" and then "pasting" it, references must be updated in two ways, as shown by the example in figure 2.11:

- References *from* the moved formula to other cells appear unchanged in the A1 format, but in the internal representation, relative references must actually be changed because they are stored as offsets. In the figure 2.11 example, the internal representation of cell reference A1 changes from R[-1]C to R[-2]C[-1].

- Cell references *to* the cell containing the formula before the move must be updated so they refer to the cell containing the formula after the move. In the example, the external as well as internal representations of the formulas in cells B1 and C1 change as a consequence of the move. Even references from other sheets in the workbook must be updated in this way. In contrast, references to cell areas that include the formula are not updated when the formula is moved. Thus, if C1 had contained a cell area reference A2:B2, then C1 would be unaffected by the move of the formula in A2 to B3.

The second point above in particular is somewhat surprising but is the semantics implemented by Excel, Gnumeric, and OpenOffice Calc.

	A	B	C			A	B	C
1	11	=A2	=$A$2		1	11	=B3	=$B$3
2	=A1+$A$1				2			
3					3		=A1+$A$1	

Figure 2.11: Formulas before (left) and after (right) moving from A2 to B3.

The moving of formulas is only partially implemented in Corecalc, by method Move on abstract class **Expr** and its concrete subclasses, and method MoveContents on abstract class **Cell** and its concrete subclasses. Currently we do not implement:

- The adjustment of all references that pointed to the old cell so that henceforth they point to the new cell. Also references from other sheets and from within the moved formula must be adjusted. This adjustment should preserve the sharing of the referring formulas. The to-be-moved cell's support set contains all (other) cells that refer to it and that may need to be adjusted.

- When a block of cells, all of which share the same underlying formula (due to virtual copying), is moved, one should maintain the sharing in the moved cells. This is not done currently.

2.19   Inserting new rows or columns

It should be possible to insert additional rows (or columns) into a given sheet. This must not only move, and hence change the numbering of, some rows within the given sheet, but it should also update references *from* cells in that sheet and in other sheets to the moved rows. (Insertion of columns is entirely similar to insertion of rows and will therefore not be discussed explicitly here.) In general, one must update references from the affected sheet as well as from other sheets.

Consider what happens when a new row 3 is inserted in the example sheet shown on the left in figure 2.12.

A row-absolute reference must be updated if it refers to a row that follows the inserted rows. In the example, this affects all the $A$3 references in the sheet (before insertion).

A row-relative reference must be updated if the reference straddles the insertion, that is, if the referring cell precedes the insert and the referred-to cell follows the insert, or vice versa. In both cases, the reference must be increased (numerically) by the number of inserted rows. In the example, this affects reference $A3 in cell B1, references $A3 and $A4 in B2, references $A1 and $A2 in B3, and reference $A2 in cell B4 (before the insertion).

	A	B
1	11	=$A$2+$A$3+$A1+$A2+$A3
2	21	=$A$2+$A$3+$A2+$A3+$A4
3	31	=$A$2+$A$3+$A1+$A2+$A3
4	41	=$A$2+$A$3+$A2+$A3+$A4

	A	B
1	11	=$A$2+$A$4+$A1+$A2+$A4
2	21	=$A$2+$A$4+$A2+$A4+$A5
3		
4	31	=$A$2+$A$4+$A1+$A2+$A4
5	41	=$A$2+$A$4+$A2+$A4+$A5

Figure 2.12: Formulas before (left) and after (right) inserting new row 3.

The insertion of a row is illegal if it would split an array formula block; this restriction is enforced in OpenOffice Calc, for instance. Therefore, we first check that no array formula straddles the insert; if one does, then the insert is rejected. To make this check, we let a cached array formula include the corner coordinates of the area of participating cells. The check is made by scanning all cells preceding the insert (if any) and checking that no array formula block in that row extends to cells following the insert.

If possible, one should avoid creating individual copies of all the formulas that are to be updated. That would lose the sharing of expressions carefully achieved by the representation of relative and absolute references (see section 2.9). However, a shared expression cannot simply be adjusted destructively because it might then be adjusted once for each cell that shares it.

Virtual formula copies near the insert may have relative references that straddle the insert and therefore require adjustment, whereas virtual copies of the same formula farther away from the insert do not have relative references that straddle the insert. Hence, even virtual formula copies on the same side of the insert may need to be adjusted in different ways. The possible versions are further multiplied if a formula contains relative references with different offsets.

Figure 2.13 shows the internal representation of the formulas from figure 2.12. The left-hand side shows that before the insertion, the B column cells in rows 0 and 1 contain virtual copies of one formula, and the B column cells in rows 2 and 3 contain virtual copies of another formula. The right-hand side shows that after the insertion, no two formulas are the same internally.

n	A	B
0	11	R1+R2+R[0]+R[+1]+R[+2]
1	21	R1+R2+R[0]+R[+1]+R[+2]
2	31	R1+R2+R[-2]+R[-1]+R[0]
3	41	R1+R2+R[-2]+R[-1]+R[0]

n	A	B
0	11	R1+R3+R[0]+R[+1]+R[+3]
1	21	R1+R3+R[0]+R[+2]+R[+3]
2		
3	31	R1+R3+R[-3]+R[-2]+R[0]
4	41	R1+R3+R[-3]+R[-1]+R[0]

Figure 2.13: Internal representation before and after inserting new row $R = 2$ (zero-based). References are in C0R0 format, but we omit the C0 prefix above, as we are interested only in the row adjustments.

> Observation 1: All virtual copies of an expression on the same row must be adjusted in the same way.

Using this observation, it is clear that sharing of copies of an expression on the same row can be obtained as follows: When processing each row, maintain a dictionary that maps old expressions to new (adjusted) expressions; if an old expression is found in the dictionary, use a virtual copy of the new expression (simply set the Expr reference in the Formula instance; formula instances are shared only in the case of array formulas); else compute the new expression, add the entry (old,new) to the dictionary, and use a virtual copy of new.

> Observation 2: One can compute the range of rows for which the adjustment is valid, as shown by the case analysis below.

Assume that $N \geq 0$ rows are to be inserted just before row $R \geq 0$. For relative references, let δ denote the offset before adjustment and δ' the offset after adjustment.

Aa An absolute reference to row $n < R$ needs no adjustment. This nonadjustment is valid regardless of the row r in which the containing expression appears.

Ab An absolute reference to row $n \geq R$ must be adjusted to $n+N$. This adjustment is valid regardless of the row r in which the containing expression appears.

Raa A relative reference to row $n < R$ needs no adjustment if the containing expression appears in row $r < R$. The reference has $\delta' = \delta = n - r$ before and after the insertion.

Rab A relative reference to row $n < R$ must be adjusted (changed from $\delta = n - r$ to $\delta' = n - r - N$) if the containing expression appears in row $r \geq R$. Insertion increases the distance between the referring and referred-to rows, and indeed subtracting $N \geq 0$ from the offset $\delta < 0$ increases its absolute value.

Rba A relative reference to row $n \geq R$ must be adjusted (changed from $\delta = n - r$ to $\delta' = n - r + N$) if the containing expression appears in row $r < R$. Insertion increases the distance between the referring and referred-to rows, and indeed adding $N \geq 0$ to the offset $\delta > 0$ increases its absolute value.

Rbb A relative reference to row $n \geq R$ needs no adjustment if the containing expression appears in row $r \geq R$. The reference has $\delta' = \delta = n - r$ before and after the insertion.

In the example on the left of figures 2.12 and 2.13, case Aa applies to all the $A$2 references, case Ab applies to all the $A$3 references, case Raa applies to the $A1 and $A2 references in cells B1 and B2, case Rab applies to the $A1 and $A2 references in cells B3 and B4, case Rba applies to the $A3 and $A4 references in cells B3 and B4, and case Rbb applies to the $A3 and $A4 references in cells B1 and B2.

The cases Raa, Rab, Rba, and Rbb for relative references can be translated into the following constraints on the offset $\delta = n - r$ and the containing row r, where $[a, b[$ denotes an interval that includes its left endpoint a but excludes its right endpoint b:

Raa If $r < R$ and $\delta + r < R$, then no adjustment is needed. The resulting expression is valid for rows r for which $r < \min(R, R - \delta)$, that is, $r \in [0, \min(R, R - \delta)[$.

Rab If $r \geq R$ and $\delta + r < R$, then adjust to $\delta' = \delta - N$. The resulting expression is valid for rows r for which $R \leq r < R - \delta$, that is, $r \in [R, R - \delta[$.

Rba If $r < R$ and $\delta + r \geq R$, then adjust to $\delta' = \delta + N$. The resulting expression is valid for rows r for which $R - \delta \leq r < R$, that is, $r \in [R - \delta, R[$.

Rbb If $r \geq R$ and $\delta + r \geq R$, then no adjustment is needed. The resulting expression is valid for rows r for which $r \geq \max(R, R - \delta)$, that is, $r \in [max(R, R - \delta), M[$ where M is the number of rows in the sheet.

The variables R, N, and r used above agree with the Corecalc implementation of row insertion in method **InsertRowCols** in class **Expr**. For relative references, we additionally have δ=rowRef and n=r+rowRef.

The adjustment of an entire expression is valid for the intersection of the rows for which the adjustments of each of its relative references is valid.

Note that an adjustment for a reference is valid for an entire sheet (Aa and Ab), for a lower (Raa) or upper (Rbb) half-sheet, for a band preceding (Rba), or for a band following (Rab) the insertion. In all cases, this range is a half-open interval, representable by its lower bound (inclusive) and upper bound (exclusive). The intersection of intervals is itself an interval (possibly empty, though not here), easily computed as $[\max(lower), \min(upper)[$.

Building further on Observation 1, we could maintain for each original expression a collection $[(r_1, e_1), \ldots, (r_m, e_m)]$ of ranges $r_1, \ldots, r_m$ and the adjusted versions $e_1, \ldots, e_m$ of the expression valid for each of those ranges.

But in fact, if we process the rows in increasing order, we only need to record, for each adjusted expression in the dictionary, the least row U not in its validity range. Once we reach a row r for which $r \geq U$, we recompute an adjusted expression and save that and the corresponding new U to the dictionary.

This scheme will preserve sharing of virtual copies completely within each row. However, sharing may be lost across rows because the same adjusted version of an expression may be valid at non-contiguous row ranges of the sheet (e.g., if a row is inserted in a range of cells, each of which depends on a cell on the immediately preceding row). The reason for this small deficiency is that our case analysis above involves the row r in which the formula appears.

This could be partially alleviated by reusing the old expression whenever the adjusted one is structurally identical. A more general solution would be to use a form of hash-consing to (re)introduce sharing of expressions that turn out to be identical after adjustment.

The insertion of new rows and new columns according to the above scheme is implemented by methods called `InsertRowCols` on class Sheet, on abstract class Cell and its subclasses, on abstract class Expr and its subclasses, and on class RARef. A generic class `Adjusted<T>` is used to store adjusted copies of Expr and RARef objects to preserve sharing as described above.

2.20   Deleting rows or columns

Deletion of rows or columns is similar to insertion. Again we consider only deletion of rows since deletion of columns is completely analogous. More precisely, we consider deleting $N \geq 0$ rows beginning with row $R \geq 0$, that is, deleting the rows numbered R through $R+N-1$. As in the insertion case, references *from* cells in rows following row $R + N$ on the affected sheet must be adjusted, as must references *to* those rows from any cell in the workbook. Moreover, references to the deleted rows cannot be adjusted in a meaningful way and must be replaced with a static error indication (class Error in section 2.7.3). Figures 2.14 and 2.15 show the same example in the ordinary A1 reference format and in the internal C0R0 format.

The cases are analogous to those of insertion in section 2.19, with two additional cases (Ac and Rc) to handle references to cells that get deleted.

	A	B
1	11	=$A$2+$A$4+$A1+$A2+$A4
2	21	=$A$2+$A$4+$A2+$A3+$A5
3	31	
4	41	=$A$2+$A$4+$A1+$A2+$A4
5	51	=$A$2+$A$4+$A2+$A3+$A5

	A	B
1	11	=$A$2+$A$3+$A1+$A2+$A3
2	21	=$A$2+$A$3+$A2+#REF+$A4
3	41	=$A$2+$A$3+$A1+$A2+$A3
4	51	=$A$2+$A$3+$A2+#REF+$A4

Figure 2.14: Formulas before (left) and after (right) deleting row 3.

n	A	B
0	11	R1+R3+R[0]+R[+1]+R[+3]
1	21	R1+R3+R[0]+R[+1]+R[+3]
2	31	
3	41	R1+R3+R[-3]+R[-2]+R[0]
4	51	R1+R3+R[-3]+R[-2]+R[0]

n	A	B
0	11	R1+R2+R[0]+R[+1]+R[+2]
1	21	R1+R2+R[0]+#REF+R[+2]
2	41	R1+R2+R[-2]+R[-1]+R[0]
3	51	R1+R2+R[-2]+#REF+R[0]

Figure 2.15: Internal representation before and after deleting row $R = 2$ (zero-based). References are in C0R0 format, but we omit the C0 prefix.

Aa An absolute reference to row $n < R$ needs no adjustment. This nonadjustment is valid regardless of the row r in which the containing expression appears.

Ab An absolute reference to row $n \geq R + N$ must be adjusted to $n - N$. This adjustment is valid regardless of the row r in which the containing expression appears.

Ac An absolute reference to row $R \leq n < R + N$ must be replaced by a #REF error indication. This adjustment is valid regardless of the row r in which the containing expression appears.

Raa A relative reference to row $n < R$ needs no adjustment if the containing expression appears in row $r < R$. The reference has $\delta' = \delta = n - r$ before and after the deletion.

Rab A relative reference to row $n < R$ must be adjusted (changed from $\delta = n - r$ to $\delta' = n - r + N$) if the containing expression appears in row $r \geq R + N$. Deletion reduces the distance between the referring and referred-to rows, and indeed adding $N \geq 0$ to the offset $\delta < 0$ reduces its absolute value.

Rba A relative reference to row $n \geq R + N$ must be adjusted (changed from $\delta = n - r$ to $\delta' = n - r - N$) if the containing expression appears in row $r < R$. Deletion reduces the distance between the referring and referred-to rows, and indeed subtracting $N \geq 0$ from the offset $\delta > 0$ reduces its absolute value.

Rbb A relative reference to row $n \geq R + N$ needs no adjustment if the containing expression appears in row $r \geq R + N$. The reference has $\delta' = \delta = n - r$ before and after the deletion.

Rca A relative reference to row $R \le n < R + N$ from row $r < R$ must be replaced by an error indication #REF!.

Rcb A relative reference to row $R \le n < R+N$ from row $r \ge R+N$ must be replaced by an error indication #REF!.

In the example on the left of figures 2.14 and 2.15, case Aa applies to all the $A$2 references, case Ab applies to all the $A$3 references, case Ac does not apply anywhere, case Raa applies to the $A1 and $A2 references in cells B1 and B2, case Rab applies to the $A1 and $A2 references in cells B4 and B5, case Rba applies to the $A4 and $A5 references in cells B1 and B2, case Rbb applies to the $A4 and $A5 references in cells B4 and B5, case Rca applies to the $A3 reference in cell B2, and case Rcb applies to the $A3 reference in cell B5.

The cases Raa, Rab, Rba, Rbb, Rca, and Rcb for relative references can be translated into the following constraints on the offset $\delta = n - r$ and the referring row r, where again $[a, b[$ is the interval that includes its left endpoint a but excludes its right endpoint b:

Raa If $r < R$ and $\delta + r < R$, then no adjustment is needed. The resulting expression is valid for rows r for which $r < \min(R, R - \delta)$, that is, $r \in [0, \min(R, R - \delta)[$.

Rab If $r \ge R + N$ and $\delta + r < R$, then adjust to $\delta' = \delta + N$. The resulting expression is valid for rows r for which $R + N \le r < R - \delta$, that is, $r \in [R + N, R - \delta[$.

Rba If $r < R$ and $\delta + r \ge R + N$, then adjust to $\delta' = \delta - N$. The resulting expression is valid for rows r for which $R + N - \delta \le r < R$, that is, $r \in [R + N - \delta, R[$.

Rbb If $r \ge R + N$ and $\delta + r \ge R + N$, then no adjustment is needed. The resulting expression is valid for rows r for which $r \ge \max(R, R + N - \delta)$, that is, $r \in [\max(R, R + N - \delta), M[$ where M is the number of rows in the sheet.

Rca If $r < R$ and $R \le \delta + r < R + N$, then the reference is invalid and must be replaced by #REF!. The resulting expression is valid for rows r for which $R - \delta \le r < \min(R, R + N - \delta)$, that is, $r \in [R - \delta, \min(R, R + N - \delta)[$.

Rcb If $r \ge R + N$ and $R \le \delta + r < R + N$, then the reference is invalid and must be replaced by #REF!. The resulting expression is valid for rows r for which $\max(R + N, R - \delta) \le r < R + N - \delta$, that is, $r \in [\max(R + N, R - \delta), R + N - \delta[$.

2.21 Summary of Corecalc implementation

This chapter has described most aspects of Corecalc, a core interpretive spreadsheet implementation. In particular it has described the representation of workbooks, sheets, and formulas and the machinery needed for recalculation (sections 2.4 through 2.16), and the effects of bulk edit operations (sections 2.17 through 2.20).

The next chapter will discuss some alternative designs for aspects of Corecalc, and chapters 4 and 5 will consider how to maintain the information necessary to recalculate those cells that may actually need it.

Chapter 3

Alternative Designs

The previous chapter presented details of the Corecalc implementation. This chapter will review some aspects of the Corecalc design, especially the recalculation mechanism, and discuss the advantages and disadvantages of some alternative implementation techniques.

3.1   Representation of references

As described in sections 2.18 through 2.20, since we use the C0R0 reference representation (section 2.9), it is necessary to perform cumbersome adjustments of referring formulas when moving a referred-to formula from one cell to another and when inserting or deleting rows or columns in an existing sheet.

3.1.1   Direct object references

The adjustments that the C0R0 reference format requires would be automatic if a cell reference such as A1 were instead represented as a direct object reference, from the abstract syntax of the referring formula, to the abstract syntax of the referred-to formula. However, such a representation would preclude sharing of virtual formula copies because different copies of relative references must refer to different cells.

Alternatively, the adjustment of referring formulas described in section 2.18 would be considerably simplified if the implementation maintained explicit knowledge of which cells directly depend on the moved cell, using a support graph as described in section 3.3.2. Currently, we perform a scan of the entire workbook to find those cells, but cell move operations are infrequent, and the extra time required to scan the workbook is small compared with the time it takes a user to perform these operations manually.

3.1.2 Reference representation in Excel

The fact that the XML export format of Excel 2003 uses the R1C1 format (section 1.3) makes it reasonable to assume that a variant of R1C1 is the internal reference format of Excel. However, patents 12 and 14 by Kaethler et al. indicate that formula copies are (or were) *not* shared by default in Excel, which seems to undermine a major advantage of using R1C1. Also, the highly efficient formula implementation described in Schlafly's patents 13 and 15 is not directly applicable to sharable formulas, unlike Thomas Iversen's implementation of run-time code generation [84].

3.2 The handling of infinities

Corecalc and Funcalc currently handle infinities the same way as Excel and OpenOffice Calc. Thus, expressions such as `1.0/0.0` and `EXP(10000)` produce overflow errors that must propagate through computations, tests, function calls, and so on. However, this is not really desirable. First, this does not agree with the IEEE 754-2008 binary floating-point standard [81]. Second, it is comparatively inefficient to treat infinities as errors. Third, infinities have many natural uses in clever computational algorithms [67] and as identities for functions such as `MAX` and `MIN`.

Hence, the treatment of infinities may change in a future version of Corecalc and Funcalc.

3.3 Minimal recalculation

In the Corecalc implementation as described so far, each recalculation evaluates every formula exactly once and follows each cell or area reference from each formula once, for a recalculation time that is linear in the sum of the sizes of all formulas. This provides efficiency comparable to that of several other spreadsheet implementations when all cells need to be recalculated [137, chapter 5].

Still, it would be desirable to improve this so that each recalculation only involves cells that depend on some changed or volatile cell, as seems to be the case in Excel. We shall call such a recalculation *minimal*, although in general it does not perform a provably minimal or optimal amount of work. Better terms might have been "parsimonious" or "frugal" recalculation.

Several solutions are frequently proposed in discussions:

- Attach update event listeners to cells (see section 3.3.1).

- Use an explicit support graph (see section 3.3.2 and chapter 4).

- Topologically sort cells in dependency order (see section 3.3.3).

- Speculatively reuse evaluation order (see section 3.3.4).

In the sections below, we will discuss the merits of each of these proposed mechanisms for minimal recalculation. To simplify discussion of space and time requirements, assume that the user has edited only one cell before a recalculation, let N_A be the number of non-null or active cells in the workbook, let F_A be the total size of formulas in the workbook, let N_D be the number of cells that depend on the changed (edited) cell in a given recalculation, and let correspondingly F_D be the total size of formulas in those cells.

3.3.1   Update event listeners

One plausible idea is to use event listeners. For instance, if the formula in cell C2 depends on cells A2 and B2 as in figure 1.2, then C2 could listen to value change events on cells A2 and B2. Whenever the value of a cell changes, a value change event is raised and can be handled by the listening cells. This makes each dependent cell an *observer* of all its supporting cells.

A design based on event listeners makes it quite easy to support level 4 liveness, in which recalculation and redisplay of results may be provoked not just by user edits (as in level 3 liveness) but also by external events such as the passing of time or the arrival of new readings from an instrument [27, 152]. One simply attaches event listeners to external data streams or to an operating system timer, just as one attaches event listeners to cells. With this approach, a spreadsheet becomes a true reactive system well suited for creating dynamic information displays.

However, there are also some difficulties in using this design:

- First, the number of event listeners may be $O(N_A^2)$, quadratic in the number of active cells. For instance, in the sheet shown in figure 3.1, the SUM formula in cell Bn must have event listeners on n cells in column A. With N such rows, the number of event listeners is $O(N^2)$, which poses two problems. It requires $O(N^2)$ space to record the event handlers associated with cells (even if the handler objects themselves can be shared), and it requires $O(N^2)$ time to call the event handlers.

- Second, one needs a separate mechanism to determine the proper recalculation order anyway. The value change event listener cannot just initiate the recalculation of the listening cell because the handler may be called at a time when some (other) supporting cells are not yet up to date. Hence, an event handler may just record that the cell needs to be recalculated and perhaps also that a particular supporting cell is now up to date.

- Third, a cell that contains a formula with a volatile function call such as NOW() or RAND() must be recalculated even if the value of no supporting cell has changed. That is, one needs to keep a separate list of such cells and recalculate them whenever anything changes, or one could introduce artificial "events" on which such cells depend.

- Fourth, a dynamic cyclic dependency will cause an infinite chain of events unless a separate cycle detection scheme is implemented.

- Fifth, event listeners would have to be attached based on static dependencies. For instance, if some cell G3 contains the formula IF(RAND()<0.5, G1, G2), then G3 would attach event handlers to both G1 and G2. However, a value change event on G1 may be irrelevant to G3, namely, when the pseudo-random number generator RAND() returns a number greater than or equal to 0.5. In general, the existence of non-strict functions means that some event handlers will be called to no avail.

- Finally, the lists of event handlers need to be maintained when the contents of cells are edited. This is fairly straightforward because the formula in a cell contains the necessary information about its directly supporting cells. So when a cell reference is added to or deleted from a formula, it is easy to find the cell(s) that must have event listeners added or removed.

3.3.2   Explicit support graph

A more general alternative to using event listeners is to build an explicit static *support graph*, whose nodes are sheet cells and where there are edges from cells A2 and B2 to cell C2 if C2 statically depends on A2 and B2 or, equivalently, A2 and B2 statically support C2. Figure 1.3 shows the entire support graph for the example sheet in figure 1.2. In fact, the arrows drawn by the formula audit feature of modern spreadsheet programs essentially show part of the support graph, as illustrated in figure 1.7.

In the support graph, each cell has edges to the cells that refer to it, called its dependents. This is the opposite of a dependency graph, in which each cell has edges to the cells that it depends on, called its precedents. Since a cell's precedents can easily be inferred from its formula, there is no need to store the dependency graph explicitly, but since the dependents cannot be easily inferred, an explicit support graph is useful. The "support" terminology, although not the concept of support graph, is used also in a Microsoft document describing recalculation in Excel [88]. Other sources call the support graph a "dependency tree" [44], although strictly speaking it is not a tree but a graph, as one cell may indirectly support another one via many different intermediate cells.

An explicit support graph suffers from some of the same problems as the use of event listeners. In fact, systematic attachment of event listeners as described above would create precisely a support graph, where the edge from B2 to C2 is represented by B2 holding a reference to an event handler supplied by C2.

Some of the challenges posed by using an explicit support graph are:

- First, as for event listeners, the support graph may have $O(N_A^2)$ edges when there are N_A active cells, witness the example in figure 3.1. Thus, the space required to explicitly represent the support graph's edges would be excessive. But note that the dependency graph, represented by the formulas in the active cells, requires space $O(F_A)$ only. The reason for this is chiefly the compact representation of sums and other formulas that take cell area arguments.

An interesting question is whether the support graph, like the dependency graph, can be represented compactly? The answer is yes, for a large set of plausible spreadsheet structures, as shown in chapters 4 and 5.

	A	B
1	0.5	=SUM(A$1:A$10000)
2	=A1*1.00001	=SUM(A$1:A$10000)
3	=A2*1.00001	=SUM(A$1:A$10000)
...	...	...
5000	=A4999*1.00001	=SUM(A$1:A$10000)
...	...	
10000	=A9999*1.00001	

Figure 3.1: A sheet with 15 000 active cells and 50 million support graph edges.

- The support graph can be used to determine the proper recalculation order. When a user has edited a cell, we can determine all the cells reachable from that cell, that is, all the cells transitively statically supported by it. Then we can linearize the subgraph consisting of those cells by a topological sort in time $O(F_D)$. The resulting linear order is suitable for a single pass recalculation.

- As for event listeners, one needs to keep a list of the cells containing formulas with volatile function calls and recalculate those cells, and all cells reachable from them, at every recalculation.

- A static cyclic dependency manifests itself as a cycle in the support graph, but such a static dependency cycle may be harmless; it does not prove that there is a dynamic dependency cycle. When there is no cycle in the support graph, there can be no dynamic cyclic dependency. When there is a cycle in the support graph, which should be rare, a full recalculation can be used to determine whether this is also a harmful dynamic cyclic dependency. However, permitting static cycles would complicate the topological sorting proposed above.

- As for event listeners, the support graph would have to be based on static dependencies, with the same consequence: some cells may be recomputed, although they do not actually (dynamically) depend on cells that have changed.

- The static support graph must be maintained when the contents of cells are edited. As for event listeners, this is fairly straightforward.

In conclusion, an explicit static support graph seems more promising than event listeners, but it is feasible only if a compact yet easily maintainable representation can be found. Two such representations are discussed in chapter 4 and 5.

3.3.3   Topological sorting of cell dependencies

A topological sorting is a linearization and approximation of the support graph. The advantage of keeping just the topological sorting is that it requires space $O(N_A)$ only, rather than space $O(N_A^2)$ for the more precise support graph. The chief disadvantage is that the topological sort can be very imprecise and hence is a poor basis for achieving minimal recalculation. Linearizations of the dependencies in the figure 3.2 example have the form A1, A2, A3, ..., B1, B2, B3, ..., C1, C2, C3, ..., D1, D2, D3, ..., E1, E2, E3, ..., F1, F2, F3, ..., with some permutation of the blocks.

	A	B	C	D	E	F
1	11	12	13	14	15	16
2	=A1+1	=B1+1	=C1+1	=D1+1	=E1+1	=F1+1
3	=A2+1	=B2+1	=C2+1	=D2+1	=E2+1	=F2+1
...	...	...	...	...	...	...

Figure 3.2: Bad control of recalculation using topological sort.

This means that if A1 changes, then not only the cells in column A supported by A1 will be recalculated, but also all the other cells following A1 in the topological sorting, most of them needlessly.

Building the topological sorting in the first place is not straightforward. Most simple algorithms for topological sorting assume a proper ordering (acyclic, that is, not just a preorder), but as shown in section 1.7.6, a spreadsheet can contain a static dependency cycle that is perfectly harmless, thanks to non-strict functions.

Rebuilding the topological sorting anew at each change to the spreadsheet is not attractive, as this requires time $O(F_A)$, in which time one can recalculate all cells, whether changed or not, anyway. Hence, it is desirable to try to incrementally adapt the topological sorting as the cells of the spreadsheet are edited. There do exist some clever rather recent algorithms for maintaining a topological sort under updates [13], but they seem to support only addition of dependency edges, not their removal, which seems equally important in the spreadsheet context. Simple edits to spreadsheet cells can radically change the topological sorting as shown in figure 3.3, which indicates that efficient maintenance of the topological sorting is not straightforward.

3.3.4   Speculative reuse of evaluation order

As an alternative to maintaining a correct topological sorting, or linearization, of the cell dependencies, one could simply record the actual order in which cells are recalculated and attempt to reuse that order at the next recalculation. Quite likely this is what Excel does (see section 3.3.5).

The idea is that the dependency structure changes very little, usually not at all, from recalculation to recalculation. Hence, the most recent bottom-up recalculation order is likely to work next time also.

	A	B	C	D
1	11	12	=SUM(B1:B9999)	14
2		=B1+A\$1		=D1+C\$1
3		=B2+A\$1		=D2+C\$1
4		=B3+A\$1		=D3+C\$1
...		...		...

Topological order before edit: A1, B1, B2, ..., C1, D1, D2, ...

	A	B	C	D
1	=SUM(D1:D9999)	12	13	14
2		=B1+A\$1		=D1+C\$1
3		=B2+A\$1		=D2+C\$1
4		=B3+A\$1		=D3+C\$1
...		...		...

Topological order after edit: C1, D1, D2, ..., A1, B1, B2, ...

Figure 3.3: Radical change in topological order after editing A1 and C2.

Most of the time, one would therefore not have to rediscover the dependency order. However, the correct amount and order of recalculation may change from recalculation to recalculation even if no cells are edited between recalculations. Again, non-strict and volatile functions are the culprits: if the sheet contains a formula such as IF(RAND()<0.5, G1, G2), then the previous recalculation order may be wrong in half the recalculations.

Nevertheless, it is quite easy to record the last recalculation order simply by dynamically chaining cells together so that each cell contains a reference to the next cell to be calculated. This is not currently done in Corecalc, but it would be worth experimenting with.

3.3.5   Recalculation in Microsoft Excel

A paper by La Penna at the Microsoft Developer Network (MSDN) website [88] describes recalculation in Excel 2002. The paper presents an example but glosses over the handling of volatile and non-strict functions. (A more recent Microsoft Support page [150] also describes Excel 2007 and 2010, but the description is superficial and doesn't look quite right, so we will ignore it here).

Recalculation is presented as a three-stage process: (1) identify the cells whose values need to be recalculated, (2) find the correct order in which to recalculate those cells, and (3) recalculate them.

The description of step (1) implies that from a given cell one can efficiently find the cells and cell areas that depend on that cell, but the paper does not say how this is implemented. Presumably this is done using the "dependency tree" described later in this section.

The paper's advice on efficiency of user-defined functions indicate that step (2) is embedded in step (3) as follows. To recalculate a cell, start evaluating its formula. If this evaluation encounters a reference to a cell that must be recalculated, then abandon the current evaluation and start evaluating the other cell's formula. When that is finished, start over from scratch, evaluating the original cell's formula. At least that is what the advice implies for user-defined VBA functions: *"One way to optimize user-defined functions is to prevent repeated calls to the user-defined function by entering them [the calls?] last in order in an on-sheet formula"*.

Interestingly, this requires a linked list (acting as a stack) to remember the yet-to-be-computed cells. This is somewhat similar to the Corecalc design, which uses the method call stack but avoids discarding any work already done.

Another interesting bit of information is that the final recalculation order is saved and reused for the next recalculation, so that it avoids discarding partially computed results. It is not discussed how this scheme works for a formula such as IF(RAND()<0.5, G1, G2), which changes the dynamic dependencies in an unpredictable way. Nevertheless, such a scheme probably works well in practice.

The paper hints that usually Excel only recalculates a cell if it (transitively) depends on cells that have changed, but no explicit guarantees are given. That paper says that one can request a standard recalculation (recalculate only cells that transitively depend on changed ones or volatile ones) by pressing F9 and force a "full recalculation" (recalculate all cells, also those not depending on changed cells) by pressing Ctrl+Alt+F9 (see also section 4.3.1).

Other sources indicate that the methods Calculate and CalculateFull from Excel interop class ApplicationClass provide other ways to perform ordinary and full recalculation [44, 109]. In addition, the method CalculateFullRebuild rebuilds the so-called "dependency tree" and then performs a full recalculation (see below). These methods and the dependency tree are not mentioned in the La Penna paper. Experiments made by Thomas Iversen [137, section 5.2.2] show that rebuilding the dependency tree can increase recalculation time considerably—by a factor of 80 in bad cases.

The Borland patents by Schlafly (numbers 13 and 15 in appendix B) give a hint about how recalculation order may be implemented in classic spreadsheet implementations. Our conjecture about this mechanism is this: Each formula (really, cell) record has a pointer to the next formula, so that all cells together make up a linked list. The implementation attempts to keep this list ordered so that a cell always precedes any cells that depend on it. If, during evaluation, a formula is found to depend on a cell that has not yet been evaluated, then the offending cell is moved from its current position in the linked list to just before the dependent formula, and evaluation starts over at the offending cell's new position in the list.

Third-party information from the company Decision Models [45] indicates that Excel 2003 does maintain a "dependency tree", probably corresponding to the support graph discussed in section 3.3.2 and chapter 4. (Note that the "tree" is typically not a proper tree but may in general be a graph with multiple paths between two nodes and may even contain cycles). The dependency tree is used to limit recalculation to those cells that depend on changed cells. However, according to the same source, in Excel 2003, there are some limitations on the representation of the dependency tree: *The number of different areas in a sheet that may have dependencies is limited to 65 536*, and *the number of cells that may depend on a single area is limited to 8192*. Excel versions 2007 and later do not have those limits, but in older versions, full recalculations will be performed rather than minimal recalculations when those limits are exceeded [44].

A 2008 blog post by Bill Seddon discusses Excel's recalculation mechanism and explains that the zip-based `.xlsx` file format contains a file `xl/calcChain.xml` that describes the recalculation order. From experiments this file seems not to contain a full support graph, just the order in which cells were processed during the most recent recalculation, as indicated in Schlafly's patent.

3.3.6 Recalculation in Gnumeric

The Gnumeric spreadsheet program [66] is open source, but we have not studied its recalculation mechanism in detail. An interesting technical note [98] by Meeks and Goldberg, distributed with the source code, discusses "the new dependency code". The purpose of that code is to find a minimal set of cells that must be recalculated when given cells have changed. Apparently two hash tables are used for individual cell dependencies, but some other form of search is needed to determine whether the value of a cell `A42` is used in a cell area reference such as `A1:A10000`.

3.3.7 Related work

One of the very first software patents, number 18 in appendix B and filed 1970, concerned the ordering of a full recalculation (by topological sorting), although in a spreadsheet concept that predates modern Visicalc-style electronic spreadsheets.

Harris and Bastian has a patent, number 17 in appendix B, on a method for "optimal recalculation". The patent assumes that there is an explicit representation of the support graph (which the patent calls the *dependency set* for a cell) and then describes how to recalculate only those formulas that need to be recalculated, and in an order that respects dependencies. Basically, this combines a filtering (consider only non-up-to-date cells) with transitive closure (cells that depend on non-up-to-date cells are themselves non-up-to-date) and topological sorting (to recalculate in dependency order), so algorithmically, this is standard. Nothing is said about volatile and non-strict functions, and the handling of cyclic dependencies is unclear. Nothing is said about how to represent the dependency set.

Burnett et al. [27] compare several mechanisms for recalculation in visual programming environments that support level 4 liveness, that is, where the passing of time or external non-user-generated events can trigger recalculation. They consider not only whether changed "input" values cause a need for recalculation, but also what "output" values (such as spreadsheet cells) are actually displayed, and how to avoid recalculating results that are not displayed. In their terminology, our "standard minimal recalculation" (see section 4.3.1) would be an "eager evaluation" or a "lazy evaluation with eager marking", and they show that both of these are non-optimal when taking into account what "output" values are actually needed. They also state [27, section 7] that what is an effective recalculation mechanism for level 3 liveness (which is what we are concerned with here) remains an open question.

Chapter 4

The Support Graph

A *support graph* shows which cells directly statically depend on a given cell. In figure 4.1, the support graph shows that cell A1 supports cells B1:B10. A support graph facilitates minimal recalculation as well as ordering of formula recalculation.

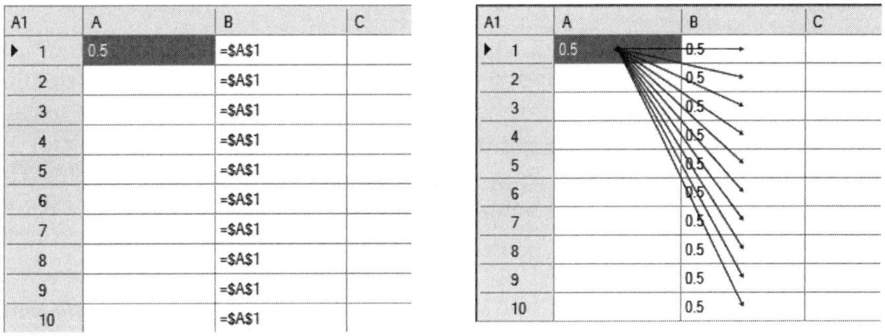

Figure 4.1: Cell A1 supports cells B1:B10. Formulas are shown on the left and the support graph on the right.

As discussed in section 3.3.2, the number of edges in the support graph may be very large relative to the number of cells in a workbook. This chapter investigates a compact representation of the support graph, as well as efficient algorithms for building, maintaining, and using it. Figure 4.2 shows a rather more dense support graph.

Corecalc implements the ideas presented in this chapter. Chapter 5 presents a more advanced support graph representation, not implemented. Minimal recalculation is achieved by a smooth extension, described in section 4.3, of the simple Corecalc mechanism (section 2.12), resulting in a mixture of bottom-up and top-down recalculation order (section 1.7.1). A support graph has a number of beneficial uses other than minimal recalculation (see section 4.4).

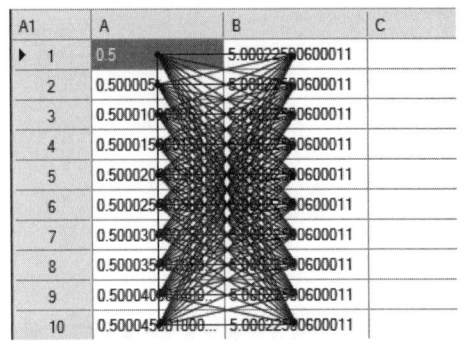

A1	A	B	C
▶ 1	0.5	=SUM($A$1:$A$10)	
2	=A1*1.00001	=SUM($A$1:$A$10)	
3	=A2*1.00001	=SUM($A$1:$A$10)	
4	=A3*1.00001	=SUM($A$1:$A$10)	
5	=A4*1.00001	=SUM($A$1:$A$10)	
6	=A5*1.00001	=SUM($A$1:$A$10)	
7	=A6*1.00001	=SUM($A$1:$A$10)	
8	=A7*1.00001	=SUM($A$1:$A$10)	
9	=A8*1.00001	=SUM($A$1:$A$10)	
10	=A9*1.00001	=SUM($A$1:$A$10)	

Figure 4.2: Cell A1 supports cells B1:B10, and so does cell A2, A3, and so on. Formulas are shown on the left and the support graph on the right. In this example, all support edges go from the A column to the B column, and from A1 to A2 to A3 and so on. When there are n populated rows, the number of support graph edges is $O(n^2)$. Note that the graph is not a tree; for instance, there are two paths from A1 to B1, both a direct one from A1 to B1 and an indirect one from A1 to A2 to B1.

4.1   Size of the support graph

As shown in section 3.3.2 and figure 3.1, there may be a large number of edges in the static support graph. There are two reasons for this: A cell area argument in a formula may refer to a large number of cells, and copying of such a formula may multiply that by a large factor. First, a cell that contains the formula SUM($A$1:$A$10000) will belong to the support of 10 000 cells. Second, that formula may be copied to 5 000 other cells, thus making each of the 10 000 cells support 5 000 cells, for a total of 10 000 · 5 000 = 50 000 000 support graph edges between only 10 000 + 5 000 = 15 000 cells. In general, there may be $O(n^2)$ support graph edges when there are n formula cells. Clearly a naive explicit representation of the support graph might require far too much memory even for modest-size spreadsheets.

Here we shall investigate how to compactly represent support graph edges from a cell to families of other cells that all hold virtual copies of the same expression. That is, we shall attack the second source of the support graph edge problem and reduce the 50 000 000 support graph edges needed above to 10 000 compactly represented families of support graph edges.

4.2   Compact representation of the support graph

We shall represent the support graph not as a separate entity but by letting each cell *cell* of the workbook maintain its *support set*, which is a set of cell addresses that includes all cells that refer to *cell*. How should we then represent each cell's support set?

If one copies the formula =$A$1 to the rectangular block of cells B2:D6, then the cell at A1 will support the cell area B2:D6, a rectangular block. Since formulas are frequently copied to rectangular cell areas in just this manner, for now we shall represent a support set as a list of such rectangular cell areas. This is the approach currently implemented; chapter 5 describes a more general approach, not implemented.

4.2.1   Copying of formulas and update of support set

All references from a formula are from its single cell references (such as $A1) and from its cell area references (such as A1:C$2). Moreover, a single cell reference can be considered a degenerate cell area reference $A1:$A1. So to study the effect on references—and hence on support sets—of copying a formula, it suffices to study cell area references, which we do now.

4.2.2   The effect of a cell area reference on support sets

Consider a cell area reference such as A1:C$2, being copied from cell K11 to cell area K11:M14, as in figure 4.3. The copied and adjusted area references all refer to cells in the A1:E4 area. The purpose of this section is to compute the support set for each cell in the A1:E4 area: the set of cells among K11:M14 that refer to that cell. The figure shows just the *size* of the support set for each cell in A1:E4.

	A	B	C	D	E	...	K	L	M	N
1	*1*	*2*	*3*	*2*	*1*	...				
2	*4*	*8*	*12*	*8*	*4*	...				
3	*2*	*4*	*6*	*4*	*2*	...				
4	*1*	*2*	*3*	*2*	*1*	...				
...	...	...	...	...	...	...	...	...	...	...
11						...	A1:C$2	B1:D$2	C1:E$2	
12						...	A2:C$2	B2:D$2	C2:E$2	
13						...	A3:C$2	B3:D$2	C3:E$2	
14						...	A4:C$2	B4:D$2	C4:E$2	
15						...				

Figure 4.3: Copying area reference A1:C$2 from cell K11 to the area K11:M14. An italic number in area A1:E4 is the cell's support set size, that is, the number of cells in area K11:M14 that refer to it. For instance, cell B1 is referred by K11 and L11 and thus supports those 2 cells, and cell C4 is referred by K14, L14, and M14 and thus supports 3 cells.

For these computations, we shall use C0R0-format references (see section 2.9). Consider in general a cell area reference $Cc_aRr_a:Cc_bRr_b$ in cell Cc_1Rr_1 copied to a target cell area $Cc_1Rr_1:Cc_2Rr_2$, in which it is the upper left corner and whose lower right corner is Cc_2Rr_2.

In the figure 4.3 example, the cell area reference is `C[-10]R[-10]:C[-8]R2` because the relative offset from column K to A is −10, the offset from row 11 to 1 is 10, and the offset from column K to C is −8. The target area is `C10R10:C12R13` in C0R0-format.

Note that the target area is always given in absolute cell coordinates. For the cell area reference, there seems to be a daunting 16 cases to consider because there are four combinations of (relative or absolute) and (column or row) references for each of the area reference's two corners, here `A1` and `C$2`. However, the row and column dimensions are independent of and analogous to each other, so it suffices to analyze just the four cases arising for each of those two dimensions, say, the row dimension. These four cases will also work for the column dimension.

So let us focus on the row dimension $Rr_a:Rr_b$ of a cell area reference and consider each of the four combinations of the row end-points r_a and r_b being relative or absolute. For the target cell area, we can ignore the column dimension as well and consider only the row dimension $Rr_1:Rr_2$. We can assume $r_1 \leq r_2$. It will be helpful to refer to figure 4.4 during the discussion below; the four columns in the figure correspond to the four cases.

Our task is to determine what cells the various copies of the cell area reference can refer to. This will tell us the effect of the formula copying on the support sets of (other) cells in the workbook.

	A	B	C	D	...
0					...
1	*supp R10:R12*	*supp R10:R12*	*supp R10:R12*	*supp R10:R10*	...
2	*supp R10:R12*	*supp R10:R12*	*supp R10:R12*	*supp R10:R11*	...
3		*supp R11:R12*	*supp R11:R12*	*supp R11:R12*	...
4		*supp R12:R12*	*supp R12:R12*	*supp R12:R12*	...
5					...
...	...	...	...	...	...
10	R1:R2	R1:R[-8]	R[-8]:R1	R[-9]:R[-8]	...
11	R1:R2	R1:R[-8]	R[-8]:R1	R[-9]:R[-8]	...
12	R1:R2	R1:R[-8]	R[-8]:R1	R[-9]:R[-8]	...
13					...

Figure 4.4: Support sets resulting from copying four kinds of row range references to rows `R10:R12`: abs-abs (column A), abs-rel (column B), rel-abs (column C), and rel-rel (column D). Each referred-to cell in rows 1 through 4 shows the range supported by that cell. For instance, column B row 3 supports the range `R11:R12` because it is referred to by rows 11 and 12 in the same column. References are in C0R0 format and assumed to refer within the same column, so for brevity, only row references are shown. Figure 4.5 shows the copied range references in A1 format for clarity.

- Case abs-abs: Single-column absolute/absolute area reference $Rr_a : Rr_b$ copied to target rows $Rr_1 : Rr_2$. Each cell row Rr in $Rr_a : Rr_b$, that is, with $r_a \leq r \leq r_b$, supports the entire area $Rr_1 : Rr_2$, that is, the cell row supports the row interval $[r_1, r_2]$. Figure 4.4, column A illustrates the abs-abs case with $r_a = 1$, $r_b = 2$, $r_1 = 10$ and $r_2 = 12$, and indeed each row $1 \leq r \leq 2$ supports the entire row range R10:R12.

- Case abs-rel: Single-column absolute/relative cell area reference $Rr_a : R[r_b]$ copied to target rows $Rr_1 : Rr_2$. Subcase 1: For a cell row r such that $r_a < r \leq r_2 + r_b$, the support set is $[\max(r_1, r - r_b), r_2]$. Subcase 2: For $r = r_a$, the support set is the interval $[r_1, r_2]$; informally, the absolute endpoint Rr_a of the cell area reference must be referred from every virtual copy of the cell area reference in target cells $[r_1, r_2]$. Subcase 3: A cell row r such that $r_1 + r_b \leq r < r_a$ supports the interval $[r_1, \min(r_2, r - r_b)]$.

  It also follows that the range of cells that support some cell in the target area is the union of $[r_a, r_2 + r_b]$ and $[r_1 + r_b, r_a]$, that is, $[\min(r_a, r_1 + r_b), \max(r_a, r_2 + r_b)]$.

  Figure 4.4, column B illustrates case abs-rel with $r_a = 1$, $r_b = -8$, $r_1 = 10$, and $r_2 = 12$. Indeed only rows $r \in [\min(1, 10 + (-8)), \max(1, 12 + (-8))] = [1, 4]$ support some cell in the target area, where rows $1 < r \leq 4$ correspond to subcase 1, row $r = 1$ corresponds to subcase 2, and the empty set of rows, with $2 \leq r < 1$, correspond to subcase 3.

  The above subcase results can be derived as follows. A cell row r supports cell row s in the target area provided s indeed is in the target area ($r_1 \leq s \leq r_2$) and r is between the bounds of the area reference ($r_a \leq r \leq s + r_b$ or $s + r_b \leq r \leq r_a$). By breaking into cases on r and splitting the inequalities and rewriting to isolate s, we get:

  - Subcase 1: When $r_a < r$, the second disjunct is false, so r supports s provided $r - r_b \leq s$ and $r_1 \leq s$ and $s \leq r_2$, that is, when s belongs to the interval $[\max(r_1, r - r_b), r_2]$. This interval is non-empty when $r - r_b \leq r_2$, that is, $r \leq r_2 + r_b$. Hence, each r with $r_a < r \leq r_2 + r_b$ supports the interval $[\max(r_1, r - r_b), r_2]$.

  - Subcase 2: When $r = r_a$, r supports s provided $r \leq s + r_b \lor s + r_b \leq r$, which is always true, so the only constraint is that s is in the interval $[r_1, r_2]$. Hence, row r_a supports the row interval $[r_1, r_2]$.

  - Subcase 3: When $r < r_a$, the first disjunct cannot be true, so r supports s provided $s \leq r - r_b$ and $r_1 \leq s$ and $s \leq r_2$, that is, when s belongs to the interval $[r_1, \min(r_2, r - r_b)]$. This interval is non-empty when $r_1 \leq r - r_b$, that is, $r_1 + r_b \leq r$. Hence, each r with $r_1 + r_b \leq r < r_a$ supports the interval $[r_1, \min(r_2, r - r_b)]$.

- Case rel-abs: Single-column relative/absolute cell area reference $R[r_a] : Rr_b$ copied to target rows $Rr_1 : Rr_2$. Subcase 1: A cell row r such that $r_1 + r_a \leq r < r_b$ supports the interval $[r_1, \min(r_2, r - r_a)]$. Subcase 2: The cell row $r = r_b$

supports the row interval $[r_1, r_2]$. Subcase 3: A cell r such that $r_b < r \leq r_2 + r_a$ supports the interval $[\max(r_1, r - r_a), r_2]$.

The range of cells that support some cell in the target area is described by the row interval $[\min(r_1 + r_a, r_b), \max(r_2 + r_a, r_b)]$.

This can be proven with reasoning very similar to the abs-rel case. In fact the abs-rel and rel-abs cases are identical because the order of endpoints in a cell area reference does not matter. There is no difference between the cell area references $Rr_a : R[r_b]$ and $R[r_b] : Rr_a$, at least in Excel and Corecalc.

Figure 4.4, column C illustrates case rel-abs with $r_a = -8$, $r_b = 1$, $r_1 = 10$, and $r_2 = 12$. Indeed only rows $r \in [\min(10 + (-8), 1), \max(12 + (-8), 1)] = [1, 4]$ support some cell in the target area.

- Case rel-rel: Single-column relative/relative cell area reference $R[r_a] : R[r_b]$ copied to target rows $Rr_1 : Rr_2$. We can assume without loss of generality that $r_a \leq r_b$. Each cell r in the interval $[r_1 + r_a, r_2 + r_b]$ supports the row interval $[\max(r_1, r - r_b), \min(r_2, r - r_a)]$.

  Figure 4.4, column D illustrates case rel-rel with $r_a = -9$, $r_b = -8$, $r_1 = 10$, and $r_2 = 12$. Indeed only rows $r \in [10 + (-9), 12 + (-8)] = [1, 4]$ support some cell in the target area, and row $r = 1$ supports target rows $[\max(10, 1 - (-8)), \min(12, 1 - (-9)] = [10, 10]$, row $r = 2$ supports target rows $[\max(10, 2 - (-8)), \min(12, 2 - (-9))] = [10, 11]$, and so on.

  The rel-rel result can be derived as follows. A cell row r supports cell row s in the target area provided s indeed is in the target area ($r_1 \leq s \leq r_2$) *and* r is between the bounds of the area reference ($s + r_a \leq r \leq s + r_b$). Isolating s in the latter inequality we get $s \leq r - r_a \wedge r - r_b \leq s$, and together with the former inequality, we see that s must belong to the interval $[\max(r_1, r - r_b), \min(r_2, r - r_a)]$. This interval is non-empty when $r_1 \leq r - r_a \wedge r - r_b \leq r_2$, that is, when $r_1 + r_a \leq r \leq r_2 + r_b$. Hence, each r with $r_1 + r_a \leq r \leq r_2 + r_b$ supports the interval $[\max(r_1, r - r_b), \min(r_2, r - r_a)]$.

	A	B	C	D	...
1					...
...	...	...	...	...	...
11	A$2:A$3	B$2:B3	C3:C$2	D2:D3	...
12	A$2:A$3	B$2:B4	C4:C$2	D3:D4	...
13	A$2:A$3	B$2:B5	C5:C$2	D4:D5	...
14					...

Figure 4.5: The range references from figure 4.4 shown in A1 format rather than C0R0 format. Because of the A1 format the row numbers are 1 higher than in figure 4.4.

As can be seen, we frequently need to represent intervals of row or column numbers. For this we use a struct type Interval:

```
public struct Interval {
  public readonly int min, max;   // Assume min<=max
  ...
}
```

Now we can implement the above analysis of the four absolute/relative cases by a C# method `RefAndSupp`, short for "references and supports", using some functional programming (see the aside in section 4.2.3 if this appears incomprehensible):

```
void RefAndSupp(bool ulAbs, bool lrAbs, int ra, int rb,
                int r1, int r2,
                out Interval referred,
                out Func<int,Interval> supported)
{
  if (ulAbs) {
    if (lrAbs) {   // case abs-abs
      SortInts(ref ra, ref rb);   // Ensure ra <= rb
      referred = new Interval(ra, rb);
      supported = r => new Interval(r1, r2);
    } else {       // case abs-rel
      referred = new Interval(Math.Min(ra,r1+rb),Math.Max(ra,r2+rb));
      supported = r => ra < r ? new Interval(Math.Max(r1, r-rb), r2)
                     : ra > r ? new Interval(r1, Math.Min(r2, r-rb))
                              : new Interval(r1, r2);
    }
  } else {
    if (lrAbs) {   // case rel-abs
      referred = new Interval(Math.Min(r1+ra, rb),Math.Max(r2+ra, rb));
      supported = r => rb > r ? new Interval(r1, Math.Min(r2,r-ra))
                     : rb < r ? new Interval(Math.Max(r1,r-ra), r2)
                              : new Interval(r1, r2);
    } else {       // case rel-rel
      SortInts(ref ra, ref rb);   // Ensure ra <= rb
      referred = new Interval(r1+ra, r2+rb);
      supported = r => new Interval(Math.Max(r1,r-rb),
                                    Math.Min(r2,r-ra));
    }
  }
}
```

This method takes as argument a row reference interval $[r_a, r_b]$, indications whether the reference endpoints r_a and r_b are relative or absolute, and an absolute copy target row range $[r_1, r_2]$. It returns two results via the `out` parameters. First, `referred` is a row interval indicating which rows may be referred from the copies of the reference $r_a : r_b$. Second, `supported` is a function such that `supported(r)` is the interval of rows supported by cell row `r`, when `r` is within the `referred` interval.

Until now we have discussed only the row dimension, but the column dimension can be handled in exactly the same way, using the exact same method `RefAndSupp`, and independently of the row dimension. This leads to the following succinct code for updating the support sets when cell area reference $Cc_aRr_a : Cc_bRr_b$ is copied to target cell area $Cc_1Rr_1 : Cc_2Rr_2$:

```
void AddToSupport(Sheet supported, int col, int row,
                  int cols, int rows)
{
  Sheet referredSheet = this.sheet ?? supported;
  Interval referredRows, referredCols;
  Func<int, Interval> supportedRows, supportedCols;
  int ra = ul.rowRef, rb = lr.rowRef, r1 = row, r2 = row+rows-1;
  RefAndSupp(ul.rowAbs, lr.rowAbs, ra, rb, r1, r2,
             out referredRows, out supportedRows);
  int ca = ul.colRef, cb = lr.colRef, c1 = col, c2 = col+cols-1;
  RefAndSupp(ul.colAbs, lr.colAbs, ca, cb, c1, c2,
             out referredCols, out supportedCols);
  referredCols.ForEach(c => {
    Interval suppCols = supportedCols(c);
    referredRows.ForEach(r =>
      referredSheet.AddSupport(c, r, supported,
                               suppCols, supportedRows(r)));
  });
}
```

This code analyzes the row and column dimensions of the cell area reference independently, using two calls to the `RefAndSupp` method shown earlier. This produces intervals `referredRows` and `referredCols` describing the referred cell area, that is, those cells that may support some copy of the cell area reference. Moreover, it produces functions `supportedRows(r)` and `supportedCols(c)` that given a row `r` or column `c` return the interval of rows or columns that the referred cell supports. Finally, the cell rectangle spanned by these row and column intervals is added to the support set of the referred cell `(c, r)` on the referred sheet by iterating over all items `(c, r)` in the product of the intervals.

4.2.3   Aside: Functional programming for code reuse

Method `RefAndSupp` shown in section 4.2.2 is a higher-order function, a function whose result is itself a function; this may require some additional explanation and motivation.

Recall that `RefAndSupp` returns two results via the `out` parameters: `referred` is a row or column interval, and `supported` is a function such that `supported(r)` is the interval of rows or columns supported by row or column `r` when `r` is within the `referred` interval. Note that the type of `supported` is `Func<int, Interval>`, that is, a function that takes an `int` and returns an `Interval`.

Concretely, consider the method's abs-abs case:

```
referred = new Interval(ra, rb);
supported = r => new Interval(r1, r2);
```

Here `supported` is the function `r => new Interval(r1, r2)`, or in words, the function that given integer argument `r` will return `Interval(r1, r2)` representing the interval $[r_1, r_2]$. This expresses exactly the conclusion of the abs-abs case on page 85: any row or column r in $[r_a, r_b]$ supports the row or column interval $[r_1, r_2]$. This illustrates the idea, but the function is trivial: the result does not depend on the argument.

Consider one of `RefAndSupp`'s more interesting cases, rel-rel:

```
referred = new Interval(r1+ra, r2+rb);
supported = r => new Interval(Math.Max(r1,r-rb), Math.Min(r2,r-ra));
```

Here `supported` is the function that given an argument r will return the interval $[\max(r_1, r - r_b), \min(r_2, r - r_a)]$, and again this corresponds exactly to the conclusion of the rel-rel case on page 86. This case shows why it would not suffice to return `supported` as an interval: since the supported interval depends on the row or column number r, `supported` must be a function, capable of returning a different interval for each r.

The two remaining cases, abs-rel and rel-abs, further underscore this point.

However, this does not explain why it is useful to return `supported` at all, rather than somehow process it inside each case of `RefAndSupp`. The motivation is *modularity* and *code reuse*. The case analysis in section 4.2.2 holds for both rows and columns, so the computations that must be performed are the same for rows as for columns; this is reflected in the many occurrences of "row or column `r`" above. Therefore, we encapsulate these computations in method `RefAndSupp` and simply call it twice whenever we need to compute support: once to compute for the rows and once to compute for the columns, as illustrated by the first two lines of this excerpt of method `AddToSupport`:

```
RefAndSupp(..., out referredRows, out supportedRows);
RefAndSupp(..., out referredCols, out supportedCols);
referredCols.ForEach(c => {
  Interval suppCols = supportedCols(c);
  referredRows.ForEach(r =>
    sheet.AddSupport(c, r, ..., suppCols, supportedRows(r)));
});
```

The rest of the above method uses further functional programming to process each combination (c,r) of referred-to column `c` and referred-to row `r`, and for each of these computes the supported range of cells by calling `supportedCols(c)` and `supportedRows(r)`.

The `referredCols.ForEach(c => ...)` call passes a function `c => ...` to higher-order function `ForEach`, which calls function `c => ...` on each column in the interval `referredCols`. This is just a functional programming equivalent of this foreach statement:

```
foreach (int c in referredCols)
  ...
```

By combining object-oriented and functional programming as possible in C#, one can obtain considerable modularity, code reuse, and brevity. In the compiler for sheet-defined functions in chapter 7, we will also combine object-oriented inheritance with higher-order compilation functions.

4.2.4 The effect of a single cell reference on support sets

Based on the analysis of copying of cell area references (albeit only in the row dimension), let us consider the special case of a single cell reference, using that a single cell reference such as A$3 is equivalent to an area reference A$3:A$3 whose two corner references are identical. Focusing again on the row dimension only, we have just two cases:

- Case abs: Single-column absolute single cell reference Rr_a, or equivalently $Rr_a:Rr_a$. From the abs-abs case in section 4.2.2, we see that each r with $r_a \le r \le r_a$, that is, just row $r = r_a$, has support interval $[r_1, r_2]$.

- Case rel: Single-column relative single cell reference $R[r_a]$, or equivalently $R[r_a]:R[r_a]$. From the rel-rel case in section 4.2.2, we see that each r with $r_1 + r_a \le r \le r_2 + r_a$ has support interval $[\max(r_1, r - r_a), \min(r_2, r - r_a)]$. But for such r, it holds that $r_1 \le r - r_a$ and $r - r_a \le r_2$, so the support interval is $[r - r_a, r - r_a]$, that is, a single cell.

The column dimension is analogous and independent of the row dimension. The machinery for finding the effect, on support sets, of copying a single cell reference can be implemented as slightly specialized versions of methods `RefAndSupp` and `AddToSupport` from section 4.2.2.

4.2.5 The effect of a formula on support sets

In sections 4.2.2 and 4.2.4, we analyzed what cells the copies of a cell (area) reference actually refer to, and we used that information to determine the support set of each such referred cell. But in general one does not just copy a cell (area) reference, but a formula, which may contain any number of cell (area) references. To find the effect of the formula copies on the support sets of referred cells, one may simply traverse the formula abstract syntax tree, processing each cell (area) reference encountered.

This works, but it is common for a formula to contain multiple occurrences of the same cell (area) reference, as in `MAX(A1:A10)-MIN(A1:A10)`, which computes the spread between minimal and maximal values, referring to area `A1:A10` twice. To avoid recording the computed support set twice, the traversal of the formula abstract syntax carries along a set of the cell area references already processed. Then the support sets are computed only on the first encounter of each reference such as `A1:A10`.

4.2.6 Representing the support sets

Conceptually, the support set for a cell is a union of rectangular cell areas (whose formulas refer to that cell). The support set is represented as an array list of SupportRange objects, where abstract class SupportRange has subclasses SupportCell (representing a single supported cell) and SupportArea (representing a rectangular cell area). This distinction is made primarily to conserve memory since a SupportCell object requires just three fields (sheet, column, row), whereas a SupportArea object requires five fields (sheet, start and end points for column interval as well as row interval).

In the current implementation, no effort is made to avoid overlapping support ranges in the array list, although overlaps cause needless administrative work during recalculation (but does not cause cells to be needlessly recalculated). Also, no effort is made to coalesce adjacent support ranges into one. Such cleanup is expected to require more effort than it saves, given that there is no simple way to ensure that support ranges that are adjacent or overlapping in the grid structure are also stored near each other in the array list. Moreover, completely avoiding overlaps between support ranges might increase the number of support ranges needed to represent the support set.

A SupportRange object has an `Apply` method that takes as argument a delegate act, and calls `act(sheet, col, row)` for each cell in the support range. This is used during minimal recalculation (section 4.3):

```
public abstract void Apply(Action<Sheet,int,int> act);
```

The SupportRange class has a static method `Make` that creates an appropriate representation of a cell range, whether the range consists of a single cell or multiple cells:

```
public static SupportRange Make(Sheet sheet, Interval colInt,
                                Interval rowInt) {
  if (colInt.min == colInt.max && rowInt.min == rowInt.max)
    return new SupportCell(sheet, colInt.min, rowInt.min);
  else
    return new SupportArea(sheet, colInt, rowInt);
}
```

The `Make` method is called from a support set's `AddSupport` method, which adds a range, given as the product of a column interval suppCols and a row interval suppRows, to the support set of cell `sheet[col,row]`:

```
public void AddSupport(Sheet sheet, int col, int row,
                       Sheet suppSheet, Interval suppCols,
                       Interval suppRows) {
  SupportRange range
    = SupportRange.Make(suppSheet, suppCols, suppRows);
  if (!range.RemoveCell(this, sheet, col, row))
    ranges.Add(range);
}
```

The `range.RemoveCell` call above removes the cell itself (at `[col,row]`) from the support set because such direct self-support causes problems when using the support graph for minimal recalculation for array formulas (section 4.3.5). Those problems could be avoided by additional run-time checks and by also requiring array formulas to have cell state, but it is more efficient to avoid such unit cycles in the support graph from the outset. The `RemoveCell` call returns true if it removed something from the range, in which case it also already added any remaining cell areas to the list `ranges` of support ranges.

Removing a single cell from a support range (also needed when updating support sets, section 4.2.7) can be done as follows:

- Removing a cell address from a single-cell support range (a SupportCell) either eliminates the support range completely, if the cell address is the one described by the support range, or else has no effect.

- Removing a cell address *ca* from a multi-cell support range (a SupportArea) either replaces the given support range with between one and four smaller support ranges, if *ca* is within the support area, or else has no effect. The smaller subranges are North, the partial column above *ca*; South, the partial column below *ca*; West, the block consisting of all rows and of the columns to the left of *ca*; and East, the block consisting of all rows and of the columns to the right of *ca*. Any one of these areas may be empty, may consist of a single cell, or may be a proper cell area, depending on the position of *ca* within the given support area.

We do not attempt to minimize the representation of a support set by joining adjacent SupportCells into a SupportArea, after removing a cell from the support set. After a large number of edits, this may cause deterioration of the support set representation. That can be mitigated by requesting a full recalculation after rebuild (section 4.3.1) to reconstruct the support graph from scratch.

4.2.7 Maintaining the support sets

The support graph must be maintained as the user edits the workbook interactively. Whenever a cell is edited, so that its contents changes from, say, 27 to 42, the cell's old support set should be transferred to the new cell contents: Editing the cell does not affect which other cells refer to it, except for direct self-references, which we avoid in this context (see section 4.2.6). Method `TransferSupportTo` in class Cell performs this support set transfer.

Editing the cell's contents clearly may change what other cells it refers to and hence what other cells support it. Specifically, if the edited cell previously did not refer to other cells, and we type, copy, or paste in a formula that does, this cell should be added to the support sets of the referred cells. Conversely, if the edited cell previously contained a formula that refers to other cells, then one can remove this cell from the support sets of the previously referred-to cells.

But note that whereas *adding* the cell is necessary for correct recalculation (otherwise the new formula will not be recalculated when the referred cells change), recalculation would not be incorrect if we neglected to *remove* the cell from those support sets. Leaving the cell there would make the support graph imprecise (but safe) and might cause the cell to be needlessly recalculated; results would still be correct, but some recalculation effort may be wasted.

However, removing the cell from those support sets and maintaining precision of the support graph brings other benefits. In particular, the support set will not contain spurious cycles, only cycles that could lead to cyclic dependencies during recalculation. The advantage of this becomes clear in section 4.3.2 when we describe how the support graph is used during minimal calculation.

So when we delete a formula from a cell *cell*, we must remove the cell from the support sets to which it belongs. But those are precisely the support sets of those cells that *cell*'s formula refers to. Hence, we can find them by traversing the formula's expression and processing each CellRef and AreaRef expression (once), removing cell *cell* from the cells referred to by these reference expressions.

Traversing the formula of *cell* is likely to be fast (because formulas are small), but the procedure has two other costs that may be significant. First, even a small formula may refer to many such cells; consider the formula =SUM(A1:Z10000), which refers to 260 000 cells. Second, the support set of each such cell may consist of many support ranges, and for each such support range, we must determine whether it contains *cell* and, if so, remove *cell* from the support range. This can be done as explained in section 4.2.6; in general, it will require the support range to be replaced by between zero and four smaller support ranges. Hence, deleting a cell from a support set may make the representation of the support set larger (although the represented set becomes smaller).

4.2.8   The support graph and array formulas

Recall that an array formula (section 1.4 and figure 1.6) is a formula whose array-valued result is distributed over a range of cells, called the display area. Array formulas require special attention in relation to support sets.

Each cell in the display area may be referred to from other cells, and so should maintain its own support set; this is in line with the treatment of all other cells. In addition, all cells in the display area share the same underlying array-valued formula (although displaying only a part of its value), so the support set of that underlying formula must include all cells in the display area. In fact, no other cell can refer directly to the underlying formula, so its support set is exactly the cells in the display area. Finally, the underlying formula may refer to other cells, and hence must be added to the support set of those cells, once. To ensure that the underlying cached formula is added only once to referred cells, we use update flags in the CachedArrayFormula objects.

This setup avoids adding every cell in the display area to every cell referred to by the shared underlying formula, which would lead to redundant work during recalculation. Section 4.3.5 describes how minimal recalculation handles array formulas.

4.2.9   Rebuilding the support graph at load-time

When loading a workbook from an externally generated file, we need to rebuild the support graph from scratch. This can be done by determining blocks of identical formulas and then treating each such block as if it resulted from copying a formula from the block's upper left corner to the entire block, using the machinery from section 4.2.2 to update support sets.

A given formula may be copied to many cells of the sheet, and ideally we want to find the minimal set of disjoint rectangles that cover all those cells. However, this is a version of the black and white Rectilinear Picture Compression problem that is NP-complete [65, problem SR25]. Therefore, we must be satisfied with determining a modest but perhaps not minimal set of rectangles that cover all the formula copies. The procedure outlined below processes an entire sheet in time $O(n)$, where n is the number of cells, and appears to work well in practice.

We scan each sheet from left to right and top to bottom, and for each formula cell not yet covered, we use a greedy approach to find a large rectangle of virtual copies with that cell as upper left corner, as follows. First, we determine the largest *square* of virtual copies with that cell as the upper left corner. Then we determine the largest extension (to the right or downward) of that square to a *rectangle* of virtual copies. The cells in that rectangle are marked as covered, and the process proceeds to the next uncovered cell in the sheet. To find a largest square of size n^2, we need at most $n^2 + 2n + 1$ operations or at most four times the number of cells in the resulting square. To extend that to a largest rectangle requires at most twice as many operations as there are cells in the final rectangle. Hence, the entire process is linear in the number of cells. Since formulas are interned (section 2.2.4) when reading them—only a single copy of each formula expression abstract syntax tree is created—a simple reference equality comparison suffices to determine whether one formula is a virtual copy of another.

As a practical matter, instead of equipping each cell with an additional Visited flag, we temporarily abuse the cell state (section 2.12) for this purpose, interpreting Uptodate as Visited and Dirty as non-Visited. The `ResetCellState` method then can be used to initialize all cells to non-Visited before the scan and to reset the cells again after the scan. Only formula cells matter in the scan, and it is precisely the formula cells that have cell state.

Support graph rebuilding may be requested also by a user (see section 4.3.1).

4.3   Minimal recalculation using a support graph

Given a support graph for a workbook, one can implement minimal or parsimonious recalculation (section 3.3) by a modest extension of the simple top-down recalculation mechanism described in section 2.12. This section describes the scheme actually implemented in Corecalc and Funcalc. This scheme is independent of the support graph representation and works with both the interval-based one presented in this chapter and the more sophisticated one presented in chapter 5.

4.3.1   Three kinds of recalculation

Here we summarize the different kinds of recalculations that can be performed in Corecalc and Funcalc, which appear to correspond closely to those of Microsoft Excel. The recalculation mechanisms rely on the cell states Dirty, Computing, and Uptodate already introduced in section 2.12 and an additional cell state Enqueued.

Let a *volatile cell* be a formula cell whose expression contains a call to a volatile function. In general, a recalculation of a workbook will reevaluate those formula cells that depend, directly or indirectly, on the *recalculation roots*. In a standard (minimal) recalculation, the recalculation roots are the newly edited cells and the volatile cells. In a full recalculation, performed just after loading the workbook or after a cycle has been discovered, all cells are recalculation roots.

- A *standard minimal recalculation* recalculates only those cells that depend on recalculation roots. It assumes that all cells are Uptodate before the recalculation, and it guarantees that all cells are Uptodate after the recalculation, unless there is a dependency cycle, which may leave some cells not Uptodate. (Hence, a standard recalculation cannot be used after a dependency cycle has been discovered).

  A standard recalculation happens whenever the user edits one or more cells, in which case the recalculation roots are the edited cells and all volatile cells. It may also be requested explicitly by pressing F9, just as in Microsoft Excel, in which case the recalculation roots are the volatile cells. In Microsoft Excel, the request is equivalent to calling Application.Calculate in a VBA macro. In Funcalc, standard recalculation is implemented by method `Recalculate` in class Workbook, as described in section 4.3.2.

- A *full recalculation* forces recalculation of all cells. It first marks all cells Dirty and then evaluates all of them in top-down order. It leaves all cells Uptodate unless there is a cycle, which may leave some cells not Uptodate. A full recalculation is automatically performed once after loading a workbook from a file. It may also be requested explicitly by pressing Ctrl+Alt+F9, just as in Microsoft Excel. Moreover, any attempt at recalculation of a workbook in which a cycle has been discovered will result in a full recalculation. Full recalculation is implemented by method `RecalculateFull` in class Workbook. In Microsoft Excel, it is equivalent to calling Application.CalculateFull in a VBA macro.

- A *full recalculation with rebuild* will rebuild the support graph as described in section 4.2.9 and then perform a full recalculation. A plausible use of this is to clean up support sets that have become overly conservative due to vigorous editing of the workbook or that have otherwise become inconsistent with the actual dependencies. There is anecdotal evidence that it serves such clean-up purposes in Microsoft Excel [96, 116]. A full recalculation with rebuild may be requested by pressing Ctrl+Alt+Shift+F9 as in MS Excel. Full recalculation with rebuild is implemented by method `RecalculateFullRebuild` in class Workbook. In Microsoft Excel it is equivalent to calling Application.CalculateFullRebuild in a VBA macro.

The discovery of a dependency cycle may leave cells in the states Dirty, Enqueued, and Computing, so the next recalculation cannot rely on cells being Uptodate. A safe solution to this problem is to force a full recalculation, which will begin by marking all cells Dirty.

It seems that a more parsimonious approach would be possible because any cell that depends on the yet unevaluated cells, including the cells involved in the cycle(s), will be in state Dirty, Enqueued, or Computing. Hence, it would suffice to reset all those to Dirty and leave the Uptodate ones in that state. The resetting would require a visit to all cells, but the subsequent recalculation would be faster because it does not affect the Uptodate cells.

However, we stick to the simpler approach of resetting and recalculating all cells because a cyclic dependency should be a mistake and hence an infrequent occurrence.

4.3.2 Standard minimal recalculation

Standard minimal recalculation is performed as a mixture of bottom-up recalculation driven by the support graph and top-down recalculation driven by one cell's need for the value of another cell that has not yet been recalculated. It is a smooth extension of the simple top-down mechanism described in section 2.12.

The mechanism relies on the cell states Dirty, Enqueued, Computing, and Uptodate, three of which were already described in section 2.12. The new state Enqueued is essentially a substate of Dirty, indicating that the cell is Dirty but in addition has been put on a recalculation queue.

A standard minimal recalculation assumes that all cells are Uptodate (in particular, no dependency cycle has been discovered, as that may leave some cells not Uptodate). Also, a set of recalculation roots is given.

The recalculation proceeds in two phases, Mark and Evaluate:

- (1) The Mark phase marks Dirty those cells transitively reachable from recalculation roots via the support graph. Cycles in the process are avoided by recursively marking only cells that are not Dirty. It can be implemented by pseudo-code like this:

```
foreach r in roots do
  MarkDirty(r)
```

where procedure `MarkDirty` is this:

```
procedure MarkDirty(c) is
  foreach d in supported(c) do
    if d.state<>Dirty then
      d.state = Dirty
      MarkDirty(d)
```

To see how the Mark phase works, assume that a user edits cell B8 in the spreadsheet shown in figures 1.1 and 1.2. It may be useful to consult the sheet's support graph, shown in figure 1.3. Initially only cell B8 is Dirty, and it is the only root, causing the call `MarkDirty(B8)`. Since cell B8 directly supports D8, C8, and B9, the call marks the three cells Dirty and also executes the calls `MarkDirty(D8)`, `MarkDirty(C8)`, and `MarkDirty(B9)`. The first call has no effect since D8 supports no cells. The second call `MarkDirty(C8)` will mark C9 Dirty and further call `MarkDirty(C11)` because C9 supports C11, and so C11 will be marked Dirty and then nothing more happens. The third call `MarkDirty(B9)` will mark D2 through D7 Dirty, but not D8 because it is already Dirty.

- (2) The Evaluate phase evaluates cells bottom-up based on support sets, but when a dependency of a Dirty cell `c` on another Dirty cell `d` is discovered, we evaluate `d` and enqueue its set of supported cells (unless they are already Enqueued, Computing, or Uptodate) instead of evaluating them eagerly. In particular, this means that `c`, which may be in the support set of `d`, will not be put on the queue or wrongly considered to cause a cycle. Whenever the evaluation of a root has finished, new cells to evaluate are taken from the queue or stack and are evaluated unless in the meantime they have become Uptodate. This can be expressed in pseudo-code like this:

```
queue = roots
while (queue is non-empty)
  c = some cell from the queue
  Eval(c)
```

The pseudo-code for procedure `Eval(c)` is this, where `c.v` is the cached value of cell `c`:

```
procedure Eval(c) is
  switch c.state on
    case Uptodate:
      break;
    case Computing:
      CYCLE detected;
      break;
    case Dirty: case Enqueued:
      c.state = Computing;
      c.v = c.e.Eval();
      c.state = Uptodate;
      foreach d in supported(c) do
        if d.state=Dirty then
          d.state=Enqueued
          put d on queue
      break;
  end switch
  return c.v
```

After the Mark phase, some formula cells are Dirty, namely, those that need recalculation. After the Evaluate phase, all formula cells are Uptodate again. To maintain this cell state invariant, a newly created cell (corresponding to a newly edited constant or formula) should be created Uptodate, so that the Mark phase will also mark cells in that cell's supported set.

The above pseudo-code is a simplification. For instance, only Formula cells (not blank, constant, or array formula cells) have state, but that saves some space (relative to maintaining state on all cells) and suffices for dynamic cycle detection because any cycle must go through a Formula. An edited cell may be a constant, not a formula, so it has no cell state, but anything that depends on the cell (or on anything else) must be a formula. Hence, to apply `MarkDirty` to a non-formula cell, we can simply apply `MarkDirty` to every cell in its support set, that is, every cell that depends on it.

This shortcut potentially would cause a problem if we did not remove support graph edges when updating a cell. Namely, consider the accidental creation of a direct cycle, such as cell A1 containing the formula =A1+2, which would cause A1's support set to contain A1 itself. Then assume we fix the mistake by editing A1 to contain the constant 99, and that the support set of A1 gets transferred to the new cell contents. Then `MarkDirty` will be called on non-formula cell A1, which will cause `MarkDirty` to be called on A1, and so on, infinitely. An analogous problem exists for longer cycles, and this is the chief reason we take care to remove edges from the support graph when editing cells (section 4.2.7).

It might seem tempting to introduce an optimization in `Eval` above so that it does not enqueue, for reevaluation, the cells supported by a cell whose value did not change. This could save a large amount of recalculation work, especially in the case of `IF`, `CHOOSE`, and `INDEX` formulas, which may appear to depend on many more cells than actually affect their value in any particular evaluation. But if we do so, the recalculation would leave those unenqueued cells artificially Dirty, confusing the subsequent Mark phase. To use this optimization, we would need a more advanced cell state representation, possibly representing the four cell states as some integer modulo 4, increment the recalculation count in increments of 4, and consider Uptodate any state s that is strictly smaller than the recalculation count.

The minimal-recalculation version of the `Eval` method for a formula cell is so similar to the simple one on page 52 that they can be unified just by treating the Enqueued cell state the same as the Dirty cell state and introducing a workbook-wide flag `UseSupportSets` to control whether a formula cell's support set should be enqueued after evaluating it:

```
public override Value Eval(Sheet sheet, int col, int row) {
  switch (state) {
    case CellState.Uptodate:
      break;
    case CellState.Computing:
      FullCellAddr culprit = new FullCellAddr(sheet, col, row);
      String msg = String.Format("CYCLE in cell {0} formula {1}",
                          culprit, Show(col, row, format));
```

```
        throw new CyclicException(msg, culprit);
      case CellState.Dirty:
      case CellState.Enqueued:
        state = CellState.Computing;
        v = e.Eval(sheet, col, row);
        state = CellState.Uptodate;
        if (workbook.UseSupportSets)
          ForEachSupported(EnqueueCellForEvaluation);
        break;
    }
    return v;
}
```

4.3.3 Keeping track of volatile cells

The recalculation roots (section 4.3.1) include all volatile cells, that is, any cell whose formula involves a volatile function. We let each workbook maintain a hash set `volatileCells` of the workbook's volatile cells' addresses. Volatility is a local property that can be determined by a simple traversal of the cell's formula expression, in contrast to the support set, which potentially is influenced by any other cell in the workbook (section 4.2.7). We therefore update the volatile set whenever a cell is edited to accurately reflect the cell's volatility.

The set-accessor of the `[col,row]` indexer on a sheet makes sure that this update is performed, as shown here. If the old cell contents were a volatile formula, the cell is removed from the volatile set; if the new cell contents are a volatile formula, the cell is added to the volatile set:

```
public Cell this[int col, int row] {
  set {
    Cell oldCell = cells[col, row];
    if (oldCell != value) {
      if (oldCell != null) {
        oldCell.TransferSupport(ref value);
        workbook.DecreaseVolatileSet(oldCell, this, col, row);
      }
      workbook.IncreaseVolatileSet(value, this, col, row);
      cells[col, row] = value;
      workbook.RecordCellChange(col, row, this);
    }
  }
}
```

To determine whether a formula is volatile, we add a readonly property `IsVolatile` to the Expr hierarchy of abstract syntax classes:

```
public abstract bool IsVolatile { get; }
```

Its only interesting override is on a function call expression (FunCall), which is volatile if the called function, or any of the arguments, is volatile:

```
public override bool IsVolatile {
  get {
    if (function.IsVolatile(es))
      return true;
    foreach (Expr e in es)
      if (e.IsVolatile)
        return true;
    return false;
  }
}
```

The built-in functions NOW and RAND are volatile (section 1.7.5). A sheet-defined function (section 6) whose definition involves a volatile function is itself volatile. An external function (section 8.7) is not itself considered volatile, but calls to it can be wrapped in the VOLATILIZE function (section 11.5) and so become volatile.

This simple treatment of volatile sheet-defined functions works for higher-order functions too. If function FOO(x, y) is volatile, then we must consider partial applications such as CLOSURE("FOO", NA(), 42) and CLOSURE("FOO", 42, NA()) volatile as well, by an appropriate definition of function.IsVolatile(es) above. Then in every recalculation, the CLOSURE expression will be reevaluated, and hence everything (i.e., any APPLY call) that depends on it will be reevaluated as well.

Finally, some very dynamic spreadsheet functions, such as Excel's INDIRECT, may depend on any cell of the workbook. Instead of adding each cell that contains such a function to the support graph, one may simply consider the INDIRECT function volatile, so it gets evaluated in every recalculation (section 5.5).

We have decided not to trace whether a sheet-defined function depends on volatile cells on ordinary sheets. Doing so would involve a fixed point computation, and makes it more expensive to accurately maintain the volatility status of cells and sheet-defined functions as cells and functions are being edited.

4.3.4   Avoiding redundant marking

As observed in section 4.1, the number of support graph edges may be large, $O(n^2)$, when there are n formula cells. Section 4.2 described how to compactly represent such a support graph using products of row and column intervals.

That solved a space consumption problem, but there is still a time consumption problem. The Mark phase described in section 4.3.2 may repeatedly mark Dirty the same cells, thus performing $O(n^2)$ marking operations where $O(n)$ would suffice. For instance, when cell A1 in figure 4.2 is edited, each of A2:A10 would be marked once, but each of the cells B1:B10 would be marked 10 times each because each is supported by all of A1:A10. If there were n rows of cells, then the n cells in column B would each be marked Dirty n times, for a total of $O(n^2)$ work.

Since marking is an idempotent operation (performing it twice makes no difference), this is clearly wasteful. It can be argued that the extra work is not a big problem since the computation of the values in column B would take time $O(n^2)$ anyway, but there is a relatively simple and efficient way to avoid it.

The core idea is that the Mark phase maintains an array list `alreadyVisited` of SupportArea objects, each representing a rectangular area already marked. Before marking a new rectangular area, the array list is traversed to see whether the area is already completely or partially marked. For each already-marked area, the following cases are considered:

- The new area may be contained in the old one. In this case, do nothing.

- The new area may contain the old one. In this case, replace the old area in the array list by the new larger area, and mark those cells in the new area but not the old one.

- The new area may form a rectangular union with the old one because they overlap and either the set of columns or the set of rows are the same in the two areas. In this case, replace the old area in the array list by the union, and mark those cells in the new area but not the old one.

- Otherwise, if the new and old areas overlap, add the new area to the array list, and mark the difference.

The four cases are easily implemented using a few functions on support ranges:

```
SupportArea old = alreadyVisited[i];
if (this.Overlaps(old)) {
  SupportArea overlap = this.Overlap(old);
  if (overlap.Count == this.Count) {          // new contained in old
    return;
  } else if (overlap.Count == old.Count) {   // new contains old
    alreadyVisited[i] = this;
    ForEachExcept(overlap, act);
    return;
  } else if (this.colInt.Equals(old.colInt) // col rectangular union
            && this.rowInt.Overlaps(old.rowInt)) {
    alreadyVisited[i] = new SupportArea(sheet, this.colInt,
                                 this.rowInt.Join(old.rowInt));
    ForEachExcept(overlap, act);
    return;
  } else if (...)                              // row rectangular union
    ... similar to column rectangular union ...
  } else { // overlap, but no containment nor rectangular union
    alreadyVisited.Add(this);
    ForEachExcept(overlap, act);
    return;
  }
}
```

The operations `Overlaps`, `Overlap`, and `new` on SupportAreas are constant-time operations implemented by simple constant-time operations on the column and row intervals `colInt` and `rowInt`. Nevertheless, it is clear that searching the array list for an overlapping interval itself takes some time, which may exceed the time saved by avoiding redundant marking. There is a straightforward way to keep the time waste within bounds, though.

Let K be the length of the array list, and let S be the size (number of cells) of the new support area to be marked. The time spent searching the array list for an overlap is $O(K)$, and the time saved by not marking the new area is $O(S)$. Hence, if we traverse the array only if $S > K$, then we make sure that the potential savings exceed the potential time wasted. It may be that $S > kK$ would be a better criterion, for some constant k, because the support range operations are more expensive than the marking operations, but it does not seem to matter much.

Moreover, since the array list is extended only after a traversal, we know that the support areas in the array list have size (number of cells) at least $1, 2, 3, \ldots, K$. In case these areas do not overlap, the total number of cells is $\theta(K^2)$, so the length K of the array list is bounded by $\sqrt{n}$ when n is the total number of cells to be marked. Note that the array list maintenance does not guarantee the absence of overlaps, but usually K is small, and when it is not, the array list is simply ignored except when a large area is to be marked.

Some practical experiments with a sheet having 10 000 formulas, 12.5 million support graph edges, and 5 000 overlapping support areas showed that the array list machinery reduced the average time for standard recalculation from 1 550 ms to 985 ms, only marginally slower than a full recalculation (in which all cells are marked exactly once) at 975 ms. For a worst-case example with 4-by-4 support ranges having lots of overlaps, none of which was rectangular, the new machinery caused a 5% slowdown of standard recalculation, from 2.75 ms to 2.9 ms.

4.3.5   Minimal recalculation and array formulas

As described in section 4.2.8, each cell of an array formula's display area maintains its own support set, any cell referenced by the underlying formula supports that formula (by supporting a specified cell in the display area), and the underlying formula supports every cell in the display area.

How do we use this information during a minimal recalculation? In other words, what should happen to an array formula during the Mark and Evaluate phases of recalculation?

- The Mark phase for array formulas. If any cell that the underlying formula depends on gets marked, then `MarkDirty` will be called on some cell (containing an ArrayFormula object) in the display area. If the underlying formula is still Uptodate, then `MarkDirty` is called on the underlying formula, making it Dirty. Since all cells in the display area are in the underlying formula's support set, `MarkDirty` will automatically be called again on all those cells. So the cell's `MarkDirty` will be called again, but now the underlying formula is already Dirty, and we proceed to call `MarkDirty` on the cell's support set (but we do not mark the array formula cell itself because it has no state). This is implemented by ArrayFormula's `MarkDirty`, where `caf.formula` is the underlying formula:

```
void MarkDirty() {
  switch (caf.formula.state) {
    case CellState.Uptodate:
      caf.formula.MarkDirty(); break;
    case CellState.Dirty:
      ForEachSupported(MarkCellDirty); break;
  }
}
```

- The Evaluate phase for array formulas. For an array formula display cell, `EnqueueForEvaluation` must perform two tasks. First, it must make sure that the underlying formula gets evaluated. Second, it must cause everything dependent on the array formula cell to be enqueued. As in the Mark phase, we exploit the general machinery and the cell state of the underlying formula `caf.formula`. If the underlying formula is still Dirty, we evaluate it by calling `Eval` on the formula. Eventually, this will cause `EnqueueForEvaluation` to be called on every cell in the underlying formula's support set, that is, on every cell in the display area. Hence, `EnqueueForEvaluation` will be called again, but now that the underlying formula is Uptodate, we proceed to enqueue all cells in the display cell's support set.

  Since only the array formulas can refer to their underlying formula, its evaluation can be initiated only via the array formulas, so a direct call to its `Eval` method will not lead to spurious detection of cycles. However, if the formula depends on one of the display area's array formulas, then the evaluation of the formula will lead to a call to `Eval` on the array formula and hence back to a call to `Eval` on the underlying formula, leading to the detection of a cycle.

  ```
  void EnqueueForEvaluation(Sheet sheet, int col, int row) {
    switch (caf.formula.state) {
      case CellState.Dirty:
        caf.Eval(); break;
      case CellState.Uptodate:
        ForEachSupported(EnqueueCellForEvaluation); break;
    }
  }
  ```

With the array formula recalculation scheme discussed above, we cannot allow the support graph to contain direct self-dependencies where a cell belongs to its own support set. Consider a cyclic array formula such as `{=TRANSPOSE(A1:B2)}` entered in cell A1 and with display area A1:B2. If we allow direct self-dependencies, the underlying formula `TRANSPOSE(A1:B2)`, at cell A1, will have support set A1:B2. Now if we call `MarkDirty` on array formula cell A1, then that will call `MarkDirty` on the underlying cell, which in turn calls `MarkDirty` on each of A1:B2, including

A1 itself. Thus, `MarkDirty` will enter an infinite recursion. This could probably be avoided by adding cell state to array formulas, but it is more easily and efficiently avoided by preventing a cell from belonging to its own support set, as discussed in section 4.2.6.

4.4 Other applications of a support graph

The support graph has several uses besides controlling minimal recalculation:

- The scheme for minimal recalculation described in section 4.3 is relatively simple and deals correctly with support graphs that have (static and/or dynamic) cycles. However, when the static support graph contains no static cycles, it might be beneficial to perform a topological sort of the reachable cells in the support graph. This produces a safe recalculation order, in which all referring expressions can assume that referred-to cells are up to date, thus saving evaluation-time checks and recalculation time and avoiding the need for a recursion stack. The Expr subclasses could have a special version of the `Eval` method for this purpose.

- The topologically sorted cell list seems especially useful in a multiprocessor implementation. A multiprocessor implementation of the scheme for minimal recalculation in section 4.3 would appear to require an expensive lock on each formula cell because multiple threads could discover dynamically that they need the value of that (as yet unevaluated) cell. With a topological sort, cells evaluated in parallel can safely refer to any cell they depend on; such a cell will already have been evaluated.

- When the static support graph contains no (static) cycles, the cycle check can be left out, thus saving recalculation time.

- If we create "efficient" versions of expressions by inter-cell type analysis, the support graph can be used to efficiently find the cells whose type analysis may be affected by a type change in a given cell.

- The support graph could help schedule recalculation for multiprocessor architectures, general-purpose graphics processors (GPGPUs), and implementations based on field-programmable gate arrays (FPGAs) [90].

4.5 Related work

It is clear that some explicit representation of the support graph is used in both Excel [44] and Gnumeric [98]. However, it seems that the representation in both cases is considerably different from what is suggested here (see section 3.3.5).

Burnett and others [29] introduced the concept of *cp-similar* cells, essentially meaning that their formulas could have arisen by a copy-paste operation from one cell to the other. This is equivalent to saying that their R1C1 representations (or C0R0 representations) are identical. They further define a region to be a group of adjacent cp-similar cells. The purpose of grouping cells into regions is not to support recalculation but to reduce the task of testing to one representative from each region.

Sajaniemi [133] says that two cells are *formula equivalent* if the formula in one cell could have arisen by copying the formula in the other one. Sajaniemi's paper uses the R1C1 representation, which he calls an absolute-direct and relative-offset (ADRO) representation, so this notion is the same as the "virtual copies" relation that our compact support graph representations rely on.

A paper by Mittermeir and Clermont proposes the highly relevant idea of a "semantic class" of cells [105], which corresponds to Burnett's notion of cp-similar cells, but the cells in a semantic class are not necessarily adjacent. As above, the paper's goal is to assist users in discovering irregularities and bugs in spreadsheets not to implement spreadsheet programs. The paper defines semantic class using first-order logic but does not suggest how to represent semantic classes and does not provide algorithms for reconstructing or maintaining semantic classes.

Abraham and Erwig [3] use the concept of cp-similarity to infer templates for spreadsheets, in the sense of Gencel [52]. That paper seems to work with regular grids of cp-similar cells, an idea very similar to arithmetic progression (AP) grids described in chapter 5, but there is no explanation of an algorithm for discovering such regular grids. The purpose of template inference (and Gencel) is to guide and limit the editing of a spreadsheet and hence to prevent the introduction of errors.

Chapter 5

Non-Contiguous Support

This chapter describes a concept of support graph that generalizes that presented in chapter 4. Instead of restricting a supported area to be a product of two *intervals* (of columns and rows), it may be the product of two *arithmetic progressions*, each of form $a, a + b, a + 2b, \ldots, a + (k - 1)b$. What we have discussed in chapter 4 is the special case where $b = 1$. This more general idea was presented in our technical report [137, chapter 4] and was tested in an experimental extension of Corecalc, as part of Morten Poulsen's and Poul Serek's MSc thesis [122].

While in principle the support graph representation presented in this chapter is more general and powerful and not much harder to implement, practical experiments indicate that few real-life spreadsheets would benefit from it. For those spreadsheets that do benefit, it can make the support graph representation dramatically more compact.

The discussion in this chapter is quite technical and is not needed to understand the subsequent chapters or the implementation, so the reader who is more interested in Funcalc sheet-defined functions may skip to chapter 6.

5.1 Arithmetic progressions and AP sets

A finite *arithmetic progression* has the form $a, a + b, \ldots, a + (k - 1)b$, where a, b, and $k \geq 0$ are integers. Arithmetic progressions are interesting because the row numbers (and column numbers) of virtual copies of an expression can be described by an arithmetic progression with $b \geq 1$ and $k \geq 1$. We shall refer to the set of elements in a finite arithmetic progression as an AP set and call a its offset, b its period, and k its cardinality. Clearly, AP sets generalize singleton sets ($k = 1$) and integer intervals ($b = 1$).

First observe that an AP set can be represented compactly by the triple (a, b, k). We shall abuse notation and denote the set itself by the triple, like this:

$$(a, b, k) = \{a, a + b, \ldots, a + (k - 1)b\}$$

For the empty set ($k = 0$) and for one-element sets ($k = 1$), the representation by a triple is not unique. We shall usually not represent the empty set by a triple at all, and we therefore say that the representation is *normalized* if $b \geq 1$, $k \geq 1$, and $k = 1$ implies $b = 1$. Figure 5.1 shows some equivalences for AP sets.

$(m, b, 0)$	$=$	$\{\}$	empty set
$(m, b, 1)$	$=$	$\{m\}$	singleton
$(m, 1, n - m + 1)$	$=$	$\{m, m+1, \ldots, n\}$	interval
$(a, b, k_1 + k_2)$	$=$	$(a, b, k_1) \cup (a + bk_1, b, k_2)$	concatenate
$(a, 1, 2k)$	$=$	$(a, 2, k) \cup (a + 1, 2, k)$	zip two

Figure 5.1: Some equivalences for AP sets. These are used to obtain compact representations of grids of equivalent formulas.

The "concatenate" equivalence in the figure describes the concatenation of two sequences of cells such as A1, A3, A5 and A7, A9 into a single sequence A1, A3, A5, A7, A9; in this example, $a = 0$ and $b = 2$ and $k_1 = 3$ and $k_2 = 2$.

The "zip two" equivalence in the figure describes the zipping of two interleaved sequences of cells such as A1, A3, A5 and A2, A4, A6 into a single sequence A1, A2, A3, A4, A5, A6; in this example, $a = 0$ and $k = 3$.

The zip two equivalence is a special case (with $b = 1$ and $n = 2$) of this "zip multiple" equivalence:

$$(a, b, k) = (a, nb, k_0) \cup (a + b, nb, k_1) \cup \ldots \cup (a + (n - 1)b, nb, k_{n-1})$$

where $k_i \geq 0$ is the greatest integer such that $n(k_i - 1) \leq k - 1 - i$, which can be computed as `k_i= (k-1-i+n) /n`. This can be used to find a non-redundant AP set representation of the union of two AP sets, in the form of a set of mutually disjoint AP sets.

For example, to represent the union of $(a_1, b_1, k_1) = (0, 2, 10)$ and $(a_2, b_2, k_2) = (0, 3, 8)$, notice that the least common multiple of b_1 and b_2 is $b = lcm(2, 3) = 6$. We use the "zip multiple" equivalence to rewrite the two AP sets to use the common period $b = 6$, with the multipliers n being $n_1 = b/b_1 = 3$ and $n_2 = b/b_2 = 2$, respectively:

$$
\begin{aligned}
(0, 2, 10) &= (0, 6, 4) \cup (2, 6, 3) \cup (4, 6, 3) \\
(0, 3, 8) &= (0, 6, 4) \cup (3, 6, 4)
\end{aligned}
$$

We see that the component AP sets $(0, 6, 4)$ are identical, whereas all the other component AP sets are disjoint. Hence, one non-redundant representation of the union of the sets is this:

$$(0, 2, 10) \cup (0, 3, 8) = (0, 6, 4) \cup (2, 6, 3) \cup (3, 6, 4) \cup (4, 6, 3)$$

In the above case, the offsets of the two AP sets were the same, namely, $a_1 = a_2 = 0$. When the offsets are distinct, there is not necessarily any overlap between component AP sets in the expansion. The two set overlap if there exist i_1 and i_2 with

$0 \leq i_1 < k_1$ and $0 \leq i_2 < k_2$ such that $a_1 + i_1 b_1 = a_2 + i_2 b_2$. To see when this is the case, let again $b = lcm(b_1, b_2)$ and further let $\beta = gcd(b_1, b_2) = b_1 b_2 / b$ so we have $n_1 = b/b_1 = b_2/\beta$ and $n_2 = b/b_2 = b_1/\beta$.

Now if the two sets overlap, then there exist $0 \leq i_1 < k_1$ and $0 \leq i_2 < k_2$ such that $a_2 - a_1 = i_1 b_1 - i_2 b_2 = i_1 \beta n_2 - i_2 \beta n_1 = \beta(i_1 n_2 - i_2 n_1)$, so $a_1 \equiv a_2 (mod\ \beta)$.

Hence, if $a_1 \not\equiv a_2 (mod\ \beta)$, then the AP sets (a_1, b_1, k_1) and (a_2, b_2, k_2) are disjoint, and there is no need to expand them to obtain an irredundant representation.

However, if $a_1 \equiv a_2 (mod\ \beta)$, it depends also on the cardinalities k_1 and k_2 whether the sets overlap. Loosely speaking, if the cardinalities are large enough, the sets will overlap; otherwise they will not. The sets overlap if and only if there are $0 \leq i_1 < k_1$ and $0 \leq i_2 < k_2$ such that $i_1 n_2 - i_2 n_1 = (a_2 - a_1)/\beta$, and whether this is the case depends on the bounds k_1 and k_2 on i_1 and i_2. Namely, since n_1 and n_2 are coprime, this equation would always have a solution if there were no bounds on i_1 and i_2.

5.2   Support graph edge families and AP sets

The core idea is to represent the family of support graph edges from a cell to virtual copies of an expression by a pair of AP sets, that is, by a pair $((a_c, b_c, k_c), (a_r, b_r, k_r))$ of triples. Namely, each copy operation giving rise to virtual copies creates a regular rectangular grid of virtual copies, and we let the triple (a_c, b_c, k_c) represent all the columns containing virtual copies, and let the triple (a_r, b_r, k_r) represent all the rows containing virtual copies. Hence, the virtual copies occupy precisely the cells with these absolute, zero-based column and row numbers:

$$\{ (c, r) \mid c \in (a_c, b_c, k_c),\ r \in (a_r, b_r, k_r) \}$$

We shall refer to such a product of AP sets as an AP grid. For a simple example, assume that cell B1 contains the formula SUM(A\$1:A\$10000) and that formula is copied to the area B2:B5000, as shown in figure 3.1.

Then cell A1 must have support graph edges to cells B1, B2, ..., B5000, and likewise for A2, ..., A10000. In each case, this family of support graph edges can be represented by this AP grid or pair of AP sets:

$$((a_c, b_c, k_c), (a_r, b_r, k_r)) = ((1, 1, 1), (0, 1, 5000))$$

of triples, that is, column 1, rows 0–4999. This representation must be used for each of the 10 000 cells in column A that support the cells in column B, but the space needed per cell in column A is now just six integers instead of 5 000 cell addresses. In this case, a single pair of triples can even be shared among all the column A cells. Clearly, in figure 3.1, cell A1 also supports A2, A2 supports A3, and so on, so the support edges must be represented as the union of families of support graph edges, where each family can be represented by a pair of triples.

For a more interesting example, let cell B1 contain the formula SUM(A\$1:A1), as in figure 1.5, and assume that formula is copied to the area B2:B5000. Then cell A1 has support graph edges to cell B1; cell A2 has support graph edges to cells B1 and B2; and, more generally, cell An has support graph edges to cells B1, B2, ..., Bn. For cell An, where $1 \leq n$, the family of support graph edges can be represented by the pair $((1, 1, 1), (n - 1, 1, 5000 - n + 1))$. Hence, six integers per cell in column A still suffice to represent the support graph edge family, although the pairs of triples can no longer be shared between all the cells in column A.

To illustrate the need for AP sets rather than just integer intervals, assume again that cell B1 contains the formula SUM($A$1:$A$30); that the cells C1, D1, B2, C2, and D2 contain other formulas; and that the 3×2 block B1:D2 of formulas is copied to the cell area B1:M30, which has 12 columns and 30 rows, or $4 \cdot 15 = 60$ virtual copies of each of the formulas from B1:D2. As outlined in figure 5.2, the virtual copies of cell B1 are in cells B1, E1, H1, K1, B3, E3, ..., K29. This family of cells can be represented by the pair of triples $((1, 3, 4), (0, 2, 15))$, where the column triple $(1, 3, 4) = \{1, 4, 7, 10\}$ represents the columns B, E, H, and K, and the row triple $(0, 2, 15) = \{0, 2, 4, \ldots, 28\}$ represents rows 1, 3, 5, ..., 29.

	A	B	C	D	E	F	G	...	M
1	0.5	$A$1:$A$30			$A$1:$A$30			...	
2	=A1							...	
3	=A2	$A$1:$A$30			$A$1:$A$30			...	
4	=A3							...	
				...					
29	=A28	$A$1:$A$30			$A$1:$A$30			...	
30	=A29							...	

Figure 5.2: Making virtual copies of a 3×2 cell area. Only the area references are shown, not the enclosing SUM function calls.

5.3   Creating and maintaining support graph edges

Let S_t be the set of absolute cell addresses of cells directly supported by the cell at address t. The support graph must have an edge (t, s) for each $s \in S_t$.

Assume that the formula f, if at cell ca, contains references to a set T of cells; that is, it directly statically depends on the cells in T. Then creation, deletion, copying, and moving of that formula affects the support set of each cell $t \in T$ as follows:

- When *creating* the formula in the cell at address ca, we must add ca to S_t for each cell $t \in T$.

- When *deleting* the formula from the cell at ca, we must remove ca from S_t for each cell $t \in T$.

- When *copying* the formula from cell $ca = (c, r)$ within a *cols* $\times$ *rows* block that is being copied to a cell area whose upper left-hand corner is (c_{ul}, r_{ul}), the pair of triples $((c_{ul} - c, cols, k_c), (r_{ul} - r, rows, k_r))$ must be added to S_t for each $t \in T$. Here k_c is the number of columns that receive copies of the formula, and k_r is the number of rows that receive copies of the formula. This is true for absolute cell references in formula f to the cell addresses in T.

Since relative references get adjusted by the copying, the story for those is a little more complicated. Define $f[c', r']$ to be the formula at target cell (c', r'), that is, with relative reference adjusted by the copying, and let $refers(f[c', r'])$ denote the set of cell addresses referenced from $f[c', r']$. Then for each $c' \in (c_{ul}, cols, k_c)$ and each $r' \in (r_{ul}, rows, k_r)$, we must add (c', r') to each S_{ca} where $ca \in refers(f[c', r'])$. If we do this naively as described here, then the support graph representation may require quadratic space. Using the technique from section 5.4.5, this can be done efficiently in a way that results in a much more compact support graph representation.

Obviously, this operation also overwrites any formulas within the target cell area of the copying operation, which affects the support graph.

- When *moving* a formula from cell ca_1 to cell ca_2, we must remove ca_1 from and add ca_2 to the support set of each cell $t \in T$.

- When *inserting* $N \geq 1$ new rows just before row $R \geq 0$, each S_t that includes a row $r \geq R$ must be adjusted.

  More precisely, when the AP set pair $((a_c, b_c, k_c), (a_r, b_r, k_r)) \subseteq S_t$ satisfies that $a_r + b_r(k_r - 1) \geq R$, S_t must be adjusted.

  When $a_r \geq R$ too, simply add N to each member of the row AP set (a_r, b_r, k_r) to obtain $(a_r + N, b_r, k_r)$.

  Otherwise, when $a_r < R \leq a_r + b_r(k_r - 1)$, we must split the row AP set into two. One set represents those rows preceding the insertion, and another set represents those rows following the insertion, and then we must add N to each element of the latter set. Determine the integer k such that $a_r + b_r(k-1) < R \leq a_r + bk$; then the resulting row AP sets are (a_r, b_r, k) and $(a_r + b_r k + N, b_r, k_r - k)$.

  Insertion of columns is completely similar.

- When *deleting* the $N \geq 1$ rows numbered $R, R + 1, \ldots, R + N - 1$, those rows must be removed from each row AP set (a_r, b_r, k_r), and for each row AP set, N must be subtracted from the numbers of any rows following the deleted ones.

  Let k_1 be the greatest integer such that $a_r + b_r(k_1 - 1) < R$. The idea is that k_1, if positive, is the number of rows in the row AP set that precede the deleted rows. Similarly, let k_2 be the least integer such that $R + N \leq a_r + b_r k_2$; then $k_r - k_2$, if positive, is the number of rows in the row AP set that follow the deleted rows.

  The original row AP set must be replaced by zero, one, or two non-empty row support sets, as follows:

– If $1 \leq k_1$, then (a_r, b_r, k_1) is part of the resulting row AP set. These are the rows preceding the deleted rows.

One can compute k_1 by the expression `k_1 = (R-a_r+b_r-1)/b_r` (see section 5.4.6).

– If $k_2 < k_r$, then $(a_r + b_r k_2 - N, b_r, k_r - k_2)$ is part of the resulting row AP set. These are the rows following the deleted rows.

One can compute k_2 by the expression `k_2 = (R+N-a_r+b_r-1)/b_r` (see section 5.4.6).

Figure 5.3 shows examples of adjustment of row AP sets for some formula `=Z1` when the shaded rows 4 through 7 are deleted. The original AP set triples (a_r, b_r, k_r) and the resulting k_1 and k_2 are shown below the spreadsheet fragment.

	A	B	C	D	E
1	=Z1				
2		=Z1			
3			=Z1		
4	=Z1			=Z1	=Z1
5		=Z1			
6			=Z1		
7	=Z1			=Z1	=Z1
8		=Z1			
9			=Z1		
10	=Z1			=Z1	
a_r	0	1	2	3	3
b_r	3	3	3	3	3
k_r	4	3	3	3	2
k_1	1	1	1	0	0
k_2	3	2	2	2	2

Figure 5.3: Effect on row AP set for $S_{=Z1}$ of deleting the grey rows ($N = 4$ and $R = 3$).

Deletion of columns is completely similar.

It seems that it is never necessary to have more than one instance of a given row AP set representation in the implementation. Namely, assume AP set S appears in the support of two different cells. If any formula in a cell in S is updated so that set S must be changed, then this change affects both cells in the same way. Hence, updates to the support graph can be made very simple; they just require some mechanism to avoid performing the update more than once.

5.4   Reconstructing the support graph

The previous section describes how the support graph can be *maintained* while inserting, deleting, moving, and copying formulas. An equally relevant challenge is
to efficiently *create* the support graph from a spreadsheet that does not have one,
such as a newly loaded spreadsheet created by an external program. It is trivial to
find a poor solution to this problem, but finding an optimal one is quite likely an
NP-complete problem, as it involves finding a kind of minimal exact set cover.

We propose a two-stage approach in which one first builds an *occurrence map* for
each formula (section 5.4.1) and then uses the occurrence map to build the support
graph (sections 5.4.2 through 5.4.5).

5.4.1   Building a formula occurrence map

The following procedure seems usable for building a reasonably compact occurrence
map for typical spreadsheets:

- Scan columns from left to right.

- In the scan of a column c, we maintain a map m from expressions e (in the internal, copy-invariant representation) to a sequence $m(e)$ of triples, each triple
  representing an AP set.

  The goal is that after scanning the column, the union of the members of the
  triples in $m(e)$ is exactly the set of those cells (in that column) that contain
  formula e.

  We maintain a map from expressions (to sequences of triples), rather than a
  map from the cells that those expressions refer to. This is because the latter
  map could have many more keys: an expression such as SUM(A1:A10000) in
  effect represents 10 000 cells, and clearly it is more efficient to map from one
  such expression than from 10 000 individual cells.

  The map from expressions to sequences of AP sets can be maintained as a
  hash dictionary, with equality being expression object reference identity or
  expression abstract syntax tree equality. The former is faster but less precise
  than the latter, but imprecision just leads to a less compact representation of
  the support graph, not to wrong results.

  At the beginning of the scan of the column, the map m is empty.

- The rows of the column are scanned in order from row 0. Assume the cell in
  row r contains a formula e, then we proceed as follows:

  - If $e \notin dom(m)$, then set $m(e) := [(r, 1, 1)]$.
    The expression e has not been seen before in this column.

  - Otherwise assume $m(e) = [\dots, (r', b', k')]$.
    The expression has been seen before, and the most recent occurrence was
    at $r' + b'(k' - 1)$.

– If $k' = 1$, then update the last item of $m(e)$ to $(r', r - r', 2)$.

The most recent AP set has only one element, and we can extend it to have $k = 2$, with the step b being the difference $r - r'$ between this row and the row in the AP set.

– Otherwise, if $r = r' + b'k'$, then update the last item of $m(e)$ to $(r', b', k'+1)$.

The new row is an additional member of the most recent AP set, so we extend that set.

– Otherwise, add a new last item $(r, 1, 1)$ to $m(e)$.

The new row is not a member of the most recent AP set, so we do not extend that sequence but begin a new one.

This simple scheme can be defeated by writing a formula in A1, copying it to A3, and then copying the block A1:A3 to many further cells. It would give alternating distances 2,1,2,1,2,1, . . .

Hence, instead we might collect the sequence of distances as above and infer the AP sets $(0, 3, k_1)$ and $(2, 3, k_2)$ from them. This is quite easy, presumably, by considering derived sequences of 2-sums, 3-sums, and so on that are constant.

Another approach would be to use a Fast Fourier Transform (FFT) [36] of the column's formula identities to find the spectrum of the formula occurrences. In the example sketched here, one would expect to find the periods 1, 2, and 3, with 3 having twice the power of 1 and 2, which would indicate that 3 is the most interesting period for that column. (Periods that are multiples of 3 would also appear but with lesser power). After noting this, one can perform a column scan that keeps for each formula up to 3 partially constructed AP sets.

A conceptually simpler auto-correlation computation might serve the same purpose as the FFT but might be slower if the correlation window needs to be large. In both cases, a possible weakness of this method is that the pattern of virtual formula copies may not be uniform over the column.

Even more speculatively, could we perform a two-dimensional Fourier Transform to find repetitive structure in columns and rows at the same time? It would seem that a two-dimensional auto-correlation function could easily be computed. However, it would increase computational cost a good deal, especially if we want to handle copying of blocks up to, say, 20x20 cells.

- Let m_c be the map resulting from scanning column c as outlined above. Now scan all columns, building a map M, from pairs (f, ts) of formulas f and triple sequences ts, to a list of set of pairs $((a_c, b_c, k_c), (a_r, b_r, k_r))$ of triples, using a scheme similar to the above.

- When we have built the map M, we can create the support graph as explained in the next section.

Instead of building a map m from formulas e to sequences of triples, we could build a map from ccars, where a ccar is a cell reference such as B7 or a cell area reference

such as `B7:D8`. The chief advantage of this would be to permit better sharing of
support graph edge descriptions. The disadvantages are that it would exacerbate
the problem mentioned in the Note above and make a solution to that problem more
urgent, and it would require a traversal of each expression $e \in dom(m)$ when processing a cell in a column, instead of just looking up the expression's reference in
m. However, even if we stick to letting m map from expressions e, the processing of
each e described in the sections below would consist of processing each ccar in e.

5.4.2   From formula occurrence map to support graph

Now let us consider how to build the support graph. This is done by two nested
loops:

- For each $e \in dom(M)$ and for each member $(C, R) \in M(e)$, find the set CA of
  absolute cell addresses that is referred by at least one occurrence of formula f
  within the grid of cells described by (C, R). This can be computed in constant
  time for each *ccar*, as shown in section 5.4.4.

- Then for each such cell address $ca \in CA$, compute the pair of triples that
  represents the subset of (C, R) that ca actually supports. For each ca, this
  computation is a constant time operation, as shown in section 5.4.5.

5.4.3   Some examples

First let us consider some concrete examples of virtual formula copies that contain
cell area references, such as those in figure 5.4. The task is to find which cells in
column A support which cells in columns B, C, and D. The formula copies in columns
B and C are described by the triple $(0, 2, 5)$; and the formula copies in column D are
described by the triple $(1, 2, 5)$.

    In column B, each of cells A1–A10 support all of the cells B1, B3, B5, B7, and B9,
which can be described by the triple $(0, 2, 5)$.

    In column C, cell A1 supports C1, C3, C5, C7, and C9, described by $(0, 2, 5)$; cells
A2 and A3 both support C3, C5, C7, and C9, described by $(2, 2, 4)$; cells A4 and A5
both support C5, C7, and C9, described by $(4, 2, 3)$; cells A6 and A7 both support C7
and C9, described by $(6, 2, 1)$; cells A8 and A9 both support C7 and C9, described by
$(6, 2, 1)$; and cell A10 supports nothing in column C.

    In column D, cells A1 and A2 both support D2, D4, D6, D8, and D10, described
by $(1, 2, 5)$; cells A3 and A4 both support D4, D6, D8, and D10, described by $(3, 2, 4)$;
cells A5 and A6 both support D6, D8, and D10, described by $(5, 2, 3)$; cells A7 and A8
both support D8 and D10, described by $(7, 2, 2)$; and cells A9 and A10 both support
D10, described by $(9, 2, 1)$.

    In continuation of the above example, consider figure 5.5 and let us find which
cells in column A support which cells in columns E, F, and G. The formula copies
in column E are described by the triple $(0, 2, 5)$; the formula copies in column F by
$(2, 2, 4)$; and the formula copies in column G by $(1, 3, 3)$.

	A	B	C	D
1	11	SUM($A$1:$A$10)	SUM($A$1:$A1)	
2	12			SUM($A$1:$A2)
3	13	SUM($A$1:$A$10)	SUM($A$1:$A3)	
4	14			SUM($A$1:$A4)
5	15	SUM($A$1:$A$10)	SUM($A$1:$A5)	
6	16			SUM($A$1:$A6)
7	17	SUM($A$1:$A$10)	SUM($A$1:$A7)	
8	18			SUM($A$1:$A8)
9	19	SUM($A$1:$A$10)	SUM($A$1:$A9)	
10	20			SUM($A$1:$A10)

Figure 5.4: Finding the support edges from each cell in column A.

In column E, cells A1 and A2 both support E1 only, described by $(0, 2, 1)$; cell A3 supports E1 and E3, described by $(0, 2, 2)$; cell A4 supports E1, E3, E5, E7, and E9, described by $(0, 2, 5)$; cell A5 supports E5, E7, and E9, described by $(4, 2, 3)$; cells A6 and A7 both support E7 and E9, described by $(6, 2, 2)$; cells A8 and A9 both support E9, described by $(8, 2, 1)$; and cell A10 supports nothing in column E.

In column F, cells A1 and A2 both support F3, described by $(2, 2, 1)$; cell A3 supports F3 and F5, described by $(2, 2, 2)$; cell A4 supports F5, described by $(4, 2, 1)$; cell A5 supports F5 and F7, described by $(4, 2, 2)$; cell A6 supports F7, described by $(6, 2, 1)$; cell A7 supports F7 and F9, described by $(6, 2, 2)$; cells A8 and A9 both support F9, described by $(8, 2, 1)$; and cell A10 supports nothing in column F.

In column G, cells A1 and A2 both support G2, described by $(1, 3, 1)$; cell A3 supports nothing in column G; cells A4 and A5 both support G5, described by $(4, 3, 1)$; cell A6 supports nothing in column G; cells A7 and A8 both support G8, described by $(7, 3, 1)$; and cells A9 and A10 support nothing in column G. In this case, with non-overlapping areas of supporting cells, each triple represents a single edge, and no space is saved by our supposedly compact support graph representation. However, the number of support graph edges is already only linear in the number of formula occurrences.

5.4.4   From occurrence map to referred cells

Now let us consider more generally the problem of finding the set of cell addresses referred to by the occurrences of a formula; this is the first step in section 5.4.2. For simplicity, we will consider this problem in one dimension only, working on the formula (or ccar) occurrences in one column at a time. Hence, we consider triples of the form (a_r, b_r, k_r), describing a pattern of occurrences of a single formula or ccar. In fact, regardless of whether the occurrence map M created in the previous section maps from formulas f or ccars $ccar$, we shall consider one $ccar$ at a time, if necessary extracted from the formulas in the domain of M.

Hence, we consider a $ccar$ that appears in a given column c and an associated

	A	...	E	F	G
1	11	...	SUM($A$4:$A1)		
2	12	...			SUM($A1:$A2)
3	13	...	SUM($A$4:$A3)	AVERAGE($A1:$A3)	
4	14	...			
5	15	...	SUM($A$4:$A5)	AVERAGE($A3:$A5)	SUM($A4:$A5)
6	16	...			
7	17	...	SUM($A$4:$A7)	AVERAGE($A5:$A7)	
8	18	...			SUM($A7:$A8)
9	19	...	SUM($A$4:$A9)	AVERAGE($A7:$A9)	
10	20	...			

Figure 5.5: Finding the support edges from each cell in column A; more cases.

triple (a, b, k) that describes the rows of that column in which the $ccar$ appears. The procedure then becomes:

(1) First we find the set CA of all those absolute cell addresses ca that are referred to by some occurrence $ccar[c, r]$ for $r \in (a, b, k)$. This set can be represented by an interval (in the one-dimensional case) or the product of two intervals (in the general case).

The point of computing CA in advance is to avoid analyzing any ca more than once in step (2). Namely, the cell areas referenced by different occurrences of the same formula may overlap, and certainly do in columns B, C, D, E, and F above, and processing each such cell area in turn could change a linear time algorithm to a quadratic time algorithm.

(2) Next, for each $ca \in CA$, we compute the triple (a', b, k') representing the subset of (a, b, k) that ca actually supports. This triple is then used to represent support graph edges from ca to cells in column c supported by ca.

Step (1) above in principle must compute $r = a + bi$ for all $0 \le i < k$ and then find the union of the sets of cells referred to by each occurrence $ccar[c, r]$ of the cell/cell area reference:

$$CA = \bigcup_{0 \le i < k} refers(ccar[c, a + bi])$$

This looks like a potentially expensive operation, but it turns out that CA is an interval and can be computed in constant time in all cases where computing it matters, namely, when the referred-to cell areas overlap, so that processing the areas one by one would duplicate work. The CA sets for the examples in figures 5.4 and 5.5 are shown in figure 5.6 in A1 and C0R0 format. The column G case shows that CA in general may not be an interval.

Formula (A1)	Formula (C0R0)	Occurs	Referred-to cells (CA)
B SUM($A$1:$A$10)	SUM(C0R0:C0R9)	$(0,2,5)$	{ A1, A2, $\ldots$, A9, A10 }
C SUM($A$1:$A1)	SUM(C0R0:C0R[0])	$(0,2,5)$	{ A1, A2, $\ldots$, A9 }
D SUM($A$1:$A2)	SUM(C0R0:C0R[0])	$(1,2,5)$	{ A1, A2, $\ldots$, A9, A10 }
E SUM($A$4:$A1)	SUM(C0R4:C0R[0])	$(0,2,5)$	{ A1, A2, $\ldots$, A9 }
F AVERAGE($A1:$A3)	AVERAGE(C0R[-2]:C0R[0])	$(2,2,4)$	{ A1, A2, $\ldots$, A9 }
G SUM($A1:$A2)	SUM(C0R[-1]:C0R[0])	$(1,3,3)$	{ A1, A2, A4, A5, A7, A8 }

Figure 5.6: Formula occurrences and referred-to cells in figures 5.4 and 5.5.

To see that the set CA can be computed efficiently, consider the four possible forms of *ccar* using C0R0-format references (figure 2.7) for the two corners. We assume here that *ccar* is a cell area reference since a simple cell reference such as A1 can be represented by a cell area reference A1:A1.

- When *ccar* is C0Ri_1:C0Ri_2, that is, both corners are absolute references, the occurrences (a, b, k) do not matter. Obviously the exact result is an interval, namely, assuming without loss of generality $i_1 \leq i_2$:

$$CA = \{i_1, \ldots, i_2\}$$

- When *ccar* is C0Ri_1:C0R[i_2], that is, one corner is an absolute reference, the other is a relative one, the occurrences do matter. Still the exact result is an interval, namely:

$$CA = \{n_1, \ldots, n_2\}$$

where

$$
\begin{aligned}
n_1 &= \min(i_1, a + i_2, a + b(k-1) + i_2) \\
n_2 &= \max(i_1, a + i_2, a + b(k-1) + i_2)
\end{aligned}
$$

- When *ccar* is C0R[i_1]:C0Ri_2, that is, one corner is a relative reference, the other is an absolute one, we have the same situation as above; simply swap i_1 and i_2 in the formulas.

- When *ccar* is C0R[i_1]:C0R[i_2] and assuming without loss of generality $i_1 \leq i_2$, the exact set is

$$CA = \bigcup_{0 \leq i < k} \{a + ib + i_1, \ldots, a + ib + i_2\}$$

This can be approximated by an interval:

$$CA \subseteq \{a + i_1, \ldots, a + i(k-1) + i_2\}$$

In fact, this interval is the exact answer when the cell areas referred to from the formula occurrences are adjacent or even overlap, that is, when $i_2 - i_1 + 1 \geq b$ as in column F of figure 5.5. When this is not the case, there is no point in building the set CA explicitly; instead step (2) described in section 5.4.5 should iterate over the ca in each set $\{a + ib + i_1, \ldots, a + ib + i_2\}$ individually, for $0 \leq i < k$. Precisely because those sets do not overlap, no ca will be analyzed twice.

For the formulas in figures 5.4 and 5.5, we find precisely the CA sets shown in figure 5.6.

5.4.5   The support graph edges from a referred cell

Now let us consider how to find the support graph edges from a given referred-to cell; this is the inner loop (2) in section 5.4.4. We consider an absolute cell address $(c', r') = ca \in CA$, where CA was computed in the previous section, and recall that the occurrences of $ccar$ are described by (a, b, k). We must find the set

$$S_{ca} = \{\, j \mid ca \in \mathit{refers}(ccar[c, j]),\ j = a + bi,\ 0 \leq i < k \,\}$$

The challenge is to compute this set efficiently and to find a compact representation of it. Preferably, we want to find a triple (a', b, k') that is equivalent to S_{ca}. Again this computation can be performed by case analysis in the form of the $ccar$.

- When $ccar$ is $\mathtt{COR}i_1\mathtt{:COR}i_2$ and $ca \in CA$, clearly ca supports every occurrence of the $ccar$, so

  $$S_{ca} = (a', b, k') = (a, b, k)$$

- When $ccar$ is $\mathtt{COR}i_1\mathtt{:COR}[i_2]$, there are three cases, according as r' equals, precedes, or follows the anchor point i_1:

  - If $r' = i_1$, then

    $$S_{ca} = (a, b, k)$$

  - If $r' < i_1$, then find the greatest $k_1 \leq k$ such that $i_2 + a + b(k_1 - 1) \leq r'$. If $k_1 \geq 1$, then the set is non-empty:

    $$S_{ca} = (a, b, k_1)$$

    The number k_1 can be computed as $\mathtt{Math.Min(k,\ (r'-i\_2-a+b)/b)}$.

  - If $i_1 < r'$, then find the least $k_1 \geq 0$ such that $r' \leq i_2 + a + bk_1$. If $k_1 < k$, then the set is non-empty:

    $$S_{ca} = (a + bk_1, b, k - k_1)$$

    The number k_1 can be computed as $\mathtt{Math.Max(0,\ (r'-i\_2-a+b-1)/b)}$.

- When *ccar* is $\texttt{COR}[i_1]\texttt{:COR}i_2$, the cases and solutions are exactly as above, only with i_1 and i_2 swapped.

- When *ccar* is $\texttt{COR}[i_1]\texttt{:COR}[i_2]$ and assuming without loss of generality $i_1 \le i_2$, determine the greatest k_1 such that $i_2 + a + b(k_1 - 1) < r'$ and the least k_2 such that $r' < i_1 + a + bk_2$, and define $k'_1 = \max(0, k_1)$ and $k'_2 = \min(k, k_2)$. If $k'_1 < k'_2$, then we have

$$S_{ca} = (a + bk'_1, b, k'_2 - k'_1)$$

The number k'_1 can be computed as $\texttt{Math.Max(0, (r'-i\_2-a+b-1)/b)}$.

The number k'_2 can be computed as $\texttt{Math.Min(k, (r'-i\_1-a+b)/b)}$.

See figure 5.8 for an example where the referred-to row ranges overlap and figure 5.9 for an example where the referred-to row ranges do not overlap.

Considering the formulas in figure 5.6, we find for each cell in column A the support graph edge families shown in figure 5.7. Fortunately, these agree with the sets of supported cells found in the informal discussion of those figures.

Cell	r'	B	C	D	E	F	G
A1	0	$(0,2,5)$	$(0,2,5)$	$(1,2,5)$	$(0,2,1)$	$(2,2,1)$	$(1,3,1)$
A2	1	$(0,2,5)$	$(2,2,4)$	$(1,2,5)$	$(0,2,1)$	$(2,2,1)$	$(1,3,1)$
A3	2	$(0,2,5)$	$(2,2,4)$	$(3,2,4)$	$(0,2,2)$	$(2,2,2)$	$\{\}$
A4	3	$(0,2,5)$	$(4,2,3)$	$(3,2,4)$	$(0,2,5)$	$(4,2,1)$	$(4,3,1)$
A5	4	$(0,2,5)$	$(4,2,3)$	$(5,2,3)$	$(4,2,3)$	$(4,2,2)$	$(4,3,1)$
A6	5	$(0,2,5)$	$(6,2,2)$	$(5,2,3)$	$(6,2,2)$	$(6,2,1)$	$\{\}$
A7	6	$(0,2,5)$	$(6,2,2)$	$(7,2,2)$	$(6,2,2)$	$(6,2,2)$	$(7,3,1)$
A8	7	$(0,2,5)$	$(8,2,1)$	$(7,2,2)$	$(8,2,1)$	$(8,2,1)$	$(7,3,1)$
A9	8	$(0,2,5)$	$(8,2,1)$	$(9,2,1)$	$(8,2,1)$	$(8,2,1)$	$\{\}$
A10	9	$(0,2,5)$	$\{\}$	$(9,2,1)$	$\{\}$	$\{\}$	$\{\}$

Figure 5.7: Support graph edge families for column A cells in figures 5.4 and 5.5.

5.4.6 Computer integer arithmetics caveats

Much of the theory in this chapter relies on integer arithmetics and inequalities. Implementing such operations requires some care, both because the algebra rules are different from those of arithmetics on reals, and because most programming languages, including C# and Java (but not Standard ML [103]), traditionally implement integer division with negative numerators in a peculiar way. Essentially, most languages let integer division truncate toward zero rather than toward minus infinity, and therefore satisfy $(-n)/d = -(n/d)$ but not $(n + d)/d = n/d + 1$ for $d > 0$.

Let an integer $d > 0$ be given.

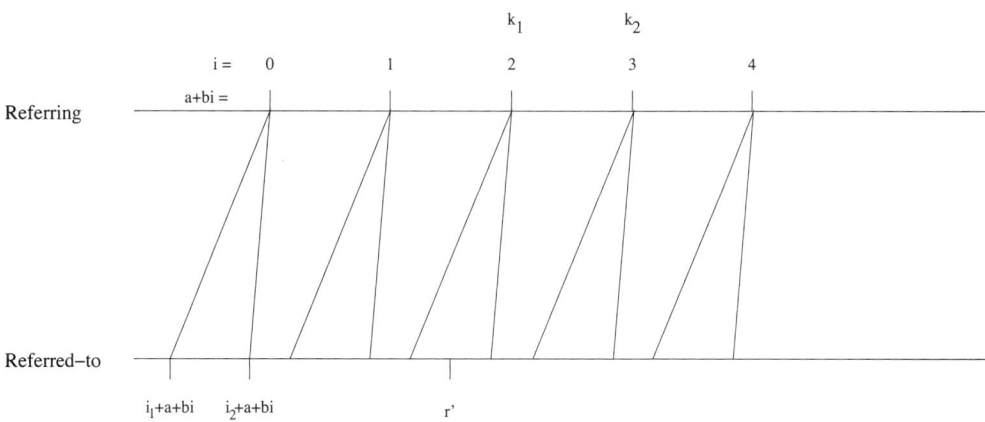

Figure 5.8: Five virtual copies of a cell area reference *ccar* of form $\text{COR}[i_1]\!:\!\text{COR}[i_2]$, that is, with both endpoints relative. Non-overlapping cell areas. The row number r' is included in the cell areas referred by i for which $k_1 \leq i < k_2$, in this case, $i = 2$.

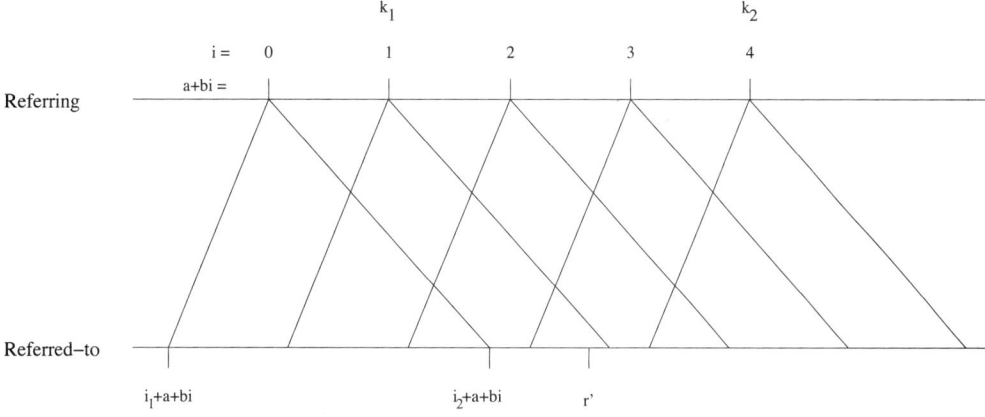

Figure 5.9: Five virtual copies of a cell area reference *ccar* of form $\text{COR}[i_1]\!:\!\text{COR}[i_2]$, that is, with both endpoints relative. Overlapping cell areas. The row number r' is included in the cell areas referred by i for which $k_1 \leq i < k_2$, in this case, $i = 1, 2, 3$.

- To find the least integer q such that $n \leq dq$, where $n \geq 0$, compute `q = (n+d-1)/d`.

- To find the greatest integer q such that $dq \leq n$, where $n \geq 0$, compute `q = n/d`.

- To find the greatest integer q such that $dq < n$, where $n \geq 0$, compute `q = (n-1)/d`.

- To find the greatest integer q such that $dq \leq n$, where $n \geq -d$, compute `q = (n+d)/d-1`.

  Computing this as `q = n/d` would be wrong because integer division in most programming languages truncates the quotient toward zero rather than toward minus infinity, and therefore does not satisfy the expected equivalence $(n+d)/d = n/d + 1$ for integers n and $d > 0$.

- To find the greatest integer q such that $dq < n$, where $n \geq -d$, compute `q = (n+d-1)/d-1`.

- To find the greatest integer q such that $d(q-1) < n$, where $n \geq -d$, compute `q = (n+d-1)/d`.

5.5   Limitations and challenges

The interval representation (chapter 4) and AP grid representation (this chapter) of the support graph provide a compact support graph for highly regular grids of formulas. Moreover, these support graph representations can be efficiently constructed and maintained. However, for spreadsheets with an irregular structure, which cannot be built using only a small number of copy operations, the representations may degenerate to a representation of all single edges. For instance, a spreadsheet to compute the discrete Fourier transform [16, 36] has a structure that cannot easily be built using copy operations, as shown in figure 5.10. It is unlikely to be worthwhile to devise a support graph representation that can compactly represent this pattern of dependencies.

   In general, and especially in the presence of SUM formulas and other functions with cell area arguments, it may be useful to supplement the AP grid representation of the support graph with other representations. One way to obtain a compact support graph representation is to maintain only an over-approximation of the actual support graph. This will not lead to wrong results, only to unnecessary work during recalculation. But an arbitrary amount of such extra work (up to recalculating the entire workbook) may be caused by including just one extraneous cell in a support set because that extraneous cell may indirectly support most of the workbook.

   In a sense, such an approximation is needed in any case to deal with various dynamic features of spreadsheet programs. In particular, the functions HLOOKUP and VLOOKUP are used to search for a given value in a range, and the function INDEX

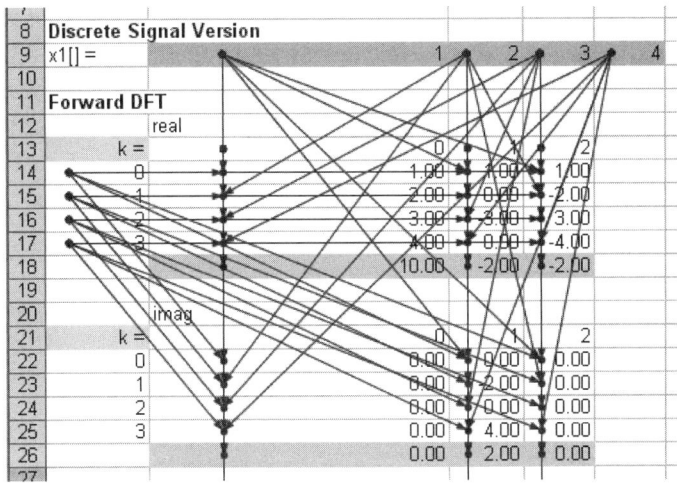

Figure 5.10: Dependencies in a discrete Fourier transform [158].

is used to retrieve a cell from a range given row and column. The exact dependencies are determined by the given value or the given row and column number. To obtain a static support graph, one must make an (obvious) over-approximation: Every cell in these functions' range argument supports the cell in which the function is used.

Similar problems are caused by Excel functions such as COUNTIF and SUMIF, whose second argument is a string that dynamically gets interpreted as a formula, as in COUNTIF(A1:A10000, "> 42"). If such a formula could contain references to arbitrary cells, then it would require parsing of the text string to find the cells supporting this formula. In Funcalc, the second argument to COUNTIF and SUMIF must be a sheet-defined function (example 6.21 and section 11.5), so the general support graph construction automatically handles this case correctly.

An even more dynamic Excel function is INDIRECT(ref), which evaluates its argument ref to a string and then interprets the string as a cell reference. In general, the value of this function depends on the entire workbook. A simple way to deal with this is to treat INDIRECT as a volatile function, just like RAND and NOW. This means that any occurrence of INDIRECT gets evaluated in every recalculation, that is, whenever anything on which it may depend could change.

5.6   Related work

As far as we know, the only other work that has considered non-contiguous grid-like formula copies is Abraham and Erwig's Gencel system [3, 52]. It seems to work with regular grids of cp-similar cells, but unlike the present chapter, it does not describe an algorithm for discovering such regular grids.

Fisher and others [59] define a "discontiguous region" as a set of copy-equivalent cells without any particular geometric structure. While in a sense this is more general than our AP grids of equivalent formulas, such a region does not admit any compact representation and hence would not be suitable for compact representation of a support graph—and indeed this was not the intention of [59].

Part II

Funcalc and Compilation

Chapter 6

Sheet-Defined Functions

6.1 Introduction

Several authors have proposed functionality that allows spreadsheet users to define new functions while staying within the sheet, cell, and formula metaphor, rather than using external languages such as Visual Basic for Applications (VBA), Python, Java, Scala, or Haskell. By a sheet-defined function, we here mean a function F that is defined by designating its input cells `in1...inn` and its output cell `out`, like this:

```
DEFINE("F", out, in1, ..., inn)
```

A call `F(v1...vn)` to sheet-defined function F assigns argument values `v1...vn` to the input cells `in1...inn` and returns the value computed by the output cell `out`, where "the value computed" is defined using completely standard spreadsheet concepts.

Sheet-defined functions must be defined on special function sheets, but they can be called from ordinary data sheets as well as from sheet-defined functions. A function sheet can define any number of sheet-defined functions.

Notable proposals for sheet-defined functions are due to Nuñez [113, section 5.2.2] and to Peyton-Jones, Blackwell, and Burnett [120]. Interpretive prototype implementations have been made by Nuñez and by Cortes and Hansen [37], who based theirs on the Corecalc infrastructure. For further discussion of related work, see section 6.5.

However, as far as we know, no implementation has exploited or investigated the opportunities for performance gains that would accrue by compiling sheet-defined functions to machine code at run-time. Here we shall do this by generating byte-code for Microsoft .NET and then letting the just-in-time compiler of the execution environment compile that to real machine code.

Our implementation supports recursive as well as higher-order sheet-defined functions, as in Cortes and Hansen's work (see section 6.5). Without recursion, sheet-defined functions add *encapsulation* of intermediate results, *abstraction* of function parameters, and *modularization* of functionality and tabular data. With recursion, they further add the ability to process inputs of arbitrary size and structure. Higher-order sheet-defined functions can be used to define general, declarative, and properly scoped versions of Excel's COUNTIF and SUMIF functions, its Goal Seek functionality, and much more.

6.2 Examples of sheet-defined functions

This section presents many examples of sheet-defined functions, all "programmed" in the Funcalc implementation described in subsequent chapters. Simple examples include computing the area of a triangle or rolling an n-sided die; and intermediate examples include calendrical, financial, and statistical calculations. Other examples show how sheet-defined functions eliminate the need for ad hoc mechanisms, such as Excel's Data Tables and text-based predicates in functions such as COUNTIF, and automatically avoids various limitations imposed by these mechanisms.

The most advanced examples show how higher-order and recursive functions allow an expert user to implement functionality, such as Goal Seek, that is available only through laborious dialogs and wizards in Excel and other spreadsheet programs.

We do not claim that the mere availability of sheet-defined functions would make every single spreadsheet user capable of inventing all the functions shown here. But we do expect that experienced spreadsheet users will be able to invent or adapt sheet-defined functions to suit their domain-specific needs, thereby liberating themselves from the straitjackets of limited built-in functions, intransigent IT departments, and unfathomable VBA code.

Example 6.1 Assume we have the side lengths of a large number of triangles in columns A, B, and C of a spreadsheet, and we want to compute the area of each triangle in column E. The area is given by the formula $\sqrt{s(s-a)(s-b)(s-c)}$, where $s = (a+b+c)/2$ is half the perimeter.

To use this formula in the spreadsheet, we could compute s in column D using the formula =(A1+B1+C1)/2, compute the area in column E using the formula =SQRT(D1*(D1-A1)*(D1-B1)*(D1-C1)), and then copy both formulas for all rows. However, this introduces the distracting extra column D, and the formulas look a little daunting even for this simple task. Alternatively, we might avoid the extra column D and inline the computation directly in the column E, resulting in the formula

```
=SQRT((A1+B1+C1)/2*((A1+B1+C1)/2-A1)
       *((A1+B1+C1)/2-B1)*((A1+B1+C1)/2-C1))
```

which computes the subexpression for s no less than four times. Even the slightly simplified version

```
=SQRT((A1+B1+C1)/2*(-A1+B1+C1)/2*(A1-B1+C1)/2*(A1+B1-C1)/2)
```

is inefficient, unwieldy, and easy to get wrong.

By encapsulating the computation in a sheet-defined function, TRIAREA say, we can hide the intermediate variable s there, use the simpler and more obviously correct formula for column E, and rely on run-time compilation to produce fast code. Then the main sheet can use the formula =TRIAREA(A1,B1,C1) to compute the area of the triangle with side lengths A1, B1, and C1.

Figure 6.1 shows the definition of function TRIAREA. The defined function can be called as TRIAREA(3, 4, 5) as shown in figure 11.1.

F7	A	B	C	D	E	F
1	'Area of...					
2	'a	'b	'c	's	'area	
3	3	4	5	=(A3+B3+C3)/2	=SQRT(D3*(D3-A3)*(D3-B3)*(D3-C3))	=DEFINE("triarea", E3, A3, B3, C3)
4						

Figure 6.1: Definition of function TRIAREA, formula view. Cells A3, B3, and C3 are input cells; cell D3 computes half the perimeter as an intermediate result; and cell E3 computes the function's output. The call to DEFINE in F3 creates the TRIAREA sheet-defined function, specifying its name, output cell, and input cells.

The bytecode generated for this definition of function TRIAREA is shown below. The code in the first column converts the three arguments (passed in CIL arguments V_0, V_1, and V_2) to floating-point numbers (stored in CIL variables V_4, V_5, and V_6), computes half the perimeter s, and stores it in variable V_7. The code in the second column computes the product of the differences, takes the square root, and wraps the result as a NumberValue:

```
0000: ldarg V_0                    0035: ldloc.s V_7
0004: call Value.ToDoubleOrNan     0037: ldloc.s V_7
0009: stloc.s V_4                  0039: ldloc.s V_4
000b: ldarg V_1                    003b: sub
000f: call Value.ToDoubleOrNan     003c: mul
0014: stloc.s V_5                  003d: ldloc.s V_7
0016: ldarg V_2                    003f: ldloc.s V_5
001a: call Value.ToDoubleOrNan     0041: sub
001f: stloc.s V_6                  0042: mul
0021: ldloc.s V_4                  0043: ldloc.s V_7
0023: ldloc.s V_5                  0045: ldloc.s V_6
0025: add                         0047: sub
0026: ldloc.s V_6                  0048: mul
0028: add                         0049: call Math.Sqrt
0029: ldc.r8 2                     004e: call NumberValue.Make
0032: div                         0053: ret
0033: stloc.s V_7
```

One call TRIAREA(15,20,25) of this function takes approximately 73 ns (measured as average of 10 million calls to on a 2.66 GHz Core 2 Duo) despite the unwrapping and wrapping. Errors are propagated correctly thanks to the NaN encoding of error values (section 2.8.1). For instance, if the function is applied to a string argument, then the `ToDoubleOrNan` function will produce a NaN representing ArgTypeError, which will propagate through the arithmetic functions, and the `NumberValue.Make` function will turn that into an ArgTypeError error value. Similarly, if the function is called on side lengths that cannot make up a triangle, `Sqrt` will be called on a negative number and produce a NaN that `NumberValue.Make` will turn into a NumError.

Example 6.2 A sheet-defined function `NDIE(n)` that simulates a general n-sided die can be defined as follows. The input cell B32 holds n, and the output cell is B33:

D13	A	B	C
31	=DEFINE("ndie",...	'General n-side die	
32	'n =	6	
33	'eyes =	=FLOOR(RAND()*B32, 1)+1	
34			

Rolls of a six-sided die are computed by calling `NDIE(6)`. Function `NDIE` is defined in file testsdf.xml; it is used in example 6.20.

Example 6.3 Calendrical calculations. Many functions concerning the Gregorian calendar, the ISO calendar, the date of Easter Sunday in Christian calendars, and so on can be found on sheet @Calendar in testsdf.xml. These are based on Dershowitz and Reingold's algorithms [46]. The initial implementations are dure to IT University MSc students Hui Xu and Mainul Liton. For a very simple example, `LEAPYEAR(year)` can be implemented like this with input cell B5 and output cell B6:

A1	A	B	C
4	=DEFINE("leapy...	'leapyear(yyyy)	'N&D: gregori
5	'yyyy =	1904	
6	'result =	=AND(MOD(B5, 4)=0, OR(MOD(B5, 100)<>0, MOD(B5, 400)=0))	
7			

The conversion `FIXDATE(yyyy,mm,dd)` from a Gregorian calendar date to the number of days since January 1, year 1, called the fixdate, can be implemented like this, with input cells B9:B11 and output cell B14:

B21	A	B	C
8	=DEFINE("fixdat...	fixdate(yyyy,mm,dd)	'N&D: fixed-fi
9	'yyyy =	1901	
10	'mm =	1	
11	'dd =	1	
12		=B9+FLOOR((B10+9)/12, 1)	
13		=12+MOD(B10-2, -12)	
14	'result =	=-306+365*(B12-1)+FLOOR((B12-1)/4, 1)-FLOOR((B12-1)/100, 1)+FLOOR((B12-1)/400, 1)+FLOOR((3*B13-1)/5, 1)+30*(B13-1)+B11	
15			

The conversion in the opposite direction—obtaining Gregorian year, month, and date from a fixdate—can be expressed with a similar amount of spreadsheet "code".

Using FIXDATE, one can implement EASTER(yyyy), a function that computes the fixdate of Easter Sunday in year yyyy, with input B122 and output B127:

B137	A	B	C
121	=DEFINE("easter...	'easter(yyyy)	
122	'yyyy =	2000	
123	'century =	=FLOOR(B122/100, 1)+1	
124	'shifted-epact =	=MOD(14+11*MOD(B122, 19)-FLOOR(3*B123/4, 1)+FLOOR((5+8*B123)/25, 1), 30)	
125	'adjusted-epact =	=IF(OR(B124=0, AND(B124=1, 10<MOD(B123, 19))), B124+1, B124)	
126	'paschal-moon =	=FIXDATE(B122, 4, 19)-B125	
127	'easterfixed =	=KDAYA(B126, 6)	

The EASTER function may look complicated, but it is a straightforward translation from the Dershowitz and Reingold book [46, section 4.3], and it is fast enough: it executes in around 640 ns per call (1 million calls, 2.66 GHz Core 2 Duo) or more than 1 560 000 calls per second. The KDAYA function (not shown) is very simple, taken from the same book, and essentially uses modulo to find the fixdate of the nearest Sunday (weekday 6) after the fixdate represented by B126.

These examples are interesting because they show that calendrical calculations can be implemented in a simple and rational manner using sheet-defined functions. Thus, one can easily find the first Monday, last Tuesday, last working day, and so on of a given month. It is also easy to implement computations with ISO week numbers, which are widely used outside the United States, yet remained unsupported by MS Excel until version 2010.

Example 6.4 The density function $\phi_{\mu,\sigma}(x)$ for the normal distribution $N(\mu, \sigma)$ is

$$\phi_{\mu,\sigma}(x) = \frac{1}{\sigma\sqrt{2\pi}} exp\left(-\frac{(x-\mu)^2}{2\sigma^2}\right)$$

It can be computed by a function NORMDENSITYGENERAL(x, μ, σ) in Funcalc like this, with input cells B8:B10 and output cell B12:

D16	A	B	C
7	=DEFINE("normd...	'The density of the normal distribution N(0,1)	
8	'x =	-2	
9	'mu =	0	
10	'sigma =	1	
11		=(B8-B9)/B10	
12	'f(x) =	=0.398942280401432*EXP(-0.5*B11*B11)/B10	

The constant $0.3989\ldots$ is $1/\sqrt{2\pi}$. See sheet @Functions in file testsdf.xml. This is the same as Excel's NORMDIST($x, \mu, \sigma, 0$).

Example 6.5 Consider the cumulative distribution function NORMDISTCDF(x) for the normal or Gaussian distribution $N(0, 1)$, and its inverse INVNORMDISTCDF(p), corresponding to Excel's built-ins NORMSDIST(x) and NORMSINV(x). These functions are widely used in statistics and other areas, for instance, in the Black-Scholes approach to options pricing in finance (example 6.18). The functions are also well suited as test cases for compilation of sheet-defined functions since they contain a mixture of conditionals and floating-point multiplication, division, and addition, and 10–25 high-precision floating-point constants. Function NORMDISTCDF can be defined like this, with input cell B6 and output cell B7:

G22	A	B	C	D	E
5	=DEFINE("normdist...				
6	'z =	-5			
7	'p =	=IF(B6<0, B11, 1-B11)			
8	'zabs =	=ABS(B6)			
9	'expntl =	=EXP(-1*B8*B8/2)			
10	'pdf =	=B9/SQRT(2*PI())			
11	'p' =	=IF(B8>37, 0, IF(B8<7.071, B9*B14/D14, B10/(B8+1/(B8+2/(B8+3/(B8+4/(B8+0.65)))))))			
12					
13	'pi		'qi		
14	220.206867912376	=A14+$B$8*B15	440.413735824752	=C14+$B$8*D15	
15	221.213596169931	=A15+$B$8*B16	793.826512519948	=C15+$B$8*D16	
16	112.07929149787	=A16+$B$8*B17	637.333633378831	=C16+$B$8*D17	
17	33.912866078383	=A17+$B$8*B18	296.564248779673	=C17+$B$8*D18	
18	6.37396220353165	=A18+$B$8*B19	86.780732202946	=C18+$B$8*D19	
19	0.700383064443688	=A19+$B$8*B20	16.0641775792069	=C19+$B$8*D20	
20	0.035262496599891	=A20	1.75566716318264	=C20+$B$8*D21	
21			0.0883883476483184	=C21	

Depending on the magnitude B8 of the input, cell B11 either computes the ratio between two polynomials (from cells B14:B20 and D14:D21) or a continued fraction; this approach is from Hart [73]. Functions NORMDISTCDF and INVNORMDISTCDF are on sheet @NormalDist in file testsdf.xml.

The bytecode generated for NORMDISTCDF in Funcalc executes in approximately 118 ns/call (1 million calls, 2.66 GHz Core 2 Duo, 32-bit mode). This compares with 1140 ns/call for the Excel 2007 built-in NORMSDIST, 64 ns/call for an implementation in C# on .NET, and 54 ns/call for an implementation in C, compiled with aggressive optimization (-O3) and gcc version 4.2.1.

Example 6.6 The binomial coefficients BINOM(a, b) = (a+b)!/(a!b!) can be computed efficiently for a range of small integers a and b by indexing into a precomputed table. For instance, BINOM(3, 49) is the number of ways to select 3 cards from a deck of 52. One can build a table of values of n! for n=0..100, say, in an ordinary sheet called Data, and then define a sheet-defined function that uses INDEX(Data!$B$3:$B$54, a+b) and so on to index into that table, like this with input cells B22 and B23 and output cell B24:

B24	A	B		C
21	=DEFINE("binom...	'Binomial coefficients		
22	'a =	49		
23	'b =	3		
▶ 24	'binom(n,k) =	=IF(AND(B22>0, B23>0), INDEX(Data!B3:B102, B22+B23, 1)/INDEX(Data!B3:B102, B22, 1)/INDEX(Data!B3:B102, B23, 1), 1)		

The complicated formula in cell B24 is somewhat difficult to read and may be considered bad style; example 6.7 illustrates the use of intermediate cells to shorten formulas and improve readability.

Function BINOM and the ordinary sheet Data are defined file testsdf.xml. The function is a special case of Excel's Analysis Toolpak function MULTINOMIAL(a,b). It takes roughly 400 ns to compute BINOM(3,49) = 22 100 using the sheet-defined function.

Example 6.7 More binomial coefficients. When we need to compute BINOM(a,b) for a and b whose sum exceeds 170, it is necessary to compute with logarithms of $n!$ instead of $n!$ because 64-bit IEEE floating-point cannot represent the result $n!$ for n greater than 170 (see section 2.8.1). When computing with logarithms, the results will be less accurate, though.

We build a table of values of log(n!) by addition of logarithms in sheet Data and define the alternative function BINOMLOG(a,b) like this, with input cells B27 and B28 and output cell B32:

C35	A	B	C
26	=DEFINE("binoml...	'Binomial coefficients using table of logarithms	
27	'a =	49	
28	'b =	3	
29		=INDEX(Data!H3:H102, B27+B28, 1)	
30		=INDEX(Data!H3:H102, B27, 1)	
31		=INDEX(Data!H3:H102, B28, 1)	
32	'binomlog(n,k) =	=IF(AND(B27>0, B28>0), ROUND(EXP(B29-B30-B31), 0), 1)	

Note the use of intermediate cells B29:B31 to obtain a short and readable formula in cell B32. Function BINOMLOG is in file testsdf.xml.

Example 6.8 Even more binomial coefficients. One can compute binomial coefficients more accurately at the cost of vastly increased space usage. Simply build Pascal's triangle in an ordinary data sheet Data by putting the number 1 in all of row 1 and all of column A, putting the formula =B1+A2 in B2, and copying that formula to a rectangular area such as B2:G9, like this:

B2	A	B	C	D	E	F	G	H
1	1	1	1	1	1	1	1	
▶ 2	1	=B1+A2	3	4	5	6	7	
3	1	3	6	10	15	21	28	
4	1	4	10	20	35	56	84	
5	1	5	15	35	70	126	210	
6	1	6	21	56	126	252	462	
7	1	7	28	84	210	462	924	
8	1	8	36	120	330	792	1716	
9	1	9	45	165	495	1287	3003	

and then use two-dimensional lookup =INDEX(Data!$A$1:$G$9, a+1, b+1) in that data sheet.

Example 6.9 A financial function. Assume that a bullet bond (one whose principal is paid only on maturity) pays a coupon of y dollars each term and pays \$100 on maturity after n terms. Then we can define a function BULLETPV(y,n,r) to compute the present value of the bullet bond by discounting future payments by the effective interest rate r, like this, with input cells B4:B6 and output cell D7:

A1	A	B	C	D	E
▶ 1	'BULLETPV(cou...				'2
2	'Present value of ...				
3	=DEFINE('bullet...				
4	'coupon =	4			
5	'n =	10			
6	'eff.int r =	6			
7	'(1+r/100)^n=	=(1+B6/100)^B5		=100/B7+B4*(B7-1)/B6*100/B7	

This function is defined on sheet @BulletLoan in workbook testsdf.xml. Example 6.23 shows how we can solve the opposite and often more interesting problem: Given the current price p, the coupon y, and the number of terms n, find the effective interest rate r.

Example 6.10 Table lookup. Excel's built-in lookup function MATCH can be implemented as a sheet-defined function. The call MATCH(x, arr) should return the number of the last column or row in array arr whose value is less than or equal to key x or return error #NA if there is no such column or row. Column and row numbers within arr start with 1. The area arr must be one-dimensional, and its values must be arranged in ascending order. If arr has multiple columns and one row, then the function returns the column number of x; if it has multiple rows and one column, then the function returns the row number of x.

We can implement MATCH(x, arr) as a sheet-defined function, using binary search or recursive bisection within arr.

Let us first consider the case where arr is a single row $arr[1, n]$, with $n \geq 1$, of ordered values. We define an auxiliary function MATCHCOLAUX(x, arr, a, b) that returns the column of x within the array segment $arr[a, b]$. This function is called as MATCHCOLAUX(x, arr, 1, COLUMNS(arr)) from MATCH(x, arr) to search all of arr.

Function MATCHCOLAUX(x, arr, a, b) can be defined as follows. If $b > a$, then it returns the error value #NA; otherwise if $arr[b] \leq x$, then it returns b; otherwise it computes $m = \text{CEILING}((a + b)/2, 1)$; and if $arr[m] \leq x$, then it calls MATCHCOLAUX(x, arr, m, b), otherwise MATCHCOLAUX(x, arr, a, m-1).

D17	A	B		C
3	=DEFINE("match...	'MATCHCOLAUX(x, arr, a, b)		
4	'x =			
5	'arr =			
6	'a =			
7	'b =			
8	'm =	=CEILING((B6+B7)/2, 1)		
9		=MATCHCOLAUX(B4, B5, B8, B7)		
10		=MATCHCOLAUX(B4, B5, B6, B8-1)		
11	'result =	=IF(B6>B7, NA(), IF(INDEX(B5, 1, B7)<=B4, B7, IF(INDEX(B5, 1, B8)<=B4, B9, B10)))		

Another function MATCHROWAUX(x, arr, a, b) is defined analogously—only the row and column arguments in INDEX are swapped—to search for x in a segment $arr[a, b]$ of a one-column array.

Then the general MATCH(x, arr) can be defined with inputs B22:B23 and output B24:

B42	A	B		C
21	=DEFINE("match...	'MATCH(x,arr)		
22	'x =			
23	'arr =			
24	'result =	=IF(ROWS(B23)=1, MATCHCOLAUX(B22, B23, 1, COLUMNS(B23)), MATCHROWAUX(B22, B23, 1, ROWS(B23)))		

See functions MATCHCOLAUX, MATCHROWAUX, and MATCH in sheet @Lookup in workbook testsdf.xml.

Example 6.11 Like MATCH, Excel's built-in VLOOKUP and HLOOKUP functions can be implemented as sheet-defined functions. Let us first consider the "horizontal" lookup function HLOOKUP(x, arr, r), which finds the first column in area arr whose first-row value is less than or equal to key x and then returns the contents of row r in that column, counting from 1. It should return error #NA if no first-row value is less than or equal to key x and error #REF! if r is not a legal row number in area tab. (Here we ignore the regular expression-style capabilities that are also built into Excel's HLOOKUP and VLOOKUP).

To implement HLOOKUP(x, arr, r), call MATCHCOLAUX to get the column c that matches x and then look up row r of column c using INDEX(arr, r, c). So we can implement HLOOKUP very easily like this, with inputs B27:B29 and output B30:

26	=DEFINE('hlook...	'HLOOKUP(x, arr, r)
27	'x =	
28	'arr =	
29	'r =	
30	'result =	=INDEX(B28, B29, MATCHCOLAUX(B27, B28, 1, COLUMNS(B28)))

Thanks to error propagation semantics, if MATCHCOLAUX returns #NA because no row matches x, then so does HLOOKUP.

The analogous "vertical" lookup function VLOOKUP(x, arr, c) is implemented in much the same way but uses MATCHROWAUX instead of MATCHCOLAUX to find the row matching x, and then returns column c of that row. See sheet @Lookup in workbook testsdf.xml.

Example 6.12 Biology, engineering, and science often need specialized statistical distributions, such as a mixture of the normal distribution $N(\mu, \sigma)$ and the Poisson distribution, defined by this integral:

$$F(\mu, \sigma, s) = \int_{-\infty}^{\infty} \phi_{\mu,\sigma}(\ell)(1 - e^{s10^\ell})d\ell$$

where $\phi_{\mu,\sigma}(\ell)$ is the density of the normal distribution (see example 6.4). Since this function is extremely small for ℓ far away from μ, the integral can be well approximated by summation from $-10\sigma + \mu$ to $+10\sigma + \mu$. This is done in function POISSONLOGNORMAL2(μ, σ, s) by calling an auxiliary function POISSONLOGNORMALAUX2($\mu, \sigma, s, b, e, \delta$), where b is the start of the summation, e is the end, and δ is the step, which can be chosen as 0.2σ.

The function $F(\mu, \sigma, s)$ can be used to describe sampling for microbiological food safety. Namely, if contaminating microorganisms (cells) appear in a food lot with a frequency whose logarithm is normally distributed with mean μ and standard deviation σ (so the frequency itself is log-normally distributed), then $F(\mu, \sigma, s)$ is the probability that a sample of size s will contain the contamination [157]. For instance, $\mu = -2 = \log_{10}(0.01)$ indicates on average 0.01 microorganisms per gram, or 1 per 100 gram, in the lot. If the standard deviation σ is 0.8, then the probability that a sample of size $s = 100$ gram contains a microorganism is $F(-2, 0.8, 100) = 0.592$ or 59.2%.

In other words, if $\mu = -2$ describes the desired maximal level of contamination, then we have a chance of 59.2% of actually discovering that a product exceeds this limit by taking a single sample of size $s = 100$ gram.

See sheet @Sampling in file testsdf.xml.

Example 6.13 The probability $F(\mu, \sigma, s)$ computed in example 6.12 can be used to design sampling plans for microbiological food safety. More precisely, assume we take n samples, each of size s grams, of which we allow $c < n$ to test positive, and we assume that the probability of an occurrence of a microbiological contaminant is log-normally distributed with mean μ and standard deviation σ as before.

Then the probability of accepting a lot whose contamination exceeds the acceptable level is $P(accept)$, where

$$P(accept) = \sum_{i=0}^{i=c} \binom{n}{i} (1 - F(\mu, \sigma, s))^{n-i} F(\mu, \sigma, s)^i$$

Namely, if $c = 3$ say, we must consider the four mutually exclusive possibilities of precisely $i = 0$, $i = 1$, $i = 2$, and $i = 3$ samples showing contamination. To find the probability of the case of $i = 1$ say, observe that the probability of $i = 1$ sample showing contamination is $F(\mu, \sigma, s)^i$ and the probability of the remaining $n - i$ samples showing no contamination is $(1 - F(\mu, \sigma, s))^{n-i}$. Finally, there are n over i ways to "choose" the sample(s) that shows contamination. This gives the summands for each $i = 0, \ldots, c$.

This computation is performed, for n up to 10, by function `ACCEPT` in sheet @Sampling of file testsdf.xml. It uses function `POISSONLOGNORMAL2` from example 6.12 and `BINOM` from example 6.6.

Having gotten this far, we can further use this function together with `GOALSEEK` from example 6.22 to find the number of samples n necessary to obtain a desired low level of risk of accepting a contaminated food lot, or to find the highest level (μ) of contamination that will go undetected with a particular probability. See sheet @Sampling in workbook testsdf.xml.

The functions in this and the preceding example are based on Schothorst et al. [157].

Example 6.14 The Excel built-in function `REPT(s,n)` returns the string s^n, that is, string s concatenated with itself n times. It can be implemented efficiently as a sheet-defined function in several ways. The `REPT` function is particularly useful for creating simple in-sheet bar charts. To graphically display the A1:A5 values in cells B1:B5, enter `REPT("|", A1)` in B1 and copy it to B2:B5. To show the numbers on a relative scale, enter instead `REPT("|", 50*A1/MAX(A1:A5))` in B1 and copy it.

First let us consider a surprising *non-recursive* implementation, `REPT1(s,n)`. Of course it can work only for a bounded range on n, say up to 1023, but that would be entirely sufficient for the bar chart example. The idea is to compute powers of two (1, 2, 4, 8, etc.) in B43:B52 and compute the corresponding powers of s (s^1, s^2, s^4, s^8, etc.) in column D43:D52 by successive squaring, for instance, $s^8 = ((s^2)^2)^2$. In column E43:E52, we calculate, from the bottom up, the number of copies of s still needed, in column F43:F52 a logical value that says whether the corresponding square of s in D43:D52 shall be included in the result, and in G42:G53 the result. The total cost of this procedure is $O(n)$. See sheet @Functions in workbook testsdf.xml.

Example 6.15 Consider a more traditional recursive implementation REPT2(s,n) of the Excel REPT function. The simplest approach is to add one copy of s in each recursive call, performing n recursive calls and n string concatenations of increasing length, for a total execution time of $O(n^2)$. Inputs B59:B60 and output B61:

A1	A	B	C
58	=DEFINE("rept2"...	'REPT2(s,n), naïve recursive implement...	
59	's =	'a	
60	'n =	3	
61	'result =	=IF(B60=0, "", B59&REPT2(B59, B60-1))	

Much better solutions exist, as shown by examples 6.16 and 9.1.

Example 6.16 A far better recursive implementation REPT3(s,n) exploits that $s^0 = \epsilon$ is the empty string, $s^1 = s$ itself, and, most importantly, $s^{2m} = (ss)^m$ and $s^{2m+1} = s(ss)^m$. Hence, s^n can be computed by REPT3(s,n) in only $O(\log n)$ recursive steps and $O(\log n)$ string concatenations, at a total cost of $O(n)$:

C72	A	B	C
63	=DEFINE("rept3"...	'REPT3(s,n), fast recursive implementation, no evaluation conditions required	
64	's =		
65	'n =		
66		=IF(B65=0, "", IF(B65=1, B64, IF(MOD(B65, 2), B64&REPT3(B64&B64, FLOOR(B65/2, 1)), REPT3(B64&B64, FLOOR(B65/2, 1)))))	

The test IF(B65=1, "", ...) is not strictly necessary for correctness, but without it, the recursion will always terminate with creating a string that is twice as long as the final result and then discarding that string, which is wasteful.

An even neater and equally efficient solution would avoid the extra test as well as the nearly identical branches of the innermost IF. Such a solution REPT4(s,n) is presented only later in example 9.1.

Example 6.17 The binary van der Corput sequence [156] is an infinite sequence of numbers, dense in the unit interval $[0, 1]$:

$$\frac{1}{2}, \quad \frac{1}{4}, \quad \frac{3}{4}, \quad \frac{1}{8}, \quad \frac{5}{8}, \quad \frac{3}{8}, \quad \frac{7}{8}, \quad \cdots$$

The sequence is used for quasi-random or quasi-Monte Carlo simulation, as in example 6.18. Using auxiliary functions ADD (inputs B5:B6, output B7) and NEXTVDC (inputs B10:B11, output B12), function VANDERCORPUT(n) with input B15 and output B17 returns a 1-row array that is a $2^{n+1}-1$ element approximation to the infinite van der Corput sequence. Thus, for $n = 0$, the result is the sequence $[0.5]$; for $n = 1$, the result is $[0.5, 0.25, 0.75]$; for $n = 2$, it is $[0.5, 0.25, 0.75, 0.125, 0.625, 0.375, 0.875]$; and so on. It can be expressed as a sheet-defined function like this:

E23	A	B	C
4	=DEFINE("add", ...	'ADD(x,y)	
5	'x	12	
6	'y	15	
7		=B5+B6	
8			
9	=DEFINE("nextv...	'NEXTVDC(x,v)	
10	'x	0.25	
11	'v	=VCAT(0.5)	
12		=HCAT(B11, B10, MAP(CLOSURE("add", B10, NA()), B11))	
13			
14	=DEFINE("vande...	'VANDERCORPUT(n)	
15	'n		
16		=VANDERCORPUT(B15-1)	
17		=IF(B15<=1, HCAT(0.5), NEXTVDC(2^-B15, B16))	

Example 6.18 Black-Scholes is a widely used model for pricing of European options [15]; see sheet @BlackScholes in file testsdf.xml. The function QMCBS estimates the price of the option given several parameters (cells B22:B27) and a probability p (cell B28). Function SIMULATE(n, f) then averages the value of QMCBS over all p values in the interval $[0, 1]$ using a van der Corput sequence (example 6.17):

21	=DEFINE("qmcb...	'QMCBS(p0,d0,r,delta,sigma,T,p)	
22	'p0	20	
23	'd0	20	
24	'r	0.08	
25	'delta	0.08	
26	'sigma	0.25	
27	'T	2	
28	'p	0.99	
29	'trendm =	=(B24-B25-B26*B26/2)*B27	
30	'sigraiz =	=B26*SQRT(B27)	
31	'vt(x) =	=B22*EXP(B29+B30*INVNORMDISTCDF(B28))	
32		=IF(B31>=B23, B31-B23, 0)	
33			
34	=DEFINE("simula...		
35	'r =	0.08	
36	'T =	2	
37	'n =	2	
38	'vdc seq =	=VANDERCORPUT(B37)	
39	'fcn =	=CLOSURE("qmcbs", 20, 20, $B$35, 0.08, 0.25, $B$36, NA())	
40	'simres =	=SUM(MAP($B$39, $B$38))/COLUMNS($B$38)*EXP(-$B$35*$B$36)	

Example 6.19 Sørensen [141, 151] reimplemented many of Excel's built-in financial functions as sheet-defined functions. Figure 6.2 lists some of these and shows that in most cases the sheet-defined function definitions are faster than or comparable to the corresponding Excel built-ins. Two exceptions are RATE and IRR, marked by an asterisk (*), whose poor performance is due to the rather simplistic general binary search root finder GOALSEEK from example 6.22.

The sheet-defined functions are based on, and tested against, Bolognese's F# implementation of financial functions [17], known to exactly mimic the Excel built-ins.

Function	Excel	Funcalc	Note
PV	1461	804	
FV	1445	1138	
NPER	1055	472	
RATE	2297	44864	*
PMT	1523	664	
FVSCHEDULE	2960	928	
IMPT	1593	1732	
PPMT	1805	1292	
CUMIPMT	3117	3400	
CUMPRINC	2742	4072	
ISPMT	468	170	
IRR	4750	79804	*
NPV	2156	2060	
MIRR	3515	8328	
SLN	125	158	
SYD	453	212	
AMORLINC	14921	2054	
AMORDEGRC	16343	4444	

Figure 6.2: Execution time for Excel 2010 built-in financial functions compared to Funcalc sheet-defined functions (ns/call). For the *-marked cases, see text in example 6.19.

Example 6.20 As shown in example 6.2, we can create a sheet-defined function NDIE(n) that produces a roll of an n-sided die.

This general die function can be partially applied to obtain function values that represent specialized dice, for instance, one with n=6 sides and another with n=20 sides, that can subsequently be rolled as many times as desired. Here are the formulas on the left and some corresponding results on the right:

28	'Die rolls	
29	=CLOSURE("ndie", 6)	=CLOSURE("ndie", 40)
30	=APPLY(A$29)	=APPLY(B$29)
31	=APPLY(A$29)	=APPLY(B$29)
32	=APPLY(A$29)	=APPLY(B$29)
33	=APPLY(A$29)	=APPLY(B$29)
34	=APPLY(A$29)	=APPLY(B$29)
35	=APPLY(A$29)	=APPLY(B$29)

28	Die rolls	
29	NDIE(6)	NDIE(40)
30	5	2
31	1	37
32	3	34
33	6	9
34	3	34
35	3	2

See sheet Results in file testsdf.xml.

Example 6.21 Generalized predicates. In Excel, the functions COUNTIF and SUMIF take as argument a cell area and a criterion, where the criterion may be a constant number such as 20, a constant string such as "apple", or a string that encodes a comparison such as ">= 18.5". However, one cannot express composite criteria and ranges such as "18.5 <= x < 25".

By passing the criterion as a sheet-defined function, we can easily express such composite criteria and obtain a much clearer semantics for COUNTIF and SUMIF. The criterion must be a one-argument function value that acts as a predicate; that is, it must return 0 to mean false and a non-zero value to mean true.

For instance, we may create a sheet-defined function NORMALBMI with input cell B92 and output cell B93 containing =AND(18.5<=B92, B92<25):

F104	A	B	C
91	=DEFINE("norma...	'NORMALBMI(bmi)	
92	'bmi =		
93	'isnormal =	=AND(18.5<=B92, B92<25)	

Then COUNTIF(C1:C100, CLOSURE("NORMALBMI")) will count the number of individuals in range C1:C100 whose body mass index (BMI) is between 18.5 and 25, that is, "normal".

Example 6.22 Numerical equation solving. Define a function GOALSEEK(f,r,a) for finding a numerical solution x to the equation $f(x) = r$ if one exists. The input is a continuous function f, a target value r, and an initial guess a at the value of x. The function uses bisection by either a recursive sheet-defined function or more simply a finite number of explicit bisection steps. Just 30 such steps seems to give better precision than Excel's built-in Goal Seek dialog; below are the first few steps. The input cells are B21, D21, and F21, and the output cell is D57 (not shown):

A1	A	B	C	D	E	F	G
20	=DEFINE("goals…						
21	f =		target =	0	'a =	1	
22							
23		'a0	'b0	'f(a0)-target	'f(b0)-target		
24		=$F$21	=FINDEND($B$21, $D$21, B24)	=APPLY($B$21, B24)-$D$21	=APPLY($B$21, C24)-$D$21		
25							
26		'Invariant: f(ai)<=target<=…					
27		'ai	'bi	'xi=(ai+bi)/2	'f(xi)-target		
28		=IF($D$24<=0, B24, C24)	=IF($D$24<=0, C24, B24)	=(B28+C28)/2	=APPLY($B$21, D28)-$D$21		
29		=IF($E$28>=0, $D28, B28)	=IF($E$28>=0, $D28, C28)	=(B29+C29)/2	=APPLY($B$21, D29)-$D$21		
30		=IF($E$29<=0, $D29, B29)	=IF($E$29>=0, $D29, C29)	=(B30+C30)/2	=APPLY($B$21, D30)-$D$21		
31		=IF($E$30<=0, $D30, B30)	=IF($E$30>=0, $D30, C30)	=(B31+C31)/2	=APPLY($B$21, D31)-$D$21		
32		=IF($E$31<=0, $D31, B31)	=IF($E$31>=0, $D31, C31)	=(B32+C32)/2	=APPLY($B$21, D32)-$D$21		
33		=IF($E$32<=0, $D32, B32)	=IF($E$32>=0, $D32, C32)	=(B33+C33)/2	=APPLY($B$21, D33)-$D$21		

An auxiliary function FINDEND(f,r,a) is needed to search for a b such that $f(b)$ and $f(a)$ are on opposite sides of the target value r, that is, $(f(b) - r)$ and $(f(a) - r)$ have opposite signs. One such function is shown in example 6.24.

See function GOALSEEK in file testsdf.xml.

Example 6.23 The effective interest rate of a bullet loan. We can use GOALSEEK from example 6.22 to solve the opposite problem of that in example 6.9: Given the current price p of the loan, the coupon y, and the number of terms n, find the effective interest rate r. This cannot be computed by a closed formula, but we can use GOALSEEK to find the r that provides a numerical solution to the equation BULLETPV(y,n,r) = p. For instance, to find the effective interest rate $r = 4.90\%$ for a bullet loan with coupon $y = 4$, $n = 10$ terms, and current price \$93, we simply compute:

```
GOALSEEK(CLOSURE("BULLETPV", 4, 10, NA()), 93, 4)
```

Above, the last occurrence of 4 is the initial guess at the solution. This computation takes 26 500 ns, so we can compute roughly 37 500 effective interest rates per second using this approach.

Example 6.24 For convenient use of function GOALSEEK above, we need an auxiliary function FINDEND(f,r,a) that tries to find and return another initial value b such that $(f(a) - r)$ and $(f(b) - r)$ have opposite signs or, more precisely, $(f(a) - r)(f(b) - r) \leq 0$. It can be implemented by bounded search: try $b = a \pm 1, a \pm 0.1, a \pm 10.0, a \pm 0.01, a \pm 100.0$, and so on; or by a recursive function as shown below. Here B5, D5, and F5 are input cells, and I5 is the output cell:

E22	A	B	C	D	E	F	G	H	I	J
4	=DEFINE("findEn...									
5	f =		target =	0	'a =	1			=I8+0	
6										
7	'a	'delta	'a-delta	'a+delta	f(a-delta)	f(a+delta)	'OK(a-delta)	'OK(a+delta)		
8	=$F$5	0.0001	=$A$8-$B8	=$A$8+$B8	=APPLY($B$5, C8)-$D$5	=APPLY($B$5, D8)-$D$5	=$A$9*E8<=0	=$A$9*F8<=0	=IF($G8, $C8, IF($H8, $D8, I9))	
9	=APPLY($B$5, $...	=B8*10	=$A$8-$B9	=$A$8+$B9	=APPLY($B$5, C9)-$D$5	=APPLY($B$5, D9)-$D$5	=$A$9*E9<=0	=$A$9*F9<=0	=IF($G9, $C9, IF($H9, $D9, I10))	
10		=B9*10	=$A$8-$B$10	=$A$8+$B10	=APPLY($B$5, C10)-$D$5	=APPLY($B$5, D10)-$D$5	=$A$9*E10<=0	=$A$9*F10<=0	=IF($G10, $C10, IF($H10, $D10, I11))	
11		=B10*10	=$A$8-$B11	=$A$8+$B11	=APPLY($B$5, C11)-$D$5	=APPLY($B$5, D11)-$D$5	=$A$9*E11<=0	=$A$9*F11<=0	=IF($G11, $C11, IF($H11, $D11, I12))	
12		=B11*10	=$A$8-$B12	=$A$8+$B12	=APPLY($B$5, C12)-$D$5	=APPLY($B$5, D12)-$D$5	=$A$9*E12<=0	=$A$9*F12<=0	=IF($G12, $C12, IF($H12, $D12, I13))	
13		=B12*10	=$A$8-$B13	=$A$8+$B13	=APPLY($B$5, C13)-$D$5	=APPLY($B$5, D13)-$D$5	=$A$9*E13<=0	=$A$9*F13<=0	=IF($G13, $C13, IF($H13, $D13, I14))	
14		=B13*10	=$A$8-$B14	=$A$8+$B14	=APPLY($B$5, C14)-$D$5	=APPLY($B$5, D14)-$D$5	=$A$9*E14<=0	=$A$9*F14<=0	=IF($G14, $C14, IF($H14, $D14, I15))	
15		=B14*10	=$A$8-$B15	=$A$8+$B15	=APPLY($B$5, C15)-$D$5	=APPLY($B$5, D15)-$D$5	=$A$9*E15<=0	=$A$9*F15<=0	=IF($G15, $C15, IF($H15, $D15, I16))	
16		=B15*10	=$A$8-$B16	=$A$8+$B16	=APPLY($B$5, C16)-$D$5	=APPLY($B$5, D16)-$D$5	=$A$9*E16<=0	=$A$9*F16<=0	=IF($G16, $C16, IF($H16, $D16, I17))	
17		=B16*10	=$A$8-$B17	=$A$8+$B17	=APPLY($B$5, C17)-$D$5	=APPLY($B$5, D17)-$D$5	=$A$9*E17<=0	=$A$9*F17<=0	=IF($G17, $C17, IF($H17, $D17, ER...	

See auxiliary function FINDEND(f,r,a) in file testsdf.xml.

Example 6.25 Adaptive quadrature is a well-known technique for numerical integration of a function $f(x)$ on an interval $[a, b]$. It can be implemented by putting $m = (a+b)/2$ and computing two approximations to the integral, for instance, Simpson's rule $(b - a)(f(a) + 4f(m) + f(b))/6$ and the midpoint formula $(b - a)f(m)$. If the two approximations are nearly equal, return one of them; otherwise recursively compute the integral of f on $[a, m]$ and the integral of f on $[b, m]$ and add the results. This implementation naturally relies on recursion and higher-order functions for passing the function f whose integral is being computed. With sheet-defined functions, the implementation of this is straightforward and quite efficient; here with input cells B75:B77 and output cell B81:

B86	A	B	C	D
74	=DEFINE("integr...	'INTEGRATE(f,a,b)		
75	f =		f(x)	
76	'a =		=APPLY($B$75, B76)	
77	'b =		=APPLY($B$75, B77)	
78	'm =	=(B76+B77)/2	=APPLY($B$75, B78)	
79	'simpson =	=($B$77-$B$76)/6*(C76+4*C78+C77)		
80	'midpoint =	=($B$77-$B$76)*C78		
81	'result =	=IF(ABS(B79-B80)<1E-07, B79, INTEGRATE(B75, B76, B78)+INTEGRATE(B75, B78, B77))		

The function is both recursive and higher order. Using only standard spreadsheet functions or VBA, one cannot define adaptive integration this way because neither supports higher-order functions. Function INTEGRATE(f,a,b) is in file testsdf.xml.

Example 6.26 Excel has a feature called a data table, activated by the menu Data > What-If Analysis > Data Table, which can calculate the values of a complex of formulas for given values of one or two "input cells", whose values are drawn from the column to the left of the table and/or the row above the table. Interestingly, this seems to provide a kind of poor man's sheet-defined function in Excel: the function from the table's input cell(s) to the tables output cells.

Let's consider an example of an Excel data table. Assume that cell B8 contains an annual interest rate r and cell B9 contains a number of years n, and that we compute in cell B10 the future value of $100 after n years at interest rate r using compound interest. Cell B10 could contain the formula =100*(1+B8)^B9 as shown in the lower left part of figure 6.3.

Now create an Excel data table as follows. Let row cells B2:D2 contain some argument values for n, let column cells A3:A6 contain some argument values for r, and insert in the "corner" A2 a reference =B10 to the future value computed in B10 (see figure 6.3, left). To create a data table, we mark A2:D6, select Data > What-If Analysis > Data Table, and choose Row input cell to be B9 and Column input cell to be B8. Now Excel will fill the cells B3:D6 with the computed future value for all $3 \cdot 4 = 12$ combinations of r and n. The formulas in B3:D6 will display as array formulas {=TABLE(B9,B8)} as seen in figure 6.3, left, and the computed results will be as shown on the right.

	A	B	C	D
1				
2	=B10	5	10	15
3	0.01	=TABLE(B9,B8)	=TABLE(B9,B8)	=TABLE(B9,B8)
4	0.02	=TABLE(B9,B8)	=TABLE(B9,B8)	=TABLE(B9,B8)
5	0.03	=TABLE(B9,B8)	=TABLE(B9,B8)	=TABLE(B9,B8)
6	0.04	=TABLE(B9,B8)	=TABLE(B9,B8)	=TABLE(B9,B8)
7				
8	r =	0.04		
9	n =	15		
10		=100*(1+B8)^B9		

	A	B	C	D
1				
2	180.0944	5	10	15
3	0.01	105.101	110.4622	116.0969
4	0.02	110.4081	121.8994	134.5868
5	0.03	115.9274	134.3916	155.7967
6	0.04	121.6653	148.0244	180.0944
7				
8	r =	0.04		
9	n =	15		
10		180.0944		

Figure 6.3: An Excel 2013 data table. The underlying formulas are shown on the left and the computed results on the right. The table B3:D6 contains values of the "function" whose input cells are B8 and B9 and whose output cell is B10.

However, using sheet-defined functions, one can create such a data table without any special machinery and with better functionality. Let SAVING(r,n) be the function computed by output cell B213 from input cells B211 and B212 in exactly the same way as above:

G218	A	B	C
210	=DEFINE("savin...	'SAVING	'Future value of $..
211	'r =	0.01	
212	'n =	10	
213	'result =	=100*(1+B211)^B212	
214			

Enter the formula =SAVING($A3,B$2) in B3 and copy it to the area B3:D6, as shown in figure 6.4, left. The relative cell references will be adjusted correctly by the copying, for instance, to =SAVING($A6,D$2) in cell D6. Thus, we achieve the same effect as the Excel data table but now using completely standard formula copying with relative and absolute references.

G9	A	B	C	D	E
1	'Savings table				
2	'r and n	5	10	15	
3	0.01	=SAVING($A3, B$2)	=SAVING($A3, C$2)	=SAVING($A3, D$2)	
4	0.02	=SAVING($A4, B$2)	=SAVING($A4, C$2)	=SAVING($A4, D$2)	
5	0.03	=SAVING($A5, B$2)	=SAVING($A5, C$2)	=SAVING($A5, D$2)	
6	0.04	=SAVING($A6, B$2)	=SAVING($A6, C$2)	=SAVING($A6, D$2)	

G9	A	B	C	D	E
1	Savings table				
2	r and n	5	10	15	
3	0.01	105.10100501	110.46221254112	116.096895537	
4	0.02	110.40808032	121.8994419994...	134.5868338324...	
5	0.03	115.92740743	134.3916379344...	155.7967416600...	
6	0.04	121.66529024	148.0244284918...	180.0943505506...	

Figure 6.4: Data table built in Funcalc using a sheet-defined function. The underlying formulas are shown on the left and the computed results on the right.

Moreover, in the Funcalc approach, further calculations based on the values of computed cells work correctly, both when a data table input depends on a computed value in the same data table and when it depends on a computed value in another data table. This is not the case in Excel (versions 2003 and 2013 at least), whose recalculation mechanism does not handle data tables correctly. First, when an input argument (column or row) of an Excel data table entry depends on some cell of the same data table, the affected dependent cells of the data table are not recalculated at all, not even when recalculation is explicitly requested by pressing F9.

Second, when an input argument (column or row) of one data table depends on the results of *another* data table, Excel's recalculation seems to not work; sometimes changes are not propagated, thus leaving the sheet in an inconsistent state. Recalculating enough times (by pressing F9 repeatedly) does seem to propagate the correct values.

Incidentally, OpenOffice Calc (version 4) does not allow data table inputs to depend on data table results at all, not even between unrelated data tables (there called `Data > Multiple Operations`). Instead an error message is produced.

Independently, Balson and Tyszkiewicz observed that user-defined functions can be simulated by data tables, but their presentation [12] does not mention the shortcomings of Excel's data table implementation described here.

Example 6.27 A curiosity: Array values can be nested to any depth, so Funcalc actually embodies a Lisp (or Scheme) implementation. Namely, we can represent a cons cell as an array with one row and two columns and then define CONS(x, y) in terms of HARRAY, define CAR and CDR in terms of INDEX, and define ATOMP in terms of ISARRAY. See sheet @Lambda in file testsdf.xml.

6.3   What is wrong with VBA functions?

Most spreadsheet programs allow users to define their own functions in some external programming language. For instance, in Excel one can use the VBA language to define functions that are callable from spreadsheets. Indeed VBA is widely used to extend Excel with new functionality and add-ins. Other spreadsheet programs offer such extensibility through other languages, such as Java, Python, or Scheme, and with Excel one can even use functional languages such as Haskell [14, 160] or F# [148].

These are powerful and in some cases elegant programming languages, and they are certainly the right tools in many contexts. However, conceptually and notationally, such "real" programming languages are very different from spreadsheets, and functions in these languages need to be developed using programming environments (such as editors and debuggers) that are unfamiliar to the majority of even experienced spreadsheet users.

Conversely, professional software developers typically lack the domain expertise that experienced spreadsheet users have, and this makes it slow and error-prone for spreadsheet users to rely on external software developers for creating functions and add-ins. Moreover, many professional software developers have a surprisingly limited understanding of spreadsheets and sometimes also little respect for the complexity and utility of the spreadsheet models built by domain experts.

Thus, historically, domain expert spreadsheet users had two options: either develop needed functions themselves in VBA or another external language, thus straddling two different conceptual worlds and very likely introduce errors and inconsistencies, or rely on professional software developers with the attendant loss of control and efficiency. Sheet-defined functions provide a third option: gradually encapsulate spreadsheet models as function definitions, without drastic changes in "programming" concepts and notation, while preserving the ability to adapt and evolve the sheet-defined functions as the real-world domain evolves.

Nardi and Miller [107, 108] show how spreadsheet users, who are often domain experts, collaborate on the gradual development and refinement of spreadsheet models. Our hope is that sheet-defined functions will allow them to collaborate on the development and refinement of domain-specific function libraries too.

Since sheet-defined functions are "live" while being developed, unlike VBA functions and similar, it is likely that mistakes will be discovered during experimentation, even without systematic testing. Moreover, existing proposals for systematic testing of spreadsheet models would immediately benefit sheet-defined functions too [129]. Further work will be required to support the "change control, static type checking, abstraction and reuse" that is "almost completely lacking" [10] from the traditional combination of spreadsheets and external functions written in VBA or C++.

6.4   Why not generate code from ordinary sheets?

This part of the book discusses how to generate code, at run-time, from function definitions. Alternatively, one could compile ordinary spreadsheet formulas to code at run-time for better performance, but we believe that the former approach is better. There are two reasons. First, ordinary sheets, with their mixture of formulas and data, are typically being edited more frequently than function definitions, so that expending too much effort compiling them to high-performance machine code could slow down interaction unacceptably. Second, function definitions (if well structured) should isolate functionality in smaller chunks that are fast to recompile on interactive editing, whereas ordinary sheets can have complex dependencies between many thousands of formulas.

Compilation of a sheet-defined function to efficient code is both simpler and more complicated than compilation of general spreadsheet models. It is simpler because a direction of computation can be assumed, from designated input cells to designated output cells. It is more complicated because evaluation of unneeded cells, which in ordinary sheet evaluation will just slow down computation, can cause nontermination of a sheet-defined function that calls itself recursively. Also, since a sheet-defined function may be invoked thousands or millions of times for each recalculation of the workbook, the memory consumption and allocation speed for constants, cells, and arrays is far more important than for evaluation of an ordinary spreadsheet model.

In the rest of this work, we distinguish function sheets, which are used to define sheet-defined functions, from ordinary sheets, which contain data and ordinary formulas.

A sheet-defined function must be defined on a function sheet and may refer to cells on ordinary sheets and on the function sheet in which it is defined but not to cells on other function sheets. An ordinary sheet can refer only to cells on ordinary sheets, not to cells on function sheets. Apart from these restrictions, function sheets support both ordinary evaluation and creation of sheet-defined functions. Thus, a sheet-defined function can be developed on a function sheet by experimenting with the formulas and various inputs and then turned into a (fast, self-contained) sheet-defined function once it works as required.

The distinction between function sheets and ordinary sheets is not strictly necessary but leads to a clearer semantics and a simpler implementation: If an ordinary sheet could refer to a function sheet cell that is affected by the input to a sheet-defined function, then what value should that reference have? One possible answer is the value most recently put in that cell by the sheet-defined function, but then the value would depend on the recalculation order and introduce an unpleasant element of nondeterminism, and also this decision would constrain the implementation of sheet-defined functions.

Since ordinary sheets are likely to be evaluated only once or a few times per edit performed on the sheets, and a single edit might affect the types of an arbitrary number of cells, we shall refrain from performing type-based optimizations in ordinary sheets. In more detail, the reasoning goes like this:

- In ordinary sheets, only a constant amount of time can be saved per cell per recalculation because each cell is evaluated at most once. (We assume that external wizards like Goal Seek, Solver, Data Table, and so on are replaced by functions operating on sheet-defined functions). In function sheets, the same cells may be evaluated thousands or millions of times per recalculation, and therefore it is more likely to be worthwhile to optimize operations there. Hence, in ordinary sheets, the time savings is limited by the size of the sheet; this is not the case in function sheets. If an ordinary sheet is large, the time savings may be large, but in that case, the time to optimize/recompile the ordinary sheet due to edits is likely to be large as well.

- The distinction between ordinary sheets and function sheets is further motivated by the assumption that function sheets will be more stable than ordinary sheets. Since ordinary sheets contain a mixture of data and computations, they are more likely to be updated due to changes in the data. Of course function sheets are likely to be playgrounds for algorithmic experimentation, but even so, after a period of experiments, the functions are likely to be used unmodified in many different computations for a long time.

- Also, because of the mixture of data and computation in ordinary sheets, they are likely to be much larger than function sheets. Although bytecode generation is quite fast, it would take a noticeable amount of time to regenerate and optimize a sheet with 10 000 non-blank cells, which would be very irritating in an environment that otherwise invites rapid experimentation.

In short, function sheets are likely to be edited less frequently than ordinary sheets, so one can afford spending more time analyzing or optimizing them for each edit. Moreover, such optimization is likely to be more worthwhile because the code generated for a function sheet is likely to be used many times per recalculation, whereas that in an ordinary sheet is not.

Therefore, we evaluate ordinary sheets using the Corecalc interpretive mechanism, with value wrapping and so on, whereas sheet-defined functions on function sheets are compiled to bytecode and evaluated by executing the bytecode, avoiding value wrapping to a large extent. That way, changes to ordinary sheets are fast and their evaluation comparatively slower, whereas changes to sheet-defined functions are relatively slow, but their evaluation is fast. Still the total time to compile a sheet-defined function, such as NORMDISTCDF from example 6.5, seems to be less than 5 ms.

6.5   Related work

Simon Peyton Jones, Alan Blackwell, and Margaret Burnett proposed in a 2003 paper [120] that user-defined functions should be definable as so-called *function sheets* using ordinary spreadsheet formulas. Their goal was to allow "lay" spreadsheet users to define their own functions without forcing them to use a separate programming language such as VBA. Rather, functions should be definable using familiar concepts such as sheets, formulas, references, and so on. To accommodate sheet-defined array functions, a spreadsheet cell should be allowed to contain an entire array. These ideas are the subject also of patent number 4 in appendix B.

Rather similar ideas seem to be incorporated in Nuñez's Scheme-based spreadsheet system ViSSh [113, section 5.2.2], the subject of his 2000 MSc thesis. However, ViSSh generalizes and modifies the spreadsheet paradigm in many other ways and would not appear familiar to most Excel users. Hence, it would possibly fail some of the design goals of Peyton Jones et al.

Wakeling shows [160] how to call the Haskell interpreter Hugs from formulas in Excel. Haskell functions are defined in Excel cell comments, and Haskell expressions are evaluated by enclosing them in quotes and passing them to a function call, as in =Haskell("ack B3 B4", 0). The function definitions and expressions are written to a file and passed to the Haskell interpreter, which runs in a separate process. The communication is likely rather slow, so this is most meaningful for somewhat long-running Haskell functions.

Daniel S. Cortes and Morten W. Hansen in their IT University of Copenhagen MSc thesis [37] set out to further elaborate and implement the concept of sheet-defined functions. Based on Corecalc, they created a series of interpretive prototype implementations of sheet-defined functions supporting array values, higher-order functions, and recursive functions. They demonstrated the utility of these features in application case studies, mostly actuarial computations relevant to the life insurance business. In all cases, sheet-defined functions led to conceptual and practical simplifications, which shows that sheet-defined functions can be added in a natural way to spreadsheet programs while maintaining their familiar look and feel. More details can be found in their thesis [37] and in [137, section 6.1].

Quan Vi Tran and Phong Ha in their MSc thesis [72] investigated whether sheet-defined functions could be implemented using the infrastructure already provided by Microsoft Excel and VBA. They created an add-in for Excel that allowed users to define functions using ordinary Excel sheets and to call them as if they were defined as macros using VBA. However, the implementation was considerably slower than calling VBA functions, most likely due to the complicated means needed to circumvent restrictions in Excel. A more detailed summary in English can be found in [137, section 6.2].

Some other work relevant to the implementation of sheet-defined functions is listed already in section 1.9. In particular, there are patents, papers, and commercial tools for compiling spreadsheets to code in various languages. For instance, Schlafly's patents (numbers 13 and 15 in appendix B) describe the run-time generation of x86 machine code from spreadsheet formulas. The patents were originally assigned to Borland and were presumably used in Borland's QuattroPro spreadsheet. Schlafly's approach exploits the NaN values of the IEEE754 floating-point representation (section 2.8.1) to propagate error codes without any wrapping of run-time values, indeed just what IEEE754 NaNs were originally designed for. It is plausible that a similar run-time code-generation technique and value representation is used in Excel but not in Gnumeric and OpenOffice Calc.

More immediately interesting for the present purposes is Francoeur's work on generating Java code from entire spreadsheet models with designated input and output cells [61].

Several patents and patent applications claim to have invented code generation for various target platforms from such models, including Khosrowshahi and Woloshin's patent (number 8), Rank and Pampuch's patent (number 2), Rubin and Smialek's patents (including number 1), Waldau's patent application (number 7), and Tanenbaum's patent applications (number 5 and 6). They present variants of the same fairly obvious algorithm: compute the transitive closure of the output cells' static dependencies, perform topological sorting, and generate code in dependency order, naming intermediate results in some way. None of the patents or patent applications describes how to deal efficiently with error values or non-strict functions (IF and CHOOSE), although Waldau's patent application stands out as especially comprehensive, describing, for instance, how to implement functions such as INDEX efficiently. We do not use Waldau's method.

There are many commercial tools for turning spreadsheet models into Java programs, web services, mobile applications, and so on. Notable examples are Formula One for Java [124] and SpreadsheetGear for .NET [146]; the lead developer for both is (or was) Joe Erickson. Two other implementations are KDCalc [82] from Knowledge Dynamics Inc. (probably based on Rubin and Smialek's patent number 1) and SpreadsheetConverter by Framtidsforum AB [60] (probably based on Waldau's patent application number 7).

Thomas Iversen's 2006 MSc thesis [84] created a version of Corecalc called Tiny-Calc that would compile ordinary sheets to .NET bytecode [91] at run-time, performing a number of optimizations. The ability to perform run-time code generation for formulas was a Corecalc design goal in 2005 and is one reason for the design of sharable expressions (section 2.9) and for preserving sharing at row or column insertions (sections 2.19 and 2.20). Run-time code generation is expensive in time and memory, and that expense should be sharable among all virtual copies of a formula.

Iversen performed a number of measurements [84], also reported in [137, chapter 5], of full recalculations on some artificial but rather large spreadsheets. They showed that the baseline interpretive Corecalc implementation was faster than Gnumeric and OpenOffice Calc (in their 2006 incarnations) but slower than Microsoft Excel. Moreover, for complex formulas, TinyCalc's run-time code generation could provide considerable speed-ups, often giving recalculation times comparable to those of Microsoft Excel. The main exception was functions that take cell areas or arrays as arguments, where the best results were only half as fast as Excel.

Chapter 7

Compiling Sheet-Defined Functions

7.1 Problem statement

This chapter and the following ones develop and describe Funcalc's implementation of sheet-defined functions. The problem is this: Given a sheet-defined function, defined using standard sheets, cells, and formulas, generate code that will execute the function. The code should be compact (no duplication of operations) and fast (no unnecessary computation), and the computed results should agree with those of the interpretive Corecalc implementation.

Technically, each sheet-defined function will be compiled to CLI or .NET bytecode (section 7.5) to create the body of a so-called DynamicMethod, from which one can obtain a delegate object of type `Func<Value...Value,Value>`, that is, a function that takes as arguments some fixed number of Value objects and returns a Value object. Such a delegate can be invoked efficiently from the interpretive Corecalc implementation.

The general goals of this implementation include:

G1 A cell's formula should be evaluated at most once to preserve efficiency of the spreadsheet model and preserve the semantics of formulas that involve volatile functions such as `RAND` and `NOW`.

G2 A cell's formula should be compiled at most once, and the code should not be duplicated at sites of use to preserve compactness of the implementation.

G3 A cell's formula should be evaluated only if needed by the sheet's output. Otherwise a sheet-defined function cannot safely contain recursive calls.

G4 Constant cells and formulas that depend only on constant cells should be pre-allocated and/or precomputed so that one can use a table of computed values in a sheet-defined function without allocating the table at each invocation of the sheet-defined function. Alternatively, require that such tables are allocated in ordinary sheets, and let the sheet-defined function refer to that sheet (e.g., using the INDEX, VLOOKUP, and HLOOKUP functions). We have chosen the latter approach here. Using an accurate recalculation mechanism, for instance, based on a support graph, the data tables will not be recalculated unless necessary.

We also make some simplifying assumptions:

- Design goal G3 will be ignored until chapter 9.

- A sheet-defined function has a fixed number of arguments. For now, a function can return only one result value; however, this may be an array containing multiple values.

- The formula cells making up a sheet-defined function must have no static cycles. This means that the output cell's dependencies on the input cells can be sorted topologically, and the variables representing the sheet-defined function's cells can be computed in the reverse of that order.

- Sheet-defined functions are stateless. A hypothetical design for stateful sheet-defined function is presented in section 8.8 but has not been implemented.

7.2   Outline of the compilation process

Before diving into the details, here is an outline of the overall compilation process:

1. Starting from the sheet-defined function's output cell, find all cells on the function sheet that it depends on. This is done by computing the transitive closure of the precedents relation (section 3.3.2) from the output cell.

2. Perform a topological sort of those cells starting from the output cell. The result is a list of function sheet cells in which every cell follows all the cells that it depends on.

3. Create a generator object of type TopoListToCGExprList, encapsulating the topologically sorted list of cell addresses.

4. Create a DynamicMethod object (section 7.7) and obtain its ILGenerator to enable generation of local variables to hold the values of cells.

   For each cell whose value is referred more than once, we convert the cell's formula's Expr into a CGExpr (section 7.8) and allocate a local variable for the cell. The result is a program list each of whose elements is a ComputeCell.

   If a cell is used only once, no variable will be allocated for it, but the conversion from Expr to CGExpr will inline the cell's CGExpr where it is used (see section 7.13).

5. If a cell's value is allocated to a local variable (of type Value) and is a number, then allocate another local variable of type `double`, generate code to unwrap the Value as a double, and insert that code right after the cell's computation in the program list (see section 7.9).

6. Traverse the program list from step 4 in forward order and call `Compile()` on each CGExpr to generate CIL code for the body of the sheet-defined function. Then use the DynamicMethod obtained in step 4 to create a Delegate; this is the CLI function generated from the sheet-defined function.

The presentation below does not follow this outline of the compilation process. Instead, it initially describes a simpler but inefficient process and then gradually improves it to avoid value wrapping (section 7.10), to correctly propagate errors from comparisons and conditionals without excess run-time tests (section 7.11), and to avoid duplicate generation of code (section 7.12). Also, some more complex aspects such as how to efficiently call functions from inside a sheet-defined function, and how to safely compile recursive function calls, are dealt with in chapters 8 and 9. Sections 9.2 and 9.3 give a more detailed outline of the compilation process.

7.3   Basic approach to code generation

To see how to compile a sheet-defined function to bytecode, let us consider this slightly contrived example function:

C9	A	B
1		
2	=ABS(A1)	
3	=EXP(-A2*A2/2)	
4	=RAND()*IF(A2>37, 1, 0.3989*A3)	

The input cell is A1 and the output cell is A4. For numeric arguments between -37 and 37, it returns the density of the normal distribution $N(0,1)$ multiplied by a random number, and for numeric arguments outside that range, it returns a random number. The example is constructed to involve floating-point constants, arithmetic operators, mathematical functions, the non-strict function IF nested inside an expression, and the volatile function RAND.

The basic idea is to create a variable v_A2 for each cell A2 to hold the value of that cell. For instance, cell A2, which contains the formula =ABS(A1), will be compiled to a variable definition of the form

```
v_A2 = Math.Abs(v_A1);
```

Similarly, cell A4, containing the formula =RAND()*IF(A2>37, 1, 0.3989*A3), will be compiled to a variable definition of the form

```
v_A4 = rnd.NextDouble() * (v_A2>37 ? 1 : 0.3989 * v_A3);
```

In total, we might get the following code from the sheet-defined function shown above:

```
v_A1 = <input>;                        <-- input cell
v_A2 = Math.Abs(v_A1);
v_A3 = Math.Exp(-v_A2*v_A2/2);
v_A4 = rnd.NextDouble() * (v_A2>37 ? 1 : 0.3989 * v_A3);
return v_A4;
```

This compilation scheme is simple, and the resulting computation model is data driven, or forward, as is usual for spreadsheets. Also, by building the variable definitions backward from the output cell by following static dependencies, one ensures that cells are computed in the correct order and that cells not needed at all will not be computed.

However, more gets computed than what is strictly necessary. For instance, cell A3 above gets computed regardless of whether its value is used by the output cell A4. We will address this problem in much detail in section 7.11.

To make our discussions a little more precise, let us adopt this terminology:

- A static use of a variable is a non-defining occurrence, such as in the right-hand side of an assignment or in a return expression.

- A dynamic use of a variable is the run-time evaluation of a non-defining occurrence.

A variable can be used dynamically at most as many times as it is used statically because no variable definition is evaluated twice. A variable may be used twice statically yet be used only once dynamically, for instance, if it is used statically in different branches of a conditional (... ? v_C2+1 : v_C2+2).

Some improvements of the above compilation scheme suggest themselves:

- If a variable is used statically exactly once, we can inline the variable's expression at its use. For instance, A3 is used only once, and its expression could be inlined in the expression for A4. We shall consider that in section 7.13.

  A variable that is used more than once statically should not be inlined, even if it is used only once dynamically. Such inlining could increase code size exponentially, unless the variable's right-hand side is just a variable or constant.

- We could use register allocation techniques to map several cells to the same generated-program variable, thus reusing local variables. For instance, A2 could be stored in the same variable as A1 because when A2 has been computed, A1 is no longer needed. This is probably not a good idea since such variable reuse may confuse the just-in-time compiler's register allocation, causing it to do a poorer job.

- We could make an effort to compute only what is necessary, respecting dynamic dependencies. For instance, we need to compute A3 above only if `NOT (A2>37)` because only in that case is A3 needed to compute A4. This is considered at length in chapter 9.

7.4   Taking value representation into account

The generated code shown at the beginning of section 7.3 is misleadingly simple:

```
v_A1 = <input>;                        <-- input cell
v_A2 = Math.Abs(v_A1);
v_A3 = Math.Exp(-v_A2*v_A2/2);
v_A4 = rnd.NextDouble() * (v_A2>37 ? 1 : 0.3989 * v_A3);
return v_A4;                           <-- output
```

We have carelessly assumed that all cells contain numbers, but spreadsheets are dynamically typed (section 1.7.7), so the value of a spreadsheet cell may also be a string, an array value, an error, and so on.

Hence, in an interpretive spreadsheet implementation such as Corecalc, all values are wrapped as objects (section 2.8), and computation code needs to be very defensive, with run-time checks, casts, and wrapping.

As a consequence, the innocent-looking computation in the second line above:

```
v_A2 = Math.Abs(v_A1);
```

will actually have to be implemented using rather complex code like this:

```
v_A2 = v_A1 is NumberValue
       ? new NumberValue(Math.Abs((NumberValue)v_A1).value)
       : v_A1 is ErrorValue
       ? v_A1
       : new ErrorValue("ArgTypeError");
```

Namely, the result in A2 will be a number only if A1 evaluates to a number (line 1). Note that in this case the actual number must be extracted from `v_A1` and its absolute value computed and wrapped as a new NumberValue object (line 2). Else if cell A1 evaluates to an error, then that should be the value of A2 as well, to propagate errors correctly (lines 3 and 4). Otherwise, if A1 is any other value, the value of A2 will be an argument type error (line 5).

In total, the naive code above must be replaced with something like this:

```
Value v_A1 = <input>
v_A2 = v_A1 is NumberValue
       ? new NumberValue(Math.Abs((NumberValue)v_A1).value)
       : v_A1 is ErrorValue
       ? v_A1
       : new ErrorValue("ArgTypeError");
```

```
v_A3 = v_A2 is NumberValue
        ? new NumberValue(Math.Exp(- ((NumberValue)v_A2).value
                                      * ((NumberValue)v_A2).value / 2))
        : v_A2 is ErrorValue
        ? v_A2
        : new ErrorValue("ArgTypeError");
v_A4 = v_A2 is NumberValue
        ? (((NumberValue)v_A2).value > 37
            ? new NumberValue(rnd.NextDouble() * 1)
            : (v_A3 is NumberValue
               ? new NumberValue(rnd.NextDouble()
                 * 0.3989 * ((NumberValue)v_A3).value)
               : v_A3 is ErrorValue
               ? v_A3
               : new ErrorValue("ArgTypeError"))
          )
        : v_A2 is ErrorValue
        ? v_A2
        : new ErrorValue("ArgTypeError")
return v_A4;
```

This of course looks cumbersome and slow, and it rather closely emulates what must happen in an interpretive spreadsheet implementation. Moreover, we have even simplified expressions slightly on the fly: in the definition of A3, we test A2 only once and then unwrap and use it twice.

A possible improvement is to introduce extra variables to avoid repeated unwrapping of values. For instance, one could replace the definition of v_A3 with this:

```
n_A2 = v_A2 as NumberValue;
v_A3 = n_A2 != null
        ? new NumberValue(Math.Exp(- (v_A2.value
                                      * (v_A2.value / 2))
        : v_A2 is ErrorValue
        ? v_A2
        : new ErrorValue("ArgTypeError");
```

or even this

```
if (v_A2 is NumberValue) {
  double d_A2 = ((NumberValue)v_A2).value;
  v_A3 = new NumberValue(Math.Exp(-d_A2*d_A2/2));
} else if (v_A2 is ErrorValue) {
  v_A3 = v_A2;
} else
  v_A3 = new ErrorValue("ArgTypeError");
```

Here we have used the convention that a variable named n_A2 is known to hold a NumberValue or null, and a variable named d_A2 is known to hold a `double`. We shall see in section 7.10 how to obtain this effect in general.

An obvious improvement is to avoid wrapping and unwrapping intermediate values where possible. That is to avoid creating a NumberValue object, only to take it apart a moment later. In particular, it is important to avoid the object creation, which involves the memory manager and garbage collector, and therefore is likely to be much slower than arithmetic operations. We consider this in detail in section 7.9.

Another seemingly useful idea is to return an error value as early as possible, when it is known beyond doubt that the function cannot produce a proper result. For instance, if A1 is not a NumberValue, then the function must return an ErrorValue. For this particular sheet-defined function, the converse holds too: If A1 is a number, then the function returns a number.

A hypothetical code sequence for this sheet-defined function might be the following, which almost gets us back to the naive code shown initially:

```
static Value Foo(Value[] input) {
  Value v_A1 = input[0];
  if (v_A1 is NumberValue) {
    double d_A1 = ((NumberValue)v_A1).value;
    double d_A2 = Math.Abs(d_A1);
    double d_A3 = Math.Exp(-d_A2*d_A2/2);
    double d_A4 = rnd.NextDouble() * (d_A2>37 ? 1 : 0.3989 * d_A3);
    return new NumberValue(d_A4);
  } else if (v_A1 is ErrorValue)
    return v_A1;
  else
    return new ErrorValue("ArgTypeError");
}
```

Such a neat result cannot in general be expected for a sheet-defined function that refers to cells in other sheets because every such reference must check whether the result has the correct type.

Also, when a sheet-defined function has multiple output cells, some of the results may be NumberValues and others may be ErrorValues, and hence it is unworkable to return an ErrorValue just because part of the computation leads to errors. So in general, the values of all output cells must be computed, and one cannot return ErrorValue early.

Moreover, some numeric operations and functions produce an ErrorValue even on NumberValue arguments. Consider, for instance, `SQRT(-1)` and `LOG(-1)` that produce NaNs, as well as `EXP(10000)` and `LOG(0)` that produce positive or negative infinities, and `1/0` or `0/0` that report division by zero. In Excel, all of these give an error value.

However, the IEEE floating-point standard saves us at this point because a NaN value can represent an error, and the standard requires arithmetic operations to preserve NaNs, as explained in section 2.8.1. In particular, when the result of an expression is a number or an error, we use variables of type `double` to uniformly represent numbers as well as errors. Only the subsequent run-time conversion of a `double` to a Value will create a NumberValue when d is proper and create an ErrorValue when d is NaN or an infinity.

7.5 Aside: CIL bytecode

In a real implementation of sheet-defined functions, we do not want to generate C# code. We will instead generate bytecode in the Common Intermediate Language (CIL), as used in the Microsoft .NET platform, also known as the Common Language Infrastructure (CLI), and standardized as Ecma Standard 335 [49]. This bytecode offers hardware independence, rather close control over the generated code, and fast compilation to real machine code. Hence, bytecode is a more attractive target for run-time code generation than both C# source code and .NET expression trees.

The run-time state of CLI or .NET consists of a garbage-collected heap for allocated objects, strings, and arrays, and a call stack for each thread (see figure 7.1); here we consider only a single thread. The call stack contains a stack frame for each active method invocation. Each such stack frame contains the values of the method's arguments and local variables, plus a local stack that holds intermediate expression evaluation results.

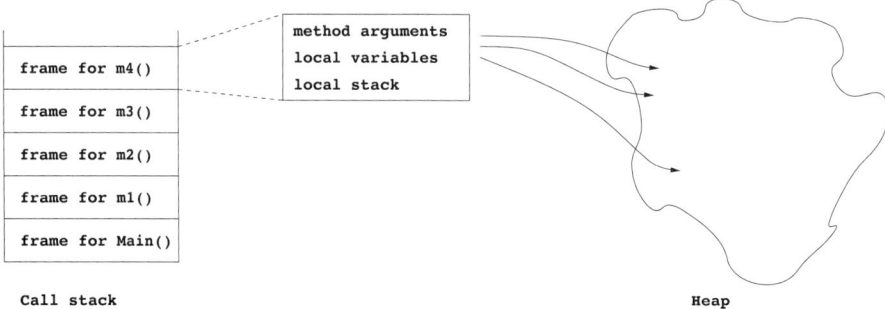

Figure 7.1: Run-time state of the Common Language Infrastructure (CLI). The call stack contains frames for calls to methods `Main`, `m1`, and so on; each frame contains method arguments, local variables, and a local stack; these in turn contain primitive data (such as `int` and `double`) and references to objects in the heap.

A bytecode instruction always executes in the context of some call stack frame. Most bytecode instructions operate on the local stack. For instance, the `add` instruction pops two numbers v_1 and v_2 from the local stack, computes their sum $v_1 + v_2$, and pushes it onto the local stack. Thus, given this local stack, where the stack top is to the right:

    ..., 23, 16

the execution of `add` will pop 23 and 16 from the stack and push their sum 39 to obtain this local stack:

    ..., 39

Other bytecode instructions operate on the frame's method arguments or local variables. For instance, the `ldarg 0` instruction will push the value of the first method argument (number zero) onto the local stack.

Some bytecode instructions operate on the heap. For instance, the `ldfld f` instruction will pop an object reference v from the local stack, retrieve the value of field `f` of object v from the heap, and push that value onto the local stack.

Figure 7.2 lists the bytecode instructions used in the Funcalc code generator.

Name	Effect
add	Pop v_1 and v_2, push $v_1 + v_2$
bgt a	Pop v_1 and v_2, if $v_1 > v_2$ go to code address a
br a	Go to code address a
brfalse a	Pop v, if $v = 0$ go to code address a
brtrue a	Pop v, if $v \neq 0$ go to code address a
call m	Pop $v_0\, v_1 \ldots v_n$, call instance method $v_0\,.\mathrm{m}(v_1 \ldots v_n)$
call m	Pop $v_1 \ldots v_n$, call static method $\mathrm{m}(v_1 \ldots v_n)$
castclass t	Pop v, if v has type t then push (t)v else throw exception
ceq	Pop v_1 and v_2, if $v_1 = v_2$ push true else false
conv.i4 d	Pop v, convert to 32-bit int, push it
conv.r8 d	Pop v, convert to 64-bit double, push it
isinst t	Pop v, if v has type t push true else false
ldarg x	Push argument x
ldc.i4 i	Push integer i
ldc.r8 d	Push double d
ldelem.ref	Pop array a and index i, push $a[i]$
ldfld f	Pop v, push field f of object or struct v
ldloc x	Push local variable x
ldsfld f	Push static field f
ldstr s	Push reference to string s
lt	Pop v_1 and v_2, if $v_1 < v_2$ push true else false
newobj c	Pop $v_1 \ldots v_n$, create object v, call constructor $\mathrm{c}(v_1 \ldots v_n)$, push v
ret	Pop v and return v as method result
stloc x	Pop v and store in local variable x
tail.	Execute subsequent call as tail call if possible

Figure 7.2: Some CIL bytecode instructions. Push and pop operations affect the local stack (see figure 7.1). Further arithmetic instructions `div`, `mul`, and `sub` behave as `add`, and compare-and-jump instructions `beq`, `bge`, and `ble` behave as `bgt`.

The assignment `z = 23.0 + Math.Sin(y) * 2.0` may be compiled to this bytecode, assuming that `y` is local variable number 0 and `z` is local variable 1:

```
ldc.r8 23.0          // load 23.0
ldloc  0             // load from y
call   Math::Sin     // compute sine
ldc.r8 2.0           // load 2.0
mul                  // multiply
add                  // add
stloc  1             // store into z
```

To understand this, note that an infix expression `Sin(y) * 2.0` may be written in postfix notation `y Sin 2.0 *`, where the operator follows its operands: The `Sin` operator is applied to `y`, and the `*` operator is applied to the result of `Sin` and to the constant `2.0`. In fact, the sequence of seven bytecode instructions above simply corresponds to the postfix version `23.0 y Sin 2.0 * +` of the infix arithmetic expression `23.0 + Math.Sin(y) * 2.0`, followed by the assignment to z.

Section 7.7 describes how to generate CIL bytecode at run-time in a C# program. More comprehensive information about the CIL bytecode and the CLI/.NET runtime system can be found in books by Richter [125] and Lidin [91] and in the freely available Ecma CLI Standard 335 [49].

7.6   The bytecode corresponding to the C# code

After the aside describing the CIL bytecode, we now return to the problem of compiling formula expressions into such bytecode rather than C# code as outlined in section 7.4. Fortunately, there is a fairly close correspondence between C# expressions and CIL bytecode.

Unfortunately, there are also some terminological clashes. The 64-bit floating-point type, which is called `double` in C#, is called `float64` in CIL and `binary64` in the IEEE 754-2008 floating-point standard [81], and is denoted R8 on CIL instruction suffixes. We shall use the C# term `double` here despite the CIL code saying `float64`.

Consider this arithmetic expression and assignment:

```
double d_A3 = Math.Exp(-v_A2*v_A2/2);
```

It is executed by loading local variable d_A2 onto the evaluation stack twice, multiplying the two numbers so that the result is on the stack, loading the constant 2.0, dividing, negating, and storing the result in local variable d_A2. The bytecode that performs this task may look like this:

```
ldloc V_2
neg
ldloc V_2
mul
ldc_r8 2.0
div
stloc V_3
```

Here we assume that d_A1 is local variable V_2 and d_A2 is local variable V_3.

A conditional expression such as

```
v_A2>37 ? 1 : 0.3989 * v_A3
```

would compile to bytecode that pushes the comparison's left-hand side and right-hand side, performs the comparison, and jumps to the false branch if the condition is false or else falls through to the true branch:

```
        ldloc V_2
        ldc.r8 37.0
        ble L1
        ldc.r8 1.0
        br L2
    L1: ldc.r8 0.3989
        ldloc V_3
        mul
    L2:
```

A class instance test is compiled to an isinst instruction, and a cast is compiled
to a castclass instruction. The isinst instruction takes an object reference from
the evaluation stack and either succeeds, leaving the reference on the stack, or fails,
leaving a null on the stack. The castclass instruction throws an InvalidCastEx-
ception in case of failure and otherwise leaves the reference on the stack.

Here is the actual CIL code generated from the C# method Foo on page 157.
We used Microsoft's C# compiler csc (with optimization enabled) and then disas-
sembled it with ildasm. The C# variables are mapped to CIL local variables as
follows:

```
    v_A1    class Value V_0
    d_A1    float64 V_1
    d_A2    float64 V_2
    d_A3    float64 V_3
    d_A4    float64 V_4
```

The CIL bytecode, commented with the corresponding source lines, is this:

```
    // Value v_A1 = input[0];
    0000:  ldarg.0
    0001:  ldc.i4.0
    0002:  ldelem.ref
    0003:  stloc.0
    // if (v_A1 is NumberValue) {
    0004:  ldloc.0
    0005:  isinst NumberValue
    000a:  brfalse.s  006a
    // double d_A1 = ((NumberValue)v_A1).value;
    000c:  ldloc.0
    000d:  castclass NumberValue
    0012:  ldfld NumberValue::value
    0017:  stloc.1
    // double d_A2 = Math.Abs(d_A1);
    0018:  ldloc.1
    0019:  call float64 [mscorlib]System.Math::Abs(float64)
    001e:  stloc.2
    // double d_A3 = Math.Exp(-d_A2*d_A2/2);
    001f:  ldloc.2
    0020:  neg
```

```
0021:  ldloc.2
0022:  mul
0023:  ldc.r8 2.
002c:  div
002d:  call Math::Exp
0032:  stloc.3
// double d_A4 = rnd.NextDouble() * (d_A2>37 ? 1 : 0.3989 * d_A3);
0033:  ldsfld rnd
0038:  callvirt Random::NextDouble()
003d:  ldloc.2
003e:  ldc.r8 37.
0047:  bgt.s 0056
0049:  ldc.r8 0.3989
0052:  ldloc.3
0053:  mul
0054:  br.s 005f
0056:  ldc.r8 1.
005f:  mul
0060:  stloc.s V_4
// return new NumberValue(d_A4);
0062:  ldloc.s V_4
0064:  newobj NumberValue::.ctor
0069:  ret
// } else if (v_A1 is ErrorValue)
006a:  ldloc.0
006b:  isinst ErrorValue
0070:  brfalse.s 0074
// return v_A1;
0072:  ldloc.0
0073:  ret
// return new ErrorValue("ArgTypeError");
0074:  ldstr "ArgTypeError"
0079:  newobj ErrorValue::.ctor
007e:  ret
```

Even if somewhat verbose, this should be quite easy to follow, line by line.

7.7   Generating bytecode with a C# program

To generate the bytecode shown above at run-time, one uses classes from the System.Reflection.Emit namespace, which we shall abbreviate SRE. This namespace is not standardized by Ecma Standard 335 [49] but is implemented by Microsoft .NET as well as Mono.

The simplest approach is to create an SRE.DynamicMethod object, obtain an SRE.ILGenerator from it and use that to generate a method body, and then extract a delegate object from the DynamicMethod object. First, we need a delegate type VA2V to describe methods that take as argument a Value and return a Value:

```
public delegate Value VA2V(Value[] arguments);
```

Then we can build, at run-time, such a method

```
static Value Foo(Value[] input) { ... }
```

as follows:

```
DynamicMethod methodBuilder =
    new DynamicMethod("Foo",                                  // Method name
                      typeof(Value),                          // Return type
                      new Type[] { typeof(Value[]) },  // Arg. types
                      typeof(MyClass).Module);                // Module

ILGenerator ilg = methodBuilder.GetILGenerator();
ilg.Emit(...);  // This creates the method's body, see below
VA2V foo = (VA2V)methodBuilder.CreateDelegate(typeof(VA2V));
```

The newly created method can then be called like any other C# delegate, for instance:

```
Value result = foo(new Value[] { new NumberValue(10.0) });
```

The body of the Foo method is built using the `ilg` object, some of whose more important methods are:

Method	Effect
`ilg.Emit(ins)`	Generate bytecode instruction
`ilg.Emit(OpCodes.Call, mth)`	Generate call instruction
`ilg.DeclareLocal(type)`	Declare local variable of the given type
`ilg.DefineLabel()`	Create a new label
`ilg.MarkLabel(lab)`	Put label on next instruction

The SRE.OpCodes class has a static readonly field corresponding to every bytecode instruction that can be used as an argument to `ilg.Emit(...)`.

Hence, to generate the bytecode shown at the end of section 7.6, one might use the following sequence of calls to `ilg` methods. First, generate objects that represent the local variables, program labels, and class fields that will be needed in the generated bytecode:

```
LocalBuilder v_A1 = ilg.DeclareLocal(typeof(Value));
LocalBuilder d_A1 = ilg.DeclareLocal(typeof(double));
LocalBuilder d_A2 = ilg.DeclareLocal(typeof(double));
LocalBuilder d_A3 = ilg.DeclareLocal(typeof(double));
LocalBuilder d_A4 = ilg.DeclareLocal(typeof(double));
Label a1NotNumberLabel = ilg.DefineLabel();
Label a4TrueLabel = ilg.DefineLabel();
Label a4EndLabel = ilg.DefineLabel();
Label a1NotErrorLabel = ilg.DefineLabel();
```

```
FieldInfo numberValueDotValue
  = typeof(NumberValue).GetField("value");
FieldInfo rndField = typeof(MyClass).GetField("rnd");
```

Then use the `ilg.Emit` method to generate the actual bytecode:

```
// Value v_A1 = input[0];
ilg.Emit(OpCodes.Ldarg, 0);
ilg.Emit(OpCodes.Ldc_I4, 0);
ilg.Emit(OpCodes.Ldelem_Ref);
ilg.Emit(OpCodes.Stloc, v_A1);
// if (v_A1 is NumberValue) {
ilg.Emit(OpCodes.Ldloc, v_A1);
ilg.Emit(OpCodes.Isinst, typeof(NumberValue));
ilg.Emit(OpCodes.Brfalse, a1NotNumberLabel);
// double d_A1 = ((NumberValue)v_A1).value;
ilg.Emit(OpCodes.Ldloc, v_A1);
ilg.Emit(OpCodes.Castclass, typeof(NumberValue));
ilg.Emit(OpCodes.Ldfld, numberValueDotValue);
ilg.Emit(OpCodes.Stloc, d_A1);
// double d_A2 = Math.Abs(d_A1);
ilg.Emit(OpCodes.Ldloc, d_A1);
ilg.Emit(OpCodes.Call,
        typeof(System.Math)
        .GetMethod("Abs", new Type[] { typeof(double) }));
ilg.Emit(OpCodes.Stloc, d_A2);
// double d_A3 = Math.Exp(-d_A2*d_A2/2);
ilg.Emit(OpCodes.Ldloc, d_A2);
ilg.Emit(OpCodes.Neg);
ilg.Emit(OpCodes.Ldloc, d_A2);
ilg.Emit(OpCodes.Mul);
ilg.Emit(OpCodes.Ldc_R8, 2.0);
ilg.Emit(OpCodes.Div);
ilg.Emit(OpCodes.Call,
        typeof(System.Math)
        .GetMethod("Exp", new Type[] { typeof(double) }));
ilg.Emit(OpCodes.Stloc, d_A3);
// double d_A4 = rnd.NextDouble() * (d_A2>37 ? 1 : 0.3989 * d_A3);
ilg.Emit(OpCodes.Ldsfld, rndField);
ilg.Emit(OpCodes.Call,
        typeof(System.Random)
        .GetMethod("NextDouble"), new Type[] { });
ilg.Emit(OpCodes.Ldloc, d_A2);
ilg.Emit(OpCodes.Ldc_R8, 37.0);
ilg.Emit(OpCodes.Bgt, a4TrueLabel);
ilg.Emit(OpCodes.Ldc_R8, 0.3989);
ilg.Emit(OpCodes.Ldloc, d_A3);
ilg.Emit(OpCodes.Mul);
ilg.Emit(OpCodes.Br, a4EndLabel);
```

```
ilg.MarkLabel(a4TrueLabel);
ilg.Emit(OpCodes.Ldc_R8, 1.0);
ilg.Emit(OpCodes.Mul);
ilg.MarkLabel(a4EndLabel);
ilg.Emit(OpCodes.Stloc, d_A4);
// return new NumberValue(d_A4);
ilg.Emit(OpCodes.Ldloc, d_A4);
ilg.Emit(OpCodes.Newobj,
         typeof(NumberValue)
         .GetConstructor(new Type[] { typeof(double) }));
ilg.Emit(OpCodes.Ret);
// } else if (v_A1 is ErrorValue)
ilg.MarkLabel(a1NotNumberLabel);
ilg.Emit(OpCodes.Ldloc, v_A1);
ilg.Emit(OpCodes.Isinst, typeof(ErrorValue));
ilg.Emit(OpCodes.Brfalse, a1NotErrorLabel);
// return v_A1;
ilg.Emit(OpCodes.Ldloc, v_A1);
ilg.Emit(OpCodes.Ret);
ilg.MarkLabel(a1NotErrorLabel);
// return new ErrorValue("ArgTypeError");
ilg.Emit(OpCodes.Ldstr, "ArgTypeError");
ilg.Emit(OpCodes.Newobj,
         typeof(ErrorValue)
         .GetConstructor(new Type[] { typeof(string) }));
ilg.Emit(OpCodes.Ret);
```

Of course one would never write a function-specific code generator like this, but it shows how the ILGenerator and other parts of the System.Reflection.Emit namespace can be used. Note in particular how labels are created (`DefineLabel`), used in branch instructions, and associated with code points (`MarkLabel`).

7.8   Translation scheme (with value wrapping)

7.8.1   The net effect principle for `Compile()`

We will adhere to the following *net effect principle* for bytecode generation from a spreadsheet expression using the `Compile()` method:

> Let `e` be a spreadsheet expression and let `ce` be the bytecode generated for `e` by calling `e.Compile()`. Then executing `ce` will leave the value of `e` on the stack top, as reference to a Value object.
>
> The execution can assume that if a cell (such as A8) is needed for the evaluation of *e*, then that cell has been evaluated. The cell's value is available in the local variable that is represented in the code generator as the LocalBuilder object `CellReferences[fca].Var` where `fca` is the full cell address corresponding to cell A8.

The full cell address, of type FullCellAddr, is an absolute reference to a particular cell on a particular (function) sheet.

The code generation for sheet-defined functions is kept separate from the original interpretive Corecalc. There is a new class hierarchy called CGExpr, for code generating expression, which parallels and refines the Expr class hierarchy (see figure 7.3).

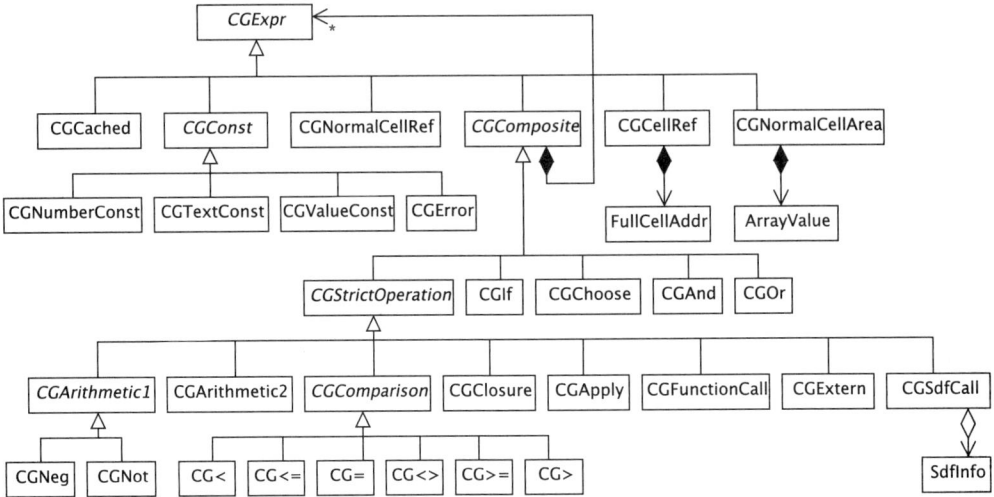

Figure 7.3: Class diagram for Funcalc's code generating expressions. The CGExpr hierarchy is a refinement of the Expr class hierarchy in figure 2.1.

The abstract base class CGExpr further derives from class CodeGenerate, which contains many shared methods for code generation and makes some data available to the code generator:

- The LocalBuilder `testValue` is an auxiliary local variable of type Value. It is used when testing whether a Value is of a particular subclass, such as NumberValue, TextValue, ArrayValue, or FunctionValue.

- The LocalBuilder `testDouble` is an auxiliary local variable of type `double`. It is used when testing whether a number is infinity or a NaN. In our later compilation schemes, the error path of floating-point computations will assume that this variable contains the latest error NaN.

- The ILGenerator `ilg` is the CIL code generator for the method currently being generated.

- Several standard ErrorValue objects are pre-allocated as static fields in class ErrorValue.

- Generated code must be able to refer to the pre-allocated NumberValue objects for 0.0, 1.0, and π. Therefore, class NumberValue has static fields `zeroField` and so on, of type FieldInfo, that reflectively represent these pre-allocated fields. The code generator will use `ilg.Emit` to emit a "load static field" instruction for the required field.

- Similarly, most subclasses of Value (section 2.8), as well as class Function (section 2.14), have public static methods that must be callable from generated code. For this purpose, the code generator obtains the methods' reflective MethodInfo representations and then use `ilg.Emit` to emit a method call to the required method.

Using these resources, we can easily generate code for a cell reference, such as A8:

```
FullCellAddr fca = new FullCellAddr("A8", "Sheet1");
ilg.Emit(OpCodes.Ldloc, CellReferences[fca].Var);
```

Cell references are stored in a dictionary that maps a FullCellAddr to a Variable object, which contains information about the cell:

- The Name of the variable, such as "dA1" or "vB7".

- A LocalBuilder representing the variable at code generation time.

- The type `Typ` of the cell, which is Value, Number, Text, Function, Array, or Error.

7.8.2　Code generation with NaNs

Basic code generation for arithmetic expressions, without wrapping/unwrapping optimizations, could be based on the following principles:

- The code for an arithmetic expression creates a `double` and then wraps this as a Value by calling method `NumberValue.Make` from section 2.8.2 and leaves this value on the stack top. The wrapping produces a NumberValue if the `double` is a number and produces an ErrorValue if the `double` is an infinity or a NaN. Which error value is produced depends on the NaN's payload.

- An arithmetic operation or mathematical function expects its operands to be present on the stack as `double`s, possibly representing errors. So operands are always pre-unwrapped by calling method `Value.ToDoubleOrNan`. This unwrapping may produce a `double` that represents a number or a NaN that represents an error value. In the latter case, the arithmetic operation or mathematical function is guaranteed to preserve the NaN's payload, so the subsequent wrapping of the result as a Value will reconstruct the original ErrorValue, if any.

Following this scheme, code for a CGNumberConst such as 42.1 will push the constant as a `double` and then convert it to a Value by calling `NumberValue.Make`:

```
void Compile() {
  ilg.Emit(OpCodes.Ldc_R8, 42.1);
  ilg.Emit(OpCodes.Call, typeof(NumberValue).GetMethod("Make"));
}
```

Code generation for a CGCellRef reference to a function sheet cell, say, at full cell
address `fca`, simply loads the variable, which has type Value:

```
void Compile() {
  ilg.Emit(OpCodes.Ldloc, CellReferences[fca].Var);
}
```

Code for `e1+e2`, or any other strict two-argument numeric operator, will evaluate `e1`
and unwrap to a `double`, evaluate `e2` and unwrap to a `double`, add the `doubles`,
and wrap the result as a NumberValue:

```
void Compile() {
  e1.Compile();
  ilg.Emit(OpCodes.Call, typeof(Value).GetMethod("ToDoubleOrNan"));
  e2.Compile();
  ilg.Emit(OpCodes.Call, typeof(Value).GetMethod("ToDoubleOrNan"));
  ilg.Emit(OpCodes.Add);
  ilg.Emit(OpCodes.Call, typeof(NumberValue).GetMethod("Make"));
}
```

Similarly, to compile `EXP(e1)` or any other strict function from `double` to `double`,
will evaluate `e1` and unwrap to `double`, call `Math.Exp`, and wrap the result as a
NumberValue:

```
void Compile() {
  e1.Compile();
  ilg.Emit(OpCodes.Call, typeof(Value).GetMethod("ToDoubleOrNan"));
  ilg.Emit(OpCodes.Call,
           typeof(Math)
           .GetMethod("Exp", new Type[] { typeof(double) }));
  ilg.Emit(OpCodes.Call, typeof(NumberValue).GetMethod("Make"));
}
```

Method `Compile` is implemented in the subclasses of CGExpr. Some `Compile()`
methods are identical except for the operator and are therefore shared in a superclass. For instance, addition, subtraction, multiplication, and division only differ
in the bytecode operation (`OpCodes.Add`, `OpCodes.Sub`, etc.) used in the previous
example. Using the template method pattern, we have implemented an abstract
`GetOperation()` method in a common superclass CGArithmetic2, representing all
arithmetic expressions that take two arguments.

The code generated by the above scheme fairly closely reflects what happens in
the interpretative Corecalc implementation, and the bytecode size is only linear in
the expression size but still far from optimal.

Code generation for IF(e1, e2, e3) would have to work along these lines to make sure that if the argument expression e1 evaluates to an error value, then that value is propagated as the result of the entire IF-expression:

```
void Compile() {
  e1.Compile();
  ilg.Emit(OpCodes.Call, typeof(Value).GetMethod("ToDoubleOrNan"));
  ilg.Emit(OpCodes.Stloc, testDouble);
  ilg.Emit(OpCodes.Ldloc, testDouble);
  ilg.Emit(OpCodes.Call, isInfinityMethod);
  Label errorLabel = ilg.DefineLabel();
  ilg.Emit(OpCodes.Brtrue, errorLabel);
  ilg.Emit(OpCodes.Ldloc, testDouble);
  ilg.Emit(OpCodes.Call, isNaNMethod);
  ilg.Emit(OpCodes.Brtrue, errorLabel);
  ilg.Emit(OpCodes.Ldloc, testDouble);
  Label falseLabel = ilg.DefineLabel();
  ilg.Emit(OpCodes.Ldc_R8, 0.0);
  ilg.Emit(OpCodes.Ceq);
  ilg.Emit(OpCodes.Brfalse, falseLabel);
  e2.Compile();
  ilg.Emit(OpCodes.Br, endLabel);
  ilg.MarkLabel(falseLabel);
  e3.Compile();
  ilg.Emit(OpCodes.Br, endLabel);
  ilg.MarkLabel(errorLabel);
  ilg.Emit(OpCodes.Ldloc, testDouble);
  ilg.Emit(OpCodes.Call, typeof(NumberValue).GetMethod("Make"));
  ilg.MarkLabel(endLabel);
}
```

To obtain correct error propagation, it is necessary to test the value of e1 for being infinity or NaN and, if so, create and push an appropriate error value; this is done after the errorLabel. If the value of e1 is a proper number, then if it is non-zero, the code for e2 must be executed, otherwise the code for e3.

Any attempt to optimize the above code by avoiding wrapping and unwrapping must be made with great care. For instance, in IEEE/C#/.NET, the expression $x>0$ is true if x is positive infinity and false if x is NaN, but in no case is it undefined. Hence, implementing IF(x>0, y, z) by the bytecode equivalent of (x>0 ? y : z), without any wrapping, would be wrong: it would not propagate errors from x.

An alternative way to achieve error propagation is to use .NET exceptions. However, this is exceedingly slow compared with floating-point arithmetics. Throwing an exception takes around 10 000 times longer than a 64-bit floating-point addition. Most of this time is spent creating a stack trace in the exception object, which is done when it is thrown, not when it is created (unlike in the Java Virtual Machine). While this overhead can be reduced by some tricks, using NaNs is a far better way to propagate errors within arithmetic code.

The code generation scheme described here is not the one we actually use because it suffers from a number of efficiency problems, which we address in the next section.

7.9   Avoiding intra-formula value wrapping

It would be desirable to improve the bytecode generated by the approach in section 7.8 in at least two respects:

- Avoid wrapping and unwrapping the results of intermediate expressions in a formula. For instance, in (A1+A2)+A3, the floating-point result of (A1+A2) should not be wrapped as a Value only to be immediately tested and unwrapped as a `double`. This is described in section 7.9.1.

- Avoid testing and unwrapping a referred-to cell more than once in a given expression. For instance, in A1+A1+A1+A1, the value of A1 should be unwrapped from a Value to a `double` only once and then be used four times. This is discussed in section 7.9.2.

7.9.1   Code generation without local wrapping

To avoid needless wrapping and unwrapping, two approaches seem feasible:

- Code that needs a `double` asks the code generator for the preceding expression to generate code that delivers a `double`.

- Code that can produce a `double` does it and tells the subsequent code whether it produced a `double` or a general Value.

The latter approach has the drawback that if the subsequent code does not need a `double` but a Value (say, because it computes the value of a cell or the return value of a sheet-defined function), then the subsequent code must wrap the `double`. But the preceding code may just have spent some effort unwrapping the value, in vain, just because it was possible.

Hence, the former approach is preferable: A `double` should be produced only when useful to the consumer, that is, the code following the computation of the value. And only the consumer knows whether it will be useful.

This leads to the following idea: In addition to the `Compile` method, class CGExpr should have an additional method `CompileToDoubleOrNan`, which generates code that leaves a `double` on the stack top. This `double` may represent a proper number or a NaN error value, as in section 2.8.1. The `CompileToDoubleOrNan` method will be called in contexts, such as the operands of the addition operator, that need a `double` operand. In fact, it should be called whenever we would otherwise have a call of the `Compile()` method immediately followed by an unwrapping, that is, by a call to `Value.ToDoubleOrNan`.

The net effect principle for the `CompileToDoubleOrNan` method is:

Let e be a spreadsheet expression and let ce be the bytecode generated by e.CompileToDoubleOrNan(). Then executing ce will leave the
value of e on the stack top, as a double. If the value is a NaN, then the
evaluation of e produced an error and the payload of that NaN explains
which error.

The CompileToDoubleOrNan method should work as follows to generate code for
a numeric constant, such as 42.1:

```
void CompileToDoubleOrNan() {
  ilg.Emit(OpCodes.Ldc_R8, 42.1);
}
```

Code generation for a CGCellRef reference to a function sheet cell, say, at full cell
address fca, loads the variable and unwraps its value:

```
void CompileToDoubleOrNan() {
  ilg.Emit(OpCodes.Ldloc, CellReferences[fca].Var);
  ilg.Emit(OpCodes.Call, typeof(Value).GetMethod("ToDoubleOrNan"));
}
```

To compile e1+e2, or any other strict two-argument numeric operator, to an expression that produces a double:

```
void CompileToDoubleOrNan() {
  e1.CompileToDoubleOrNan();
  e2.CompileToDoubleOrNan();
  ilg.Emit(OpCodes.Add);
}
```

Similarly, generating code for EXP(e1) or any other strict function of from type
double to double:

```
void CompileToDoubleOrNan() {
  e1.CompileToDoubleOrNan();
  ilg.Emit(OpCodes.Call,
           typeof(Math)
           .GetMethod("Exp", new Type[] { typeof(double) }));
}
```

What if e1+e2 or EXP(e1) or another arithmetic operation is used in a context that
expects a Value, not a double? Such compilation is the responsibility of Compile(),
which simply calls CompileToDoubleOrNan to generate code that is then followed
by code that wraps the double in the stack top:

```
void Compile() {
  CompileToDoubleOrNan();
  ilg.Emit(OpCodes.Call, typeof(NumberValue).GetMethod("Make"));
}
```

As explained in section 2.8.2, `NumberValue.Make` turns a proper `double` into a NumberValue instance and turns infinities and NaNs into ErrorValue instances.

The compilation of `IF(e1, e2, e3)` should have a `CompileToDoubleOrNan` variant also for when `IF` is used in a calculation such as `5*IF(A2<>0, 1/A2, A5)`. The main difference from the `Compile` method sketched earlier is that the branches `e2` and `e3` must be compiled with `CompileToDoubleOrNan` because of the double-expecting context. Of course the condition `e1` should be compiled by CompileToDoubleOrNan also to avoid a wrapping and unwrapping.

```
void Compile() {
  e1.CompileToDoubleOrNan();
  ilg.Emit(OpCodes.Stloc, testDouble);
  ilg.Emit(OpCodes.Ldloc, testDouble);
  ilg.Emit(OpCodes.Call, isInfinityMethod);
  Label errorLabel = ilg.DefineLabel();
  ilg.Emit(OpCodes.Brtrue, errorLabel);
  ilg.Emit(OpCodes.Ldloc, testDouble);
  ilg.Emit(OpCodes.Call, isNaNMethod);
  ilg.Emit(OpCodes.Brtrue, errorLabel);
  ilg.Emit(OpCodes.Ldloc, testDouble);
  Label falseLabel = ilg.DefineLabel();
  ilg.Emit(OpCodes.Ldc_R8, 0.0);
  ilg.Emit(OpCodes.Ceq);
  ilg.Emit(OpCodes.Brfalse, falseLabel);
  e2.CompileToDoubleOrNan();
  ilg.Emit(OpCodes.Br, endLabel);
  ilg.MarkLabel(falseLabel);
  e3.CompileToDoubleOrNan();
  ilg.Emit(OpCodes.Br, endLabel);
  ilg.MarkLabel(errorLabel);
  ilg.Emit(OpCodes.Ldloc, testDouble);
  ilg.MarkLabel(endLabel);
}
```

Finally, if `e1` evaluates to a NaN, representing an error, then that should not be converted to an ErrorValue (just before the `endLabel`).

7.9.2 Unwrap variables early

To avoid repeated unwrapping of cells stored as Values, we shall perform two passes. First, we analyze the formulas of the sheet-defined function to find the set of cells that are used as numbers. Basically, this is the set of cells whose reference will be immediately followed by an unwrapping in the generated code. For this purpose, we consider only cells that are used strictly in some cell formula, that is, will be used in any evaluation of that formula. For instance, A2 is used strictly, but A5 is not, in this expression:

```
5*IF(A2<>0, 1/A2, A5)
```

A cell that is used in both branches of a conditional, such as A6 below, is used strictly:

```
IF(RAND()>0.5, A6, A6*10)
```

The second pass then uses the information gathered in the first pass to generate code that tests and unwraps all cells that are used strictly, writing each such cell C to a new local variable `d_C` of type double. If the subsequent code generation need the contents of a cell C as a double, it checks whether the variable `d_C` is available and loads that variable. This way any cell that is used strictly in the expression can be tested and unwrapped once regardless of how often it is used in the expression. Since the cell is used strictly, early unwrapping incurs no loss of efficiency because the cell must be tested and unwrapped during expression evaluation in any case.

Concretely, the first pass builds a dictionary `NumberVariables` that records that a variable of type `double` was allocated for a given cell by mapping the cell's FullCellAddr to the Variable. This is used as follows in `CompileToDoubleOrNan` for a cell reference:

```
public override void CompileToDoubleOrNan() {
  Variable doubleVar;
  if (NumberVariables.TryGetValue(cellAddr, out doubleVar))
    ilg.Emit(OpCodes.Ldloc, doubleVar.Var);
  else {
    Variable var = CellReferences[cellAddr];
    if (var.Type == Typ.Value) {
      ilg.Emit(OpCodes.Ldloc, var.Var);
      UnwrapToDoubleOrNan();
    } else if (var.Type == Typ.Number)
      ilg.Emit(OpCodes.Ldloc, var.Var);
    else
      LoadArgTypeErrorNan();
  }
}
```

If an unwrapped (`double`) variable has been allocated, load that; otherwise, if the variable has type Value, load that and unwrap; if the cell has been declared as type Number (see section 7.10), then load that; otherwise load an error because the variable must be of an incompatible type.

The above scheme means that each unwrapped cell gets to be stored twice, once as a Value object and once as a double. Apart from space consumption, this does not matter because cells are never updated.

The code generation scheme proposed in sections 7.9.1 and 7.9.2 will only avoid intra-formula wrapping and unwrapping, and the generated will therefore look like a somewhat neater version of the (C#) code shown in section 7.4. In particular, it would avoid multiple unwrappings such as `((NumberValue)v_A2).value` seen in the definition of `v_A3` there.

7.10   Avoiding inter-formula wrapping

Section 7.9 showed how to reduce the amount of wrapping and unwrapping performed in the code generated for a single formula. Ideally, one should avoid unnecessary wrapping and unwrapping between formulas. For instance, in our example sheet-defined function, the value of cell A2 is used only in contexts that expect a double. Hence, there is no need to wrap the value of A2 as a NumberValue; it would be better to store it as a double in a variable d_A2 as in the C# code in section 7.4.

There are several ways to achieve this:

A. Perform an inter-cell type analysis. It should discover the possible types of a cell's formula. If a formula's value must be a NumberValue or an ErrorValue, represent it as a `double` and use NaN to represent ErrorValue.

B. Create two CIL local variables for each cell C, one called v_C of type Value and one called d_C of type `double`. When v_C holds a NumberValue, d_C holds the corresponding floating-point value; otherwise it holds a NaN or plus or minus infinity. When a reference to cell C appears in a context that expects a double, d_C is used, otherwise v_C.

The current implementation uses approach A. Option B is simpler to implement because it does not need a type analysis, but it will often perform some useless work and use twice as many local variables as needed.

7.10.1   Types of Funcalc values

Below we describe how the type analysis (A) could be implemented. We assume that the cells of the sheet-defined function have been sorted topologically according to dependencies as described in section 7.2.

First, we need an enumeration to describe the possible types of expressions:

```
enum Typ { Error, Number, Text, Array, Object, Function, Value };
```

The meaning of types, in terms of possible run-time values, is the following:

M[Typ.Error]	=	{ ErrorValue }
M[Typ.Number]	=	{ ErrorValue, NumberValue }
M[Typ.Text]	=	{ ErrorValue, TextValue }
M[Typ.Array]	=	{ ErrorValue, ArrayValue }
M[Typ.Function]	=	{ ErrorValue, FunctionValue }
M[Typ.Object]	=	{ ErrorValue, ObjectValue }
M[Typ.Value]	=	{ ErrorValue, NumberValue, TextValue, ArrayValue, ObjectValue, FunctionValue }

Hence, the subtype ordering is as shown in figure 7.4.

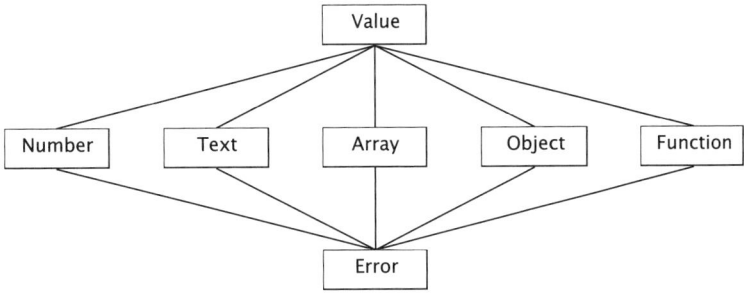

Figure 7.4: Lattice of atomic types.

7.10.2   Using types during compilation

The idea is that the sheet-defined function's input cells will have type Typ.Value, and then we compute the Typ for all other cells in the dependency order as determined by the topological sort.

This type information is then used as follows:

- If a cell gets assigned the type Typ.Number, we store its value in a local variable of type `double`, which holds a proper number to represent an unwrapped NumberValue, or NaN or plus or minus infinity to represent an ErrorValue.

- If a cell gets assigned the type Typ.Text, we store its value in a local variable of type Value, which holds a TextValue or an ErrorValue. Alternatively, we could unwrap to a value of type String, but then we could represent only one error value (using null), and it would not improve efficiency much because String objects are heap-allocated anyway, unlike doubles.

- If a cell gets assigned the type Typ.Array, we store its value in a local variable of type Value, which holds an ArrayValue or an ErrorValue. As for Strings, we forgo the modest efficiency gains that would accrue from representing the array as Value[][] instead.

- When, during subsequent compilation, we refer to a cell ca of type Typ.Number in a context that expects a `double`, we simply load that floating-point number. When referring to it in a context that expects a Value, we wrap the number as a NumberValue. When referring to it in a context that expects a String, we convert the number to a String if it is a proper number, or else to an Error-Value.

- When, during subsequent compilation, we refer to a cell ca of type Typ.Value in a context that expects a double, we generate code to test and then unwrap the number (using method `UnwrapToDoubleOrNaN` in class `CodeGenerate`).

The computation of a cell's type is done by a new method in class Expression:

```
public abstract Typ Type()
```

The implementation maintains a dictionary `CodeGenerate.cellReferences` that maps a cell address to a Variable object. This object contains the cell's type as well as its LocalBuilder for use during code generation.

The type of a NumberConst is Typ.Number:

```
public Typ Type{} {
   return Typ.Number;
}
```

The type of a TextConst is Typ.Text:

```
public Typ Type{} {
   return Typ.Text;
}
```

The type of a cell reference to `cellAddr` is found in the `CellReferences` dictionary (due to the topological sorting the `CellReferences[cellAddr]` entry has been defined already):

```
public override Typ Type() {
   return CellReferences[cellAddr].Type;
}
```

The type of an addition or any other arithmetic function is Typ.Number. The type of a string function is Typ.Text. In general, types are computed from inputs to outputs, treating the different CGExpr constructs as needed. For instance, `IF(e1, e2, e3)` should be treated like this:

```
public Typ Type() {
   return Lub(e2.Type(), e3.Type());
}
```

Here, `Lub` is a static method that computes the least upper bound of two Typ values in the ordering shown in figure 7.4:

```
public static Lub(Typ t1, Typ t2) {
  if (t1==t2)
    return t1;
  else
    switch (t1) {
    case Typ.Error:
      return t2;
    case Typ.Number: case Typ.Text:
    case Type.Array: case Type.Function:
      return t2==Typ.Error ? t1 : Typ.Value;
    case Typ.Value:
      return Typ.Value;
    default:
      throw new ImpossibleException("Lub(Typ, Typ)");
    }
}
```

This means that if one branch of an IF has type Typ.Number and the other has type Typ.Text, then the whole IF-expression has type Typ.Value, namely, the least upper bound of Typ.Number and Typ.Text.

7.11   Compilation of comparisons and conditions

7.11.1   Compilation of comparisons

As explained in section 7.8.2, care must be taken to obtain proper Excel semantics of comparisons e1<e2 and conditionals IF(e1<e2, ...) in the presence of improper numbers such as infinities and NaNs. An error arising during the evaluation of e1 or e2 must be propagated as the result of the comparison e1<e2 and as the result of the entire conditional IF(e1<e2, ...). This can be done by introducing in CGExpr a method

```
void CompileToDoubleProper(Gen ifProper, Gen ifOther)
```

that generates code that tests for NaN and infinities and continues with the code generated by ifOther if one of those values are encountered, or else it continues with the code generated by ifProper.

For now, Gen is just a delegate type for encapsulating a statement block:

```
public delegate void Gen()
```

One can think of the arguments ifProper and ifOther as code generators that may or may not be invoked by CompileToDoubleProper. In all cases, they will be generators of code that represent possible continuations of the current expression being compiled.

In general, this method could be implemented by compiling to a double and testing for the result being proper, like this:

```
void CompileToDoubleProper(Gen ifProper, Gen ifOther) {
  CompileToDoubleOrNan();
  Label otherLabel = ilg.DefineLabel();
  ilg.Emit(OpCodes.Stloc, testDouble);
  ilg.Emit(OpCodes.Ldloc, testDouble);
  ilg.Emit(OpCodes.Call, isInfinityMethod);
  ilg.Emit(OpCodes.Brtrue, otherLabel);
  ilg.Emit(OpCodes.Ldloc, testDouble);
  ilg.Emit(OpCodes.Call, isNaNMethod);
  ilg.Emit(OpCodes.Brtrue, otherLabel);
  ilg.Emit(OpCodes.Ldloc, testDouble);
  ifProper();
  Label endLabel = ilg.DefineLabel();
  ilg.Emit(OpCodes.Br, endLabel);
  ifOther();
  ilg.MarkLabel(endLabel);
}
```

Note the use of a temporary local variable `testDouble` instead of duplicating a value that would subsequently need to be popped. The advantage of this approach is that multiple occurrences of `ifOther()` should be representable by one piece of code, and we should be able to avoid some code duplication and some jumps to jumps. A single such intermediate variable suffices because no other code intervenes between its definition and its last use.

For a number constant, the test for infinities and NaN can be performed at compile-time, so the generated code will be simpler:

```
void CompileToDoubleProper(Gen ifProper, Gen ifOther) {
  if (double.IsInfinity(number.value) || double.IsNaN(number.value)){
    ilg.Emit(OpCodes.Ldc_R8, number.value);
    ilg.Emit(OpCodes.Stloc, testDouble);
    ifOther();
  } else {
    ilg.Emit(OpCodes.Ldc_R8, number.value);
    ifProper();
  }
}
```

In the code generated by first (failure) branch, the constant is stored into variable `testDouble` so that the `ifOther` code can retrieve and analyze it.

The `CompileToDoubleProper` methods may be used as follows in the compilation of a comparison operation such as `e1 < e2` to make it error-preserving:

```
void CompileToDoubleProper(Gen ifProper, Gen ifOther) {
  e1.CompileToDoubleProper(
    delegate {
      e2.CompileToDoubleProper(
        delegate {
```

```
            ilg.Emit(OpCodes.Lt);
            ilg.Emit(OpCodes.Conv_R8);
            ifProper();
          },
          delegate {
            ilg.Emit(OpCodes.Pop);
            ifOther();
          });
      },
      ifOther());
  }
```

By contrast, arithmetic operators and functions such as (*), (+), Math.Sin, and so on, which are already error-preserving thanks to IEEE floating-point semantics, can be compiled using the simpler approach in CompileToDoubleOrNan as shown in section 7.9.1.

7.11.2   Compilation of conditions

Compilation of conditions should be performed by a special method in each AST class. This way one can avoid the repeated comparisons with zero and obtain better code for composite logic expressions involving NOT, AND, and OR. For instance, for AND(e1,e2), one can distinguish between the context 10+AND(e1,e2) and the context IF(AND(e1,e2),11,22) and generate code for the former case that pushes 1.0 or 0.0 on the stack, whereas in the latter case, it pushes 11.0 or 22.0 without first pushing and testing 1.0 or 0.0.

```
    void CompileCondition(Gen ifTrue, Gen ifFalse, Gen ifOther)
```

In general, this method can be implemented in terms of CompileToDoubleProper as follows:

```
    void CompileCondition(Gen ifTrue, Gen ifFalse, Gen ifOther) {
      CompileToDoubleProper(
        delegate {
          Label falseLabel = ilg.DefineLabel();
          ilg.Emit(OpCodes.Ldc_R8, 0.0);
          ilg.Emit(OpCodes.Ceq);
          ilg.Emit(OpCodes.Brfalse, falseLabel);
          ifTrue();
          Label endLabel = ilg.DefineLabel();
          ilg.Emit(OpCodes.Br, endLabel);
          ilg.MarkLabel(falseLabel);
          ifFalse();
          ilg.MarkLabel(endLabel);
        },
        ifOther);
    }
```

This would be the default version, used for general arithmetic operations, for cell references where the `CompileToDoubleProper` method takes care of determining whether the referred-to cell needs unboxing, and so on.

But for most abstract syntax nodes, better code can be generated. In the case of a number constant `CGNumberConst(value)`, one can decide the test statically:

```
void CompileCondition(Gen ifTrue, Gen ifFalse, Gen ifOther) {
  if (Double.IsInfinity(value) || Double.IsNaN(value)) {
    ilg.Emit(OpCodes.Ldc_R8, number.value);
    ilg.Emit(OpCodes.Stloc, testDouble);
    ifOther();
  } else if (value != 0)
    ifTrue();
  else
    ifFalse();
}
```

Again, the failure branch generates code to load the offending number into the `testDouble` local variable for subsequent use by the `ifOther` code.

In the case of the unary logical operator `NOT(e0)`, one simply swaps the `ifTrue` and `ifFalse` delegates:

```
void CompileCondition(Gen ifTrue, Gen ifFalse, Gen ifOther) {
  es[0].CompileCondition(ifFalse, ifTrue, ifOther);
}
```

You may say that nobody in his right mind writes `IF(NOT(e1),e2,e3)`, but first, there may be reasons to do so, and second, the above code also optimizes `AND(e1, NOT(e2), e3)` and `OR(e1, NOT(e2), e3)` which is more plausible. Finally, such code is very likely generated by the evaluation condition generator presented in chapter 9.

In the case of a two-argument logical operator `AND(e0,e1)`, one could chain the delegates as follows to obtain short-circuit evaluation (as in C, Java, and C# but actually not Excel):

```
void CompileCondition(Gen ifTrue, Gen ifFalse, Gen ifOther) {
  es[0].CompileCondition(
    delegate {
      es[1].CompileCondition(ifTrue, ifFalse, ifOther);
    },
    ifFalse,
    ifOther);
  }
}
```

so in `AND(e0,e1)`, the code generated by `ifTrue` gets executed only if both `e0` and `e1` evaluate to a proper and non-zero `double`.

To obtain the actual Excel semantics, in which `AND(e0,e1)` is strict in both its arguments and evaluates to an error when `e1` does even if `e0` is false, we should evaluate e1 and test it for being proper also in the false branch of e0. It could be done like this (but it is not the approach we are taking):

```
void CompileToDoubleProper(Gen ifProper, Gen ifOther) {
  es[0].CompileToDoubleProper(
    delegate {
      ilg.Emit(OpCodes.Ldc_R8, 0.0);
      ilg.Emit(OpCodes.Ceq);
      es[1].CompileToDoubleProper(
      delegate {
        ilg.Emit(OpCodes.Ldc_R8, 0.0);
        ilg.Emit(OpCodes.Ceq);
        ilg.Emit(OpCodes.Or);
        ilg.Emit(OpCodes.Ldc_I4, 0);
        ilg.Emit(OpCodes.Ceq);
        ilg.Emit(OpCodes.Conv_R8);
        ifProper.Gen(ilg);
      },
      ifOther)
    },
    ifOther);
}
```

Actually, the above evaluates AND(e0,e1) as NOT(OR(NOT(e0),NOT(e1))) using de Morgan's laws, using IL instruction Ceq to compare a double for being zero (resulting in an integer on the stack), and using And to form the bitwise "and" of two integers. The CIL instruction set does not allow bitwise logical operations on doubles and does not have an instruction that pushes integer 1 when a double is non-zero.

Our implementation actually supports AND(e1,...,en) with arbitrary arity $n \geq 0$. Code generation for short-circuit evaluation can be implemented elegantly by compiling the conjuncts e1,...,en backward to build up ifTrue code generation continuation:

```
void CompileCondition(Gen ifTrue, Gen ifFalse, Gen ifOther) {
  for (int i = es.Length - 1; i >= 0; i--)
    ifTrue = delegate { es[i].CompileCondition(ifTrue, ifFalse,
                                               ifOther); };
  ifTrue();
}
```

The above code generation scheme builds up a code generator backward to achieve the following effects:

- If $n = 0$, then the code generated by the original ifTrue is executed unconditionally. This reflects that if $n = 0$, then AND() must evaluate to true.

- If $n > 0$, then code is generated to evaluate and test e1; if true, execution continues with code generated as if for AND(e2,...,en); if false, then execution continues with the code generated by `ifFalse`; and if error, with `ifOther`. This reflects that if $n > 0$, then `AND(e1,e2,...,en)` has the same meaning as `AND(e1,AND(e2,...,en))`.

Also note that if some conjunct `ei` is constant false, then no code is generated for the subsequent conjuncts `e(i+1),...,en` because the AND-expression cannot be true; the `ifTrue` code continuation of `ei` is ignored by

    ei.CompileCondition(ifTrue,ifFalse,ifOther)

However, code for the preceding conjuncts `e1,...,e(i-1)` will—and must—be generated, for if one of those evaluate to an error, then so must the AND-expression. If some conjunct `ei` is constant true, then no code is generated for it because only the `ifTrue` code continuation will be used by the `ei.CompileCondition` call.

   However, the otherwise elegant loop above does not quite work. When a delegate or anonymous method in C# refers to an outside variable such as `i`, it captures the lvalue (the variable `i` itself), not the rvalue (the variable's current value, such as 3). As a consequence, when the call `ifTrue()` is performed after the loop, the value of `i` is −1, so the indexing `es[i]` throws an IndexOutOfRangeException. Even disregarding this problem, the generated code would not work because the occurrence of `ifTrue` inside the delegate refers to the final value of `ifTrue`; so if `es[i]` happens to evaluate to true, then the code goes into an infinite loop.

   To capture the rvalues of `i` and `ifTrue`, one may introduce local loop body variables `ie` and `localIfTrue` like this:

```
void CompileCondition(Gen ifTrue, Gen ifFalse, Gen ifOther) {
  for (int i = es.Length - 1; i >= 0; i--) {
    CGExpr ei = es[i];
    Gen localIfTrue = ifTrue;
    ifTrue = delegate { ei.CompileCondition(localIfTrue, ifFalse,
                                            ifOther); });
  }
  ifTrue();
}
```

Note that all arguments `ei` have the same `ifFalse` and `ifOther` code generators.

   To compile a disjunction `OR(e1,...,en)` of arbitrary arity $n \geq 0$ with short-circuit evaluation, we use exactly the same code generation scheme, but we update the `ifFalse` code generator instead of the `ifTrue` code generator:

```
void CompileCondition(Gen ifTrue, Gen ifFalse, Gen ifOther) {
  for (int i = es.Length - 1; i >= 0; i--) {
    CGExpr ei = es[i];
    Gen localIfFalse = ifFalse;
    ifFalse = delegate { ei.CompileCondition(ifTrue, localIfFalse,
                                             ifOther); };
  }
  ifFalse();
}
```

All the subexpressions of OR have the same ifTrue and ifOther code generators. Again one might consider a more Excel-like semantics, without short-circuit evaluation, but we shall not do that here.

The code for a comparison e0<e1 (and similarly for =, <>, <=, >=, <, and >) must evaluate the two subexpressions, check that both are proper (and, failing that, use ifOther), and then test whether the stated relation between them holds (ifTrue) or not (ifFalse).

```
void CompileCondition(Gen ifTrue, Gen ifFalse, Gen ifOther) {
  es[0].CompileToDoubleProper(
    delegate {
      es[1].CompileToDoubleProper(
        delegate {
          Label falseLabel = ilg.DefineLabel();
          ilg.Emit(OpCodes.Lt);     // Or other comparison
          ilg.Emit(OpCodes.Brfalse, falseLabel);
          ifTrue();
          Label endLabel = ilg.DefineLabel();
          ilg.Emit(OpCodes.Br, endLabel);
          ilg.MarkLabel(falseLabel);
          ifFalse();
          ilg.MarkLabel(endLabel);
        },
        delegate {
          ilg.Emit(OpCodes.Pop);
          ifOther();
        });
    },
    ifOther);
}
```

This way, if any of the operands is a non-number or a non-proper number, the code generated by ifOther() will be executed. Only if both operands are proper numbers, the comparison will be performed and the result tested.

Note: Here we have focused on numerical comparisons. In general, these comparison operators should also work on TextValue and perhaps other values, using the type analysis to help generate efficient code when it is known statically that the operands are NumberValues. This is not currently implemented.

7.11.3 Compilation of conditional expressions

Using the `CompileCondition` method, the various compilation methods for `IF(e0, e1, e2)` can be implemented as shown here.

To compile `IF(e0, e1, e2)` in a context that expects a Value, we use `Compile`:

```
void Compile() {
  es[0].CompileCondition(
    delegate { es[1].Compile(); },
    delegate { es[2].Compile(); },
    delegate {
      ilg.Emit(OpCodes.Ldloc, testDouble);
      WrapDoubleToNumberValue();
    });
}
```

To compile `IF(e0, e1, e2)` in a context that expects a result of type `double`, such as `10*IF(e0, e1, e2)`:

```
void CompileToDoubleOrNan() {
  es[0].CompileCondition(
    delegate { es[1].CompileToDoubleOrNan(); },
    delegate { es[2].CompileToDoubleOrNan(); },
    delegate { ilg.Emit(OpCodes.Ldloc, testDouble); }
  );
}
```

To compile `IF(e0, e1, e2)` in a context that expects a proper `double`, such as `IF(e0, e1, e2) > 50`:

```
void CompileToDoubleProper(Gen ifProper, Gen ifOther) {
  es[0].CompileCondition(
    delegate { es[1].CompileToDoubleProper(ifProper, ifOther); },
    delegate { es[2].CompileToDoubleProper(ifProper, ifOther); },
    ifOther);
}
```

To compile `IF(...)` in a context where it is used as a condition, such as the inner `IF` in `IF(IF(e00, e01, e02), e1, e2)`:

```
void CompileCondition(Gen ifTrue, Gen ifFalse, Gen ifOther) {
  es[0].CompileCondition(
    delegate { es[1].CompileCondition(ifTrue, ifFalse, ifOther); },
    delegate { es[2].CompileCondition(ifTrue, ifFalse, ifOther); },
    ifOther);
}
```

Due to the duplication of the code generation continuations `ifTrue`, `ifFalse`, and `ifProper`, the latter case basically gets compiled as `IF(e00, IF(e01, e1, e2)`,

IF(e02, e1, e2)). This may expose some optimization opportunities when e01 or e02 are constants or comparison operations.

It may also cause code duplication unless the techniques shown in section 7.12 are used. If those techniques generate good enough code, we could simply treat AND(e1, e2) as shorthand for IF(e1, e2, FALSE) and treat OR(e1, e2) as shorthand for IF(e1, TRUE, e2), thus avoiding some special cases in the code generation. We shall not do that, though.

There is still room for improving the code generated for a nested IF-expression IF(e11,e12,IF(e21,e22,IF(e31,e32,e33))). Namely, if the conditions e11, e21, e31, ... are comparisons a11<b11 and so on, then their "other" branches for compiling ai1 to a proper double could be shared, and similarly for all the bi1. But currently each gets its own identical code continuation, which creates some jumps to jumps, but no code duplication.

7.12   Avoiding duplicate generation of code

The code generation schemes shown above may call each code generation function, such as ifOther, multiple times, and hence generate multiple copies of functionally identical bytecode. This is undesirable and can be avoided by wrapping each code generation action inside a caching object. The first time the cache is asked to generate the code, it labels and generates it; any subsequent request for code generation simply generates a jump to that label. The cache can also return the label (for use in conditional jumps to the generated code) and can be queried whether the code has already been generated (this sometimes can avoid generating a superfluous jump around it).

The design described above is our third attempt at designing such a code generation cache while also to some extent avoiding the generation of dead code and of jumps to jumps. The first two attempts failed in this respect because they did not integrate the label generation and the label marking with the cache, and hence were difficult to use correctly in the compilation functions. Also, they required the compilation functions to test prematurely for the code being generated (namely, when the label was created), which led to many unnecessary jumps to jumps.

How much sharing of generated code is actually permissible? Clearly, it would be wrong to share, by address, code copies that should have appeared in different contexts; that is, with different continuations. But so far all our compilation functions have a simple property: every code fragment generated by a delegate argument appears in tail position. That is, the actions performed by the code generated by the delegate are the last actions performed by the code generated by the compilation function, except possibly for jumps that brings the flow of control to the end of the generated code. From this observation, it follows that all copies of generated code would have the same continuation.

Another view of this continuation argument follows. One could pass program labels instead of code generation functions, effectively representing each continuation by its label. That would have the advantage of being more transparent, and the code block sharing would be more obviously correct. However, it also has the disadvantage of introducing a jump to code where none is needed, namely, where the code could simply be generated in-line as in the current compilation functions. Also, it would become more complicated to avoid generating code that is not needed, such as the infinity/NaN test in a comparison that involves a constant.

In the final design, the cache for a code generator has three states, with state 1 being the initial one:

1. Code created but not yet labeled (`label == null`)

2. Code labeled but not yet generated (`label != null && !generated`)

3. Code generated (`label != null && generated`)

The comments refer to the states of the actual implementation in the class Gen:

```
class Gen {
  private readonly Action generate;
  private Label? label;
  private bool generated;  // Invariant: generated==>label.HasValue
  public Gen(Action generate) {
    this.generate = generate;
    label = null;
    generated = false;
  }
  public Label GetLabel(ILGenerator ilg) {
    if (!label.HasValue)
      label = ilg.DefineLabel();
    return label.Value;
  }
  public bool Gend { get { return generated; } }
  public void Gen(ILGenerator ilg) {
    if (generated)
      ilg.Emit(OpCodes.Br, GetLabel(ilg));
    else {
      ilg.MarkLabel(GetLabel(ilg));
      generated = true;
      generate();
    }
  }
}
```

If ever `Gen(ilg)` is invoked, then the `label` will be defined and marked in the bytecode. Thanks to the flag called `generated`, this happens at most once, and likewise the inner `generate()` delegate will be called at most once. Note that if `Gen(ilg)` is called before the first call to `GetLabel(ilg)`, then a fresh label will be created, to be returned by any future calls to `GetLabel`.

Even if, in some strange circumstances, the execution of the `generate()` delegate would cause further recursive calls to `Gen(ilg)`, such recursive calls would simply generate jumps to the beginning of the code currently being generated.

Class Gen could be used as follows in the general version of CompileCondition:

```
void CompileCondition(Gen ifTrue, Gen ifFalse, Gen ifOther) {
  CompileToDoubleProper(
    new Gen(delegate {
      ilg.Emit(OpCodes.Ldc_R8, 0.0);
      ilg.Emit(OpCodes.Beq, ifFalse.GetLabel(ilg));
      ifTrue.Gen(ilg);
      if (!ifFalse.Generated) {
        Label endLabel = ilg.DefineLabel();
        ilg.Emit(OpCodes.Br, endLabel);
        ifFalse.Gen(ilg);
        ilg.MarkLabel(endLabel);
      }
    }),
    ifOther);
}
```

If ifFalse.Generated is true, then definitely the falseLabel has been marked—
either prior to the ifFalse.GetLabel call or as a side effect of the ifTrue.Gen
call. If ifFalse.Generated is false, the label belonging to ifFalse will next be
marked as a consequence of the call ifFalse.Gen.

Here is how class Gen is used within the general CompileToDoubleProper
method:

```
void CompileToDoubleProper(Gen ifProper, Gen ifOther) {
  CompileToDoubleOrNan();
  ilg.Emit(OpCodes.Stloc, testDouble);
  ilg.Emit(OpCodes.Ldloc, testDouble);
  ilg.EmitCall(OpCodes.Call, isInfinityMethod, null);
  ilg.Emit(OpCodes.Brtrue, ifOther.GetLabel(ilg));
  ilg.Emit(OpCodes.Ldloc, testDouble);
  ilg.EmitCall(OpCodes.Call, isNaNMethod, null);
  ilg.Emit(OpCodes.Brtrue, ifOther.GetLabel(ilg));
  ilg.Emit(OpCodes.Ldloc, testDouble);
  ifProper.Gen(ilg);
  if (!ifOther.Generated) {
    Label endLabel = ilg.DefineLabel();
    ilg.Emit(OpCodes.Br, endLabel);
    ifOther.Gen(ilg);
    ilg.MarkLabel(endLabel);
  }
}
```

The current code generation scheme occasionally generates unreachable bytecode
instructions (typically an unconditional jump preceded by an unconditional jump).
While a little inelegant, this is explicitly permitted by the CLI standard [49, section
III.1.7.1]. We suspect the unreachable code is due to, say, ifProper.Gen(ilg)

above generating an unconditional jump because `ifProper` has already been generated, and then, because `ifOther` has not yet been generated, an unreachable jump to `endLabel` will be generated. The code generation scheme also generates a few jumps to jumps. Both could possibly be avoided by further complicating the Gen class and the code that uses it. For instance, the call `ifProper.Gen(ilg)` above may tell whether it generated an unconditional jump, and in that case, we can avoid generating the jump to `endLabel` and then avoid generating `endLabel` at all.

To see the effect of the various code generation functions from sections 7.9 to 7.11 and of the Gen class above, let us compare the code generated within different contexts for a logical expression involving comparisons. In the first case, the truth value should be produced as the number 1.0 or 0.0:

```
=AND(A1<0.001, 5>B1*C1)
```

In the second case, the truth value will be used in a conditional and should not be generated on the stack:

```
=10*IF(AND(A1<0.001, 5>B1*C1), 11, 22)
```

In both cases, A1, B1, and C1 are input cells, and the formula shown is that of the output cell.

First, consider `AND(A1<0.001, 5>B1*C1)`. The entire formula is compiled by `Compile`, which invokes `CompileCondition` with an `ifTrue` continuation that pushes `NumberValue.ONE`, an `ifFalse` continuation that pushes `ZERO`, and an `ifOther` continuation that pushes an `ErrorValue` based on `testDouble`.

The `CompileCondition` method in turn invokes `CompileCondition` on the conjuncts `A1<0.001` and `5>B1*C1`, which then invokes `CompileToDoubleProper` on the operands (A1, 0.001, 5, B1*C1) of the comparisons. This method invokes `CompileToDoubleOrNan` to compile the subexpressions and then issues the `IsNaN` and `IsInfinity` tests on A1 and on the product `B1*C1` but not on the constants `0.001` and `5`. Note that if `B1*C1` is not proper, then the left operand (5) will be popped from the stack by instruction 009d.

Thanks to the Gen machinery, the `ifFalse` continuation at instruction 0093 is shared between the two conjuncts of `AND(...)`, witness the conditional branch instructions at 004f and 0084. Also, the outer `ifOther` continuation at 009e is shared, in the sense that the `ifOther` continuation of `5>B1*C1` consists of the `pop` instruction at 009d with a fall-through to the outer `ifOther` continuation at 009e. This fall-through is a consequence of the test `!ifOther.Generated` in the general `CompileToDoubleProper` method shown above.

```
0000: ldarg.0          002f: ldloc.0          006e: call IsInfinity
0001: ldc.i4 0         0030: call IsInfinity  0073: brtrue 009d
0006: ldelem Value     0035: brtrue 009e      0078: ldloc.0
000b: stloc.3          003a: ldloc.0          0079: call Double.IsNaN
000c: ldarg.0          003b: call IsNaN       007e: brtrue 009d
000d: ldc.i4 1         0040: brtrue 009e      0083: ldloc.0
0012: ldelem Value     0045: ldloc.0          0084: ble 0093
0017: stloc.s V_4      0046: ldc.r8 0.001     0089: ldsfld NumberValue.ONE
0019: ldarg.0          004f: bge 0093         008e: br 0098
001a: ldc.i4 2         0054: ldc.r8 5         0093: ldsfld NumberValue.ZERO
001f: ldelem Value     005d: ldloc.s V_4      0098: br 00a4
0024: stloc.s V_5      005f: call ToDoubleOrNan 009d: pop
0026: ldloc.3          0064: ldloc.s V_5      009e: ldloc.0
0027: call ToDoubleOrNan 0066: call ToDoubleOrNan 009f: call NumberValue.Make
002c: stloc.2          006b: mul              00a4: ret
002d: ldloc.2          006c: stloc.0
002e: stloc.0          006d: ldloc.0
```

Next consider =10*IF(AND(A1<0.001, 5>B1*C1), 11, 22). The entire expression is compiled by method Compile, which invokes CompileToDoubleOrNan on the IF(...) expression. Method CompileToDoubleOrNan is invoked on the expression AND(...) with an ifTrue continuation that pushes 11.0 as a double, an ifFalse continuation that pushes 22.0 as a double, and an ifOther continuation that pushes testDouble.

```
0000: ldarg.0          0037: stloc.0          0076: ldloc.0
0001: ldc.i4 0         0038: ldloc.0          0077: call IsInfinity
0006: ldelem Value     0039: call IsInfinity  007c: brtrue 00ae
000b: stloc.3          003e: brtrue 00af      0081: ldloc.0
000c: ldarg.0          0043: ldloc.0          0082: call IsNaN
000d: ldc.i4 1         0044: call IsNaN       0087: brtrue 00ae
0012: ldelem Value     0049: brtrue 00af      008c: ldloc.0
0017: stloc.s V_4      004e: ldloc.0          008d: ble 00a0
0019: ldarg.0          004f: ldc.r8 0.001     0092: ldc.r8 11
001a: ldc.i4 2         0058: bge 00a0         009b: br 00a9
001f: ldelem Value     005d: ldc.r8 5         00a0: ldc.r8 22
0024: stloc.s V_5      0066: ldloc.s V_4      00a9: br 00b0
0026: ldloc.3          0068: call ToDoubleOrNan 00ae: pop
0027: call ToDoubleOrNan 006d: ldloc.s V_5    00af: ldloc.0
002c: stloc.2          006f: call ToDoubleOrNan 00b0: mul
002d: ldc.r8 10        0074: mul              00b1: call NumberValue.Make
0036: ldloc.2          0075: stloc.0          00b6: ret
```

Finally, consider =10*IF(IF(A1, 0, 6), 11, 22), where A1 is an input cell, to see the effect of applying CompileCondition to the inner IF(A1, 0, 6). The resulting code unwraps A1 as a double, tests whether it is an infinity or NaN, and if so multiplies it with 10 and creates the requisite ErrorValue. Otherwise it tests whether A1 is 0, and if so pushes 11, otherwise 22, and finally multiplies 10 with this number. The intermediate 0 and 6 have been compiled away:

```
0000: ldarg.0            001d: call IsInfinity   004a: br 0058
0001: ldc.i4 0           0022: brtrue 005d       004f: ldc.r8 11
0006: ldelem Value       0027: ldloc.0           0058: br 005e
000b: stloc.2            0028: call IsNaN         005d: ldloc.0
000c: ldc.r8 10          002d: brtrue 005d        005e: mul
0015: ldloc.2            0032: ldloc.0           005f: call NumberValue.Make
0016: call ToDoubleOrNan 0033: ldc.r8 0          0064: ret
001b: stloc.0            003c: beq 004f
001c: ldloc.0            0041: ldc.r8 22
```

7.13 Reduce the use of local variables

Until now we have assumed that every cell that contains a formula would have an associated local variable in the generated code. When the value of the formula is used exactly once in the computation, this is wasteful. In fact, the value will be computed and stored to a local variable only to be immediately loaded (due to the topological sort) and then never used again. Hence, in code generated by an earlier implementation, this pattern was seen frequently:

```
stloc.s V_6
ldloc.s V_6                // This is the only use of V_6
```

Clearly, it would be safe to compute the cell's value on the stack instead and never store it in a local variable.

Hence, we change the translation from Expr to CGExpr so that no local variable is allocated for a cell that is referred exactly once. Instead, the translation (in the CGExpressionBuilder visitor) will inline the CGExpr at the single point of use.

If a cell C has two or more dependents (cells that statically refer to it) according to the dependency graph, then C is used more than once, and a local variable will be allocated for it. If the cell has exactly one dependent cell (it cannot have only zero dependents; in that case, it would not be in the dependency graph), then we need to count the number of references inside the dependent's formula. This is done by a new CountUseVisitor. If there are two or more uses, then C is used more than once, and a local variable will be allocated for it.

If cell C has only one dependent cell, whose formula has only one occurrence of C, then no variable is allocated for it. When subsequently the CGExpressionBuilder visitor's CallVisitor(CellRef cellRef) compiles a reference to cell C, it will find that it is not a key in the addressToVariable map, and it will use a new CGExpressionBuilder instance to compile the formula in cell C to a CGExpr that is then inlined into the CGExpr built for the dependent cell.

This works and generates correct, shorter, and faster code. Apparently it is beneficial to compute a subexpression only at the last moment, and the Microsoft .NET JIT seems better able to deal with rather deep stack use than with superfluous local variables. Perhaps the large number of local variables confuses the JIT and upsets register allocation, although the live ranges are short and not overlapping.

Chapter 8

Functions and Calls

8.1 Calling built-ins from sheet-defined functions

Built-in functions such as SQRT or RAND can be called from formulas in sheet-defined functions, just as from formulas in ordinary sheets. Code generation for built-in functions, corresponding to the interpretive Expr subclass FunCall, is performed by the CGExpr subclass CGFunctionCall.

8.1.1 Different kinds of built-in functions

Since class FunCall is used to represent a wide range of operations and functions, they must be compiled in very different ways. Method Make in CGFunctionCall makes the following distinctions:

- Arithmetic operations (+, *, −, /) are represented by subclasses CGArithmetic1 and CGArithmetic2 and are compiled to their corresponding bytecode instructions, like this:

  ```
  ilg.Emit(OpCodes.Add);
  ```

- Comparison operations (=, <>, <, >, <=, >=) are represented by subclasses of abstract class CGComparison. Compilation of comparisons implement error propagation from the operands, as well as optimizations when operands are constants.

- Non-strict functions (IF, AND, OR, and CHOOSE) are represented by classes CGIf, CGAnd, CGOr, and CGChoose. Compilation implements error propagation, avoids evaluating unneeded arguments, and performs some optimizations.

- The NOT and NEG functions are represented by classes CGNot and CGNeg to expose some optimization opportunities and to generate efficient bytecode instructions for them.

- Most mathematical functions supported by the .NET libraries and even by hardware (SQRT, SIN, etc.) are compiled to calls to static functions in the .NET System.Math class, in principle as follows:

```
ilg.Emit(OpCodes.Call, typeof(Math).GetMethod("Sqrt"));
```

- A few mathematical functions (ATAN2, FLOOR, MOD, ROUND) are compiled as calls to static methods in the Function class to obtain Excel-compatible behavior. The same static methods are used by the interpretive implementation in class Functions, in principle as follows:

```
ilg.Emit(OpCodes.Call, typeof(Function).GetMethod("ExcelMod"));
```

- Some special built-ins, notably APPLY, CLOSURE, ERR, and EXTERN, are represented and compiled by specific classes CGApply, CGClosure, CGErr, and CGExtern (section 8.7).

- Any other strict built-in function, whether of variable arity (AVERAGE, HARRAY, HCAT, etc.) or fixed arity (INDEX, SLICE, etc.), is represented as a CGFunction-Call object. This object contains a FunctionInfo object, which contains among other things a Signature object describing the function's argument types and return type (see section 8.1.2).

  Compilation of the argument expressions emits the relevant argument checking code, guided by the function's signature. If the return type according to the signature is Typ.Number, then method CompileToDoubleOrNan can avoid creating unwrapping code. This machinery is described in more detail in section 8.1.3 and is quite similar to the machinery for compiling EXTERN calls.

- A call to a sheet-defined function is represented by class CGSdfCall, as described in section 8.2.1.

In all cases, care is taken to perform the reflective lookup of MethodInfo objects only once and to create signatures only once, regardless of how many occurrences there are of calls to the function.

8.1.2   The Signature and FunctionInfo classes

Class Signature describes argument types and result type of built-in functions, where Typ is discussed in section 7.10.1:

```
public class Signature {
  public readonly Typ retType;
  public readonly Typ[] argTypes;    // null means variadic
  ...
}
```

Each built-in function is described by a FunctionInfo object, which contains the function's name, signature (for compilation of arguments and conversion of result value), MethodInfo object (when generating bytecode to actually call the function), and applier (used during partial evaluation; see chapter 10):

```
public class FunctionInfo {
   public readonly String name;           // For lookup and display
   public readonly MethodInfo methodInfo; // For code generation
   public readonly Signature signature;   // For arg. compilation
   public readonly bool isSerious;        // Cache it or not?
   public readonly Applier applier;       // For specialization

   private static readonly IDictionary<String, FunctionInfo>
     functions = new Dictionary<String, FunctionInfo>();
   ...
}
```

The FunctionInfo class also maintains a static pre-allocated table of all built-in functions so that there will be a single FunctionInfo object for each function, rather than one for each call to the function.

8.1.3   Compilation of calls to built-ins using signatures

A call such as INDEX(e1, e2, e3) to a built-in function is compiled by first generating code for the argument expressions using the CompileArgumentsAndApply method in class CGFunctionCall. Then code is generated to call the function and finally to convert the function's result value from a .NET value to a Funcalc value.

The compilation of argument expressions and the conversion of the function's result is guided by the types specified in the function signature (section 8.1.2). To compile an argument expression, first code is generated to evaluate the expression, then code to check that the argument value is of the required type (for instance, Typ.Number), and then code to convert the Funcalc value to a .NET value (for instance, a double).

8.2   Calling a sheet-defined function

8.2.1   Calling from a sheet-defined function

A sheet-defined function should be able to call other sheet-defined functions and even itself. There are at least four different ways to compile a call to a sheet-defined function:

1. The first approach is to generate code that looks up the sheet-defined function by name in a table to get the delegate representing it and then calls that delegate. This immediately allows sheet-defined functions to be recursive and mutually recursive but incurs the cost of the table lookup at each invocation,

which is slower than a call to a built-in function from an interpreted formula (which would call the function directly by its delegate reference).

2. The second approach is to retrieve, at generation time, the MethodInfo object corresponding to the delegate compiled for the sheet-defined function, and then generate a bytecode call straight to that MethodInfo object. This avoids the table lookup at call time but precludes recursive and mutually recursive sheet-defined functions because we cannot generate a call to a sheet-defined function before its definition has been compiled. Also, after a modification and recompilation of a sheet-defined function, all functions calling it would have to be recompiled as well.

3. A third and intermediate approach is to maintain a map from names of sheet-defined functions to indexes $0, 1, 2, \ldots$ of sheet-defined functions and a global array `sdfDelegates[]` that maps an index to the DynamicMethod delegate generated for that sheet-defined function. We can then compile a call to the sheet-defined function with index `i` into an array access followed by an invocation as in `sdfDelegates[i]()`. After modification and recompilation of the sheet-defined function with index `i`, we must update the `sdfDelegates[i]` entry but need not recompile any other function. This permits recursive and mutually recursive sheet-defined functions and replaces hash table lookup by array indexing, which is faster.

4. A fourth approach would be to store a direct reference to the delegate within the sheet-defined function object to be called. To keep these references up to date, we would need to add a modification event to every sheet-defined function and add event listeners that update the delegate fields after (re)compilation. This would save one array indexing per call to the sheet-defined function but is more likely to go wrong and harder to debug.

We have implemented approach number (3) in classes SdfManager and SdfInfo in file CGManager.cs.

8.2.2 Passing arguments to a sheet-defined function

When calling a sheet-defined function, we need to pass its evaluated arguments to it somehow. Two approaches suggest themselves immediately:

A. Compile every sheet-defined function, regardless of argument count, as a delegate that takes an array of Values and returns a Value, of type `SdfDelegate`:

```
delegate Value SdfDelegate(Value[])
```

Then we could call a sheet-defined function `f(e1, ..., en)` at index `sdfIndex` as follows:

– Allocate a Value[] array `arguments` with n elements.

- Evaluate arguments e1, . . . , en and store their values into the `arguments` array.
- Call the function as `sdfDelegates[index](arguments)`.

B. Alternatively, to avoid allocating an argument array, use different delegate types for different numbers of arguments. We can use the delegate types from section 2.14, where zero-argument functions have type `Func<Value>`, one-argument functions have type `Func<Value,Value>`, and so on. All of these are subtypes of type System.Delegate, so we can still store all function in a common array of type System.Delegate[].

Then we could call a sheet-defined function `f(e1, . . . ,en)` at index i as follows:

- Get the delegate `sdfDelegates[i]` from the array of delegates.
- Based on the arity n, cast the delegate to the correct type. For instance, when n=1 cast to type `Func<Value,Value>` to obtain a delegate `dlg`.
- Evaluate arguments e1, . . . , en and push them onto the stack.
- Call instance method `dlg.Invoke` from the requisite delegate type, such as `Func<Value,Value>`. This is equivalent to the C# delegate call syntax `dlg(v1, . . . ,vn)`, where v1, . . . ,vn are the values on stack.

We have chosen approach (B) because it is faster. Experiments show that (B)'s cast takes only 3 ns, whereas (A)'s allocation of an array and storing arguments into it takes 30 ns for a one-element array and 150 ns for a ten-element array. Moreover, method (B) makes it easier to further differentiate sheet-defined functions by their argument types, which opens the way for further optimizations, especially the avoidance of wrapping and unwrapping of argument values.

The main drawback of the chosen approach (B) is that it works only for limited argument counts; so far the implementation supports sheet-defined functions with zero to nine arguments. Higher numbers of arguments could be supported by falling back on the (A) approach, passing the arguments in an array.

Another drawback of (B) is that it requires a fair amount of (rather trivial) code duplication to implement calls from ordinary sheets to a sheet-defined function (see section 8.2.3).

However, it is easy to generate good code for approach (B) to call a sheet-defined function from a sheet-defined function, and it is easy to support tail calls as shown in section 8.3.

8.2.3   Speculation: Using more type information

We could further optimize calls to a sheet-defined function by generating a delegate with more specific argument types than just Value, thus avoiding argument wrapping and unwrapping. For instance, a function such as REPT2(s,n) in example 6.15 could be compiled to a delegate of type `Func<String,double,String>` rather than `Func<Value,Value,Value>`.

It is easier to detect the actual argument types in generated code when calling a sheet-defined function from a sheet-defined function than when calling it from an ordinary sheet. Hence, we could create two versions of each sheet-defined function: a worker and a wrapper. The worker would be a delegate that takes specific argument types, and the wrapper would be a delegate that takes Value arguments, unwraps them to the specific argument types, calls the worker, and wraps its result. Within compiled code generated for a sheet-defined function, the worker can be called directly. Within ordinary sheets, the wrapper would be called instead.

We could refine the function sheet type analysis (section 7.9.2) as outlined in section 8.5 to discriminate FunctionValues based on their argument and return types, as in `Function<Number,Number>` and `Function<Number,Text>`. For instance, a more refined type analysis may find that a function sheet needs one of its argument types to be not only a FunctionValue but of type `Func<double,double>` and may unwrap it early to a local variable of that type, just as it does for Number-Value arguments. The unwrapping of the sheet-defined function would retrieve `worker[sdfInfo.index]`, perform an `IsInst` check on a suitable instance of `Func<...>` built using reflection at code generation time, and store the value in a local variable of that type. A call to the worker can then be performed without any wrapping and unwrapping of arguments or results.

We have not currently implemented the worker-wrapper distinction.

8.2.4 Calling from an ordinary sheet

To compile a call to a sheet-defined function from an ordinary sheet formula, we use method number (3) from section 8.2.1 combined with argument passing approach (B) from section 8.2.1. First, we use a hash dictionary to convert the name of the sheet-defined function into its index `i`. Then each call is executed as follows:

- Get the delegate `sdfDelegates[i]` from the array of delegates.

- Based on the arity n, cast the delegate to the correct type. For instance, when n=1, cast to type `Func<Value,Value>` to obtain a delegate `dlg`.

- Evaluate arguments `e1,...,en` and store them in local variables `v1,...,vn`.

- Call the delegate as `dlg(v1,...,vn)`.

For n=1, this corresponds to `((Func<Value,Value>)(sdfDelegates[i]))(v0)` when expressed as C# code. The implementation uses a `switch` statement and 10 auxiliary functions to distinguish the 10 different cases corresponding to zero to nine arguments because each case requires a different typecast of the delegate retrieved from the `sdfDelegates` table.

8.3 Recursive calls and tail calls

Funcalc supports recursive functions, including mutually recursive ones, even when the functions are defined in different worksheets. Moreover, Funcalc ensures that tail calls to known functions are executed in constant space, so that recursion can be used to implement iteration (loops) without risk of stack overflow (see section 8.3.3).

8.3.1 Mutually recursive functions

To support mutually recursive sheet-defined functions, loading a workbook from file requires two passes. The first pass considers only cells that contain a call to `DEFINE` and simply registers all sheet-defined functions without compiling them. The second pass then compiles the sheet-defined functions, using the registry from the first pass to generate code for calling other sheet-defined functions.

8.3.2 Aside: Tail calls

A function call that is the last action of the enclosing function is a *tail call*. For instance, in the function below, the recursive call `sumi(n-1.0, 1.0/n + r)` is a tail call because it is the last action of the function, if executed:

```
let rec sumi(n, r) =
    if n<=0.0 then r else sumi(n-1.0, 1.0/n + r)
```

By contrast, the recursive call `sum(n-1.0)` below is not a tail call because `1.0/n` must be added to the result of that call after it returns:

```
let rec sum(n) =
    if n<=0.0 then 0.0 else 1.0/n + sum(n-1.0)
```

Whereas an ordinary function call `sum(...)` must create a new frame for function `sum` on the call stack (see figure 7.1), a tail call can be executed by discarding the current frame and replacing it with a frame for the called function. Thus, an arbitrarily long sequence of tail calls can be executed using only a bounded amount of call stack space, whereas a long sequence of ordinary function calls would eventually run out of stack space.

The execution of tail calls in bounded stack space is vital for the implementation of pure functional languages, including our language of sheet-defined functions. Since a pure functional language does not allow mutable variables, it makes no sense to have for- or while-loops. All iteration has to be implemented by recursive function calls, so it is essential that arbitrarily long sequences of recursive calls can be executed without stack overflow.

In bytecode, a tail call can usually be recognized as a call instruction immediately followed by a return instruction, like this:

```
call f
ret
```

In this case, the call is the last action of the enclosing method because it will return immediately after the call to `f`, and the result of the called method `f` will also be the result of the enclosing method. The CLI or .NET platform does not automatically execute such a call in constant space (by replacing the stack frame), but one can request tail call execution by adding the "`tail.`" prefix immediately before the `call` instruction:

```
tail.
call f
ret
```

This is the only legal use of that prefix, according to the CLI specification [49, section III.2.4].

8.3.3   Tail recursive functions

The sheet-defined functions in Funcalc do not allow mutable variables, so the only way to perform iterative computations is through recursive function calls. Hence, tail call optimization is important when writing recursive sheet-defined functions. The current structure of the CGExpr compilation functions does not support tail call optimizations well because the (code) continuation is not always available.

However, tail calls can be supported by separately analyzing the CGExpr compiled for the sheet-defined function's output cell before invoking `Compile` on it. The compiler may perform this analysis right after it has converted the output cell's expression into a CGExpr.

Any tail call must be a last action executed by the expression in the output cell. That may include a function call that is actually in another cell but whose only use is in (a branch of) the output cell, like this:

```
A6=...
A7=FOO()
A8=IF(A6,A7,42)    <-- output cell
```

In this case, the A7 formula would be inlined in the A8 formula and would become a tail call. Note that for code size reasons, this would not be the case here:

```
A6=...
A7=FOO()
A8=IF(A6,A7,A7)    <-- output cell
```

Because the multiple (static) occurrences of A7 would mean that the code for `FOO()` is followed by a store to the local variable for A7, so `FOO()` is no longer in tail position. By manual code duplication, the calls could be turned into tail calls again, like this:

```
A6=...
A8=IF(A6,FOO(),FOO())    <-- output cell
```

This code duplication seems rather harmless, and hence the use of auxiliary cell A7 seems pointless. But `FOO(...)` may have a long list of complicated argument expressions and moreover may appear multiple times in different branches of the final `IF`-expression, like this:

```
A8=IF(..., FOO(), IF(..., ..., IF(..., FOO(), IF(..., FOO(), ...))))
```

In this case, it is meaningful to use the auxiliary A7 to save space, ensure consistency between the `FOO(...)` expressions, and hence improve maintainability. However, we shall not attempt to recognize tail position in such auxiliaries.

Which positions are tail positions? Assuming that the entire expression e is in tail position, the subexpressions in tail position are as follows:

- If e is `IF(e1,e2,e3)`, then `e2` and `e3` are in tail position.

- If e is `CHOOSE(e0,e1,...,en)`, then `e1,...,en` are in tail position.

If the processing is done during the conversion from Expr to CGExpr, then the CG-ExpressionBuilder.FunCall would have to distinguish `IF` and `CHOOSE` from other cases, which is unpleasant. It seems better to traverse the resulting CGExpr and decorate CGSdfCall and CGApply expressions with an `isTail` property.

We therefore add a Boolean field `isInTailPosition` to classes CGSdfCall and CGApply, which are the only ones that can perform recursive call. The compilation functions in CGSdfCall and CGApply must take the `isInTailPosition` flag into account when generating code, emitting the "`tail.`" prefix before the call and a return instruction after it, as shown in section 8.3.2.

Also, we add a virtual method `NoteTailPosition` to CGExpr hierarchy, which does nothing except in the overrides in classes CGIf, CGChoose, CGSdfCall, and CGApply. The method should be called (only) on the CGExpr generated for the output cell in method `ConvertExprToCGExpr` in class TopoListToCGExprList.

We need to perform calls to sheet-defined functions directly in bytecode for the tail call optimization to work as intended. It does not work to perform the calls through an auxiliary C# method, say. Even if that method were tail recursive, the C# compiler would not care and therefore never emit the "`tail.`" prefix.

8.3.4 No tail call optimization in `APPLY`

Ideally, tail calls should be optimized also when a sheet-defined function is called via `APPLY(fv,b1,...,bm)`. Unfortunately, this would require generating a large amount of bytecode for each occurrence of `APPLY`.

The reason is that we do not know, at compile-time, the full arity N of the sheet-defined function encapsulated in the function value `fv`, except that it must be at least `m`. Hence, we cannot generate a single instruction to correctly cast the sheet-defined function's delegate to its run-time type `Func<Value,...,Value>`, and we cannot find the single correct `Invoke` method token corresponding to that delegate type.

Alternatively, we could code to detect the arity of the sheet-defined function encapsulated in `fv`, perform the relevant cast, and call the corresponding `Invoke` method, all at run-time. However, this would generate a large amount of bytecode for each `APPLY`, which could be detrimental to performance of the CIL just-in-time compiler.

What we shall do instead is to implement the arity detection, cast, and `Invoke` call once and for all in C# rather than CIL bytecode, and call on the C# code to perform the requisite run-time tests. This precludes true tail call optimization because the C# compiler does not optimize tail calls. Presumably this is less of a problem for `APPLY` than for direct calls to a sheet-defined function. Non-constant space recursion through `APPLY` can happen only if a function value calls itself recursively, directly or indirectly; and this in turn can happen only if the function value was called with itself as argument. Consider this function `TAILREC3` with input cells B139 and B140 and output cell B140:

```
B139 = <input f>
B140 = <input n>
B141 = <output>
     = IF(B140, APPLY(B139, B139, B140-1), 117)
```

This function performs a tail call to the function value in B139. If we call `TAILREC3` with itself as argument, then the tail call becomes a self-recursive call:

```
B150 = TAILREC3(CLOSURE("TAILREC3",#NA,#NA), 1000000)
```

Although this looks rather contrived, there are nevertheless some plausible uses. Should these uses turn out to be frequent, tail call optimization for `APPLY` could still be achieved in two ways. First, one could manipulate the CIL code generated by the C# compiler to make the requisite C# methods properly tail recursive. Second, one could generate the complex version of the `APPLY` code only when `APPLY` is actually in tail position, falling back on the C# code in other cases.

8.3.5 The performance of tail-recursive functions

The simplest terminating tail-recursive function is this, `LOOP(n)`:

```
B3 = <input>
B4 = <output>
   = IF(B3, LOOP(B3-1), 117)
```

We investigate the performance calls `LOOP(n)` for a range of values of n and both with and without the tail recursion optimization in place.

The results are shown in figure 8.1. Without the tail call optimization, the time per recursive call is almost linear in the recursion depth n. This is probably because (1) one `Value[]` object and one NumberValue object is allocated per recursive call, so the .NET garbage collector must run frequently; and (2) the garbage collector must scan the execution stack for each minor collection, which takes time linear in the stack depth, which grows linearly with the recursion depth. On the Microsoft MS .NET 3.5 run-time, the Funcalc implementation works correctly up to a call depth of at least 30 000, but at call depth 40 000, it throws a StackOverflowException after a computing for nearly one minute.

n	Without optimization		With tail call optimization	
	Time (ns)	Time/n (ns)	Time (ns)	Time/n (ns)
1 000	415 000	415	131 000	131
2 000	1 410 000	705	254 100	127
5 000	6 310 000	1 262	635 200	127
30 000	190 000 000	6 333	3 740 000	125
40 000	stack overflow		4 866 000	122
10 000 000	stack overflow		1 159 360 000	116

Figure 8.1: Performance impact of the tail call optimization. The left columns show execution time without optimization, the right ones with tail call optimization. Each pair of columns shows the total time for performing n calls and the time per call. Without optimization the time per call grows linearly in the call depth; with optimization the time per call is constant.

With the tail call optimization, the time per recursive call is constant, unaffected by the recursion depth because the stack depth is constant. This constancy of course is expected for any positive n, and we have verified it for n up to 10 000 000 iterations. The optimized implementation takes around 116 ns per iteration, which allows for 8.6 million calls per second. This is quite good, but there is still considerable room for improvement, especially in getting rid of the NumberValue wrapping. Also, for comparison, a For loop VBA loop takes roughly 25 ns per iteration, which is almost five times faster than our tail recursive calls.

Here is the generated code for the tail recursive call LOOP(B3-1):

```
0033: ldsfld SdfManager.sdfDelegates
0038: ldc.i4 22               // LOOP's offset in sdfDelegates array
003d: ldelem.ref              // Load delegate for function LOOP
003e: castclass Func<Value,Value>
0043: ldloc.3                 // Load B3
0044: call Value.ToDoubleOrNan
0049: ldc.r8 1
0052: sub                     // B3-1
0053: call NumberValue.Make
0058: tail.
005a: call Fun`2[Value,Value].Invoke
005f: ret
```

8.4   Higher-order sheet-defined functions

8.4.1   Closures, or sheet-defined functions as values

How can we handle sheet-defined functions as values and how can we call them, and hence implement higher-order sheet-defined functions? Clearly, we could pass the name of a sheet-defined function as a text string and look up the name in Sdf-Manager's dictionary at every invocation. However, this provides very late binding, incurs overhead for lookup in the dictionary, and gives no opportunity for type-based optimization, more efficient calling conventions, and so on.

A more general and efficient approach is to introduce a new kind of value, namely, a *closure* or *function value*. A closure name(a1,...,an) consists of the name of an underlying sheet-defined function and some values a1,...,an for that function's arguments. Some of the ai may be the special value #NA, which is used to represent arguments not yet supplied. The closure is itself a function that may subsequently be called by supplying values for those #NA arguments.

For instance, ADD(42,#NA) is a closure whose underlying function is ADD and whose first argument is fixed as 42. Applying this closure to the argument 27 will compute ADD(42,27).

It is essential that one can form closures in which a sheet-defined function is applied to some but all of its arguments; otherwise we do not obtain the full power of higher-order functions.

Implementation-wise, a closure is represented as a FunctionValue, which is a subclass of Value. A FunctionValue object contains an index into the sdfDelegate table (representing the underlying sheet-defined function) and an array of zero or more already-given arguments: the a1,...,an.

To create a closure, we introduce a new built-in function CLOSURE("name", a1, ..., an). It returns the closure name(a1,...,an), where n is the arity of the sheet-defined function. Those argument values ai that are #NA represent arguments that will be provided later; think of #NA as "not available" (yet). The arity k of the resulting closure equals the number of #NA values among the ai.

The resulting closure fv can be called as APPLY(fv, b1, ..., bk) where APPLY is another new built-in function. This call will execute the underlying sheet-defined function on the values of all its arguments, using the non-#NA arguments from the ai, and using the bj in order of appearance as replacements for the #NA arguments among the ai.

Moreover, one can supply further arguments b1,...,bk to a given closure fv using the call CLOSURE(fv, b1, ..., bk). The resulting new closure is created from fv by replacing the #NA values among fv's ai with the bj values. The arity of the resulting closure equals the number of #NA values among the bj.

In the basic version of CLOSURE("name", a1, ..., an), we require the function name to be a string constant and not just a string-valued expression. This improves efficiency of compiled code: when CLOSURE is used within a sheet-defined function, it suffices to look up the name at compile-time, resolving it to an index into the sdfDelegate array. This also enables (in future versions of Funcalc) better type analysis for sheet-defined functions, and hence less argument wrapping and unwrapping and better speed.

Once we have a more general name mechanism for Funcalc, presumably the string "name" could be replaced by just the name. Moreover, CLOSURE("name") could be replaced by name when no arguments are given.

8.5   Speculation: Type analysis for function calls

An execution of `APPLY(e0,e1,...)` must check that the value of `e0` is a Function-Value. When `e0` is just an (input) cell reference, one can avoid multiple checks by an early check and unwrapping as done for NumberValue cells. This would be particularly valuable for the `GOALSEEK` and `FINDEND` functions (examples 6.22 and 6.24), which call the same function many times. However, the savings are not nearly as big as for NumberValues, where an object indirections and a field offset are replaced by a simple load.

More significant speedups would accrue from avoiding the wrapping (as Value objects, in a Value[] array) and, subsequent unwrapping, of function arguments. To do this systematically for both first-order and higher-order sheet-defined functions, one needs richer types, and presumably either explicit type specification or type inference by unification, respecting the subtypes. The following infinite family of types seem to be needed, as a generalization of the type Typ in section 7.9.2:

```
type Typ =
  | Error
  | Number
  | Text
  | Array
  | Value
  | Function of Typ list * Typ
```

with this ordering

```
Error <= { Number, Text, Array, Function(_,_) } <= Value
```

The question is whether there should be an induced ordering of Function types (covariance of return types and contravariance of argument types) so that:

```
Function([Value],Number) < Function([Number],Value)
```

This says that a function `f` accepting a Value argument and returning a Number result can be used wherever a function accepting a Number argument and returning a Value is expected—because the Number argument can be wrapped as a Value before being passed to `f`, and the Number result can be wrapped as a Value after being returned by `f`.

The answer to this is determined by the kinds of coercions that can be performed efficiently at run-time. For purposes of type inference, we seem to need a notion of subtyping so that a function that is used inconsistently can be assigned a type involving Value. This is both useful and in line with the dynamic typing used in most spreadsheet programs.

Similarly, one could parametrize the Array type to obtain a family of uniform-element array types like this:

```
type Typ =
  ...
  | Array of Typ
  ...
```

The most interesting case here is Array(Number) because such values could be represented by dense two-dimensional `double[,]` arrays. But note that, perhaps surprisingly, .NET computations involving such rectangular arrays are sometimes slower [138] than computations using arrays of arrays of type `double[][]`. Again, whether it is useful to have a subtype relation on Array types depends on the computational impact this has. Quite likely, some inspiration could be drawn from the OCaml type analysis of floating-point computations [89].

We have not currently implemented type analysis to support efficient function calls, but Poul Brønnum's MSc thesis [24] presents an unboxing technique based on a monomorphic type system and shows that performance can be improved by a factor of 2 or 3 relative to the implementation presented here.

8.6 Dynamic sheet indexing

Most spreadsheet programs, including Microsoft Excel, support dynamic indexing into a sheet using various built-in functions, a good representative of which is the INDEX function. The call INDEX(arr, r, c) returns the contents of the cell at row r and column c in cell area arr. Other functions in this family are HLOOKUP, VLOOKUP, MATCH, and the even more dynamic INDIRECT.

What these functions have in common is that they consider part of the sheet as an array that can be accessed using indexes dynamically. However, the compilation schemes for sheet-defined functions we have proposed above will represent each cell by a (stack allocated) local variable, which precludes efficient indexing and search.

A simple implementation scheme for the above indexing and lookup functions would allocate an array to hold the values of the area argument of each of the lookup/index function calls that appear in the function sheet. Then, as each of the sheet cells gets evaluated, its value must also be stored in any array of which the cell is a member. This works because cells are immutable: once calculated (in a particular invocation of the sheet-defined function), the value of a cell is not updated, so it is unproblematic to store the value multiple locations.

In case of the INDIRECT function, the entire sheet is the target area and hence in general needs to be indexable and represented as an array. In some particular cases, this could be optimized; for instance, INDIRECT("B" & A1) can refer only to columns whose name begins with "B", but it is unlikely that this kind of optimization is worthwhile. Hence, a single occurrence of INDIRECT is likely to ruin the efficiency of a sheet-defined function. The obvious choice is to not implement it for the time being and to focus on the other functions, or to require the target of INDIRECT to be on ordinary sheets.

In case of the INDEX, HLOOKUP, VLOOKUP, and MATCH functions, it is likely that the area contains many constant values, in which case the argument area array could be allocated once and for all and associated with the sheet-defined function. This is unproblematic if (1) all cells of the array are constants, or (2) there is ever only one active instance of the sheet-defined function, that is, no recursive calls. In the former case, there will never be updates to the array, and all instances can share it; in the latter case, array locations can be updated as needed and subsequently used in computations on the same sheet-defined function. In the general case where the target area contains non-constant cells, and the sheet-defined function may call itself recursively, one may create and initialize a fresh copy of the array holding the target area for each recursive call. If the area is large and the sheet-defined function performs little computation, this may be very slow; but in general table lookups are probably leaf functions and hence non-recursive, in which case a fast implementation is feasible.

One drawback of the above scheme is that the same cell value may be a member of a large number of target areas, and its value would need to be stored in each of these arrays. For instance, a sheet-defined function may contain 100 copies of a formula such as `=MATCH(x, $A$1:$A100)`, in which case cell A1 appears in 100 arrays. Such multiple storage could be avoided by allocating a single array representing the "maximal" area, storing the values into that array as they are computed, and then having the implementations of `HLOOKUP` and so on work from some offsets into that array.

A simpler solution is to allow dynamic indexing only into ordinary (non-function) sheets, which would actually cover a large number of plausible use cases. We can implement `INDEX(Sheet!<area>, dRow, dCol)` in a compiled sheet-defined function rather easily, provided the `Sheet!<area>` reference is to an ordinary sheet, not a function sheet. We simply add to class ArrayValue a public method

```
Value Index(double r, double c)
```

that accesses the cell row at row `r` and column `c` of the array value. Then we maintain a global static cache of array values that are really just views of ordinary sheets and compile an area reference such as `Sheets!B3:C14` to an index into this global cache. We use hashing to ensure that each such ArrayView is allocated only once regardless of how many times the area appears: a sheet-defined function may contain many copies of a formula such as `INDEX(Data!$A$1:$A$100,B1,B2)`, but only one ArrayView object is needed to evaluate all of these copies.

The implementation of CGNormalCellArea generates code to load the requisite ArrayView object. A subsequent call to `INDEX` computes the row and column offsets and calls `arrayView.Index(r, c)`.

An ArrayView consists of a non-null Sheet (which must be a non-function sheet) and two CellAddr objects `ulCa` and `lrCa`, which are normalized so that `ulCa` is to the left and above `lrCa`. The `Index` method performs a bounds check on `r` and `c` and returns error value `#REF!` in case one of the indices is illegal.

In summary, we make class ArrayValue abstract, with two concrete subclasses: one called ArrayExplicit that represents an array explicitly as an array of type `Value[,]`, and one called ArrayView that represents it by an absolute (`ulCa`,`lrCa`) window onto an ordinary sheet.

8.7   Calling external library functions

In some spreadsheet implementations, such as Excel with VBA, external function calls are very slow, as documented in section 8.7.6. Because of the dynamic nature of spreadsheets, an external function call must use some form of reflection to locate the function to be called, check argument types and wrap (or "marshall") argument values to call the function, and unwrap (or "unmarshall") the result value.

Sheet-defined functions in Funcalc provide an opportunity to drastically reduce both costs. The reflective lookup of the external function can be performed once and for all during code generation for the sheet-defined function. Static type information also allows the code generation stage to perform much of the argument type checking early and can reduce the marshalling and unmarshalling costs. For instance, when calling external function `Math.Sinh` on an arithmetic expression, inside an arithmetic expression, the argument and result can be passed as native double values rather than NumberValues or Objects, hence eliminating the need for call-time type checking, marshalling, and unmarshalling.

As a consequence, by wrapping a call to an external function inside a sheet-defined function, one can reduce the call cost by at least an order of magnitude relative to Funcalc's (already rather efficient) interpreted external function calls. Overall, a compiled call to an external (.NET) function in Funcalc seems to be 33 times faster than a VBA call from Excel.

In addition, the ability to call external functions is particularly valuable in Funcalc. In a purely interpretive spreadsheet implementation, a new built-in function can usually be added just by extending some table of functions, used when interpreting expressions of the form `FOO(...)`. In Funcalc, however, each built-in function must have both an interpreted implementation for use in ordinary sheets and a compiled implementation for use in sheet-defined functions. These two implementations must agree, or else users will be confused. By providing a single mechanism for calling external functions from both ordinary sheets and sheet-defined functions, the need to painstakingly implement built-in functions in Funcalc is reduced considerably.

A word of caution: Unbridled external function calls, like macros in Microsoft Excel and Microsoft Word, can be abused by malicious spreadsheet programmers. For instance, a single external function call can wipe out an entire directory (folder) structure. A serious implementation of external function calls should require certificates of authorship or disallow most external calls by default.

8.7.1   Possible mechanisms for external function calls

In this chapter, we describe the implementation of a mechanism to call .NET library functions and other external managed functions. This can be done in two ways:

1. By a direct call mechanism that specifies the name and signature of the method to call, for instance:

```
EXTERN("System.Math.Cos$(D)D", 1.2)
```

This would retrieve the method with the given name `System.Math.Cos` and signature `(D)D`, evaluate the argument 1.2, and call the function. In the implementation of sheet-defined functions, this can be done very efficiently because the compilation performs reflection and interpretation of the signature string once, and then the method can be called efficiently any number of times without reflection.

Within ordinary interpreted sheets, it would be inefficient to use reflection at every call. To avoid this, one could (1A) rewrite the expression to some internal optimized form on first evaluation, but this would add complications to the formula evaluation, and it should be done in a way that coexists peacefully with the internal sharing of (copied) formulas. Alternatively, one could (1B) disallow the use of this function within ordinary sheets, so if an ordinary sheet needs to call a .NET function, then one must first create a sheet-defined function that wraps it and then call the sheet-defined function. This would appear rather cumbersome to users and could lead to abuse of function sheets for hosting ordinary interpreted computations. Yet another possibility is to (1C) perform the interpretation of the signature and the reflective lookup of the method only once and cache the MethodInfo object and argument conversions in a dictionary for all subsequent uses. An `EXTERN` call would still incur the cost of argument value wrapping and reflective method call, but this is likely to be much less than the reflective method lookup. The caching dictionary could simply map the concatenation of name and signature to a structure that contains the MethodInfo object, the argument converters, and the result converter.

2. Instead of a direct `EXTERN` call, one could force the user to carry out a two-step invocation by having a built-in function that retrieves the function without calling it. For instance:

```
GETEXTERN("nameAndSignature", e1, ..., em)
```

This would be similar to `CLOSURE("name", e1, ..., em)`, except that the returned function value `fv` is a partially applied .NET method, not a sheet-defined one. The `GETEXTERN` function would use the `nameAndSignature` and reflection to obtain a MethodInfo object that can be called from both generated bytecode and ordinary interpreted sheets. An application of the method must use `APPLY(fv, ...)`, and this call only needs to consider the argument unwrapping and the result wrapping, but needs no reflective lookup. The given signature should also be used for creating type tests and avoiding value wrapping when generating bytecode. Hence, ideally, one should be able to do this:

```
A1 = GETMETHOD("System.Math.Cos$D(D)")
A2 = <input>
A3 = APPLY(A1, A2*2)/7
A4 = DEFINE("mycos",A3,A2)
```

to create a sheet-defined function that calls the raw `System.Math.Cos` without performing any wrapping of `A2*2` or any unwrapping of the result before the division by 7.

Alternative (1A) cannot be implemented by letting the Function object within the FunCall expression update the `applier` field of the `EXTERN` function because the applier is shared among all occurrences of `EXTERN`. Early reflective lookup of the MethodInfo object might instead be performed when constructing a `FunCall(...)` abstract syntax tree node in the parser; a special Extern node type might be constructed containing the MethodInfo object and the argument and result conversions. However, this may complicate compilation of `EXTERN` calls within sheet-defined functions, where performance could otherwise be very good. Hence, we disregard (1A) for now.

We do not want alternative (1B) either because the whole point of sheet-defined functions is that one can experiment with (interpreted) computations before turning them into (compiled) functions.

The two-stage approach required by alternative (2) is undesirable because it is relevant only for efficiency in ordinary sheet evaluation and therefore an unnecessary complication within sheet-defined functions.

Hence, we are left with (1C), that is, one-stage reflective evaluation in ordinary sheets, with caching of parsed signature, MethodInfo object, and argument and result converters.

This may be somewhat slow in ordinary interpreted sheets but it is usable and actually 5 times faster than calls from Excel to VBA functions (see section 8.7.6).

8.7.2   The implementation of external function calls

We adopt alternative (1C), so `EXTERN("nameAndSignature", e1, ..., en)` is implemented as follows:

- Split the text constant `nameAndSignature` into name and signature. If they are separated by `$`, then the method is static; otherwise it is a (possibly virtual) instance method.

- Parse the signature to obtain a `Type[]` array for the arguments.

- Check that the arity of the signature agrees with the number n of given arguments. An instance method must have one additional argument for the receiver object.

- Split the name into type name (System.Math) and method name (Cos), and use reflection on type name, method name, and argument type array to obtain a MethodInfo object.

- Analyze the argument types and return type to produce argument value conversion methods and a return value conversion method. This is necessary because the conversion of a Funcalc NumberValue argument depends on the corresponding formal parameter type, which could be `int`, `double`, or `bool`.

- Allocate an n-element array of type `Object[]` for the argument values.

- Evaluate `e1, ..., en` and convert each resulting Value `vi` to an Object that is stored in the argument array.

- Call the MethodInfo object reflectively on the argument array.

- Convert the returned Object to a Value and return it.

The argument value conversion and return value conversion methods are delegates of these types

```
Func<Value, Object>
Func<Object, Value>
```

For instance, class NumberValue could define static conversions from NumberValue to `double` (boxed as Object) and, conversely, from `double` (boxed as `Object`) to NumberValue, like this:

```
public static Object ToDouble(Value v) {
  NumberValue nv = v as NumberValue;
  return nv != null ? (Object)nv.value : null;       // Causes boxing
}

public static Value FromDouble(Object o) {
  if (o is double)
    return Value.MakeNumberValue((double)o);
  else
    ErrorValue.numErrorValue;
}
```

We need to map each argument and return type (of type System.Type) to an appropriate converter. A flexible solution is to use a HashDictionary to perform this mapping:

```
IDictionary<Type,Func<Value,Object>> toObjectConverter
    = new HashDictionary<Type,Func<Value,Object>>();
toObjectConverter.Add(typeof(System.Int32), NumberValue.ToInt32);
toObjectConverter.Add(typeof(System.Double), NumberValue.ToDouble);
...
```

and so on, and similarly in the opposite direction:

```
IDictionary<Type,Func<Object,Value>> fromObjectConverter
    = new HashDictionary<Type, Func<Object,Value>>();
fromObjectConverter.Add(typeof(System.Int32), NumberValue.FromInt32);
fromObjectConverter.Add(typeof(System.Double), NumberValue.FromDouble);
...
```

It is useful to allow an external function to return an "abstract" value (such as a handle to an external stream of data) that Funcalc cannot manipulate in any way except pass to another external function. We use subclass ObjectValue of class Value to wrap such "abstract" values.

We create a class ExternalFunction to contain the necessary cached information about each external function, as well as the above dictionaries of conversion methods. To call the external function from within an ordinary sheet, it must store:

- An array of argument value conversion functions, of type `Value -> Object`.

- A return value conversion function, of type `Object -> Value`.

- The MethodInfo object for the external method.

To avoid repeated reflective method lookup and so on, a cache of external functions is maintained using a dictionary that maps the `nameAndSignature` string to an ExternalFunction object. We do this using static members in class ExternalFunction. In particular, there is a static method

```
ExternalFunction Make(String nameAndSignature)
```

that checks whether an external function is in the cache. If it is, then it is returned; otherwise it is created, added to the cache, and returned.

8.7.3   Specifying the type of an external method

To write a method signature as a string, we use the compact format inspired by that used internally in Java bytecode [92]. The sequence of parameter type abbreviations is enclosed in parentheses, followed by the return type abbreviation. For instance, the signature `String foo(double d, int i)` is written like this:

```
(DI)T
```

where `T` means text or String. Since C# and .NET have many more types than the JVM, notably `uint`, other unsigned integers, and `decimal`, we use a non-standard set of abbreviations, shown in figure 11.5 on page 281 in the Funcalc user manual. Using those abbreviations, the signature of a hypothetical method `String Format(String s, int[] i, bool b)` would be written

```
(LString;[IZ)LString;
```

or more compactly as

```
(T[IZ)T
```

To parse a method signature, we create a tokenizer that takes a string and produces a stream of signature tokens:

```
private static IEnumerable<SigToken> Tokenizer(String signature)
```

A small handwritten recursive descent parser turns the token stream into a representation of the method signature. For the purpose of EXTERN, this is simply a pair of an array of argument types and a return type, where all types are .NET types. For the purpose of possibly specifying the types of sheet-defined functions, an argument type or return type may also be a function type, giving rise to signatures such as these:

(D)(D)D	corresponding to	D -> (D -> D)
((D)D)D	corresponding to	(D -> D) -> D

We also provide the abbreviation W for the .NET type void, although it can be used only for return types, and there seems to be little point in calling a void method from a spreadsheet. Nevertheless, it may be useful for tracking evaluation by calling System.Console.WriteLine or for other logging or tracing during development.

To be able to call both instance and static methods, we use the following convention. If the name and signature are separated by a dollar sign ($), then the method is static; otherwise it is a (possibly virtual) instance method. Mnemonically, the dollar sign ($) is familiar to spreadsheet users as a way to indicate an absolute reference, here to a class, and also looks like the "s" in static. When calling a static method, all n arguments e1, ..., en of EXTERN are passed to the method as ordinary arguments, the receiver argument in the reflective Invoke call is null, and the CLI call instruction is used. When calling an instance method, the first argument e1 is the receiver, passed as the first argument of the Invoke method, whereas the remaining arguments e2, ..., en are passed to the method, and the CLI callvirt instruction is used.

8.7.4   Speculation: Type notation for sheet-defined functions

The same type notation could be useful later for specifying the types of sheet-defined functions. That is the reason we use the letter W for the .NET type void; this allows us to use the letter V for the Funcalc type called Value. The following abbreviations will be especially useful:

Example	Meaning
N	number, double
T	text, String
V	value
[N	row (1D array) of numbers
{N	array (2D) of numbers
()N	argument-less function that returns a number
(N)N	function from a number to a number
(NN)N	function from two numbers to a number
(N)T	function from a number to a text

Then one could imagine the following example definitions of typed sheet-defined functions:

```
DEFINE("DIE6", "()N", A1)
DEFINE("NDIE", "(N)N", B37, B36)
DEFINE("BINOM", "(NN)N", B24, B22, B23)
DEFINE("WEEKDAYNAME", "(N)T", B41, B40)
DEFINE("REPT", "(TN)T", B46, B44, B45)
DEFINE("GOALSEEK", "((N)NNN)N", D55, B19, D19, F19)
```

We could overload the DEFINE function for this purpose because the second argument must be a cell reference in the untyped case and a text constant in the typed case.

The type notation still has two shortcomings: It cannot be used to specify functional arguments that return more than one result, and we do not yet have a design for generic or parametric polymorphic types.

8.7.5 Compiling EXTERN calls in a sheet-defined function

Now let us turn to code generation for a call to an external method within a sheet-defined function. We need a new CGExtern subclass called CGExtern to represent an EXTERN("nameAndString", e1, ..., en) call. The constructor of this class should call Make in ExternalFunction to obtain a ExternalFunction object representing the external function; prior interpretive evaluation of the function sheet has most likely created and cached that object. For purposes of code generation, the ExternalFunction object additionally needs to store:

- A MethodInfo object representing the return value conversion function for this external method.

- An array of System.Type objects representing the argument types.

- A System.Type object representing the return type.

The two latter fields are used to eliminate argument and return value conversions in the compiled code when possible, as follows.

If the type of an external method argument is System.Double, then the argument expression is compiled using CompileToDoubleOrNan and no conversion is needed; if it is System.Single, then a conv.r4 conversion to 32-bit float is performed; if it is an integer type or Boolean, then the argument expression is compiled using CompileToDoubleProper, where an appropriate integer conversion is performed in the ifProper continuation, and the ifOther continuation produces an ArgTypeError. If the argument type is System.String, then the argument is compiled using Compile and then unwrapped from TextValue to String. If the argument type is System.Object, then the argument is compiled using Compile and a Value-specific conversion to Object is performed. In summary, an argument to the external function is compiled and unwrapped as follows depending on the specified argument type:

Argument type	Compilation and conversion
System.Double	`CompileToDoubleOrNan`
System.Single	`CompileToDoubleOrNan`, `conv.r4`
System.Int32	`CompileToDoubleProper`,`conv.i4`; ditto all `int` types
System.UInt32	`CompileToDoubleProper`, `conv.u4`; ditto all `uint` types
System.Int64	`CompileToDoubleProper`, `conv.i8`
System.UInt64	`CompileToDoubleProper`, `conv.u8`
System.Boolean	`CompileToDoubleProper`, `ldc.r8 0.0`, `ceq`
System.String	`Compile`, unwrap to System.String
System.Object	`Compile`, Value-specific conversion to Object

Conversely, the result of the external function must be wrapped for use in Funcalc. This unwrapping depends on the specified argument type as well as which method is used to compile the EXTERN call.

When the EXTERN call is compiled using `CompileToDoubleOrNan`, the return value is converted as follows:

Return type	Conversion
System.Double	No conversion
System.Single	`conv.r8`
System.Int32	`conv.r8`; same for other `int` types
System.UInt32	`conv.r8`; same for other `uint` types
System.Int64	`conv.r8`
System.UInt64	`conv.r8`
System.Boolean	`conv.r8`
System.Decimal	[not implemented]
Any other type	return ArgTypeError

When the EXTERN call is compiled using `Compile`, a return value conversion is emitted unconditionally, using the MethodInfo handle for the return value conversion function. The conversions are as follows:

Return type	Conversion
System.Double	`NumberValue.Make`
System.Single	`conv.r8`, `NumberValue.Make`
System.Int32	`conv.r8`, `NumberValue.Make`; same for other `int` types
System.UInt32	`conv.r8`, `NumberValue.Make`; same for other `uint` types
System.Int64	`conv.r8`, `NumberValue.Make`
System.UInt64	`conv.r8`, `NumberValue.Make`
System.Decimal	[not implemented]
System.Boolean	`conv.r8`, `NumberValue.Make`
System.String	`TextValue.Make`
`void`	load the text "`<void>`"
All other types	`Value.ToObject`

When the EXTERN call is compiled using CompileCondition, the default implementation (section 7.11.2) in terms of CompileToDoubleOrNan is perfectly adequate. The Boolean return value is represented by an int32 (namely, 0 or 1) on the stack, and CompileToDoubleOrNan will emit conv.r8 to convert this to a double, which will then be tested. By special implementation of the CompileCondition case, we could avoid executing one conv.r8 instruction, but this is insignificant compared with the cost of calling the external function.

The argument compilation can be performed by compiling the argument expressions backward, starting with a success code continuation that calls the external method and using a common error code continuation that represents the case where an argument value cannot be converted to the required argument type:

```
for (int i = argCount - 1; i >= 0; i--) {
  if (ef.ArgType(i) == typeof(System.Double))
    ifSuccess = new Gen(
        delegate {
          es[i+1].CompileToDoubleOrNan();
          ifSuccess.Gen(ilg);
        });
  else if (ef.ArgType(i) == typeof(System.Single))
    ifSuccess = new Gen(
        delegate {
          es[i+1].CompileToDoubleOrNan();
          ilg.Emit(OpCodes.Conv_R4);
          ifSuccess.Gen(ilg);
        });
  else if (signed32.Contains(ef.ArgType(i)))
    ifSuccess = new Gen(
        delegate {
          es[i+1].CompileToDoubleProper(
            new Gen(delegate {
              ilg.Emit(OpCodes.Conv_I4);
              ifSuccess.Gen(ilg);
            }),
            errorCont[i]);
        });
  else if (unsigned32.Contains(ef.ArgType(i)))
    ...
}
ifSuccess.Gen(ilg);
```

Here we have ignored the notational problems caused by C#'s capturing lvalues rather than rvalues in anonymous methods (see page 182).

When called from Compile, the success code continuation ifSuccess must end with a call and a conversion from the external result type to Value.

When called from CompileToDoubleOrNan and when the external result has type double, the success continuation ifSuccess ends with a call but no conversion.

When called from `CompileToDoubleOrNan` and when the external result has an integer, 32-bit floating-point, or Boolean type, the success code continuation ends with a conversion to `double` (`conv.r8`).

As to the error continuation, we in fact need a whole family `errorCont[]` of those. Namely, assume that the first m argument evaluations succeed, each pushing an argument value on the stack, and then the $(m + 1)$'st conversion fails. Then we need to pop the m computed argument values from the stack before returning ArgTypeError. So each argument expression is evaluated and converted with a different failure continuation, but of course some code should be shared between these failure continuations.

8.7.6 Speed of EXTERN calls

As a consequence of the implementation outlined above, calls from Funcalc spreadsheets to external .NET methods are very fast, considerably faster than calls from Excel to VBA functions. Figure 8.2 gives some results for calling a simple external function to square a number. In the benchmark, we measure the time to evaluate 1000 cells containing the formula `SQUARE(RAND())`, which calls a VBA function defined like this:

```
Public Function square(ByVal x As Double) As Double
    Let square = x * x
End Function
```

In Funcalc we measure the time for evaluation of 1000 cells containing the formula `EXTERN("System.Math.Pow$(DD)D",RAND(),2)`, which calls the external .NET method `Pow` in class System.Math. This shows how much faster interpretive external calls are in Funcalc.

We also measure the time for evaluation of 20 000 cells containing the formula `EXTSQUARE(RAND())`, where `EXTSQUARE` is a sheet-defined function that contains a call `EXTERN("System.Math.Pow$(DD)D",A1,2)` where A1 is the function's sole input cell. This shows how much faster compiled external calls are.

Finally, for comparison we measure the time for evaluation of 20 000 cells containing the formula `SQUARE(RAND())`, where `SQUARE` is a sheet-defined function with output cell =A1*A1 where A1 is the function's sole input cell.

Call	Time/ns
Excel to VBA	19 000
Funcalc interpreted EXTERN	3 900
Funcalc compiled EXTERN	511
Funcalc sheet-defined function	350

Figure 8.2: Execution time for simple external function calls in Excel and Funcalc. All times are nanoseconds per call.

8.8 Speculation: Functions with state

This section investigates how to add a notion of state to spreadsheets and sheet-defined functions. The ideas have not been implemented, both because we want to preserve the clean spreadsheet concepts and because we have not found a simple and useful semantics for the combination of state and recursive functions.

8.8.1 Why state?

Although the declarative, side effect-free, computation model of spreadsheets makes them easy to understand and relatively safe to use, some functionality is hard to implement without state and side effects. For instance, a pseudo-random number generator typically needs to store a seed, which is updated for each number generated and used to generate the next random number.

Several mechanisms for maintaining state, such as a seed, are possible:

1. Introduce built-in functions such as GET("var") and SET("var", value) to get and set sheet-local variables, thus introducing imperative side-effects. This raises the question of when and in what order such side-effecting function calls are evaluated when there are multiple calls to SET or calls to both GET and SET.

2. Distinguish some cells as persistent so that they retain their values between calls to the sheet-defined functions. (Similar to "own" variables in Algol 60 blocks and procedures).

Henceforth, we consider only the second possibility because each call to the function can perform only one "assignment" to a persistent cell; namely, the cell's (new) value is given by the formula contained in the cell.

One possible notation is to have a pseudo-function DELAY that must be the topmost one in a cell formula, as in =DELAY(init, next). It could be implemented by a sheet-specific field that is initialized from the expression init.

A plausible semantics might be as follows: In any execution of the sheet-defined function, the value of such a delay cell would be the value *previously* computed for it (or the value of init, at the first call); but also, the expression next will be evaluated, and its value will be the next value of the cell.

Probably the next expression of a DELAY cell should be (re)computed in each invocation of the enclosing sheet-defined function regardless of whether there is another cell that needs its value in this computation. For instance, we may want to use a DELAY cell to count the number of times a sheet-defined function has been called, like this:

```
A1 = DELAY(0, A1+1)
```

If a DELAY cell were to be evaluated only if its value is being used, then we would have to "use" its value in some artificial way to make sure the evaluation takes place.

If the value of a delay cell were not uniformly the value computed and cached in the previous invocation of the sheet-defined function, then the result of definitions such as these:

```
A1 = DELAY(0, A2+1)
A2 = DELAY(0, A1+1)
```

would depend on the relative evaluation order of the cells, breaking the simple and declarative spreadsheets semantics. Would A1 and A2 be incremented by 1 or by 2 in each iteration? This is unclear unless we require that a reference to a delay cell returns its old value, as proposed above, and gets updated in each invocation of the enclosing sheet-defined function. In that case, we see that A1 and A2 proceed in lockstep, increasing by 1 in each call to the sheet-defined function. This also ensures that all cells in the sheet have a consistent view of the delay cell's contents in any given invocation of the sheet-defined function.

When the new value of a persistent cell B1 depends on the cell's old value because the `next` expression refers to B1, as in the case of the random number generator above, we have what looks like a static dependency cycle from B1 to B1. But this is harmless because the formula's B1 would refer to the old value, not the new one. Hence, a static dependency cycle in a sheet-defined function should be considered legal if it involves at least one persistent cell.

8.8.2 Further design questions

What limits must be imposed on the `init` expression in `DELAY(init,next)`? It is clear that the `init` expression should not call the enclosing sheet-defined function (directly or indirectly); that could make the value of `init` depend on itself. Moreover, `init` should be evaluated before the first call to the sheet-defined function, and therefore `init` should not (directly or indirectly) refer to the function's input cells, but may well contain calls to built-in functions. The first call to the sheet-defined function should be accompanied by the first evaluation of `next`.

Another design question is whether a `DELAY` cell should be shared among multiple sheet-defined functions on the same sheet. This would probably correspond to users' expectations and intentions, if they let two or more sheet-defined functions have `DELAY` cells in common. So we shall permit this but have so far not investigated the consequences. In implementation terms, if a `DELAY` cell can be shared among multiple sheet-defined functions, then it cannot be allocated inside each function, but must be allocated in some common state object that those functions refer to. Such a state can conveniently be shared among sheet-defined functions by creating and encapsulating a reference to it using the .NET library method

```
DynamicMethod.CreateDelegate(typeof(Delegate), state)
```

to create the Delegate, thus encapsulating the state reference in the delegate. There should be a single such state object for each function sheet, containing all the sheet's `DELAY` cells. The state object should be an extensible array (and `DELAY` cells referred to by index) because new DELAY cells may be added to the sheet after some sheet-defined functions have been created, and new sheet-defined functions may refer to the old as well as the new DELAY cells.

A third design question is whether it would be reasonable to allow the pseudo-function DELAY(init, next) to appear anywhere in an expression, not only as a formula's outermost function call. In this case, its value at first evaluation would be that of init, while also evaluating next; and in every subsequent evaluation, its value would be the previous result of next, while also evaluating next (for use in the next evaluation of that DELAY expression). This would be potentially rather confusing in a context such as IF(A1, DELAY(0, B1), ...); will the DELAY-expression be evaluated only if A1 is true? That makes a difference for the next invocation of the sheet-defined function. Probably this generalization is not desirable; DELAY should be allowed to appear only as a formula's outermost function call.

8.8.3   Examples of stateful sheet-defined functions

Example 8.1 A one-step delay line; the function returns the argument with which it was last called; returns 0 the first time:

```
A1 = <input>
B1 = DELAY(0, A1)
<output> = B1
```

Example 8.2 A two-step delay line; the function returns the argument with which it was last called; returns 0 the first two times:

```
A1 = <input>
B1 = DELAY(0, A1)
B2 = DELAY(0, B1)
<output> = B2
```

Example 8.3 A "counter" function that starts at zero, returns 1 at the first call, returns 2 at the second call, and so on:

```
B1 = DELAY(0, B1+1)
<output> = B1
```

Let's assume this function is called COUNTER(). Obviously, there is an evaluation order dependency when a formula depends on multiple calls to COUNTER(). For instance, in the ordinary sheet

```
A1 = COUNTER()
A2 = COUNTER()
A3 = (A1<=A2)
```

the value of A3 may be true or false depending on the evaluation order, but this is not different from calls to volatile functions such as NOW() or RAND(). We shall make no attempt to control this form of nondeterminism. However, one *might* stipulate that an expression such as COUNTER()<=COUNTER() must be true; that is, that expressions are evaluated left to right as in Standard ML, Java, and C#. Standard spreadsheet programs hardly make such guarantees, and we shall not either. In any case, the inter-cell recalculation order is unspecified, so making intra-cell guarantees would not be very useful.

Example 8.4 A "counter" sheet that starts at zero, returns 1 at the first call, returns 2 at the second call, and so on; and can be reset to 0 by calling the sheet-defined function with the argument "reset":

```
A1 = <input>
B1 = DELAY(0, IF(A1="reset", 0, B1+1))
<output> = B1
```

Example 8.5 An efficient generator of the Fibonacci numbers, returning 1, 1, 2, 3, 5, 8, ...:

```
B1 = DELAY(1, B1+B2)
B2 = DELAY(1, B1)
<output> = B2
```

Example 8.6 A linear congruential random number generator as specified for the Java class library, here seeded with 117:

```
B1 = DELAY(117, MOD(B1*25214903917+11, 281474976710656))
<output> = B2 = B1/281474976710656
```

One might replace the fixed seed 117 with FLOOR(86400000*NOW(),1), which would obtain the seed from the system clock at millisecond resolution.

Example 8.7 For another example that needs state, a sheet-defined function implementing the Box-Muller generator would consume two uniformly distributed random numbers on $[0, 1[$ to generate two normally distributed $N(0, 1)$ random numbers; one of these should be returned and the other one stored, so it can be returned at the next call to the function:

```
<no input>
A1 = DELAY(FALSE, NOT(A1))
A2 = SQRT(-2 * LN(RAND()))
A3 = 2 * PI() * RAND()
A4 = A2 * COS(A3)
A5 = DELAY(999, A2 * SIN(A3)) // cache
<output> = B1 = IF(A1, A5, A4)
```

The idea is that A1 toggles between false and true for each call to the function, and that A1 is true precisely when there is an unused normal deviate in cell A5. But the implementation is not really correct: namely, the second argument of DELAY cell A5 is evaluated in every invocation of the sheet, so A2 and A3 get evaluated, and the RAND and SQRT functions get executed once more, even if A1 is true and there is a usable random number in the A5 cache. The value 999 is a dummy value, never used.

One could fix it by redefining A5 like this:

```
A5 = DELAY(999, IF(A1, 999, A2*SIN(A3)))
```

where the IF makes sure that if A1 is true, then the expression A2*SIN(A3) is not recomputed and hence A2 and A3 need not be computed either. This programming technique may not seem too transparent and shows that stateful sheet-defined functions should probably be used sparingly and with caution.

Example 8.8 One recursive or stateful sheet-defined function may control the "iterations" of another stateful sheet-defined function, for instance, to perform a state change until some convergence criterion holds or until the controlled stateful function has reached a fixed point. This can be detected by further use of persistent cells as shown below. Persistent cell C2 contains the updatable state, and cell B2 computes the next state—that is, the expression eNext computes the function from old state to new state and presumably refers to C2. Cell D2 detects when the state does not change in a computation step:

```
B2=eNext
C2=DELAY(eInit, B2)
D2=(B2=C2)
<output> = HARRAY(D2, B2)
```

The output HARRAY(D2, B2) of this sheet-defined function is an array with one row and two columns, or a pair. The first component indicates whether a fixed point has been reached, and the second component is the most recent state. This sheet-defined function would need to be called until the first component of the result is true, in which case the second component is the fixed point. The example can easily be adapted for computational states that consist of multiple persistent cells C2, C3, and so on and corresponding computations in B2, B3, and so on.

Example 8.9 The above function could be generalized to take as input in A1 the function whose fixed point is to be calculated (rather than hardwiring it in expression eNext), and to take as input in A2 the initial state (rather than hardwiring it as expression eInit). A new third input cell A3 is used to signal whether the fixed point computation should be reset from the A2 parameter:

```
A1=<input: function>
A2=<input: initial state>
A3=<input: reset if TRUE>
B2=IF(A3, A2, APPLY(A1, C2))
C2=DELAY(999, B2)
D2=(B2=C2)
<output> = { D2, B2 }
```

Here cell B2 computes the next state (or the initial one, if A3=TRUE), cell C2 holds the previous state, and D2 is true if a fixed point has been reached.

Example 8.10 A stateful sheet-defined function may also be used to control the execution and tallying of multiple simulations, each such simulation being performed by another sheet-defined function. However, doing this in a highly stateful way may preclude parallelization and multicore utilization; it is better to perform multiple simulations by a higher-order operation that creates an array of simulations and then tally them afterward.

8.8.4   Related concepts

The DELAY function, permitted only at the top level in a cell and unconditionally updated at every recalculation of the sheet, gives a computation model similar to a fragment of Chandy and Misra's UNITY [32] or Staunstrup's Synchronized Transitions [149].

Namely, the DELAY cells hold the state, and the next-state transition is implemented by the next argument of the DELAY function, like this:

```
A1 = DELAY(a1init, a1next)
A2 = DELAY(a2init, a2next)
```

This corresponds to a transition, in Synchronized Transitions, of the form

```
INITIALLY
  A1=a1init
  A2=a2init
BEGIN
  <<A1,A2 := a1next,a2next>>
END
```

The main difference, though, is that a stateful sheet-defined function corresponds to a single such transition, where UNITY and Synchronized Transitions support any number of guarded transitions that may be executed in any order. In contrast, with stateful sheet-defined functions, the right-hand sides can contain arbitrarily complex expressions, including conditions, which are allowed only on as guards on the transitions of UNITY and Synchronized Transitions. A sheet-defined function seems to correspond to the notion of a "cell" in Synchronized Transitions.

8.8.5   The interaction of persistence and recursion

How would persistent cells interact with recursive sheet-defined functions? There is a potentially confusing interaction between:

- the evaluation of the `next` expression of each `DELAY` cell in every invocation of a sheet-defined function,

- the possibility of recursive calls to sheet-defined functions,

- the desire not to specify the order of evaluation of cells and recursive calls,

- the desire to maintain the spreadsheet computation model where the values of cells appear consistent within each evaluation, and

- the desire to have a simple and efficient implementation model with each `DELAY` cell represented by one field belonging to the function sheet function, plus possibly a local variable to hold the intermediate value of the cell.

Several implementation models seem plausible:

A. Let all references to the old value of a delay cell be to a field, shared among all invocations of the sheet-defined function. At the end of each invocation, `DELAY` fields are overwritten with new values computed in local variables. Pro: Simple. Con: A sheet-defined function with delay cells cannot be properly tail-recursive. Con: A sheet-defined function may see inconsistent old values (before and after recursive invocation of self). Con: Does not support an invocation counter because an earlier invocation will lose increments from recursively called function sheets.

B1. Let each invocation of the sheet-defined function copy old values from fields to local variables and overwrite the shared fields with new values as they are computed. Pro: Each invocation sees consistent old values. Pro: Can be implemented properly tail-recursively. Con: An invocation may overwrite updates performed by a recursive call, thereby losing updates. Hence, it does not support an invocation counter. Con: A recursively called sheet-defined function may see partially updated old values.

B2. Let each invocation of the sheet-defined function copy old values from fields (initial invocation) or local variables (all recursive invocations) to local variables and overwrite the shared fields with new values as they are computed. Pro: Each invocation sees consistent old values, and all invocations see the same value. Pro: Can be implemented properly tail-recursively. Pro: A recursively called sheet-defined function never sees partially updated old values. Con: An invocation may overwrite updates performed by a recursive call, thereby losing updates. Hence, it does not support an invocation counter.

C. Sidestep the issue by disallowing the combination of state and recursion: A recursive invocation chain cannot involve any stateful sheet-defined function. One can still count the number of invocations of a recursive function sheet by letting it call a separate counting sheet once.

At this time, option (C)—prohibiting a stateful sheet-defined function from calling itself—seems to be the only reasonable one because the other ones lead to a counter-intuitive semantics. However, reliably enforcing this prohibition requires a global analysis of which functions a sheet-defined function can call, and in the presence of function values and APPLY, this analysis can only be approximate. A cruder but simpler approach is to prohibit all function calls and APPLY in stateful functions.

Chapter 9

Evaluation Conditions

With the compilation model described so far, one can implement a wide range of useful sheet-defined functions, as shown by the examples in section 6.2. However, recursive sheet-defined functions must be programmed with great care to avoid infinite loops, and also some non-recursive functions perform much more computation than is strictly needed.

This chapter demonstrates how these problems can be avoided by computing a so-called *evaluation condition* for each cell in the function and using that condition to sometimes avoid evaluating the cell's formula. This might sound like a small improvement only, but if the formula involves calls to other functions, whether sheet-defined or external, the amount of wasted computation may be arbitrarily large; and if the formula involves a call to the sheet-defined function itself, the amount of wasted computation may be infinite.

9.1   Why evaluation conditions?

To see why evaluation conditions are needed, recall the function `REPT3(s,n)` from example 6.16, which returns string s concatenated with itself n times. That function was efficient enough but contained some code duplication. In its output cell B66, the expression `REPT3(B64&B64, FLOOR(B65/2,1))` occurs twice but is evaluated only once because the occurrences are in different branches of a conditional.

The next example shows a different and neater solution to the same problem, but one that challenges the compilation of sheet-defined functions.

Example 9.1 This function `REPT4(s,n)` computes string s concatenated with itself n times, is just as efficient as `REPT3` from example 6.16, and avoids the code duplication as well as the test `B65=1`:

A1	A	B	C
68	=DEFINE("rept4"...	'REPT4(s,n), fast recursive implementation, relies on eval...	
69	's =		
70	'n =		
71	'rept4(s,n/2) =	=REPT4(B69, FLOOR(B70/2, 1))	
72	'result =	=IF(B70=0, "", IF(MOD(B70, 2), B69&B71&B71, B71&B71))	

The implementation challenge is that the recursive call to REPT4 in cell B71 does not appear inside an IF-expression. Our compilation scheme needs to realize that it should evaluate B71 and the recursive call only when B70=0 is false. Note that it should not just inline the B71 formula into the branches of the inner IF in B72 because that would duplicate the recursive call, increase the number of recursive calls from $O(\log n)$ to $O(n)$, and increase the total computation time from $O(n)$ to $O(n^2)$.

9.2   The basic compilation process

First, let us summarize the basic compilation process without evaluation conditions. The compilation of sheet-defined functions is implemented in a number of stages, primarily in the classes SdfManager, DependencyGraph, TopologicalSorter, CodeGenerate, ProgramLines, and the CGExpr hierarchy. It works in the following steps:

1. Starting from the sheet-defined function's output cell, find all cells on this function sheet that its formula (as an Expr) depends on. This is done by computing the transitive closure of the "precedents" relation from the output cell.

    This also builds the static dependency graph whose nodes are function sheet cells and where a node has arrows to all its *precedents*: the cells that it directly depends on; and to all its *dependents*: the cells that directly depend on it.

    If the static dependency graph is cyclic, this is discovered and reported during construction.

2. Perform a topological sort of this graph starting from the output cell. The result is a list of function sheet cells, encapsulated in a ProgramLines object, so that every cell follows all the cells that its formula depends on. Constant cells are not included in the topologically sorted list, which means that they will become inlined in the referring expression(s) in step 4a.

3. Create a generator object of type TopoListToCGExprList, encapsulating the topologically sorted list of cell addresses.

4a. Create a DynamicMethod object and obtain its ILGenerator to enable generation of local variables to hold the values of cells.

For each cell whose value is referred (statically) more than once, we convert the cell's formula's Expr into a CGExpr (using method CGExpression-Builder.BuildExpression), allocate a local variable of appropriate type for the cell, and record this local variable in the cellToVariable map. This builds a program list each of whose elements is a ComputeCell, a pair whose first component is a cell formula of type CGExpr and whose second component is the local variable destined to hold the cell's value.

This means that no local variable is allocated for a cell that is used only once statically (it has one dependent cell, whose formula refers it statically only once). The conversion from Expr to CGExpr will create and inline the referred-to cell's CGExpr where it is used.

5. If a cell's value is allocated to a local variable (of type Value) and is a number, then allocate another local variable of type double, generate code to unwrap the Value as a double, and insert that code right after the cell's computation in the program list.

   This is slightly wasteful and could be optimized a bit by checking numbers of uses as in step 4a: If the cell is used only as a number, then there's no need to allocate it as Value also; and if it is used as number only once statically, there's no need to allocate it to a local of type double (this can happen only if it is an input cell).

   One could consider reusing local variables by allocating them from a pool and returning a variable to the pool when its live range ends. However, this may confuse the CLI just-in-time compiler's register allocation and do more harm than good, so we shall not do that.

6. Traverse the program list in forward order and call `Compile()` on each CG-Expr to generate CIL code for the body of the sheet-defined function. Then create a Delegate from the DynamicMethod obtained in step 4a.

As part of the process, we register the cells that belong to this sheet-defined function. This is used to determine when the function needs to be recompiled after edit to one of its cells and to color function sheet cells in the user interface.

9.3   The improved compilation model

What we shall do in this chapter is to add some more steps between the step 4a conversion and inlining and the step 5 construction of the program list and the actual code generation, namely:

4b. Compute the evaluation condition for each CGExpr cell in the reverse order of the topologically sorted dependency graph, that is, starting from the output cell (see section 9.6). Attach the evaluation condition to the CGExpr as well as the local variable that it should initialize.

4c. Analyze each cell's CGExpr and its evaluation condition for dependencies to build a new dependency graph, which makes sure that every cell needed for evaluation of the evaluation condition or the CGExpr has been evaluated before the evaluation condition or the CGExpr gets evaluated.

4d. Perform a topological sort of this new dependency graph, starting from the output cell, to obtain a new program list, each of whose elements holds a cell formula, a variable for the cell, and the cell's evaluation condition.

Moreover, the code generation in step 6 now must take the evaluation condition into account:

6'. Traverse the new program list in forward order and generate code for the evaluation condition and the cell's formula, and a conditional test that evaluates the cell's formula only if the evaluation condition is true, like this:

```
if (evalcond)
   var = formula;
```

Of course, if the evaluation condition is constant true, just generate code for the formula as before.

Consider again the example from section 7.3 with input cell A1 and output cell A4:

C9	A	B
1		
2	=ABS(A1)	
3	=EXP(-A2*A2/2)	
4	=RAND()*IF(A2>37, 1, 0.3989*A3)	

To avoid evaluating A3 unless it is needed by the output cell A4, we could enclose its evaluation in a conditional like this:

```
v_A1 = <input>;                          <-- input cell
v_A2 = Math.Abs(v_A1);
if (!(v_A2>37))
   v_A3 = Math.Exp(-v_A2*v_A2/2);
v_A4 = rnd.NextDouble()*(v_A2>37 ? 1 : 0.3989*v_A3);
return v_A4;
```

Here we assume that variable v_A3 is initialized with some value, and indeed this is easily done in CIL using a .locals init directive.

In this particular case, the same effect could be obtained by inlining A3 into A4, as is actually done by our implementation (step 4a in section 9.2), notionally resulting in this code:

```
v_A1 = <input>;                         <-- input cell
v_A2 = Math.Abs(v_A1);
v_A4 = rnd.NextDouble()
       * (v_A2>37 ? 1 : 0.3989 * Math.Exp(-v_A2 * v_A2 / 2));
return v_A4;
```

But this does not work if A3 is used dynamically more than once because A3 may involve volatile functions so that each evaluation could produce a different result, violating spreadsheet semantics.

Some special cases:

- A3 is needed unconditionally elsewhere anyway and hence must be computed unconditionally

- A3 is needed in both branches of the conditional and hence must be computed unconditionally

- A3 is needed only in one branch of one conditional and hence must be computed as determined by that conditional

- A3 is needed in one branch of one conditional and one branch of another and hence is needed under the logical "or" of those conditionals

- A3 is needed in one branch of a conditional, which in turn is needed by one branch of another conditional, and hence is needed under the logical "and" of those conditionals

An alternative would be to calculate lazily those variables that may or may not be needed by the result cells. That is, we associate a status of not-yet-calculated or already-calculated with each such variable, and we calculate it only the first time it is needed. This avoids the potentially complex determination of the conditions under which variables such as A3 must be computed. However, it introduces new overhead in the form of flags and run-time tests and is somewhat similar to the machinery used in Cortes and Hansen's interpretive implementation [37] (see section 6.5). It is exactly such run-time overhead that we want to avoid.

9.4   Determining evaluation conditions

To determine evaluation conditions for a sheet-defined function, we conceptually start with the function's conditional dependency graph. This is a refined version of a dependency graph in which each edge is labeled with a logical condition. There is an edge from cell d to cell c labeled with condition b_{dc} if cell d depends on cell c only when condition b_{dc} holds. Figure 9.1 shows the conditional dependency graph for function REPT4 in example 9.1. It shows that the output cell B72 depends on intermediate cell B71 only if the condition NOT(B70=0) holds.

The labels on the edges of the conditional dependency graph are used to determine the conditions under which a given cell, conditionally needed by the output,

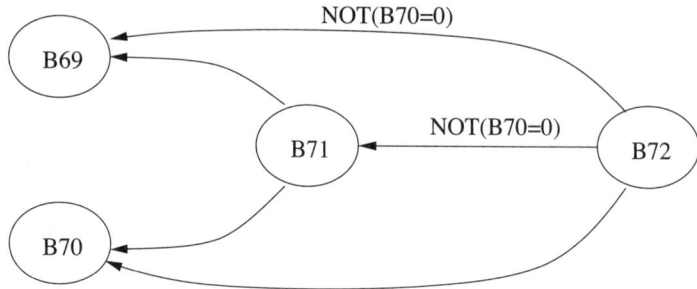

Figure 9.1: The conditional dependency graph for the `REPT4` function in example 9.1. Cell B72 depends on cell B71 only if the condition `NOT(B70=0)` holds. Unlabeled edges have condition true.

must be evaluated. Multiple dependencies along different paths give rise to logical disjunction of the labels, and chains of dependencies give rise to logical conjunction of the labels.

More precisely, consider a given cell c and let P be the set of labeled dependency paths from the output to cell c. For a path $p \in P$ and edge $e \in p$, let b_e be the label (logical expression) on edge e. Let b be the disjunction over all paths p of the conjunctions of all edge labels in p:

$$b = \bigvee_{p \in P} \bigwedge_{e \in p} b_e$$

Then the formula in cell c must be evaluated exactly when b is true; b is the *evaluation condition* for cell c. Hence, we must generate code like this for computing cell c:

```
if (b)
    v_c = ...;
```

Obviously, when b is constant true, only code to compute and assign `v_c` should be generated, no code for the condition and test, no code should be generated at all. Code for the variables should be generated in dependency order, respecting the augmented dependency graph.

Note the following special cases and optimizations, which agree with our intuition:

- Formally, there is a single empty path from the output cell to itself; the conjunction of labels along this path is true, and the singleton disjunction is true also. Intuition: the output cell's evaluated condition is true because its formula must always be evaluated.

- Formally, if there is no path from the output to a cell c, then the resulting empty disjunction is equivalent to false. Intuition: a cell on which the output does not depend has evaluation condition false because it should not be evaluated.

- Formally, if a path set P contains two paths p and q where p's label sequence is $b_1 \wedge \ldots \wedge b_i \wedge \ldots \wedge b_k$ and q's label sequence is $b_1 \wedge \ldots \wedge \neg b_i \wedge \ldots \wedge b_k$, then p and q can be replaced by a single path where b_i and its negation have been left out: $b_1 \wedge \ldots \wedge \ldots \wedge b_k$. Intuition: if a cell is needed by both the true-branch and the false-branch of a conditional, then it is needed by the conditional.

The resulting evaluation conditions may be rather complicated: long conjunctions may appear due to a cell conditionally depending on a cell conditionally depending on a cell and so on, and long disjunctions may appear due to many cells conditionally depending on the same cell but with different conditions. This is likely to cause the same subexpression to appear in conditions on a large number of edges, so subexpressions should be preserved, and one should make sure they are computed only once and the value reused (which is easy to do correctly thanks to the declarative semantics of spreadsheets).

Even with a naive syntactic treatment of the logical conditions on dependencies, the above approach would generate code that computes the correct values. However, the generated code may be needlessly complicated. For instance, consider

```
C1= ...                          <-- input cell
C2=C1+5
C3=IF(C1>0, C2, 10) + IF(C1>0, 10, C2)
```

which would give these dependencies:

```
C2====>C1
C3==C1>0==>C2
C3==!(C1>0)==>C2
```

corresponding to this generated code

```
if (d_C1>0 || !(d_C1>0)) {
   d_C2=d_C1+5;
}
d_C3=(d_C1>0 ? d_C2 : 10) + (d_C1>0 ? 10 : d_C2);
```

Clearly, the above set of dependencies could be reduced to these simpler dependencies, using that $p \vee \neg p$ equals true:

```
C2====>C1
C3====>C2
```

These simple dependencies would cause d_C2 to be computed unconditionally:

```
d_C2=d_C1+5;
d_C3=(d_C1>0 ? d_C2 : 10) + (d_C1>0 ? 10 : d_C2);
```

(Clearly, the definition of d_C3 could be optimized as well, but that is another matter.) Covering all such simplifications can become rather complicated, though, and is replete with pitfalls. For instance, consider this variant of C3:

```
C4=IF(C1>0, C2, 10)  +  IF(C1<5, C2, 10)
```

Here it seems that since every number is either greater than 0 or less than 5, or both, this could be optimized just like the C3 binding above. However, if C1 is an error value, then the value of C2 will actually not be used anyway. Hence, we refrain from using facts about numbers.

This performs no unnecessary computations but a rather large number of tests. It is essential that the individual conditional expressions (from the spreadsheet) are evaluated only once and that their results are cached; duplicating a conditional expression that involves volatile functions such as RAND()>0.5 will produce wrong results. However, order of evaluation need not be preserved. First, it should not be observable unless NOW() has nanosecond resolution, and second, usual spreadsheet semantics does not postulate a particular order of evaluation.

9.5   Representing evaluation conditions

We associate a single logical expression with each cell used by the sheet-defined function; this expression describes the conditions under which the cell should be evaluated. We can use a dictionary to associate a conditional expression with each cell. For the output cell(s) the condition is true; for all other cells it is initially set to false. We compute the conditions incrementally by updating them in reverse topological order of the augmented dependency graph, that is, starting from the output cell(s).

If cell c_1 has condition p_1, cell c_2 has condition p_2, and c_1 uses cell c_2 under condition q, then we update the condition of c_2 to $p_2 \vee p_1 \wedge q$. Due to the visit in topological order (and of course the absence of cycles), the condition of c_1 will be correct when we visit it, and hence the update of c_2's condition will be the relevant one.

For a given cell c, the evaluation condition is found as the disjunction over all references r from dependent cells, of the conjunction of the evaluation condition $cond_d$ of the cell d in which r appears, and the condition under which reference r in d gets evaluated. Note that in this description, there may be multiple references from a cell d to cell c; each such reference contributes to disjunction.

An evaluation condition is a logical expression, using "and" and "or", whose atoms are (possibly negated) formula expressions of type CGExpr. How shall we represent evaluation conditions? There are two obvious possibilities:

- Use the standard CGExpr subclasses CGAnd, CGOr, and CGNot.

- Introduce a specialized representation as another class hierarchy.

The advantage of the first option is that the code generation is already in place, and the advantage of the second option is that we have a separate place to implement logical reductions, a special representation that supports such reductions, common subexpression elimination, and similar features. Moreover, for reasons that become clear later, the short-circuit evaluation of CGAnd and CGOr may not be appropriate for evaluation conditions.

So we create a specialized representation of logical expressions, using an abstract superclass PathCond with subclasses CachedAtom for encapsulating a (possibly negated CGExpr), Conj for multi-conjunctions, and Disj for multi-disjunctions. Note that negation needs to be applied only to atoms not to composite logical expressions.

The "atomic" subexpressions are CGExprs because they arise from the conditions in non-strict expressions such as `AND(...)`, `OR(...)`, `IF(...)`, and `CHOOSE(...)`. For now we will not further analyze these atoms. But observe that we could rewrite `IF(IF(A,B,C),D,E)` as `IF(OR(AND(A,B),AND(NOT(A),C)),D,E)` by converting the inner `IF(...)` from a CGExpr into a logical expression, although at the expense of duplicating the A subexpression.

We use multi-disjunctions $\bigvee$(PathCond*) and multi-conjunctions $\bigwedge$(PathCond*), where PathCond* denotes a sequence of path conditions of type PathCond. The constant false is represented by the empty multi-disjunction and the constant true by the empty multi-conjunction.

So, in grammar terms, path conditions P have the form:

			Class
PathCond	::=	CGExpr	CachedAtom(CGExpr)
	|	$\bigvee$ PathCond*	Disj(PathCond*)
	|	$\bigwedge$ PathCond*	Conj(PathCond*)

This naturally gives a class hierarchy with superclass PathCond and three subclasses. We make the representation functional, with immutable fields, so that subexpressions can be shared freely. This means that operations on logical expression should not destructively update existing structure but should construct new object structures, possibly incorporating existing ones.

This allows object structures (subexpressions of the logical expressions) to be shared between multiple evaluation conditions; that would be impossible or very hard to get right if the operations were destructive. Since each cell has its own evaluation condition, and the evaluation conditions are built in topological order from simpler expressions to more complex ones, the substructure sharing should be quite effective in saving space.

The PathCond classes should support a method to convert the path condition to a CGExpr, which can subsequently be compiled using the usual machinery:

```
CGExpr ToCGExpr()
```

9.6 Generating evaluation conditions

To hold the evaluation condition for each cell, we create a dictionary `evalConds` that maps a FullCellAddr to a PathCond. This is initialized to false for all cells except the output cell(s), for which it is true.

Then we process the cells in reverse topological order, starting from the output cells as follows. A cell that has CGExpr `expr` and evaluation condition `cond` will be processed by a call to method `expr.EvalCond(evalCond, evalConds)`. This method will traverse expression `expr`, and for each cell reference `fca` in `expr` that gets evaluated under condition `cond`, it will update `evalConds[fca]` to hold `evalConds[fca].Or(cond)`.

For instance, if `expr` consists simply of a cell reference to cell C1, we will

- Update `evalConds[C1]` to hold `evalConds[C1].Or(evalCond)`.

For another example, if `expr` is an `IF`-expression `IF(e1,C1,C2)`, then we will:

- Compute `e1.EvalCond(evalCond, evalConds)` recursively.

- Update `evalConds[C1]`
  to hold `evalConds[C1].Or(evalCond.And(e1))`.

- Update `evalConds[C2]`
  to hold `evalConds[C2].Or(evalCond.AndNot(e1))`.

More generally, if `expr` is an `IF`-expression `IF(e1,e2,e3)`, then we will:

- Compute `e1.EvalCond(evalCond, evalConds)`.

- Compute `e2.EvalCond(evalCond.And(e1))`.

- Compute `e3.EvalCond(evalCond.AndNot(e1))`.

Finally, if `expr` is an `CHOOSE`-expression `CHOOSE(e0,e1,e2,...,en)`, then we will:

- Compute `e0.EvalCond(evalCond, evalConds)`.

- Compute `ei.EvalCond(evalCond.And(e0=i))` for each i from 1 to n.

Concretely, the implementation of `EvalCond` on `IF(es[0], es[1], es[2])` in class CGIf works roughly like this:

```
void EvalCond(PathCond evalCond, IDictionary<...> evalConds) {
  es[0].EvalCond(evalCond, evalConds);
  es[1].EvalCond(evalCond.And(es[0]), evalConds);
  es[2].EvalCond(evalCond.AndNot(es[0]), evalConds);
}
```

In actual fact, the duplication of expression es[0] implied above would be wrong, as shown in section 9.6.1. The true implementation of EvalCond for IF is given in section 9.6.2.

To generate evaluation conditions, the PathCond class provides exactly the operations Or, And, and AndNot:

```
public abstract class PathCond : IEquatable<PathCond> {
    public static readonly PathCond FALSE = new Disj();
    public static readonly PathCond TRUE = new Conj();

    public abstract PathCond And(CachedAtom expr);
    public abstract PathCond AndNot(CachedAtom expr);
    public abstract PathCond Or(PathCond other);
    ...
}
```

The CachedAtom machinery is used to ensure that expressions are evaluated at most once and is explained in section 9.6.2.

9.6.1   Conditions must be evaluated at most once

As shown above, for IF(e1,e2,e3) we generate evaluation conditions involving e1 as well as NOT(e1), and each of these may be duplicated in case there are further non-strict function calls in e2 or e3. However, for correctness (as well as efficiency), we must evaluate e1 at most once, and in particular when e1 may contain calls to volatile or external functions. Similarly, for CHOOSE(e0,e1,...,en) we generate conditions of the form e0=1, e0=2, ..., e0=n, yet we must evaluate e0 at most once.

Example 9.2 To see that we must cache expressions in evaluation conditions, consider this example where cell B180 should evaluate to $\sin(\pi/2) = 1$ with probability 20% and evaluate to 10 with probability 80%:

```
B179 = EXTERN("System.Math.Sin$(D)D", PI()/2)
B180 = IF(RAND()<0.2, B179*B179, 10)
```

The evaluation condition of B179 is RAND()<0.2, but since RAND is volatile, each evaluation may produce a different result. Hence, we should compute that expression once, cache it, and reuse the value, like this:

```
if (cache#0[RAND()<0.2])
   v_B179 = EXTERN("System.Math.Sin$(D)D", PI()/2);
v_B180 = cache#0[RAND()<0.2] ? v_B179 * v_B179 : 10.0;
```

Here the notation cache#0[RAND()<0.2] means that cache number 0 evaluates RAND()<0.2 at most once and caches its result. If, instead of caching RAND()<0.2, we computed it twice, then v_B179 would be correctly initialized only in 20% of its subsequent uses.

Example 9.3 The previous example shows that we should be careful not to duplicate the evaluation of expressions that are used in evaluation conditions. However, it would also be wrong to cache too aggressively, thereby folding or coalescing computations that should be kept separate. Consider this example, wherein cell B186 should evaluate to $\sin(\pi/2) = 1$ with probability $36\% = 0.2 + 0.8 \cdot 0.2$ and evaluate to 10 with probability 64%:

```
B185 = EXTERN("System.Math.Sin$(D)D", PI()/2)
B186 = IF(RAND()<0.2, B185*B185, IF(RAND()<0.2, B185*B185, 10))
```

If we mistakenly create only one cache variable for the two structurally identical but distinct expressions RAND()<0.2, then the function would return 1 with probability 20% instead of 36%, which clearly would be wrong. We must create a distinct cache for each subexpression, like this:

```
if (CACHE#1[RAND()<0.2]
    || (!CACHE#1[RAND()<0.2] && CACHE#0[RAND()<0.2]))
  { v_B185 = EXTERN("System.Math.Sin$(D)D", PI()/2); }
v_B186 = CACHE#1[RAND()<0.2]
          ? v_B179 * v_B179
          : CACHE#0[RAND()<0.2] ? v_B179 * v_B179 : 10.0;
```

9.6.2 Implementation of expression caching

The previous section shows that for correctness we must evaluate an expression e that is used as condition in IF(c, ..., ...) or CHOOSE(e, ...) at most once. Therefore, when such an expression is also used in an evaluation condition, we must cache the result of its first evaluation and reuse it. Therefore, we allocate a local cache variable for each such subexpression. Upon the first use, we evaluate the expression and store the result in the variable; all subsequent uses refer to that variable.

We use the following scheme. Each CGExpr expression e that must be evaluated at most once gets wrapped in a stateful CGCachedExpr object, which may then be incorporated multiple times in PathCond expressions. Also, we overwrite the original occurrence of the expression e in the abstract syntax tree with its cached version. For example, in IF(es[0], es[1], es[2]), we overwrite the condition expression es[0] with its cached version like this:

```
void EvalCond(PathCond evalCond, IDictionary<...> evalConds) {
  CachedAtom atom = new CachedAtom(es[0]);
  es[0].EvalCond(evalCond, evalConds);
  es[0] = atom.cachedExpr;
  es[1].EvalCond(evalCond.And(atom), evalConds);
  es[2].EvalCond(evalCond.AndNot(atom), evalConds);
}
```

Each compilation of a CGCachedExpr abstract syntax tree node checks whether the expression has already been evaluated and, if so, simply returns the result;

otherwise it evaluates the expression e, stores the result in the local cache variable, and returns it.

We generate code for the cached expressions in static order of use. This is not necessarily the dynamic order of use, although the dynamic order is embedded in the static order: there are no loops or other back edges. Since the statically first use may be executed only conditionally, we cannot simply compute the expression and save it to the cache at the statically first use and let all subsequent uses load from the cache. This is because we compile composite evaluation conditions using short-circuit "and" and "or". Indeed we must use short-circuit logical operations when compiling the evaluation conditions. Consider a function FOO whose output cell contains this formula:

```
IF(e1, C11*C11, IF(e2, C12*C12..., ...))
```

Here the evaluation condition of C11 is e1, which must be evaluated. The evaluation condition of C12 is NOT(e1) && e2, and we *must* avoid evaluating e2 in case e1 is true. Namely, the condition e2 may involve a recursive call to function FOO itself, like this:

```
IF(e1, ..., IF(FOO(...), ..., ...))
```

If we were to evaluate e2 unconditionally, then we would create an infinite loop. So evaluation conditions must be compiled for short-circuit evaluation, and we cannot rely on the statically first occurrence of a cached expression being evaluated before the other ones. Hence, we must be able to look at a cache variable and determine whether its expression has evaluated (and the result stored).

This leads to the following design for evaluation of cached expressions. Since an expression e is cached only because it was used as a condition in IF or as an index in CHOOSE, it must evaluate to a number (or an error). So the cache variables should have type double, and so we can use a special NaN value to denote "cache not yet filled". Concretely we use the NaN in which the 32 least significant bits of the payload is 1, corresponding to ErrorValue.MakeNan(-1).

At each occurrence of the cached expression, we test the value of the cache variable. If it is this particular NaN, we evaluate the expression and save its value in the cache; otherwise we just produce the value from the cache. Even if the expression happens to evaluate to this particular NaN, this scheme would give the correct result, but it may cause the cached expression to be evaluated more than once. All the cache variables must be initialized with the indicated NaN at the beginning of a function's code.

Unfortunately, it does seem necessary to create a copy of the code of the cached expression e at every use of the cached expression. It would be desirable to create a form of subroutine for its evaluation, in the style of the Java Virtual Machine's infamous "local subroutines" [92, 3.13]. Most of this could be done in .NET bytecode by passing to the local subroutines a number that indicates which of the finitely many call sites it would have to return to and use a CIL switch instruction to jump to the indicated one. But it would not work in general because such a "local subroutine" may be called from different expression nestings, and hence different stack depths, and this violates CLI verification conditions. The CLI standard says, "The type state of the stack (the stack depth and types of each element on the stack) at any given point in a program shall be identical for all possible control flow paths" [49, section I.12.3.2.1]. The power (and implementation complexity) of the Java Virtual Machine local subroutines stem precisely from their stack depth polymorphism.

Hence, it seems that we have to duplicate the code (but not the evaluation) for the cached expression e at each use. Since this cannot happen recursively, the risk in terms of code size growth is small, and in practice it seems not to cause a problem.

9.6.3 Avoiding caching

As an important optimization, note that even if an expresion e gets incorporated into an evaluation condition, and so potentially will need to have a cache created for it, it may happen that e is used (statically) at most once. This is because an enclosing evaluation condition may be reduced to true or ignored (see section 9.7). When the expression *e* is used (statically) at most once, we do not need to cache it or allocate a local variable for it. We can perform this optimization by introducing an extra stage:

- Wrap the CGExpr as an object of class CGCachedExpr and create an object of class CachedAtom (subclass of PathCond) with mutual references between the CGCachedExpr and the CachedAtom object.

- The `CachedAtom.ToCGExpr` conversion just returns the CGCachedExpr object but counts the total number of times it is asked to return it.

- The `CGCachedExpr.Compile` method allocates a local variable for caching only if the count is two or more.

9.7 Refining evaluation conditions

9.7.1 Reducing evaluation conditions

While it is fairly easy to correctly create the evaluation condition as the disjunction of conjunctions over the paths from the output cell, the resulting expressions may be unwieldy. For good run-time performance, it is essential to reduce the evaluation conditions as much as possible, ideally to the constant true—so the evaluation condition need not be evaluated at all at run-time.

The PathCond classes implement the following reductions:

$$
\begin{array}{lcl}
\neg\neg p & \Longrightarrow & p \\
p \wedge false & \Longrightarrow & false \\
p \wedge true & \Longrightarrow & p \\
p \vee false & \Longrightarrow & p \\
p \vee true & \Longrightarrow & true \\
p \wedge \neg p & \Longrightarrow & false \\
p \vee \neg p & \Longrightarrow & true \\
p \wedge q \vee p \wedge r & \Longrightarrow & p \wedge (q \vee r) \\
p \vee (p \wedge q) & \Longrightarrow & p
\end{array}
$$

The last reduction is especially important because it will likely appear frequently during the construction of evaluation conditions. Namely, if cell B3, which has evaluation condition p, has both an unconditional and a conditional dependency on B2, then B2 has evaluation condition $p \vee (p \wedge \ldots)$, which should reduce to p.

To preserve the evaluation order of conditions, we represent multi-conjunctions and multi-disjunctions as lists of PathConds, and to implement the optimizations efficiently, we further use hash indexes on the arraylists. More precisely, we use a class HashList<T>, which is an aggregation of the .NET 4.0 List<T> and Hash-Set<T> classes. Nevertheless, the optimizations are somewhat painful to express in our object-oriented implementation language C#; using a language such as F# with pattern matching would probably have felt more comfortable.

9.7.2 Cells with trivial formulas

In some cases, a cell that contains a rather simple formula has a complex evaluation condition, and the effort to evaluate the condition exceeds the effort to evaluate the cell's formula. In such cases, it would be better to simply set the cell's evaluation condition to constant true (after finding the evaluation conditions of all cells) and thus evaluate it unconditionally.

We call an expression *trivial* if it is a constant or a cell reference or a call to a trivial function with trivial arguments, and its abstract syntax tree has less than a certain number of nodes. Trivial functions include arithmetic operations and mathematical functions such as SIN. Non-trivial functions are array operations (which may be time-consuming), sheet-defined functions, and APPLY (which may involve recursion) and EXTERN (which may be time consuming and have side effects).

Since a trivial cell may depend on a non-trivial one that has a non-true evaluation condition, the trivial cell may refer to local variables that hold default values (null or 0.0). This should cause no problems, since the trivial cells do not call sheet-defined or external functions.

9.7.3 Do not take short-circuit evaluation into account

In Corecalc and Funcalc, the AND(...) and OR(...) functions are strict only in their first argument. Hence, to generate precise evaluation conditions for AND(e1, e2, ..., en), we could proceed as follows (OR is completely analogous, only dual to AND):

- Define evalCond1 to be evalCond

- Compute e1.EvalCond(evalCond1, evalConds)

- Set evalCond2 equal to AND(evalCond1,e1)

- Compute e2.EvalCond(evalCond2, evalConds)

- Set evalCond3 equal to AND(evalCond2,e2)

- Compute e3.EvalCond(evalCond3, evalConds)

- ... and so on.

Namely, e2 would be evaluated (and the cell references inside it would be needed) only in case evalCond is true and e1 is true, and similarly for e3 and so on.

In implementation terms, here is CGAnd's current EvalCond method, which considers all operands e1, ..., en to have the same evaluation condition, effectively considering AND strict:

```
void EvalCond(PathCond evalCond, IDictionary<...> evalConds) {
    for (int i = 0; i < es.Length; i++)
        es[i].EvalCond(evalCond, evalConds);
}
```

We could replace it by this version, which updates the evaluation conditions for e2, ..., en as indicated above:

```
void EvalCond(PathCond evalCond, IDictionary<...> evalConds) {
    for (int i = 0; i < es.Length; i++) {
        es[i].EvalCond(evalCond, evalConds);
        CachedAtom atom = new CachedAtom(es[i]);
        evalCond = evalCond.And(atom);
        es[i] = atom.cachedExpr;
    }
}
```

However, this generates very complex evaluation conditions, which moreover appear unpleasantly cyclic. For instance:

```
evalConds[@Functions!B23] =
    (@Functions!B22>0 || AND(@Functions!B22>0,@Functions!B23>0))

evalConds[@Functions!B28] =
    (AND(@Functions!B27>0,@Functions!B28>0) || @Functions!B27>0)
```

All of the above have the form $p \lor p \land q$, where the self-dependency appears in the term q and therefore could be eliminated because the expression is equivalent to just p. In all cases, such reduction would require us to take into account the semantics of CGExprs, for instance, by expanding CGExpr AND, OR, NOT, IF as PathCond terms. But that should be done with great care to avoid duplicating (or folding) expressions that involve volatile functions or have side effects, so we have not done that.

A simple way to eliminate the problem, at least for all the sheet-defined functions we consider, is to ignore short-circuit evaluation of AND and OR when generating evaluation conditions. This change eliminates all the self-dependencies listed above. It also means that too much gets computed, and that clever programming idioms such as defining ALLTRUE(xs) recursively as

```
ALLTRUE(xs) = OR(LENGTH(xs)=0, AND(CAR(xs), ALLTRUE(CDR(xs))))
```

will not work. Instead one must use an explicit test:

```
ALLTRUE(xs) =
   IF(LENGTH(xs)=0, TRUE, IF(CAR(xs), ALLTRUE(CDR(xs)), FALSE))
```

9.7.4   No new dependency cycles

How can we be sure that the new dependency graph contains no cycles incurred by the extra dependencies? Simply by considering dependencies from the evaluation condition only if there is not already a dependency the other way?

For instance, it would seem that the following situation could arise. The evaluation condition for cell B2 involves cell B2 itself; this would create a cyclic dependency:

```
if (B2)
   B2 = B1+1;
```

However, this could arise only if somewhere the use of B2 depends on B2, as in

```
B3 = IF(B2, B2, 42);
```

But in that case, B2 is unconditionally needed (assuming B3 is), and the condition on B2 *should* be true. More generally, if the evaluation condition on B3 is p, then the evaluation condition on B2 will be p too, reduced from $p \lor (p \land B2)$.

An apparent problem is that in some cases the inferred evaluation condition for a cell appears to involve the cell itself, which is not very meaningful. A case in point is @Functions!B23:

```
evalConds[@Functions!B23] =
   (@Functions!B22>0 || AND(@Functions!B22>0,@Functions!B23>0))
```

Of course, this could be reduced to

```
evalConds[@Functions!B23] =
  @Functions!B22>0
```

in which the condition evaluation for B23 does not depend on B23 itself. However, this reduction would require the logical reductions to take into account the semantics of CGExpr AND(...), and in general we can hardly be sure to cover all such cases.

So is there a simpler approach we could take? Note that if the evaluation condition of a cell really depends on the cell itself, then the sheet-defined function would already contain a cyclic dependency, as in

```
B23 = IF(B23>0, ..., ...)
```

So one way to deal with this problem is to generate evaluation conditions as outlined in section 9.6 and simply set to true those subexpressions of each evaluation condition that refer to cells that have not been computed yet.

9.7.5 Speculation: Sharing condition subexpressions

When the evaluation of multiple cells depends on the same logical expression, it is desirable to perform that test once and evaluate all the cells in one go. Even if the logical expression itself has been pre-evaluated, we should reduce the number of conditional jumps to avoid pipeline stalls caused by branch misprediction. More generally, it might be desirable to use nested conditions rather than more complex logical expressions to control conditional evaluation. We have not yet implemented such improvements.

9.8 Example evaluation conditions

Returning to the REPT4 function from section 9.1 and example 9.1, we find that the evaluation condition for cell B71 is exactly what it should be, namely:

```
NOT(CACHE#0[NOT(@Functions!B70)])
```

Here NOT(@Functions!B70) is another way of saying B70=0, the CACHE#0 is a cache variable created for that expression, and the outer NOT says that B71 should only be evaluated if B70 is non-zero.

The NORMDISTCDF from example 6.5 has a single not-true evaluation condition, namely, for cell @NormalDist!B9:

```
NOT(CACHE#1[@NormalDist!B8>37])
```

However, the formula =EXP(-B8*B8/2) in cell B9 is trivial; it is probably no slower to evaluate that formula than to evaluate and cache the evaluation condition. Hence, our implementation sets the evaluation condition to true and caches nothing.

The "unrolled" version of function FINDEND from example 6.24 has no less than 28 non-true evaluation conditions, some of which are very complex. However, they all control cells containing trivial formulas, such as $A$7+$B10, and we can therefore ignore these evaluation conditions. If we laboriously evaluate and cache all evaluation conditions, also for the 28 cells with trivial formulas, then GOALSEEK, which uses FINDEND as a subroutine, is slowed down by a factor of 1.65.

For the "unrolled" version of function GOALSEEK from example 6.22, all evaluation conditions reduce to constant true, except that non-trivial cell @Goalseek!C24 has this evaluation condition:

```
CACHE#58[@Goalseek!D24<=0] || NOT(CACHE#59[@Goalseek!D24<=0])
```

This condition is equivalent to true, of course. It was not reduced to true because the two conditions @Goalseek!D24<=0 originate from different spreadsheet cells, as indicated by the distinct caches CACHE#58 and CACHE#59 created for them. This happens because cell B28 contains the formula =IF(D24<=0,B24,C24) and cell C28 contains =IF(D24<=0,C24,B24). Regardless of the value of D24, cell C24 must be evaluated.

We can further improve the evaluation condition generator to reduce this evaluation condition to true. We would need to define a notion of equality of CGExpr that describes when two expressions will evaluate to the same value. It would suffice to require that they are structurally equal and that they contain no calls to volatile, external, or sheet-defined functions.

Chapter 10

Partial Evaluation

The function call CLOSURE("name", a1, ..., an) constructs a closure fv, in the form of a so-called partial application of sheet-defined function name. The closure fv is just a package of the underlying function name and some early, non-#NA, arguments for it. Applying the closure using APPLY(fv, b1, ..., bk) simply inserts the values of b1...bk instead of the closure's #NA arguments and then calls the underlying sheet-defined function; this is no faster than calling the original function.

However, if the closure fv is to be called more than once, it may be worthwhile to perform a *specialization* or *partial evaluation* of the underlying sheet-defined function with respect to the non-#NA values among the arguments a1...an. In Funcalc, this can be done by the built-in function SPECIALIZE(fv), which will produce a specialized function spfv that can be used exactly like fv. In particular, the specialized function can be called using APPLY(spfv, b1, ..., bk).

Often the specialized function is faster than the general one, and often the specialized function can be generated once and then applied many times.

This chapter explains how we implemented the SPECIALIZE function in Funcalc and shows some examples of its use. Much of the presentation is based on [139]. The Funcalc manual also gives a brief description of how to use specialization (see section 11.6).

10.1 Aside: What is partial evaluation?

Partial evaluation is a technique to partially execute a function when only some of its inputs are available. Consider a function $f(x_1, x_2) = \ldots$ having two parameters, x_1 and x_2. When specific values d_1 and d_2 are given for the two parameters, we can fully evaluate the function call $f(d_1, d_2)$, producing a result. When only one input value d_1 is given, we cannot fully evaluate a call to f, but we can *partially evaluate* it, producing a version f_{d_1} of function f that is specialized for the case where $x_1 = d_1$.

When some value d_2 for the remaining parameter x_2 becomes available, we can apply the specialized function f_{d_1} to d_2 by evaluating $f_{d_1}(d_2)$. This application of the specialized function f_{d_1} must produce the same result as the full call $f(d_1, d_2)$ to the original function f.

Thus, partial evaluation may look like a complicated way to compute a result that one could have obtained directly. However, the specialized function f_{d_1} may be considerably faster than the original unspecialized one: those computations inside $f(x_1, x_2)$ that depend only on the value d_1 of x_1 may be performed once and for all by the partial evaluator when creating the specialized function f_{d_1}, so that they need not be performed by each application $f_{d_1}(d_2)$ of the specialized function. This is especially useful if we need to compute $f(d_1, d_2)$ for a single value d_1 and many different values d_2, so we need to perform just one partial evaluation to obtain f_{d_1}, which can then be called any number of times on different values d_2.

For a concrete example, consider the C# function `Power(n, x)` which efficiently computes x^n, that is, x to the nth power:

```
static double Power(int n, double x) {
  double p;
  p = 1;
  while (n > 0) {
    if (n % 2 == 0)
      { x = x * x; n = n / 2; }
    else
      { p = p * x; n = n - 1; }
  }
  return p;
}
```

In this example, function f is `Power`, parameter x_1 is n, and x_2 is x. Partial evaluation of `Power` with a known value $d_1 = 7$ for n and an unknown value for x may automatically produce this specialized C# function:

```
static double Power_7(double x) {
  double p;
  p = 1;
  p = p * x;
  x = x * x;
  p = p * x;
  x = x * x;
  p = p * x;
  return p;
}
```

The specialized function contains no computations that depend on n because they were performed by the partial evaluation process. In particular the `while` loop and its test have vanished. It is not hard to see that the calls `Power(7, x)` and `Power_7(x)` compute the same result because they perform the exact same computations on variable p, which produces the return value.

Partial evaluation is an instance of *program specialization*. The early argument d_1 is called a *static value*, the late argument d_2 is called a *dynamic value*, and the specialized version f_{d_1} of f is called a *residual function*.

In the Funcalc context, partial evaluation starts with a closure f(a1, ..., an) (see section 8.4.1). Partial evaluation will specialize the closure's underlying sheet-defined function f with respect to the closure's non-#NA arguments; these are the static arguments. The result will be a new closure fd(#NA...#NA) whose underlying function fd is a specialized version of f and where the number of #NA arguments equals the number of #NA arguments in the original closure (see also figure 11.4).

10.2   Partial evaluation in a spreadsheet context

Automatic specialization, or partial evaluation, has been studied for a wide range of languages in many contexts and for many purposes [85, 75]. Yet specialization in the context of sheet-defined functions appears to offer new opportunities for several reasons:

- The declarative computation model makes specialization fairly easy. All values are immutable, and all expressions are side effect free (except possibly external calls). The main sources of complication are (1) operations that are volatile or that update or rely on external state, and (2) recursive function calls. In both respects, one can draw on a large body of experience from specialization of other dynamically typed languages, notably Scheme, as developed by Bondorf and Danvy [18, 19] and Ruf, Weise, and others [130, 131, 162].

- Actual bytecode generation for a specialized function can use the same machinery as for non-specialized ones; in particular, specialized functions are not penalized by poorer code generation.

- Specialization of sheet-defined functions that involve volatile functions, such as RAND and NOW, requires some care. A volatile function's result should always be considered dynamic; the randomness or external state inherent in a volatile function is similar to a side effect and hence should be residualized as realized already by Bondorf and Danvy [19].

- The language of sheet-defined functions is a higher-order functional language, and a function can be specialized with respect to a function.

- The spreadsheet environment is interactive, and all evaluation and specialization takes place in the same environment, containing data, the original program, and the specialized program. Any value produced during evaluation of a Funcalc spreadsheet can be represented by a CGValueConst expression (figure 7.3), which is an abstract syntax tree node that simply holds a reference to that (immutable) value. Hence, there is no need to marshall higher-order (function-type) values as data, nor to subsequently restore them as function values. This avoids the problem of cross-stage persistence [111] and the problem of finding which functions appear in dynamic context [130, section 3.3.5] when constructing a residual program in text form.

- The seemingly cumbersome split of specialization (SPECIALIZE) from closure creation (CLOSURE) has the advantage that an already-specialized function may be further partially applied using CLOSURE and then specialized using SPECIALIZE (see example 10.6 and figure 11.4). It also means that a higher-order library function may specialize an unknown closure passed to it as an argument. Using the timing function BENCHMARK (page 277), it may even measure whether the specialized function is faster than the original one.

Automatic specialization of sheet-defined functions permit generality without performance penalties. For instance, a company or a research community can develop general financial or statistical functions and rely on automatic specialization to create efficient specialized versions, removing the need to develop and maintain hand-specialized ones.

10.3   Partial evaluation of a sheet-defined function

Specialization or partial evaluation of a sheet-defined function is performed through a single additional built-in function SPECIALIZE(fv) that takes as argument a function closure fv. It then generates a specialized version of fv's underlying sheet-defined function based on the early arguments included in the closure fv.

Partial evaluation of a sheet-defined function works on its representation as a list of ComputeCell objects, as produced by steps 1 through 4a in section 9.2. The result is a new ComputeCell list containing specialized versions of the existing expressions. Section 10.4 describes the processing of most expressions, except for function calls, the main source of complications, which are described in section 10.5.

The specialized ComputeCell list is subsequently used to generate bytecode for the specialized function via the machinery already in place for this purpose. Furthermore, the ComputeCell list is saved to permit further specialization of the newly specialized sheet-defined function; this rather unusual functionality comes for free.

We use classical polyvariant specialization [25], so the residual program consists of any number of specialized variants of existing sheet-defined functions. Such specialized variants may call each other, thus permitting loops and (mutual) recursion in the residual program.

Each specialized function is given a unique name. For instance, if the display value of the given closure fv is ADD(42,#NA), then the result of SPECIALIZE(fv) may be named ADD(42,#NA)#117, where #117 is a unique internal function number.

The specialized functions will be cached so that two closures that are equal (based on underlying function and argument values) will give rise to a single shared specialized function. That avoids some wasteful specialization and also is the obvious way to allow for loops (via recursive function calls) in specialized functions.

The specialization of CGExpr expressions, described in section 10.4, takes place in a partial evaluation environment `pEnv` that is initialized and updated as follows. Initially, `pEnv` maps the cell address of each static (non-`#NA`) input cell to a constant representing that input cell's value. Moreover, `pEnv` maps each remaining (dynamic or `#NA`) input cell address to a new CGCellRef expression representing a residual function argument.

During partial evaluation of a pair `(ca,e)` in the ComputeCell list, consisting of a cell address and an expression, the `pEnv` is extended as follows. If the result of partially evaluating the formula `e` in cell `ca` is a CGConst, then we extend `pEnv` so it maps `ca` to that constant; then the constant will be inlined at all subsequent occurrences. Otherwise, create a fresh local variable as a copy of the existing cell variable `ca` and add a ComputeCell to the resulting list that will, at run-time, evaluate the residual expression and store its value in the new local variable. Also, extend `pEnv` to map `ca` to the new local variable, so that subsequent references to cell `ca` will refer to the new local variable and thereby at run-time will fetch the value computed by the residual expression.

When the residual ComputeCell list is complete, the dependency graph is built, a topological sort is performed, use-once cells are inlined, evaluation conditions are recomputed, and code is generated, as for a normal sheet-defined function (sections 9.2 and 9.3).

10.4   Partial evaluation of CGExpr terms

Partial evaluation of a given cell's formula expression proceeds by rewriting a given CGExpr term (figure 7.3) to a residual CGExpr term as follows:

- Partial evaluation of an expression of class CGConst or one of its subclasses produces that expression itself.

- Partial evaluation of a function-sheet cell reference CGCellRef(c) produces a CGConst static value if cell c is a static input cell or another cell that has been reduced to a CGConst subclass; otherwise it produces the given expression CG-CellRef(c) itself. This avoids inlining and duplication of residual computations while still exposing static values to further partial evaluation.

- Partial evaluation of an ordinary-sheet cell reference CGNormalCellRef(c) produces that expression itself, not the value currently found in the referred ordinary-sheet cell c, because that value might change before the residual sheet-defined function gets called. This allows cells on an ordinary sheet to be used as "external parameters" of a specialized function.

- Partial evaluation of an area reference CGNormalCellArea(area) to an ordinary sheet produces that expression itself, not the values currently found in the referred cells, because those values might change before the residual sheet-defined function gets called.

- Partial evaluation of expressions of class CGStrictOperation and most of its subclasses proceeds uniformly as follows. Partially evaluate the argument expressions and, if they are all constants, then evaluate the operation as usual; otherwise residualize the operation. In particular, this holds for CGArithmetic1, CGArithmetic2, CGComparison, and CGFunctionCall, except for volatile functions. A volatile function such as NOW() and RAND() should always be residualized, not evaluated, during partial evaluation. For instance, a sheet-defined function might perform a stochastic simulation, using the condition RAND()<0.2 to choose between two scenarios, as in example 10.1. Early evaluation of RAND()<0.2 would make all executions of the residual function choose the same scenario, which would make the specialized closure behave differently than the original one.

  The exceptions to the general partial evaluation of CGStrictOperation are CGApply and CGSdfCall (residualize to avoid infinite loops; see section 10.5), CGFunctionCall (residualize when the called built-in function is volatile), and CGExtern (residualize to avoid specialization-time side effects).

- Partial evaluation of a CGClosure expression follows the general CGStrictOperation scheme for partial evaluation. First, it reduces its argument expressions. If all are constant, then it calls the interpretive applier corresponding to built-in function CLOSURE and produces a CGValueConst that wraps a FunctionValue containing the given sheet-defined function and the given parameters; otherwise it residualizes.

- Partial evaluation of a call to a sheet-defined function (CGSdfCall) is discussed separately in section 10.5.

- Partial evaluation of a CGApply(e0, e1, ..., en) expression should first reduce all operands, both the function expression e0 and its arguments. If the function expression in e0 is static and is a FunctionValue wrapped in a CGValueConst, then partial evaluation can produce a CGSdfCall expression; otherwise it must residualize to a CGApply based on the residual operand expressions. Even if both the function and all the arguments are static values, it is dangerous to actually call the indicated sheet-defined function, as this could result in an infinite loop.

  It is worth pondering whether a more aggressive evaluation is possible when the function expression e0 is static and hence is a known FunctionValue. Could we simply further process it as if partially evaluating a CGSdfCall expression using the exact same machinery?

- Partial evaluation of CGIf(e0, e1, e2) or CGChoose(e0, e1, ..., en) should produce the result of partially evaluating the relevant branch ei if the first expression e0 is a static value. Otherwise, they must residualize to a CGIf or CGChoose constructed from the residual argument expressions.

- Partial evaluation of a CGAnd expression, short-cut style, can proceed as follows. Each argument is partially evaluated in turn, from left to right. If the result is constant false (zero), then the residual expression for the entire CGAnd is the constant false; if the result is constant true (non-zero), then it is ignored; and if the result is non-constant, then it is kept for possible inclusion in the residual expression. If no argument reduces to false, then the residual expression for the entire CGAnd is the conjunction of the residual expressions of the non-true arguments. In case all constant arguments were true, the result is the empty conjunction, that is, true.

- Partial evaluation of a CGOr expression is dual to CGAnd: just swap false and true, and zero and non-zero, in the description above.

- A CGCachedExpr expression may be wrapped around the conditions of `IF` and `CHOOSE` for use in evaluation conditions. Since we ignore evaluation conditions during partial evaluation, partial evaluation of a CGCachedExpr should simply partially evaluate the enclosed expression.

10.5   Partial evaluation of function calls

Partial evaluation of a function call, whether a direct call CGSdfCall of a named sheet-defined function or a call CGApply of a function closure via `APPLY`, poses special challenges that may cause partial evaluation to fail to terminate. There are two ways that partial evaluation may go on indefinitely:

- *Infinite unfolding* happens when a call to a function F is encountered during partial evaluation of the same function F, indefinitely, just as in ordinary non-terminating recursion.

- *Infinite specialization* happens when partial evaluation attempts to create an infinite number of specialized versions of some function, such as `ADD(1,#NA)`, `ADD(2,#NA)`, `ADD(3,#NA)`, and so on.

Moreover, we would like to avoid generating a finite but large number of specialized versions of a function, when these turn out to be nearly identical and offer no significant speed-up. This particular problem is discussed in section 10.5.3.

Some of the problems we need to address are:

- When should we create further specializations of a sheet-defined function while already in the process of creating one specialization?

- More precisely, given a sheet-defined function and static values of some of its arguments, which of these arguments should actually be used when specializing the function? Specializing with respect to all-#NA arguments should be equivalent to not specializing the function at all, thus making `SPECIALIZE` idempotent. This is convenient when both a higher-order library function and its caller attempt to specialize an argument closure.

- When all arguments to a sheet-defined function, encountered during partial evaluation, are static, should we then attempt to fully evaluate the function or should we specialize it?

10.5.1   Principle 1: Residualize all function calls

When the result of a function would be non-static (because some arguments are non-static or because the function body contains a call to a volatile or external function), then we would lose little information by not unfolding the call but reducing it to a call to a residual function. This decision does not affect the meaning or termination properties of the partial evaluation process.

However, when the result of partially evaluating the function body would be a concrete static value, unfolding would propagate the concrete value to the call context, thus enabling further computation, whereas residualizing the call will lose the information held in that static value.

Nevertheless, we decide to always residualize and never unfold a function call:

- Principle 1: The result of partially evaluating a function call is a residual function call.

This ensures that the only source of non-termination during partial evaluation is infinite specialization.

We residualize a function call also when all its arguments are static, even though in Funcalc it would be trivial to invoke the standard evaluation machinery and then wrap the resulting Value as a GCConst object (figure 7.3). However, using the standard evaluation machinery during partial evaluation would be wrong because it will evaluate any volatile and external functions prematurely: even when all needed arguments are static, the result may be a residual expression instead of a value. To see this, consider the function in example 10.1.

Example 10.1 Function EXPSAMPLE permits sampling from the exponential distribution:

```
EXPSAMPLE(p,n) = IF(p<=0.0, ERR("P"),
                    IF(RAND()<p, n, EXPSAMPLE(p,n+1)))
```

Function EXPSAMPLE(p,n) either terminates immediately with probability p, or otherwise performs one more recursive call. Thus, EXPSAMPLE(1,1) will return 1 immediately, and EXPSAMPLE(0.5,1) will return 1 with probability 0.5, will return 2 with probability 0.25, will return 3 with probability 0.0125, and so on, that is, on average will return 2; EXPSAMPLE(p,1) will on average return $1/p$, the mean value of the exponential distribution with parameter p, when $0 < p \leq 1$.

When both arguments to EXPSAMPLE(p,n) are static, the arguments of the recursive call will be static too. But since the condition RAND()<p is volatile and will be

residualized, the IF-expression will be residualized too, and unfolding of the recursive function call would go on indefinitely in an attempt to construct an infinite tree of residual conditionals.

To avoid such construction of infinite residual terms, we decide never to unfold function calls.

10.5.2   Principle 2: Generalize under dynamic control

In the EXPSAMPLE case, the decision never to unfold a function call will avoid infinite unfolding, but it might cause infinite specialization instead in an attempt to create specialized versions for n being 1, 2, 3, and so on.

To avoid this, we need to *generalize* one or more static arguments, here n, by reclassifying them as dynamic, that is, consider them to be #NA in further specialization. This works as follows.

We say that an expression is under *dynamic control* if some conditional (IF, CHOOSE) with dynamic condition has been encountered before the expression during the specialization process. Whether an expression appears under dynamic control can be determined by passing a context argument along with the partial evaluation environment pEnv in the recursive calls to the partial evaluator.

If, in the process of specializing a sheet-defined function F with respect to values v1...vn, we encounter a recursive call to F(...) under dynamic control and with arguments w1...wn, then we specialize F in the recursive call only with respect to those static arguments wj that have the same constant value wj=vj in both calls; the remaining static wj are made dynamic, that is, considered #NA when specializing the called function.

Although this may seem draconically conservative, it will serve one large class of specialization cases well, namely, when some static "configuration" or "problem" parameters are passed to the function initially and passed on unchanged in all recursive calls. Such static parameters will be inlined (and possibly cause IF and CHOOSE expressions to be reduced), but the part of the control structure that depends also on dynamic parameters will be preserved. The draconic policy could be loosened a little by permitting specialization with respect to literal constants given in the function (since there are only finitely many of those), but it is unclear whether this is worthwhile in general, and we currently do not do it.

To implement the above policy, we need a partial evaluation context (an evaluation stack) that says which functions are currently being specialized with respect to which constant arguments, the value of those arguments (so we can deal with mutually recursive functions), and an indication of whether the current expression (especially a call) is under dynamic control. A partial evaluation context must tell us (1) whether the expression being partially evaluated is under dynamic control, so we can decide what to do with calls CGApply or CGSdfCall; (2) which functions are currently being partially evaluated, so we can recognize recursive calls; and (3) the arguments given to the functions that are currently being partially evaluated.

Property (1) is a local property of a subexpression of a ComputeCell, determined by the cell's evaluation condition and the conditions enclosing that subexpression in the cell. This notion of context could therefore be represented by an argument IsDynamicControl passed in as an argument of the partial evaluation process. For an evaluation condition, it is initially false; and for the expression in a ComputeCell, it is true if and only if its evaluation condition is dynamic. For CgIf and CGChoose, it is determined as one might expect—by the first argument. Note the difference from the partial evaluation environment pEnv, which grows monotonically while processing the list of ComputeCells belonging to a given sheet-defined function.

Properties (2) and (3) are somewhat more global. They too could be represented by a parameter to the partial evaluator but would need much broader scope: not only the partial evaluation of a given sheet-defined function but a family of such functions.

To see the effect of the simple generalization technique, consider these examples.

Example 10.2 Ackermann's function is sometimes used to illustrate partial evaluation of recursive functions [85, section 17.3]. It may be defined like this:

```
ackA(m,n) = IF(m=0, n+1, IF(n=0, ackA(m-1,1), ackA(m-1,ackA(m,n-1))))
```

If we assume that m is static and equal to 2 and n is dynamic, then the outer IF is static but the inner one is dynamic. Using the generalization strategy outlined above, we get the following specialized function:

```
ackA2(n) = IF(n=0, ackA(1,1), ackA(1, ackA2(n-1)))
```

which basically specializes only with respect to the first value of m and only at the top-most call to ackA and therefore misses significant optimization opportunities. But to make sure that the specialization of ackA with respect to static first argument m-1 will terminate, we really need to know that the first argument is descending and bounded from below (as in several static termination analyses). This requires a somewhat sophisticated static analysis, made even more complicated by the dynamically typed spreadsheet formulas, so we prefer to avoid it.

The next example shows that by rewriting the Ackermann function in a slightly different style, we achieve much better specialization under the same generalization scheme.

Example 10.3 Now define Ackermann's function like this, pushing the inner conditional inside the recursive call:

```
ackB(m,n) = IF(m=0, n+1, ackB(m-1, IF(n=0, 1, ackB(m, n-1))))
```

Then we get the following much better specialization for m=2 static and n dynamic:

```
ackB2(n) = ackB1(IF(n=0, 1, ackB2(n-1)))
ackB1(n) = ackB0(IF(n=0, 1, ackB1(n-1)))
ackB0(n) = n+1
```

This is just as we would like it and similar to what one would get from an off-line partial evaluator and a binding-time analysis, even on the original source program in example 10.2.

10.5.3 Termination

The simple principles of (1) never unfold and (2) generalize aggressively when under
dynamic control, together ensure fairly good termination properties of the partial
evaluator. The downside is that the partial evaluator is somewhat conservative, although it achieves reasonably good results on examples such as those in section 10.7.

Termination is far from guaranteed, though, and the partial evaluator is far
from fool-proof. For instance, specialization can still fail to terminate due to infinite
specialization. To see this, consider a function definition such as the "counting-down
factorial" function [162, page 172]:

```
FACD(N) = IF(N=0, 1, N * FACD(N-1))
```

and assume that we attempt to specialize `FACD(-1)`. Since there is no dynamic control, the specializer will not generalize the static argument and will attempt to create an infinite number of specialized functions corresponding to the calls `FACD(-1)`,
`FACD(-2)`, `FACD(-3)`, and so on. However, standard evaluation of `FACD(-1)` would
also fail to terminate.

If the call `FACD(-1)` were under dynamic control, then the generalization mechanism would ensure that the argument gets generalized, and only one specialized
version will be generated.

Holst's "poor man's generalization" [77] [85, section 7.2.2] is a generalization
technique that will generalize any static parameter that is not used to evaluate a
conditional such as `IF` or `CHOOSE`. The reasoning is that such a parameter will
have little effect on the residual program's size and that knowing its value will not
help termination of specialization but might still give rise to an excessive number of
residual functions. Using poor man's generalization will not help ensure termination but could help keep the number of specialized versions in check, avoiding fruit-
less and costly code generation that gives little performance benefit. However, it is
comparatively difficult to implement. We would need a backward data flow analysis to properly determine which parameters may (or must) eventually determine a
conditional. Moreover, this analysis must be interprocedural and the language is
higher-order, so this is not entirely straightforward, and we consider it too much
complexity for a modest gain.

More advanced generalization schemes and termination analyses, such as home-
omorphic embedding, seem hard to use in the spreadsheet context because most
data are numbers or arrays of numbers. Although tree-structured data are representable as nested arrays this is not natural to the spreadsheet context. Hence, we
currently do not use flow analysis-based generalization, only the online generalization mechanism described above.

A simple expedient would be to put an arbitrary limit on the number of specializations created for any given function. Since the original function is available
anyway, it can be used as a fallback when the limit is reached (see also section 10.8).

10.6 Simplification of arithmetic expressions

During partial evaluation, it is natural to use mathematical identities to simplify arithmetic expressions. For instance, $e + 0$ may be reduced to e. The full list of reductions, implemented in class CGArithmetics2, is shown in figure 10.1.

Some "obvious" mathematical identities, such as reducing $e * 0$ to 0, do not in general preserve spreadsheet semantics because $e * 0$ will evaluate to an error if e does, whereas 0 will not. Nevertheless, we have implemented all the listed reductions. Also, it may seem wrong in general to replace $e\hat{\ }0$ and $1\hat{\ }e$ with 1, but the IEEE754 floating-point standard [81, section 9.2.1] does prescribe these identities for all values of e, even NaN.

Original		Simplified	Note
$0 + e$	$\longrightarrow$	e	
$e + 0$	$\longrightarrow$	e	
$e - 0$	$\longrightarrow$	e	
$0 - e$	$\longrightarrow$	$-e$	
$e * 0$	$\longrightarrow$	0	(*)
$0 * e$	$\longrightarrow$	0	(*)
$1 * e$	$\longrightarrow$	e	
$e * 1$	$\longrightarrow$	e	
$e / 1$	$\longrightarrow$	e	
$e\hat{\ }1$	$\longrightarrow$	e	
$e\hat{\ }0$	$\longrightarrow$	1	(**)
$1\hat{\ }e$	$\longrightarrow$	1	(**)

Figure 10.1: Arithmetic simplifications performed by partial evaluation. Those marked (*) or (**) may not preserve spreadsheet semantics; those marked (**) do agree with the IEEE754 floating-point standard.

When specializing NORMDENSITYGENERAL from example 6.4 to $\mu = 0$ and $\sigma = 1$, the arithmetic simplifications in figure 10.1 ensure that the resulting bytecode is exactly the same as that of the "hand-specialized" NORMDENSITY function (example 6.4).

10.7 Partial evaluation examples

Here we consider the result of partially evaluating some small sheet-defined functions.

Example 10.4 Function MONTHLEN(y,m) computes the length of month m in year y, taking leap years into account:

```
MONTHLEN(y,m) =
  CHOOSE(m, 31,
         28+OR(AND(NOT(MOD(y, 4)), MOD(y, 100)), NOT(MOD(y, 400))),
         31, 30, 31, 30, 31, 31, 30, 31, 30, 31)
```

Specializing this function to a fixed month m will either leave only the leap year logic, eliminating the switch (when m is 2), or eliminate both the logic and the switch (when m is not 2). Here is the residual function for MONTHLEN(#NA,3):

```
0000: ldc.r8      31
0009: call        NumberValue.Make(Double)
000e: ret
```

Specializing MONTHLEN to a given year, such as 2012, produces a function where partial evaluation has removed all the logic concerning leap years. This is the bytecode for the specialization of MONTHLEN(2012,#NA); note in line 007f the result 29 of computing 28+1 at specialization time:

```
0000: ldarg      V_0
0004: call       Value.ToDoubleOrNan
0009: stloc.0
000a: ldloc.0
000b: call       IsInfinity(Double)
0010: brtrue     0150
0015: ldloc.0
0016: call       IsNaN(Double)
001b: brtrue     0150
0020: ldloc.0
0021: conv.i4
0022: ldc.i4     1
0027: sub
0028: switch     (006c, 007f, 0092, 00a5, 00b8, 00cb,   // CHOOSE
                  00de, 00f1, 0104, 0117, 012a, 013d)
005d: ldc.i4     5
0062: call       ErrorValue.FromIndex(Int32)
0067: br         014b
006c: ldc.r8     31
0075: call       NumberValue.Make(Double)
007a: br         014b
007f: ldc.r8     29                              // reduced from 28+...
0088: call       NumberValue.Make(Double)
008d: br         014b
0092: ldc.r8     31
00ae: call       NumberValue.Make(Double)
... and so on for April through November ...
0138: br         014b
013d: ldc.r8     31
0146: call       NumberValue.Make(Double)
014b: br         015a
0150: ldc.i4     2
0155: call       ErrorValue.FromIndex(Int32)
015a: ret
```

Example 10.5 Function REPT4(s,n) from example 9.1, which computes string s concatenated with itself n times, can be specialized with respect to a given string s or with respect to a given number n.

Specialization with respect to a given string, as in REPT4("abc",#NA), achieves nothing useful. The bytecode for the resulting specialized function is nearly identical to that for the original REPT4. Both are 123 bytecode instructions long (some of which implement evaluation conditions) and identical except that the specialized function loads the string "ABC" from a table of string values, whereas the original one takes it from the first function argument.

Specialization with respect to a given n, as in REPT4(#NA,7), is much more interesting. Since the second parameter n is static and determines all conditionals, that parameter and all tests on it will be eliminated. The result is not one but four specialized functions, corresponding to the values of n encountered in the recursive calls, namely 7, 3, 1, and 0.

This is REPT4(#NA,7)#201 corresponding to n being 7:

```
0000: ldsfld      SdfManager.sdfDelegates
0005: ldc.i4      202
000a: ldelem.ref
000b: castclass   System.Func`2[Value,Value]
0010: ldarg       V_0                        // load arg s
0014: call        Invoke                     // call #202(s) giving r
0019: stloc.3
001a: ldarg       V_0
001e: ldloc.3
001f: call        Function.ExcelConcat       // r & r
0024: ldloc.3
0025: call        Function.ExcelConcat       // (r & r) & s
002a: ret
```

Function #201 above computes s^7 for any string s by calling function #202 to compute s^3 and then concatenating the result r with itself and with s to obtain s^7.

Function #202 corresponds to n being 3 and has exactly the same structure. It calls function #203 to compute s^1 and then concatenates the result with itself and with s to obtain s^3.

Function #203 corresponds to n being 1 and has the same structure as the previous two. It calls function #204, which computes s^0, that is, the empty string:

```
0000: ldsfld      TextValue.EMPTY
0005: ret                                    // return ""
```

Whereas calling the original function REPT4("abc",7) takes 1200 ns/call, calling the specialized closure REPT4(#NA,7) on argument "abc" takes only 524 ns/call. Further speedup could be achieved by inlining the calls to the auxiliary specialized functions.

Example 10.6 To illustrate multistage specialization, consider the three-argument function ADD3(x,y,z):

```
ADD3(x,y,z) = x+y+z
```

The original bytecode for the unspecialized ADD3 is this:

```
0000: ldarg      V_0
0004: call       Value.ToDoubleOrNan        // Unwrap arg x
0009: ldarg      V_1
000d: call       Value.ToDoubleOrNan        // Unwrap arg y
0012: add
0013: ldarg      V_2
0017: call       Value.ToDoubleOrNan        // Unwrap arg z
001c: add
001d: call       NumberValue.Make(Double)   // Wrap result
0022: ret
```

The function ADD3(11,#NA,#NA)#20, resulting from specializing ADD3 to its first argument having value 11, is this two-argument function:

```
0000: ldc.r8     11
0009: ldarg      V_0
000d: call       Value.ToDoubleOrNan        // Unwrap arg y
0012: add
0013: ldarg      V_1
0017: call       Value.ToDoubleOrNan        // Unwrap arg z
001c: add
001d: call       NumberValue.Make(Double)   // Wrap result
0022: ret
```

The function ADD3(11,#NA,#NA)#20(23,#NA)#21, resulting from further specializing that function to its first remaining argument having value 23, is this one-argument function:

```
0000: ldc.r8     34
0009: ldarg      V_0
000d: call       Value.ToDoubleOrNan        // Unwrap arg z
0012: add
0013: call       NumberValue.Make(Double)   // Wrap result
0018: ret
```

Finally, the function ADD3(11,#NA,#NA)#20(23,#NA)#21(32)#22, resulting from specializing the above function to its last remaining argument having value 32, is this zero-argument function:

```
0000: ldc.r8     66
0009: call       NumberValue.Make(Double)   // Wrap 66 as result
000e: ret
```

The execution times of the above four functions are the following: 59, 45, 39, and 35 ns/call. Much of this cost, roughly 23 ns/call, arises not from parameter passing, parameter unwrapping, or the addition operations, but from the final wrapping of a floating-point result as a NumberValue object.

Example 10.7 Specializing EXPSAMPLE(0.15,1) from example 10.1 with respect to static values of *both* its arguments does not produce a number because the original function involves the volatile RAND() function. Instead we get this argument-less residual function (#25):

```
0000: call        ExcelRand()
0005: ldc.r8      0.15
000e: bge         001d                         // if RAND() < 0.15
0013: ldsfld      NumberValue.ONE              //    return 1
0018: br          0043
001d: ldsfld      SdfManager.sdfDelegates      // else
0022: ldc.i4      26
0027: ldelem.ref
0028: castclass   System.Func`2[Value,Value]
002d: ldc.r8      2
0036: call        NumberValue.Make(Double)
003b: tail.                                    //    tail call
003d: call        Invoke(Value)               //    call #26 on 2
0042: ret
0043: ret
```

The original EXPSAMPLE function from example 10.1 calls itself recursively with arguments (0.15,2), where the static argument 2 differs from the previous value 1. Since the recursive call is under dynamic control (section 10.5), the second argument gets generalized to #NA, so the recursive call becomes a call to the specialization of EXPSAMPLE(0.15,#NA). The call appears above as a call to function #26, which has this bytecode:

```
0000: call        ExcelRand()
0005: ldc.r8      0.15
000e: bge         001c                         // if RAND() < 0.15
0013: ldarg       V_0                          //    return n
0017: br          004c
001c: ldsfld      SdfManager.sdfDelegates      // else
0021: ldc.i4      26
0026: ldelem.ref
0027: castclass   System.Func`2[Value,Value]
002c: ldarg       V_0
0030: call        Value.ToDoubleOrNan(Value)
0035: ldc.r8      1
003e: add
003f: call        NumberValue.Make(Double)
```

```
0044: tail.                                       //   tail call
0046: call          Invoke(Value)                 //   call #26 on (n+1)
004b: ret
004c: ret
```

This residual function calls itself recursively, as function `#26`. This result makes perfect sense because different calls to the argument-less result of

```
SPECIALIZE(CLOSURE("EXPSAMPLE", 0.15, 1))
```

will produce different samples from the exponential distribution with parameter 0.15.

10.8   Perspectives on partial evaluation

It would be desirable to have a better generalization strategy, especially one whose termination properties are well understood. Also, the generation of useless specializations should be prevented. As a less desirable alternative, there could be mechanisms to interactively control and tame excess generation of specialized functions. For instance, there might be a way to turn off specialization once a certain number of specialized functions have been generated or a way to manually interrupt specialization.

Likewise, one may ask whether the resulting specialized function is correct. This clearly depends on the expected semantics of sheet-defined functions, which in turn depends on the expected semantics of spreadsheet computations. Although formalized nowhere, to our knowledge, this semantics is mostly obvious, with the exception of (1) error values and their propagation, and (2) the meaning of volatile functions such as `RAND()` and `NOW()`. We believe our treatment of these, described in section 10.4, is sensible but would like to use the formal semantics from section 1.8, for instance, to underpin this claim.

In general-purpose languages, it is difficult to estimate the cost (specialization time, residual code size) and benefit (speedup) of partial evaluation. In the context of spreadsheets, where "iteration" is often implemented simply by making a sufficient number of copies of a computation, it may be easier to estimate whether specialization is worthwhile. For instance, it may be evident from a worksheet that the function obtained by `CLOSURE("name",a1,...,aM)` will be called from, say, 500 cells due to replicated formulas. A support graph (chapters 4 and 5) provides an estimate of this very cheaply; just count the number of cells directly supported by the cell that evaluates the `CLOSURE` expression. Such estimates are far harder in general functional and procedural languages. Of course, the more sophisticated the spreadsheet model is, the harder it may be to obtain good estimates. If users replace explicit formula replication with recursive functions, then the advantages relative to traditional languages are diminished.

It seems that partial evaluation could be especially beneficial in connection with code generation for general-purpose graphics processors. A graphics processor can efficiently run many instances of the same straight-line numeric code in parallel, but it is poorly equipped for executing branching code, such as that resulting from the translation of IF(...) and CHOOSE(...) in spreadsheet formulas. So whereas partial evaluation, with inlining of constants and early evaluation of conditionals, offers modest speed-ups on a general CPU, it may offer more impressive speedups when the code is to be executed on graphics processors.

Chapter 11

Funcalc User Manual

Funcalc is a spreadsheet implementation that supports sheet-defined functions: functions created using ordinary formulas and cells and no external language.

D2	A	B	C	D
1	a	b	c	area
► 2	3	4	5	=TRIAREA(A2, B2, C2)
3	30	40	50	600
4	100	100	100	4330.12701892219
5	6	8	10	24
6	1	1	1	0.433012701892219
7	0.293834217495...	0.553379801825...	0.554259783380...	0.0784500449670554

Figure 11.1: Ordinary sheet. Cells D2:D7 call sheet-defined function TRIAREA.

=DEFINE("triarea", E3, A3, B3, C3)							
F3	A	B	C	D	E	F	G
1	Area of a triangle						
2	a	b	c	s	area		
► 3	3	4	5	6	6	=DEFINE("triarea...	
4							
5							

Figure 11.2: Function sheet, values view. Figure 6.1 shows the underlying formulas.

A sheet-defined function may be invoked from a formula simply by writing its name and a list of arguments, as in =TRIAREA(A2, B2, C2). See figure 11.1, cell D2. The TRIAREA function is defined in a function sheet using standard spreadsheet formulas and cell references (see figure 11.2). More examples of sheet-defined functions can be found in section 6.2.

11.1   Funcalc features

The current version of Funcalc has the following features:

- A reasonably fast core spreadsheet implementation, using a support graph for minimal recalculation after any cell update.

- Many of the built-in operators and functions known from Excel are available, including array formulas. In Funcalc, functions such as SUMIF from Excel can be made considerably more robust and general simply because they can take functions rather than strings as arguments.

- Additional functions may be defined (with function DEFINE, page 279) without resorting to any external programming language; only standard spreadsheet concepts are needed. Such functions are compiled to very efficient .NET byte-code at run-time. If any part of such a user-defined function is edited, it will automatically be recompiled, and the workbook will be recalculated.

- A user-defined function may be turned into a function value, or closure (using function CLOSURE, page 279), which is a value exactly like the other kinds of spreadsheet values: a number, a text, an external object, an error value, or an array of values. Thus, Funcalc supports higher-order functions as well as nested values, just like any proper (dynamically typed) functional language.

- User-defined functions may be mutually recursive (within the same function sheet), and tail calls to known functions are executed in constant space. Hence, unbounded iteration is possible even without a loop construct.

- A user-defined function may be automatically specialized, or partially evaluated, with respect to known values of some arguments, to obtain a faster version of the function (function SPECIALIZE, page 279). A specialized function can be used in exactly the same way as other sheet-defined functions.

- External .NET instance methods and static methods may be called from formulas with very low overhead; this makes the entire .NET class library accessible from the spreadsheet formulas and from sheet-defined functions.

- Excel workbooks saved in the Excel 2003 XMLSS format (.xml files) may be imported fast. Excel cell formats, pivot tables, charts, and many other Excel features are currently ignored.

- Funcalc includes facilities for benchmarking workbook recalculation (using menu Benchmarks, page 268), benchmarking a particular sheet-defined function (using function BENCHMARK, page 277), and inspecting the CIL bytecode generated for a sheet-defined function (using menu Tools > SDF, page 268).

This user manual is intended for those who wish to experiment with the Funcalc prototype and investigate its inner workings. The manual and implementation are not suitable for general spreadsheet end-users.

11.1.1   Ordinary sheets and function sheets

In Funcalc, ordinary formulas are evaluated interpretively as in Corecalc, whereas sheet-defined functions are compiled to efficient .NET bytecode and therefore execute faster.

We distinguish between ordinary sheets and function sheets. An *ordinary sheet* may contain data and formulas but no definitions of sheet-defined functions and no references to cells on function sheets. An ordinary sheet is shown with gray row and column headers. A *function sheet* may contain definitions of sheet-defined functions as well as ordinary data and formulas and may refer to ordinary sheets but not to other function sheets; it has pink row and column headers.

In other words, whereas sheet-defined functions may be called from anywhere, there can be no cell references from other sheets into a function sheet. One advantage of this is that there cannot be external references to the cells used by a sheet-defined function, and so no confusion can arise about the value of such a cell.

Further rationale for distinguishing function sheets from ordinary sheets is that whereas ordinary sheets are edited frequently and each formula evaluated rarely (once at each recalculation), the opposite holds for function sheets: they will be edited rarely, but each formula may be evaluated thousands of times in each recalculation because the formula may be part of a function called thousands of times. Thus, it makes sense to evaluate ordinary sheets interpretively (requiring no recompilation upon edits) and to compile function sheets (obtaining better evaluation speed for those).

Because function sheets support ordinary formulas and computations, a sheet-defined function can be developed by experimenting with ordinary formulas; once they are satisfactory, they can be turned into one or more sheet-defined functions by adding a call to `DEFINE` (section 11.6).

11.1.2   Installing Funcalc

Funcalc consists of a .NET executable `funcalc.exe` and two .NET external libraries ILReader.dll and ILVisualizer.dll implementing bytecode inspection [94] (see appendix A).

11.2   Funcalc user interface

Funcalc has a rudimentary user interface, shown in figure 11.3, that allows the creation of workbooks containing ordinary sheets and function sheets, entry of data and formulas, definition of sheet-defined functions, recalculation, and benchmarking. There is currently no mechanism for saving a workbook. The most convenient way to experiment with sheet-defined functions therefore is:

- Use Excel to create and edit a workbook.

- Save the workbook in XMLSS format from Excel using `File > Save As > Save as type > XML Spreadsheet 2003 (*.xml)`.

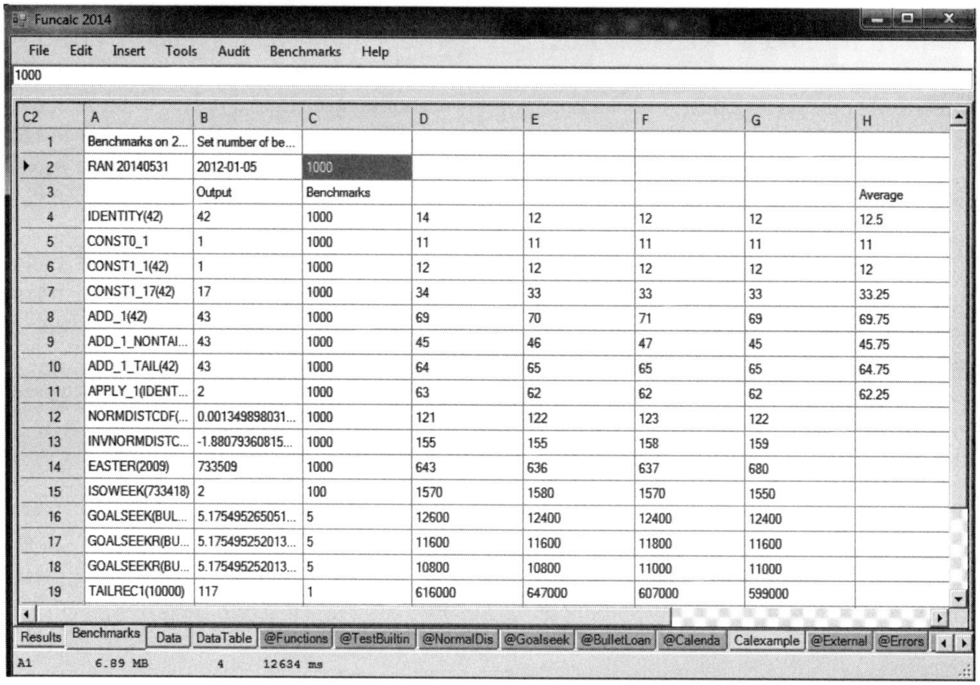

C2	A	B	C	D	E	F	G	H
1	Benchmarks on 2...	Set number of be...						
2	RAN 20140531	2012-01-05	1000					
3		Output	Benchmarks					Average
4	IDENTITY(42)	42	1000	14	12	12	12	12.5
5	CONST0_1	1	1000	11	11	11	11	11
6	CONST1_1(42)	1	1000	12	12	12	12	12
7	CONST1_17(42)	17	1000	34	33	33	33	33.25
8	ADD_1(42)	43	1000	69	70	71	69	69.75
9	ADD_1_NONTAI...	43	1000	45	46	47	45	45.75
10	ADD_1_TAIL(42)	43	1000	64	65	65	65	64.75
11	APPLY_1(IDENT...	2	1000	63	62	62	62	62.25
12	NORMDISTCDF(...	0.001349898031...	1000	121	122	123	122	
13	INVNORMDISTC...	-1.880793608l5...	1000	155	155	158	159	
14	EASTER(2009)	733509	1000	643	636	637	680	
15	ISOWEEK(733418)	2	100	1570	1580	1570	1550	
16	GOALSEEK(BUL...	5.175495265051...	5	12600	12400	12400	12400	
17	GOALSEEKR(BU...	5.175495252013...	5	11600	11600	11800	11600	
18	GOALSEEKR(BU...	5.175495252013...	5	10800	10800	11000	11000	
19	TAILREC1(10000)	117	1	616000	647000	607000	599000	

Figure 11.3: The Funcalc user interface.

- The workbook must be closed from Excel using `File > Close` or Ctrl+F4 before opening it in Funcalc, otherwise Windows may complain that the workbook file is already in use.

- Load the workbook into Funcalc using `File > Import Workbook` or Ctrl+O. A worksheet whose name begins with an at-sign (`@`) is considered a function sheet; all other sheets are considered ordinary sheets.

- There are a few limitations to the use of Excel as "editor" for Funcalc workbooks. Namely, if the name of a sheet-defined function, such as `ISODD`, happens to coincide with one from an Excel add-in library, then it may be rendered as `ATPVBAEN.XLA!ISODD` or similar in the XML file, which confuses Funcalc.

The Funcalc user interface offers the following menu points:

- `File` or Alt+F

  - `File > Import Workbook` or Ctrl+O: Loads a workbook from file in the XML Spreadsheet 2003 (XMLSS) format (`*.xml`). This discards, without warning, any workbook already loaded.

  - `File > Exit` or Alt+F4: Terminates Funcalc without saving anything. It is currently not possible to save anything from Funcalc.

- `Edit` or Alt+E: Excel-style operations on formulas in cells, with adjustment of relative references within the formulas.

  - `Edit > Copy` or Ctrl+C: Mark one cell whose contents are to be copied.

  - `Edit > Cut` or Ctrl+X: Delete cell contents and enable pasting them into another cell. [Not implemented]

  - `Edit > Paste` or Ctrl+V: Copy or paste into one or more marked cells.

  - `Edit > Delete` or Del: Delete cell contents. Currently can delete only one cell at a time.

- `Insert` or Alt+I

  - `Insert > New sheet` or Ctrl+N: Inserts an ordinary sheet after the existing sheets.

  - `Insert > New function sheet` or Ctrl+M: Inserts a function sheet after the existing sheets.

  - `Insert > Column`: Inserts a new column before the cell that has focus, adjusting references to all cells that get shifted right as a consequence of the insertion.

  - `Insert > Row`: Inserts a new row before the cell that has focus, adjusting references to all cells that get shifted down as a consequence of the insertion.

- `Tools` or Alt+T

  - `Tools > Recalculate` or F9 for a standard recalculation: Recalculate only cells that depend on volatile built-ins (such as `RAND()` or `NOW`) or volatile user-defined or external functions.

  - `Tools > Recalculate full` or Ctrl+Alt+F9: Recalculate all cells in the workbook.

  - `Tools > Recalculate full rebuild` or Ctrl+Alt+Shift+F9: Rebuild the support graph, and then recalculate all cells in the workbook.

  - `Tools > Reference format`: Determine how cell and area references should be displayed. The standard Excel and Funcalc display format is A1; the XMLSS files use R1C1; and Corecalc and Funcalc use C0R0 internally. See section 1.3 for a definition of the A1, C0R0, and R1C1 formats.

  - `Tools > Show formulas`: Toggles between showing cells' values (the default) and showing their formulas. Use this to investigate the anatomy of a sheet-defined function or make screenshots of function definitions with Alt+PrtSc or similar.

  - `Tools > SDF` or Ctrl+I: Opens a dialog that shows an alphabetical list of all sheet-defined functions. Double-clicking a function in the list switches to the function sheet on which it is defined and scrolls to its definition. Press the "Show bytecode" button to open a window that shows the function's CIL code. The window is readonly and modal, so you cannot interact with Funcalc while the window is open; to close it, press ESC or Alt+F4.

- `Audit`: Traces the precedent and dependent cells for a given cell, that is, the cells to which it refers and the cells that refer to it. A precedent cell is indicated by an arrow pointing *from* the precedent cell; a dependent cell is indicated by an arrow pointing *to* the dependent cell, as in Excel. Precedents and dependents on other sheets are not shown.

  - `Audit > More precedents` or Ctrl+P extends the trace of arrows from precedent cells to this one (and from their precedents to them and so on).

  - `Audit > Fewer precedents` or Ctrl+Shift+P shrinks the trace of arrows pointing from precedent cells.

  - `Audit > More dependents` or Ctrl+D extends the trace of arrows pointing to dependent cells (and further to their dependents and so on).

  - `Audit > Fewer dependents` or Ctrl+Shift+D shrinks the trace of arrows pointing to dependent cells.

  - `Audit > Erase arrows` or Ctrl+E erases all arrows from precedents and dependents. Changing focus to another cell or switching to another sheet also erases all arrows.

- `Benchmarks` or Alt+B: Use the textbox to specify the number of recalculations to perform for benchmarking. Then choose one of the following:

– Click `Benchmarks > Standard recalculation` to measure the average wall-clock time for a standard recalculation of the workbook (as if
requested by pressing F9).

– Click `Benchmarks > Full recalculation` to measure the average
wall-clock time for a full recalculation of the workbook (as if requested by
Ctrl+Alt+F9).

– Click `Benchmarks > Full recalculation rebuild` to measure the
average wall-clock time for a support graph rebuild followed by a full recalculation of the workbook (as if invoked by Ctrl+Alt+Shift+F9).

To benchmark the code for a single sheet-defined function (and other sheet-
defined functions that it calls), use instead the `BENCHMARK` built-in function
(see section 11.6).

• `Help > About`: Display version number and other elementary information
about Funcalc.

The status line below the Funcalc cell grid shows the current reference format (A1,
C0R0, or R1C1); the current memory consumption, which may fluctuate due to
garbage collection; the number of recalculations performed so far; and the wall-clock
time consumed by the most recent recalculation (or, after a recalculation benchmarking run, the average recalculation time).

If there is a cyclic dependency in the workbook, then the status line will give the
address and formula of one cell involved in the cycle, and that cell will be marked
with an error symbol in the cell grid.

If an interactively edited cell has a syntax error, then an error dialog will be
shown, and you must edit the cell until it is correct or cancel the edit by pressing
ESC. Hence, it is not possible to leave syntactically incorrect formulas in the sheet.

11.2.1 Array formulas

Like Excel, Funcalc supports array formulas, which display an array of values distributed over a range of individual cells. To create an array formula within an
ordinary sheet, select a cell area, type an array-valued formula (such as a cell area
reference A1:B2 or a call to `TRANSPOSE`), and then finish the formula just by typing Enter; it is not necessary to type Ctrl+Shift+Enter as in Excel and OpenOffice
Calc. Array formulas are not available within sheet-defined functions, but array-
valued expressions are available, and sheet-defined functions can take array values
as argument, compute array values as intermediate results, and return an array
value.

Array-related Funcalc functions follow the Excel convention of having the row
number r before the column number c, as in `INDEX(arr, r, c)` in section 11.5.
An index value is truncated to an integer by rounding toward zero.

11.3 Built-in functions

Funcalc provides many built-in functions known from Excel (section 11.5), as well as a few special functions for defining and using sheet-defined functions (section 11.6). In addition, it is easy and efficient to call external .NET functions (section 11.7).

Moreover—and this is one of the main objectives of the work described in the previous chapters—many functions and tools from Excel can be defined by the user as sheet-defined functions within Funcalc and often in a more general, robust, or efficient way. For instance, section 6.2 shows that one can use sheet-defined functions to create analogs of Excel's NORMSDIST, REPT, MATCH, HLOOKUP, and VLOOKUP functions, as well as the Goal Seek and Data Table tools.

The logical value false is represented by the number 0.0 and true by any non-zero number, typically 1.0.

All operators and functions propagate errors from their arguments to the result, even comparisons. Non-strict functions such as AND, OR, IF, and CHOOSE propagate errors only from the arguments that are actually evaluated.

11.4 Funcalc built-in operators

These operators are mostly as in Excel, except that when the (+) operator is applied to a number and a quoted text, Excel will try to interpret the text as a number and perform the addition; Funcalc will not. Also, in Funcalc the comparisons (=, <>, <, <=, >=, >) currently only work on numbers, not texts or other values. To determine the equality of general Funcalc values, use EQUAL(v1,v2).

- x ^ y returns x^y, that is, x to the power y. Unlike in Excel, 0^0 gives 1, as required by IEEE754 [81].

- x * y returns x times y.

- x / y returns x divided by y.

- x + y returns x plus y.

- x - y returns x minus y.

- s & t returns the text concatenation of the values s and t, converting s and t to texts first, if necessary.

- x < y returns true if x is less than y and returns false if x is not less than y. Currently works only for numbers, not texts; this is also the case for the other comparisons.

- x <= y returns true if x is less than or equal to y and returns false if x is not less than or equal to y.

- x >= y returns true if x is greater than or equal to y and returns false if x is not greater than or equal to y.

- x > y returns true if x is greater than y and returns false if x is not greater than y.

- x = y returns true if x equals y and returns false if x does not equal y.

- x <> y returns true if x is different from y and returns false if x is not different from y.

11.5   Funcalc built-in standard functions

These built-in functions are mostly as in Excel, although with function-related improvements in COUNTIF and SUMIF.

- **ABS**(x) returns the absolute value of x. As in Excel.

- **ACOS**(x) returns the arc cosine of x, in radians. As in Excel.

- **AND**(e1, e2, ..., en) returns the logical "and" (conjunction) of e1, ..., en. More precisely, if n is 0, then it returns true. If n>0, then it evaluates e1 and returns false if the result was false, returns AND(e2, ..., en) if the result was true, and returns an error if the result was an error. Note that unlike Excel, the case n=0 is legal and works as intended, and that if some ej evaluates to false, the final result is false, even if some subsequent ei with i>j would have produced an error.

- **ASIN**(x) returns the arc sine of x, in radians. As in Excel.

- **ATAN**(x) returns the arc tangent of x, in radians. As in Excel.

- **ATAN2**(x,y) returns ATAN(y/x) taking signs of x and y into account. As in Excel.

- **AVERAGE**(e1, ..., en) returns the average of the values of e1, ..., en, where each ei may evaluate to a number or an array, which is then processed recursively. Returns error #NUM! if n is zero. When used within a sheet-defined function, any array-valued arguments and ranges must refer to ordinary sheets. Generalizes the corresponding Excel function.

- **CEILING**(x, signif) returns the nearest multiple of signif that is equal to or larger than x when signif is positive (i.e., rounds toward plus infinity) and returns the nearest multiple of signif that is equal to or smaller than x when signif is negative (i.e., rounds toward minus infinity). Returns error #NUM! when signif is 0.0. Almost as in Excel.

- **CHOOSE**(e0, e1, e2, ..., en) evaluates e0 to a number and truncates it to an integer i; then evaluates ei and returns the value if 1<=i<=n; otherwise returns error value #VALUE!. As in Excel.

- **COLMAP**(fv, arr) calls function value fv on each column arr[-,c] of the array arr and returns a new array containing the values of fv(array[-,c]) for c=1,...,COLUMNS(arr). The resulting array will have one row and the same number of columns as arr. Returns ArgType error if fv is not a function and returns ArgCount error if the arity of fv is different from ROWS(arr). The COLMAP function does not exist in Excel.

- **COLUMNS**(arr) evaluates arr to an array and returns its number of columns. As in Excel.

- **CONSTARRAY**(v, rows, cols) returns an array with rows rows and cols columns, all of whose elements are the value v. Returns error value SIZE if cols or rows is negative.

- **COS**(x) returns the cosine of x, with x in radians. As in Excel.

- **COUNTIF**(fv, arr) applies the fv predicate to all values in the array arr and returns the number of times it returns true. The predicate fv must be a one-argument function value that returns a number. This considerably generalizes Excel's COUNTIF, which allows only restricted forms of predicates. When used within a sheet-defined function, the array argument must refer to an ordinary sheet.

- **EQUAL**(v1, v2) returns 1 (i.e., true) if values v1 and v2 are equal; otherwise it returns 0 (i.e., false). This works for numbers, strings, arrays, and function values, in contrast to the "=" operator, which works only for numbers. Returns an error value if any of v1 and v2 is an error; hence, it cannot be used to compare error values.

- **ERR**("message") produces an error value such as #ERR: message; the given message must be a text constant. This allows sheet-defined functions to return custom errors.

- **EXP**(x) returns e^x, that is, $e = 2.71828\ldots$ raised to the power x. As in Excel.

- **EXTERN**("nameAndSignature", e1, ..., en) evaluates e1,...,en to values v1...vn, where n >= 0, and calls the external .NET method with the given name and signature on these argument values. The method may be a static or instance method. External calls are particularly fast inside sheet-defined functions, but even in an interpreted ordinary sheet, they are much faster than Excel-to-VBA calls. See section 11.7 for more information about EXTERN. It is intended for calling external functions whose results are completely determined by their arguments and that have no external effects; for other external functions, use VOLATILIZE(EXTERN(...)).

- **FLOOR**(x, signif) returns the nearest multiple of signif that is equal to or smaller than x when signif is positive (i.e., rounds toward minus infinity) and returns the nearest multiple of signif that is equal to or greater than x when `signif` is negative (i.e., rounds toward plus infinity). Returns error `#NUM!` when signif is 0.0. Almost as in Excel.

- **HARRAY**(e1, ..., en) returns a one-row horizontal array whose elements are the values v1...vn of the arguments. The resulting array has one row and n columns. In particular, any array value among v1...vn is simply inserted as an element of the resulting array; unlike in HCAT(e1, ..., en), its columns are not made into columns of the resulting array.

- **HCAT**(e1, ..., en) horizontally concatenates the values v1...vn of the arguments (side-by-side), returning an array value. Each ei must evaluate to either an atomic value or an array value. All array values among v1...vn must have the same number of rows. An atomic value vj among the arguments v1...vn will be replicated to make a one-column array with that number of rows. If n is zero, the result has zero rows and zero columns. If there are only atomic arguments, the result has 1 row and n columns. This can be used to concatenate a new constant column to an array.

- **HSCAN**(fv, c1, n) creates an $(n+1)$-column matrix whose first column is c1, whose second column is fv(c1), and whose ith column is $fv^{(i-1)}(c1)$, where i is $1, ..., n+1$. Argument c1 must be a one-column array. Function fv must accept a one-column array as argument and return a one-column array of the same length, that is, ROWS(fv(x)) must equal ROWS(x).

- **IF**(e1, e2, e3) evaluates e1; if the result of e1 is true, evaluates e2 and returns the result; if the result of e1 is false, evaluates e3 and returns the result. As in Excel.

- **INDEX**(arr, row, col) evaluates row and col to numbers and truncates them to an integer row number r and an integer column number c. Then returns the value of the cell at row r, column c, in the array value arr, with base offset 1. Returns 0.0 for empty array cells. Returns error `#REF!` unless 1 <= r <= ROWS(arr) and 1 <= c <= COLUMNS(arr). When using INDEX on a function sheet, arr must be a cell area in an ordinary sheet. As in Excel, but cannot be used to retrieve whole rows or columns; use SLICE instead.

- **ISARRAY**(e) evaluates e and returns true if the result is an array, false otherwise.

- **ISERROR**(e) evaluates e and returns true if the result is an error (including `#NA`), false otherwise. As in Excel.

- **LN**(x) returns the natural (base $e = 2.71828...$) logarithm of x. As in Excel.

- **LOG**(x) returns the base 10 logarithm of x. As in Excel.

- **LOG10**(x) returns the base 10 logarithm of x. As in Excel.

- **MAP**(fv, arr1, ..., arrn) computes fv(arr1[r,c],...,arrn[r,c]) for each index (r,c) in the arrays arrk and returns a new array containing the resulting values. The given arrays arr1,...,arrn must all have the same shape, which is then also the shape of the resulting array; otherwise, it returns an array shape error. Returns ArgType error if fv is not a function or if some arrk is not an array and returns ArgCount error if n is zero or if fv does not take exactly n arguments.

- **MAX**(e1, ..., en) returns the maximum of the values of e1,...,en, where each ei may evaluate to a number or an array, which is then processed recursively. When used within a sheet-defined function, any array-valued arguments and ranges must refer to ordinary sheets. Generalizes the corresponding Excel function.

- **MIN**(e1, ..., en) returns the minimum of the values of e1,...,en, where each ei may evaluate to a number or an array, which is then processed recursively. When used within a sheet-defined function, any array-valued arguments and ranges must refer to ordinary sheets. Generalizes the corresponding Excel function.

- **MOD**(x,y) returns the signed remainder of x by y, that is, x-FLOOR(x/y,1)*y. Returns error #NUM! if y is 0.0. As in Excel.

- **NA**() returns the special error value #NA.

- **NEG**(x) returns minus x.

- **NOT**(e) evaluates e and returns true if the result was false and returns false if the result was true. As in Excel.

- **NOW**() returns the current date and local time measured as the number of days and fractional days since the beginning of December 30, 1899. As in Excel on Windows; Excel on MacOS is slightly different.

- **OR**(e1, e2, ..., en) returns the logical "or" (disjunction) of e1, ..., en. More precisely, if n is 0, then it returns false. If n>0, it evaluates e1 and returns true if the result was true, returns OR(e2, ..., en) if the result was false, and returns an error if the result was an error. Note that unlike Excel, the case n=0 is legal and works as intended, and that if some ej evaluates to true, the final result is true, even if some subsequent ei with i>j would have produced an error.

- **PI**() returns $\pi = 3.14159\ldots$, the ratio of the circumference to the diameter of a circle. As in Excel.

- **RAND**() returns a pseudo-random number x from a uniform distribution such that $0 <= x < 1$. As in Excel.

- **REDUCE**(fv, x1, arr) folds function fv over the elements of array value arr with x1 as starting value. More precisely, if the values of arr's elements in row-major order are $a_{11}, a_{12}, \ldots, a_{1c}, a_{21}, \ldots, a_{rc}$, and we think of function fv as a left-associative operator $\star$ then it computes $x1 \star a_{11} \star a_{12} \star \ldots \star a_{21} \star \ldots \star a_{rc}$. Function fv must take two arguments; otherwise ArgCountError is returned.

- **ROUND**(x, d) returns x rounded to d decimal digits. That is, rounds to nearest integer when d is 0, to nearest multiple of 0.1 when d is $+1$, to nearest multiple of 10 when d is -1, and so on. In case of a tie, rounds away from zero. First d is truncated (toward zero) to obtain an integer. As in Excel.

- **ROWMAP**(fv, arr) calls function value fv on each row arr[r, -] of the array arr and returns a new array containing the values of fv(array[r, -]) for r=1,...,ROWS(arr). The resulting array will have one column and the same number of rows as arr. Returns ArgType error if fv is not a function and returns ArgCount error if the arity of fv is different from COLUMNS(arr).

- **ROWS**(arr) evaluates arr to an array and returns its number of rows. As in Excel.

- **SIGN**(x) returns the sign of x, that is, $+1$ when x is positive, -1 when x is negative, and 0 when x is zero. As in Excel.

- **SIN**(x) returns the sine of x, with x in radians. As in Excel.

- **SLICE**(arr, r1, c1, r2, c2) returns an array value representing a slice of array arr that has upper left-hand corner (r1,c1) and lower right-hand corner (r2,c2), where row and column indices are 1-based and truncated to integers (toward zero). The slice has r2-r1+1 rows and c2-c1+1 columns and is a view of the underlying array, not a copy of it. The slice will have zero rows if r2=r1-1 and zero columns if c2=c1-1. It must hold that 1 <= r1 <= r2 + 1 and r2 <= ROWS(arr) and 1 <= c1 <= c2 + 1 and c2 <= COLUMNS(arr); otherwise error value #REF! is returned. Evaluation takes constant time because the function returns a view on the given array arr, not a copy of its values.

  To return row number r, call SLICE(arr, r, 1, r, COLUMNS(arr)). To return column number c, call SLICE(arr, 1, c, ROWS(arr), c).

- **SQRT**(x) returns the square root of x. As in Excel.

- **SUM**(e1, ..., en) returns the sum of the values of e1,...,en, where each ei may evaluate to a number or an array, which is then processed recursively. When used within a sheet-defined function, any array-valued arguments and ranges must refer to ordinary sheets. Generalizes the corresponding Excel function.

- **SUMIF**(`fv`, `arr`) applies the predicate `fv` to all values in the array `arr` and returns the sum of those values (which must be numbers) for which the predicate returns true. The predicate `fv` must be a one-argument function value that returns a number, interpreted as a truth value. This considerably generalizes Excel's `SUMIF`, which allows only restricted forms of predicates. When used within a sheet-defined function, the array argument must refer to an ordinary sheet.

- **TABULATE**(`fv`, `rows`, `cols`) returns an array with `rows` rows and `cols` columns, both truncated to integers, where the value at row `r` and column `c` is computed by `APPLY(fv,r,c)`, with row and column indexes starting at 1. Hence, `fv` must be a function value taking two numeric arguments. Returns error value #SIZE if `cols` or `rows` is negative.

- **TAN**(`x`) returns the tangent of `x`, with `x` in radians. As in Excel.

- **TRANSPOSE**(`arr`) evaluates `arr` to an array and returns its transpose, whose value at row `r` and column `c` is `arr[c,r]`. When used within a sheet-defined function, the array argument must refer to an ordinary sheet. As in Excel.

- **VARRAY**(`e1`, `...`, `en`) returns a one-column vertical array whose elements are the values `v1...vn` of the arguments. The resulting array has one column and `n` rows. In particular, any array value among `v1...vn` is simply inserted as an element of the resulting array; unlike in `VCAT(e1, ..., en)`, its rows are not made into rows of the resulting array.

- **VCAT**(`e1`, `...`, `en`) vertically concatenates, or stacks, the values `v1...vn` of the arguments (one atop the next one), returning an array value. Each `ei` must evaluate to either an atomic value or an array value. All array values among `v1...vn` must have the same number of columns. An atomic value `vj` among the arguments `v1...vn` will be replicated to make a one-row array with that number of columns. If `n` is zero, then the result has zero rows and zero columns. If there are only atomic arguments, then the result has `n` rows and one column. This can be used to concatenate a new constant row to an array.

- **VOLATILIZE**(`e1`) has the same result as its argument `e1` but marks the expression as volatile, so that it will be reevaluated in every recalculation (section 11.2), even if no argument expression has changed.

  A typical use is `VOLATILIZE(EXTERN(...))`, to call an external function that depends on external state (such as the time, temperature, stock quotes, etc.) or that has external effects (such as writing to a log, console, database, or similar). Another use is for experimenting with the recalculation mechanism, where `VOLATILIZE(0.5)` is the natural way to make a constant volatile, less obscure than `0.5+0*RAND()`. A better name would be `VOLATILE`, but that name is illegal in MS Excel.

- **VSCAN**(fv,r1,n) creates an $(n+1)$-row matrix whose first row is r1, whose second row is fv(r1), and whose ith row is $\text{fv}^{(i-1)}$(r1), where i is $1,\ldots,n+1$. Argument r1 must be a one-row array. Function fv must accept a one-row array as argument and return a one-row array of the same length, that is, COLUMNS(fv(x)) must equal COLUMNS(x).

11.6 Functions that manipulate functions

The entire machinery of sheet-defined functions is made available through only three new built-in functions: DEFINE, CLOSURE, and APPLY. In addition, there is a function BENCHMARK for measuring performance of sheet-defined functions and a function SPECIALIZE for creating optimized closures, both described in this section, and finally a function EXTERN for calling general .NET functions, described in section 11.7. Figure 11.4 gives an overview of how the function-manipulating functions can be used.

- **APPLY**(fv, e1, ..., ek) evaluates expression fv to a function value, or closure, and evaluates e1, ..., ek to values b1...bk. Then it applies the closure to these values, that is, completes the early argument values stored in the closure with the additional late argument values b1...bk and calls the closure's underlying sheet-defined function on this full set of arguments. The closure fv must have arity k.

  The APPLY function itself is not error-strict. Any error values among the arguments will be passed to the underlying function so it can test for them using the ISERROR built-in function.

- **BENCHMARK**(fv, count) evaluates fv to a closure, evaluates count to a number and truncates it to an integer n, and then performs n calls to the internal representation of fv and returns the average number of wall-clock nanoseconds per call. The function value fv must have arity zero, that is, it must be a sheet-defined function that has been given all its arguments, otherwise an ArgCount error is returned. If n <= 0, then error #NUM! is returned. For instance, BENCHMARK(CLOSURE("NORMDISTCDF", -3), 100000) will return the per-call cost of 100 000 calls of NORMDISTCDF(-3). The result of this particular call should be in the 80–200 ns range on modern hardware.

  Note that one can also benchmark residual functions resulting from partial evaluation (chapter 10). Let BINOM be a two-argument function that we partially evaluate with respect to static argument 17, and assume we want to measure the execution time of the residual function when applied to argument 42, measured as the average of 10 000 calls. This can be done by the expression
  =BENCHMARK(CLOSURE(SPECIALIZE("BINOM",17,NA()),42), 10000).

  Some advice on benchmarking:

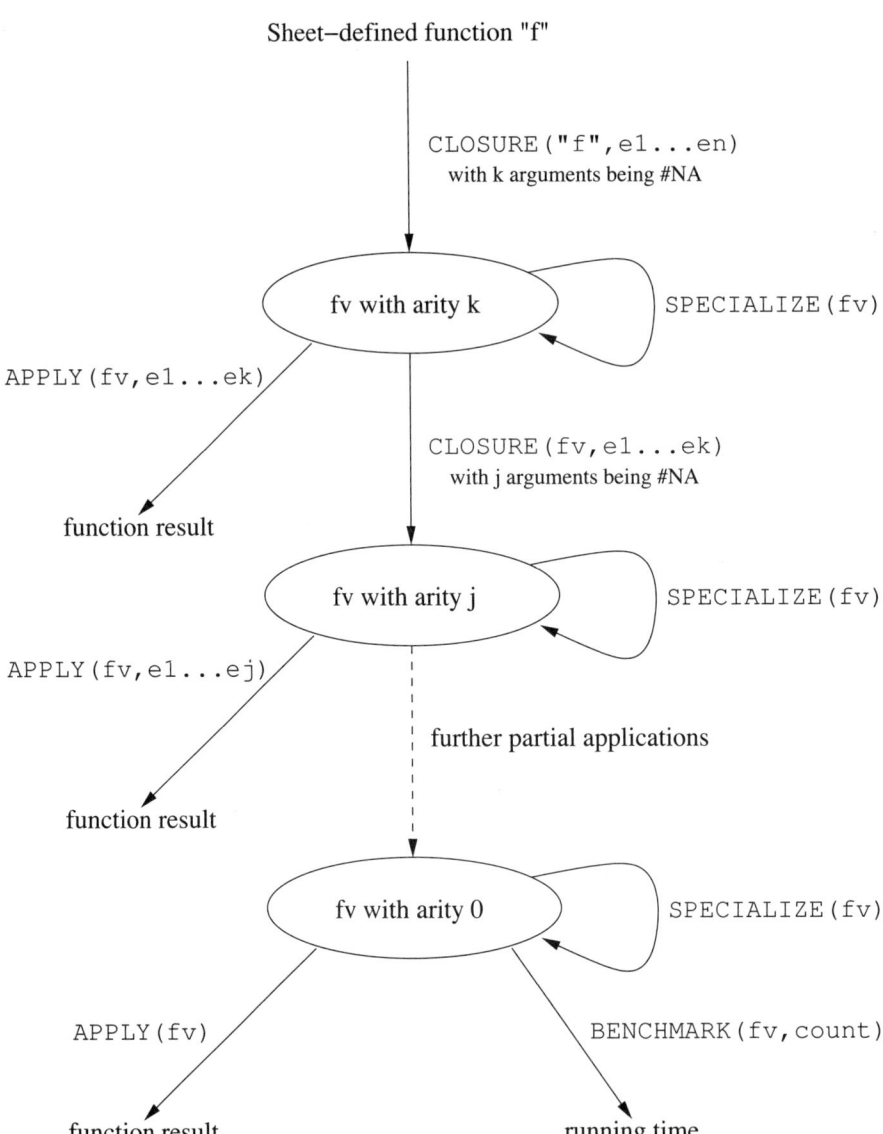

Figure 11.4: Functions to create and manipulate function values.

    – Run Funcalc from the command line, not from Visual Studio. Even in Release builds, the latter is noticeably slower.

    – Before running the benchmark, close other applications, such as browsers, database servers, and mail clients, that may consume CPU cycles.

    – If you are using a laptop system, note that the power savings scheme in force may seriously influence benchmark results.

- **CLOSURE** ("name", e1, ..., en) or **CLOSURE** (fv, e1, ..., en) evaluates e1...en to values a1...an and returns a closure, or function value, for the named sheet-defined function or the given function value fv but does not call the function or evaluate any part of it.

  An argument ai that is not #NA is called an *early* argument and will become part of the closure. An argument whose value is #NA indicates a *late* argument, that is, one that will remain a parameter of the resulting function value. Hence, if k is the number of late (#NA) arguments, then the resulting function value will have arity k.

  When no arguments are given, so n=0 and the call has form CLOSURE(e0), all arguments will be considered late (#NA). If any arguments are given, so n>0, n must equal the given function's arity.

  The resulting function value can be applied using the APPLY function and can be benchmarked using the BENCHMARK function. Moreover, it can be supplied with further arguments using the CLOSURE function or specialized using the SPECIALIZE function.

  A function value displays as name(a1,...,an), for instance, ADD(42,#NA), that is, the function name followed by a list of the argument values, where #NA values represent arguments yet to be supplied.

  The function given as first argument to CLOSURE must be a text constant "name" or an expression that evaluates to a function value fv.

  The CLOSURE function itself is not error-strict. Any non-#NA error values among the arguments are simply stored in the closure and passed to the underlying sheet-defined function when the closure is applied; this allows the function to test for them using ISERROR.

- **DEFINE** ("name", out, in1, ..., inn) creates a sheet-defined function with the given name, result cell out, and input cells in1, ..., inn, where n >= 0. The given "name" must be a text constant. The DEFINE function can be used only on a function sheet, and the out, in1, ..., inn must all be cell references within that same function sheet. A sheet-defined function can currently have at most nine arguments. Function DEFINE cannot be called from within a sheet-defined function.

- **SPECIALIZE** (fv) takes as argument a closure fv and returns a new closure representing a specialized function. The result of SPECIALIZE(fv) is functionally equivalent to fv, but SPECIALIZE performs *partial evaluation* (see chapter 10) of the given closure `fv` with respect to the values of its non-`#NA` arguments, thereby producing a specialized or residual function value. Calling this resulting function should be faster than calling the functionally equivalent closure `fv`.

Like any other function value, the resulting function can be called using `APPLY`, benchmarked using `BENCHMARK`, and provided with further arguments using `CLOSURE`.

When `fv` is a closure, all of whose enclosed arguments are `#NA`, the result of `SPECIALIZE(fv)` is just `fv`.

The given function value `fv` will often be the result of a call to `CLOSURE`, such as `CLOSURE("ADD",42,NA())`. For convenience, `SPECIALIZE(e0,...,en)` is treated as a syntactic sugar for `SPECIALIZE(CLOSURE(e0,...,en))` when `n>=1`.

The result of `SPECIALIZE(fv)` displays almost as `fv` but with `#f` added at the end, where `f` is an internal function number. For instance, if `fv` is the result of `CLOSURE("ADD",42,NA())`, then `fv` will display as `ADD(42,#NA)`, and `SPECIALIZE(fv)` may display as `ADD(42,#NA)#117`.

11.7   Calling external .NET methods

External methods, properties, indexers, and constructors can be called using the **EXTERN** built-in function, like this, where n >= 0:

```
EXTERN("nameAndSignature", e1, ..., en)
```

Such a call evaluates `e1, ..., en` to values `v1...vn` and calls the external .NET method with the given name and signature on these argument values. The text constant `nameAndSignature` is a concatenation of the method's *name* and its *signature*. The method may be a static or instance method. Due to minimal recalculation, an `EXTERN` function will only be called when one of its arguments changes. Use the idiom `VOLATILIZE(EXTERN(...))` to call an external function if it must be called at every recalculation; for instance, if it depends on volatile external state (such as stock quotes) or is intended to update external state (such as a log file).

The *name* must include the method's namespace and class. To call a method that is not in the currently executing assembly, nor in mscorlib.dll, qualify the name with the name of the assembly also. The latter is easier said than done in .NET 4.0 and later. Probably Funcalc should be modified to use the Microsoft Extensibility Framework [100] or Microsoft Composition [99] for dynamic discovery and loading of externally defined .NET functions.

A constructor is called as if it were a static method called `new`. The `get` and `set` accessors of a property `P` of type `t` are called as methods `t get_P()` and `void set_P(t value)`. The `get` and `set` accessors of an indexer `this[...]` of type `t` are methods `t get_Item(...)` and `void set_Item(t value, ...)`, where the ellipsis (`...`) denotes the "normal" arguments to the indexer.

The *signature* describes the method's argument types and return type, using a notation inspired by Java's bytecode format, where the argument types are enclosed in parentheses and followed by the return type. Thus, " (DI) T" is the signature of a method that takes two arguments, of type `double` and `int`, and returns a result of type String (text). The type codes are shown in figure 11.5.

Code	.NET type	Funcalc type
Z	`bool`	Number
B	`byte`	Number
b	`sbyte`	Number
S	`short`	Number
s	`ushort`	Number
I	`int`	Number
i	`uint`	Number
J	`long`	Number
j	`ulong`	Number
D	`double`	Number
N	`double`	Number
F	`float`	Number
M	`decimal`	(None)
C	`char`	Text
T	String, equivalent to `LSystem.String;`	Text
O	Object, equivalent to `LSystem.Object;`	Object
V	Value	Value
W	`void`, only for return type	<void>
Lc;	class c	Object
[t	1D row array of t, that is, `t []`	Array
{t	2D array of t, that is, `t [,]`	Array
(args) ret	(None)	Function

Figure 11.5: Type codes for external method signatures in Funcalc.

Method `String Format(String s, int[] i, bool b)` takes arguments of type String, integer array (`[I`), and Boolean (`Z`) and returns a String, so its signature can be written

```
(LSystem.String; [IZ) LSystem.String;
```

or, more compactly, as

```
(T[IZ)T
```

The signature of a static method must begin with a dollar sign (`$`). For instance, "`System.Math.Sinh$(D)D`" specifies the static method in class System.Math that computes hyperbolic sine:

```
static double Sinh(double)
```

To denote an instance method or a virtual method, leave out the dollar sign and specify only the method's parameter types, not the receiver type, in the signature. For instance, `"System.String.IndexOf(T)I"` specifies the instance method `int IndexOf(String)` in class System.String.

Example 11.1 Much functionality is already provided by the .NET library classes and can easily be accessed through EXTERN calls. For instance, to compute the logarithm to base 2, call this two-argument static Math method:

```
EXTERN("System.Math.Log$(DD)D", 1024, 2)
```

To format number as a string with six digits after the decimal point, call a two-argument static String method:

```
EXTERN("System.String.Format$(TO)T", "x={0:F6}", RAND())
```

To format year, month, and date as an ISO date, such as `"2014-04-17"`:

```
EXTERN("System.String.Format$(TOOO)T",
       "{0:0000}-{1:00}-{2:00}", 2014, 4, 17)
```

To obtain a .NET random number generator with a particular seed such as 37, call the Random constructor:

```
EXTERN("System.Random.new$(I)O", 37)
```

Example 11.2 Most of the string operations usually built into spreadsheet programs are already provided by the .NET System.String class; some examples are given below. Since these can be encapsulated as sheet-defined functions without loss of efficiency, Funcalc really does not need to provide them as built-in functions.

To concatenate two strings, call this two-argument static String method:

```
EXTERN("System.String.Concat$(TT)T", "abc", "def")
```

To search for string `"bcde"` in another string, call String instance method with integer result:

```
EXTERN("System.String.IndexOf(T)I", "abcdefg", "bcde")
```

To return a substring, call String instance method with integer arguments and string result:

```
EXTERN("System.String.Substring(II)T", "abcdef", 2, 3)
```

To compute the length of a string, call instance property Length with no arguments and integer result:

```
EXTERN("System.String.get_Length()I", B44)
```

To convert a string to upper case, call String instance method with no arguments and String result:

```
EXTERN("System.String.ToUpper()T", B35)
```

To test whether a string starts with a given substring, call a String instance method with Boolean result:

```
EXTERN("System.String.StartsWith(T)Z", B30, B31)
```

Example 11.3 For good and bad, external functions can access and manipulate the operating system environment through the .NET library. For instance, to read a (Windows) environment variable describing the processor architecture, call a static method with string argument and string result:

```
EXTERN("System.Environment.GetEnvironmentVariable$(T)T",
       "PROCESSOR_IDENTIFIER")
```

Printing a string to the console has a side effect but no return value and therefore return type `void`:

```
EXTERN("System.Console.WriteLine$(T)W", "Hello world!")
```

To obtain the number of bytes currently allocated, call static function with `bool` argument and `long` result:

```
EXTERN("System.GC.GetTotalMemory$(Z)J", 0)
```

To make sure that the above `EXTERN` call is evaluated in every recalculation so it reflects the current memory usage, it may be wrapped in a `VOLATILIZE` function call (see page 276).

To delete a file from the current directory:

```
EXTERN("System.IO.File.Delete$(T)W", "thesis-final.tex")
```

CAUTION: The latter example shows that external methods should be used with care; an external method can do anything, even erase your file system. Loading a workbook will evaluate all its external method calls, even those within function sheets. A security model for external methods is needed, but we have not implemented one in Funcalc yet. Don't accept workbooks from strangers.

11.8   Inspecting generated bytecode

To inspect the bytecode generated for a sheet-defined function, choose `Tools > SDF` in the menu or use shortcut Ctrl+I, select a function in the list, and click the "Show bytecode" button. Then the function's CIL bytecode will be shown in a modal dialog. Hence, you must close it before you can continue interacting with Funcalc.

This is implemented using Haibo Luo's ILVisualizer in its VS2012 incarnation [94], with a very modest addition to its MethodBodyViewer class so that it can display the bytecode of a MethodBase object. This object is obtained from the function's Delegate object, which in turn is fetched from the static array `sdfDelegates` in class `SdfManager`. Note that we do not use ILVisualizer as a debugger plug-in within Visual Studio but as a component that gets called directly from Funcalc.

11.9   Funsheet, an experimental add-in for Excel

While the Funcalc user interface is adequate for experimenting with sheet-defined functions, to do actual work one would need to integrate the Funcalc compiler infrastructure with a real spreadsheet implementation such as Microsoft Excel.

Recently, Jonas Druedahl Rask and Simon Eikeland Timmermann have created an add-in for Microsoft Excel that does just that. The add-in, called Funsheet, allows Excel users to create, apply, specialize, and benchmark Funcalc sheet-defined functions from within the standard Excel user interface.

The Funsheet add-in is still a prototype, but looks promising. It was implemented using the open source tool Excel DNA [55] and is described in Rask and Timmermann's MSc thesis [123].

Appendix A

Source File Organization

The source code of Corecalc and Funcalc is organized as a Visual Studio 2012 "solution" called Corecalc that contains a "project" also called Corecalc. Most of the machinery for compiled sheet-defined functions is in namespace Corecalc.Funcalc (figure A.1), whereas the core interpretive spreadsheet functionality is in namespace Corecalc (figure A.2).

File	Contents	Classes
CGExpr.cs	Compilable AST	*CGExpr* and subclasses (figure 7.3), FunctionInfo, Gen, Signature
CellsInFuns.cs	Track SDF cells	CellsUsedInFunctions
CodeGenerate.cs	CIL generation utilities	*CodeGenerate*, Typ
DependencyGraph.cs	Dependency graph	DependencyGraph
ExprToCGExpr.cs	From Expr to GCExpr	CGExpressionBuilder
PathConditions.cs	Evaluation conditions	*PathCond* (CachedAtom, Conj, Disj)
ProgramLines.cs	Sequenced expressions	ComputeCell, IDepend, ProgramLines, UnwrapInputCell
SdfManager.cs	SDF management	SdfInfo, SdfManager
SdfTypes.cs	Types for SDFs	ExternalFunction, *SdfType* (ArrayType, FunctionType, SimpleType)
Variable.cs	Variables in SDFs	*Variable* (LocalVariable, LocalArgument)

Figure A.1: Source files for compiling sheet-defined functions (Funcalc), all in namespace Corecalc.Funcalc, and all in subdirectory Funcalc. Abstract types are in *italics*. Local subtypes are shown in parentheses.

The current (June 2014) size of the source code is around 12,200 lines, including sparse comments. When compiled for Microsoft .NET [101], the size of the funcalc.exe executable and supporting libraries is just over 300 KB.

File	Contents	Classes
CellAddressing.cs	Cell addresses	CellAddr, FullCellAddr, Interval, RARef, *SupportRange* (SupportArea, SupportCell)
Cells.cs	Sheet cell contents	ArrayFormula, CachedArrayFormula, *Cell*, CellState, *ConstCell* (BlankCell, NumberCell, QuoteCell, TextCell), Formula
Expressions.cs	Expression AST	CellArea, CellRef, *Const* (Error, NumberConst, TextConst, ValueConst), *Expr*, FunCall, IExpressionVisitor, RefSet
Functions.cs	Built-in functions	Function
Program.cs	Main program	Program
Sheet.cs	Worksheets	Sheet
Types.cs	Auxiliary types	Applier, CyclicException, Formats, HashBag, HashList, ValueCache, ValueTable
Values.cs	Run-time values	*ArrayValue* (ArrayDouble, ArrayExplicit, ArrayView), ErrorValue, FunctionValue, NumberValue, ObjectValue, TextValue, *Value*
Workbook.cs	Workbooks	Workbook
Coco/Spreadsheet.ATG	Parser specification	
GUI/AboutBox.cs	An "about" dialog	AboutBox
GUI/GUI.cs	Cell grid, sheet tabs	ClipBoardCell, SheetTab, WorkbookForm
GUI/SDF.cs	SDF list	SdfForm
IO/WorkbookIO.cs	Spreadsheet import	IOFormat, XMLSSIOFormat

Figure A.2: Source files for core interpretive spreadsheet functionality (Corecalc), all in namespace Corecalc.

Appendix B

Patents and Applications

This is a list of U.S. patents (label USnnnnnnn) and U.S. patent applications (label USyyyynnnnnn) cited in this book, each with a brief summary. The date shown in the format yyyy-mm-dd is the date granted for patents and the date of submission for applications.

A list of all U.S. patents and patent applications that seem related to spreadsheet implementation, not just spreadsheet application, can be found in an accompanying technical report [140] from the IT University of Copenhagen.

The full text of the patent documents themselves can be obtained in PDF from the European Patent Office [114], in HTML from the U.S. Patents and Trademarks Office [154], and in multiple formats at Google Patents [69]. Simply search using the patent number USnnnnnnn or the patent application number USyyyynnnnnn.

Disclaimer: Neither the author nor the IT University of Copenhagen nor MIT Press can assume any responsibility for the completeness of the list or the correctness and completeness of the summaries, nor for any legal, technical, or monetary consequences of using the list and the summaries.

1. Parser, code generator, and data calculation and transformation engine for spreadsheet calculations; US8209661; 2012-06-26. By Michael Rubin and Michael Smialek. Describes compilation of spreadsheets to Java source code. There are other patents with the same title and by the same authors: US7010779 and US7836425.

2. Method and apparatus for formula evaluation in spreadsheets on small devices; US7793210; 2010-09-07. By Paul Rank and John Pampuch. Describes the idea, but few technical details, of cross-compilation of spreadsheet formulas for space-conserving execution on small mobile devices, such as a personal digital assistant (PDA). This involves, for instance, leaving out unused library functions.

3. Method and system for multithread processing of spreadsheet chain calculations; US7533139; 2009-05-12. By Bruce Jones and others; assigned to Microsoft. Describes multiprocessor recalculation of spreadsheet formulas and, by the way, also describes a uniprocessor implementation, probably similar to that of Excel.

4. User-defined spreadsheet functions; US7266763; 2007-09-04. By Simon Peyton Jones, Alan Blackwell, and Margaret Burnett; application by Microsoft. Describes the concepts presented also in their paper [120].

5. Program/method for converting spreadsheet models to callable, compiled routines; US2006090156; 2006-04-27. By Richard Tanenbaum. Closely related to application 6.

6. Program/method for converting spreadsheet models to callable, compiled routines; US2005193379; 2005-09-01. By Richard Tanenbaum. How to compile spreadsheet formulas to C source code. Closely related to application 5.

7. Method in connection with a spreadsheet program; US2003226105; 2003-12-04. By Mattias Waldau. Describes cross-compilation to another platform, such as a mobile phone or web service. This is a technically substantial patent with references to relevant prior art, such as Schlafly's patents, numbers 13 and 15 in this list. It describes compilation to dynamically typed and statically typed languages (JavaScript and Java), and how to present the generated code as a WML service, say. Probably the technology described by this application is that used in the SpreadsheetConverter product [60].

8. Methods and systems for generating a structured language model from a spreadsheet model; US6766512; 2004-07-20. By Farzad Khosrowshahi and Murray Woloshin at JP Morgan & Co; assigned to Furraylogic Ltd. Compiling a spreadsheet model, with designated input cells and output cells, to code for a function in a procedural programming language.

9. Methodology for testing spreadsheet grids; US6766509; 2004-07-20. By Andrei Sheretov, Margaret Burnett, and Gregg Rothermel; assigned to University of Oregon. Two methods for using definition-use-associations to test spreadsheets; in the more advanced method, the testing of a single representative cell can increase the testedness of a range of cells containing similar formulas.

10. Methodology for testing spreadsheets; US6948154; 2005-09-20. By Gregg Rothermel, Margaret Burnett, and Lixin Li; assigned to University of Oregon. Uses du-associations to gradually test a spreadsheet, displaying each cell's degree of testedness.

11. Constraint-based spreadsheet system capable of displaying a process of execution of programs; US5799295; 1998-08-25. By Yasuo Nagai; assigned to Tokyo Shibaura Electric Co. A spreadsheet based on constraints in addition to formulas.

12. Method and system of sharing common formulas in a spreadsheet program and adjusting the same to conform with editing operations; US5742835; 1998-04-21. By Richard Kaethler; assigned to Microsoft. Very similar to patent 14. First, describes a technique to identify identical formulas in a contiguous block of cells and to share a single representation of the formula between all cells in the block. The need for this presupposes a particular formula representation, which is not made explicit but clearly is different from that chosen in Corecalc. Second, notes that the sharing makes insertion and deletion of entire rows and columns more complicated, should they happen to intersect with a block.

   This problem is the same as that discussed in section 2.19, but the patent's solution makes a point of creating small cell blocks, distinguishing between blocks with 1 to 4, 5 to 16, and 16 or more columns; and with 1 to 15, 16 to 31, 31 to 48, and 49 to 200 rows. The point of this distinction is not clear.

   Maybe a faulty implementation of this approach caused bugs number KB171339 ("Some values not recalculated when using multiple formulas") and KB154134 ("Functions in filled formulas may not be recalculated") in Excel'97 [110].

13. Methods for compiling formulas stored in an electronic spreadsheet system; US5633998; 1997-05-27. By Roger Schlafly; assigned to Borland. Related to patent 15.

14. Method and system of sharing common formulas in a spreadsheet program and adjusting the same to conform with editing operations; US5553215; 1996-09-03. By Richard

Kaethler; assigned to Microsoft. Very similar to patent 12.

15. Electronic spreadsheet system and methods for compiling a formula stored in a spreadsheet into native machine code for execution by a floating-point unit upon spreadsheet recalculation; US5471612; 1995-11-28. By Roger Schlafly; assigned to Borland. Unusually well written and technically substantial (see sections 1.11 and 6.5).

16. Method of bidirectional recalculation; US5339410; 1994-08-16. By Naoki Kanai; assigned to IBM. Proposes to replace the standard unidirectional computation by bidirectional constraints. This seems to require formulas to be inverted, which isn't possible in general.

17. Method for optimal recalculation; US5276607; 1994-01-04. By Bret Harris and Lewis Bastian; assigned to WordPerfect Corporation (see section 3.3.7).

18. Process and apparatus for converting a source program into an object program; US4398249; 1983-08-09. By Rene K. Pardo and Remy Landau. Describes a procedure to compile spreadsheet-like definitions in dependency order; essentially an implementation of topological sorting, although that term is not used. Patent application filed 1970, granted 1983, and ruled unenforceable 1996 (see section 1.11 and [86]).

Bibliography

[1] Robin Abraham, Margaret Burnett, and Martin Erwig. Spreadsheet programming. In B.J. Wah, editor, *Encyclopedia of Computer Science and Engineering*, pages 2804–2810. Wiley, 2009.

[2] Robin Abraham and Martin Erwig. Header and unit inference for spreadsheets through spatial analyses. In *IEEE Symposium on Visual Languages and Human-Centric Computing (VL/HCC'04)*, pages 165–172, 2004. At http://web.engr.oregonstate.edu/~erwig/papers/HeaderInf_VLHCC04.pdf on 9 June 2013.

[3] Robin Abraham and Martin Erwig. Inferring templates from spreadsheets. In *ICSE '06: Proceeding of the 28th international conference on Software engineering*, pages 182–191. ACM Press, 2006.

[4] Robin Abraham and Martin Erwig. Type inference for spreadsheets. In *PPDP '06: Proceedings of the 8th ACM SIGPLAN Symposium on Principles and Practice of Declarative Programming*, pages 73–84. ACM Press, 2006.

[5] Robin Abraham and Martin Erwig. Ucheck: A spreadsheet type checker for end users. *Journal of Visual Languages and Computing*, 18(1):71–95, February 2007.

[6] Yanif Ahmad, Tudor Antoniu, Sharon Goldwater, and Shriram Krishnamurthi. A type system for statically detecting spreadsheet errors. In *18th IEEE International Conference on Automated Software Engineering (ASE'03)*, pages 174–183, 2003.

[7] A.V. Aho, M. Lam, R. Sethi, and J.D. Ullman. *Compilers: Principles, Techniques, and Tools*. Addison-Wesley, 2006.

[8] Tudor Antoniu et al. Validating the unit correctness of spreadsheet programs. In *ICSE '04: Proceedings of the 26th International Conference on Software Engineering*, pages 439–448. IEEE Computer Society, 2004.

[9] SpreadSheets as a Programming Paradigm. Project homepage. Website. At http://ssaapp.di.uminho.pt/ on 10 May 2014.

[10] Lennart Augustsson, Howard Mansell, and Ganesh Sittampalam. Paradise: A two-stage DSL embedded in Haskell. In *International Conference on Functional Programming (ICFP'08)*, pages 225–228. ACM, September 2008.

[11] Yirsaw Ayalew. *Spreadsheet Testing Using Interval Analysis*. PhD thesis, Institut für Informatik-Systeme, Universität Klagenfurt, 2001. At http://www.isys.uni-klu.ac.at/PDF/2001-0125-YA.pdf on 9 June 2013.

[12] Dermot Balson and Jerzy Tyszkiewicz. User defined spreadsheet functions in Excel. Presentation, EuSpRiG 2012, July 2012. At http://www.eusprig.org/presentations-2012.htm on 5 January 2014.

[13] Michael A. Bender, Jeremy T. Fineman, Seth Gilbert, and Robert E. Tarjan. A new approach to incremental cycle detection and related problems. Preprint, December 2011. At http://arxiv.org/abs/1112.0784 on 15 June 2013.

[14] Lee Benfield. FMD: functional development in Excel. At Commercial Users of Functional Programming (CUFP), Edinburgh 2009 ACM SIGPLAN. Video presentation, 2009. At http://cufp.org/videos/fmd-functional-development-excel on 12 January 2014.

[15] Fischer Black and Myron Scholes. The pricing of options and corporate liabilities. *Journal of Political Economy*, 81(3):637–654, 1973.

[16] Sylvan C. Bloch. *Excel for Engineers and Scientists*. Wiley, second edition, 2003.

[17] Luca Bolognese. Excel financial functions for .NET. Website, 2009. At http://archive.msdn.microsoft.com/FinancialFunctions on 9 June 2013.

[18] Anders Bondorf. Automatic autoprojection of higher order recursive equations. *Science of Computer Programming*, 17:3–34, 1991.

[19] Anders Bondorf and Olivier Danvy. Automatic autoprojection of recursive equations with global variables and abstract data types. *Science of Computer Programming*, 16:151–195, 1991.

[20] Borland. Antique software: Turbo Pascal v1.0. Website. At http://edn.embarcadero.com/article/20693 on 9 June 2013.

[21] Dan Bricklin. Visicalc information. Website. At http://www.danbricklin.com/visicalc.htm on 9 June 2013.

[22] Dan Bricklin. *Bricklin on technology*. John Wiley and Sons, 2009.

[23] Chris Browne. Linux spreadsheets. Website. At http://linuxfinances.info/info/spreadsheets.html on 5 January 2014.

[24] Poul Brønnum. Type analysis for sheet-defined functions. Master's thesis, IT University of Copenhagen, 2009.

[25] Mikhail A. Bulyonkov Polyvariant mixed computation for analyzer programs. *Acta Informatica*, 21:473–484, 1984.

[26] William H. Burge *Recursive Programming Techniques*. Addison-Wesley, 1975.

[27] Margaret Burnett, John Attwood, and Zachary Welch. Implementing level 4 liveness in declarative visual programming languages. In *1998 IEEE Symposium on Visual Languages*, pages 126–133. IEEE, 1998.

[28] Margaret Burnett et al. Forms/3: A first-order visual language to explore the boundaries of the spreadsheet paradigm. *Journal of Functional Programming*, 11(2):155–206, March 2001.

[29] Margaret Burnett, Andrei Sheretov, Bing Ren, and Gregg Rothermel. Testing homogeneous spreadsheet grids with the "what you see is what you test" methodology. *IEEE Transactions on Software Engineering*, 28(6):576–594, 2002.

[30] Rommert J. Casimir. Real programmers don't use spreadsheets. *ACM SIGPLAN Notices*, 27(6):10–16, June 1992.

[31] Chris Chambers and Martin Erwig. Dimension inference in spreadsheets. In *IEEE Symposium on Visual Languages and Human-Centric Computing, VLHCC'08*, pages 123–130. IEEE Computer Society, 2008.

[32] Mani Chandy and Jayadev Misra. *Parallel Program Design*. Addison-Wesley, 1988.

[33] Tie Cheng and Xavier Rival. An abstract domain to infer types over zones in spreadsheets. In Antoine Miné and David Schmidt, editors, *Static Analysis - 19th International Symposium, SAS 2012, Deauville, France. Lecture Notes in Computer Science, vol. 7460*, pages 94–110. Springer, 2012.

[34] Chris Clack and Lee Braine. Object-oriented functional spreadsheets. In *Proceedings of the 10th Glasgow Workshop on Functional Programming (GlaFP'97)*, September 1997.

[35] Michael Coblenz. Using objects of measurements to detect spreadsheet errors. Technical Report CMU-CS-05-150, School of Computer Science, Carnegie Mellon University, July 2005. At http://reports-archive.adm.cs.cmu.edu/anon/2005/CMU-CS-05-150.pdf on 9 June 2013.

[36] James W. Cooley and John W. Tukey. An algorithm for the machine calculation of complex Fourier series. *Mathematics of Computation*, 19:297–301, 1965.

[37] Daniel S. Cortes and Morten Hansen. User-defined functions in spreadsheets. Master's thesis, IT University of Copenhagen, September 2006.

[38] Jácome Cunha et al. MDSheet: A framework for model-driven spreadsheet engineering. In *International Conference of Software Engineering (ICSE)*, pages 1412–1415, 2012.

[39] Jácome Cunha, João Saraiva, and Joost Visser. From spreadsheets to relational databases and back. In *Partial Evaluation and Program Manipulation (PEPM)*, pages 179–188. ACM, 2009.

[40] Tony Davie and Kevin Hammond. Functional hypersheets. In *Eighth International Workshop on Implementation of Functional Languages*, pages 39–48, 1996. At http://www-fp.dcs.st-and.ac.uk/~kh/papers/Hypersheets/Hypersheets.html on 9 June 2013.

[41] Walter de Hoon. Designing a spreadsheet in a pure functional graph rewriting language. Master's thesis, University of Nijmegen, 1993.

[42] Walter de Hoon, Luc Rutten, and Marko van Eekelen. Implementing a functional spreadsheet in Clean. *Journal of Functional Programming*, 5(3):383–414, 1995.

[43] Stefano de Pascale and Eero Hyvönen. An extended interval arithmetic library for Microsoft Excel. Research report, VTT Information Technology, Espöö, Finland, 1994.

[44] Decision Models. Excel pages – calculation secrets. Website. At http://www.decisionmodels.com/calcsecrets.htm on 22 October 2013.

[45] Decision Models. Homepage. Website. At http://www.decisionmodels.com/ on 9 June 2013.

[46] Nachum Dershowitz and Edward M. Reingold. *Calendrical calculations*. Cambridge University Press, third edition, 2008.

[47] Jack Doweck. Inside Intel core microarchitecture and smart memory access. Whitepaper, 2006. At http://software.intel.com/sites/default/files/m/3/4/d/6/3/18374-sma.pdf on 11 June 2013.

[48] Weichang Du and William W. Wadge. The eductive implementation of a three-dimensional spreadsheet. *Software Practice and Experience*, 20(11):1097–1114, 1990.

[49] Ecma TC39 TG3. *Common Language Infrastructure (CLI). Standard ECMA-335*. Ecma International, sixth edition, June 2012.

[50] John English. *Ada 95: The Craft of Object-Oriented Programming*. Prentice-Hall, 1997. At http://faculty.cs.wwu.edu/reedyc/AdaResources/bookhtml/contents.htm on 9 June 2013.

[51] Martin Erwig and Margaret M. Burnett. Adding apples and oranges. In Shriram Krishnamurthi and C. R. Ramakrishnan, editors, *PADL '02: Proceedings of the 4th International Symposium on Practical Aspects of Declarative Languages. Lecture Notes in Computer Science, vol. 2257*, pages 173–191. Springer-Verlag, 2002.

[52] Martin Erwig et al. Gencel: A program generator for correct spreadsheets. *Journal of Functional Programming*, 16(3):293–325, 2006.

[53] European Spreadsheet Risks Interest Group. Homepage. Website. At http://www.eusprig.org/ on 9 June 2013.

[54] EUSES Consortium. End users shaping effective software. Website. At http://eusesconsortium.org/ on 5 January 2014.

[55] Excel DNA Project. Homepage. At http://exceldna.codeplex.com/ on 28 February 2014.

[56] Raphael A. Finkel and Jon L. Bentley. Quad trees as a data structure for retrieval on composite keys. *Acta Informatica*, 4(1):1–9, 1974.

[57] Marc Fisher et al. Integrating automated test generation into the WYSIWYT spreadsheet testing methodology. *ACM Transactions on Software Engineering Methodology*, 15(2):150–194, 2006.

[58] Marc Fisher and Gregg Rothermel. The EUSES spreadsheet corpus: A shared resource for supporting experimentation with spreadsheet dependability mechanisms. In *First workshop on end-user software engineering (WEUSE)*, pages 1–5. ACM, 2005.

[59] Marc Fisher, Gregg Rothermel, Tyler Creelan, and Margaret Burnett. Scaling a dataflow testing methodology to the multiparadigm world of commercial spreadsheets. In *17th International Symposium on Software Reliability Engineering*, pages 13–22. IEEE, 2006.

[60] Framtidsforum. SpreadsheetConverter. Website. At http://www.spreadsheetconverter.com/ on 9 June 2013.

[61] Joe Francoeur. Algorithms using Java for spreadsheet dependent cell recomputation. Technical Report cs.DS/0301036v2, arXiv, June 2003. At http://arxiv.org/abs/cs.DS/0301036 on 9 June 2013.

[62] Joe Francoeur. Personal communication, August 2006.

[63] Bob Frankston. Implementing VisiCalc. Website, April 2003. At http://www.frankston.com/public/?name=implementingVisicalc on 9 June 2013.

[64] Erich Gamma et al. *Design Patterns: Elements of Reusable Object-Oriented Software*. Addison-Wesley, 1994.

[65] Michael R. Garey and David S. Johnson *Computers and Intractability. A Guide to the Theory of NP-Completeness*. W.H. Freeman, 1979.

[66] Gnumeric. Homepage. Website. At http://projects.gnome.org/gnumeric/ on 9 June 2013.

[67] David Goldberg. What every computer scientist should know about floating-point arithmetic. *Computing Surveys*, 23(1):5–48, March 1991.

[68] Google. Google docs and spreadsheets. Website. At http://docs.google.com/ on 9 June 2013.

[69] Google. Google patent search. Website. At http://patents.google.com/ on 9 June 2013.

[70] Vincent Granet. The XXL spreadsheet project. *Linux Journal*, April 1999. At http://www.linuxjournal.com/article/3186 on 9 June 2013.

[71] Sumit Gulwani, William R. Harris, and Rishabh Singh. Spreadsheet data manipulation using examples. *Communications of the ACM*, 55(8):97–105, August 2012.

[72] Phong Ha and Quan Vi Tran. Brugerdefinerede funktioner i Excel (User-defined functions in Excel). Master's thesis, IT University of Copenhagen, June 2006. In Danish.

[73] John F. Hart et al. *Computer Approximations*. Wiley, 1968.

[74] Haskell. Homepage. Website. At http://www.haskell.org/ on 9 June 2013.

[75] John Hatcliff, Torben Mogensen, and Peter Thiemann, editors. *Partial Evaluation: Practice and Theory: DIKU 1998 International Summer School*, volume 1706 of *Lecture Notes in Computer Science*. Springer-Verlag, 1998.

[76] Felienne Hermans. *Analyzing and visualizing spreadsheets*. PhD thesis, Technical University of Delft, September 2012. At http://figshare.com/articles/Analyzing_and_Visualizing_Spreadsheets/658936 on 5 January 2014.

[77] Carsten Kehler Holst. Poor man's generalization. Note, August 1988. 2 pages.

[78] Eero Hyvönen and Stefano de Pascale. Interval computations on the spreadsheet. In R. B. Kearfott and V. Kreinovich, editors, *Applications of Interval Computations, Applied Optimization*, pages 169–209. Kluwer, 1996.

[79] Eero Hyvönen and Stefano de Pascale. A new basis for spreadsheet computing. Interval Solver(TM) for Microsoft Excel. In *11th Conference on Innovative Applications of Artificial Intelligence (IAAI-99)*, pages 799–806. AAAI Press, 1999. At http://www.mcs.vuw.ac.nz/~elvis/db/references/NBSSC.pdf on 9 June 2013.

[80] I-Nth. Bibliography of spreadsheet errors and testing literature. Website. At http://www.i-nth.com/resources/bibliography on 5 January 2014.

[81] IEEE. IEEE standard for floating-point arithmetics. IEEE Std 754-2008, 2008.

[82] Knowledge Dynamics Inc. Kdcalc. Website. At http://www.kdcalc.com/ on 9 June 2013.

[83] Tomás Isakowitz, Shimon Schocken, and Henry C. Lucas. Toward a logical/physical theory of spreadsheet modeling. *ACM Transactions on Information Systems*, 13(1):1–37, 1995.

[84] Thomas S. Iversen. Runtime code generation to speed up spreadsheet computations. Master's thesis, DIKU, University of Copenhagen, August 2006. At http://www.itu.dk/people/sestoft/funcalc/Iversen2006.pdf on 9 June 2013.

[85] Neil D. Jones, Carsten Gomard, and Peter Sestoft. *Partial Evaluation and Automatic Program Generation*. Prentice Hall, 1993. At http://www.itu.dk/people/sestoft/pebook/pebook.html on 9 June 2013.

[86] Brian Kahin. The software patent crisis. *Technology Review, MIT*, April 1990. At http://antipatents.8m.com/software-patents.html on 9 June 2013.

[87] Gilles Kahn. Natural semantics. In F.J. Brandenburg, G. Vidal-Naquet, and M. Wirsing, editors, *STACS 87. 4th Annual Symposium on Theoretical Aspects of Computer Science, Passau, Germany (Lecture Notes in Computer Science, vol. 247)*, pages 22–39. Springer-Verlag, 1987.

[88] Loreen La Penna. Recalculation in Microsoft Excel 2002. Web page, October 2001. At http://msdn.microsoft.com/en-us/library/office/aa140058(v=office.10).aspx on 9 June 2013.

[89] Xavier Leroy. The Zinc experiment: An economical implementation of the ML language. Rapport Technique 117, INRIA Rocquencourt, France, 1990. At http://gallium.inria.fr/~xleroy/publi/ZINC.pdf on 9 June 2013.

[90] Art Lew and Richard Halverson. A FCCM for dataflow (spreadsheet) programs. In *FCCM '95: Proceedings of the IEEE Symposium on FPGA's for Custom Computing Machines*, pages 2–10. IEEE Computer Society, 1995.

[91] Serge Lidin. *.NET 2.0 IL Assembler*. Apress, 2006.

[92] Tim Lindholm, Frank Yellin, Gilad Bracha, and Alex Buckley. *The Java Virtual Machine Specification*. Oracle, Java SE 7 edition, 2013. At http://docs.oracle.com/javase/specs/jvms/se7/jvms7.pdf on 15 June 2013.

[93] Björn Lisper and Johan Malmström. Haxcel: A spreadsheet interface to haskell. In *14th International Workshop on the Implementation of Functional Languages*, pages 206–222, 2002. At http://www.mrtc.mdh.se/publications/0435.pdf on 9 June 2013.

[94] Haibo Luo. ILVisualizer. Homepage. At http://blogs.msdn.com/b/haibo_luo/archive/2010/04/19/9998595.aspx on 9 June 2013.

[95] Martin Manns. Pyspread. Website, 2013. At http://manns.github.io/pyspread/ on 5 January 2014.

[96] Bill Manville. Update linked cells within a workbook??? ExcelBanter online forum posting, reply 20 January, 2005. At http://www.excelbanter.com/showthread.php?t=557 on 13 June 2013.

[97] Chuck Martin. sc. Website. At http://freecode.com/projects/sc on 9 June 2013.

[98] Michael Meeks and Jody Goldberg. A discussion of the new dependency code, version 0.3. Code documentation, October 2003. File doc/developer/Dependencies.txt in Gnumeric source distribution. At http://www.gnome.org/projects/gnumeric/.

[99] Microsoft. Microsoft Composition. Website. At http://www.nuget.org/packages/microsoft.composition on 13 January 2014.

[100] Microsoft. Microsoft Extensibility Framework. Website. At http://mef.codeplex.com/ on 13 January 2014.

[101] Microsoft. .NET framework. Website. At http://msdn.microsoft.com/en-us/vstudio/aa496123 on 9 June 2013.

[102] Microsoft. Office online. Website. At http://office.microsoft.com/ on 9 June 2013.

[103] Robin Milner, Mads Tofte, Robert Harper, and David B. MacQueen *The Definition of Standard ML (Revised)*. The MIT Press, 1997.

[104] Vincens Riber Mink and Daniel Schiermer. Collaborative spreadsheet. BSc thesis, IT University of Copenhagen, May 2010.

[105] Roland Mittermeir and Markus Clermont. Finding high-level structures in spreadsheet programs. In Arie van Deursen and Elizabeth Burd, editors, *Proceedings of the 9th Working Conference in Reverse Engineering, Richmond, VA, USA*, pages 221–232. IEEE Computer Society, 2002.

[106] Hanspeter Mössenböck, Albrecht Wöß, and Markus Löberbauer. The compiler generator Coco/R. Website. At http://www.ssw.uni-linz.ac.at/Coco/ on 9 June 2013.

[107] Bonnie A. Nardi and James R. Miller. The spreadsheet interface: A basis for end-user programming. In D. Diaper et al., editors, *IFIP TC13 Third International Conference on Human-Computer Interaction (INTERACT)*, pages 977–983. North-Holland, 1990. At http://www.miramontes.com/writing/spreadsheet-eup/ on 5 May 2014.

[108] Bonnie A. Nardi and James R. Miller. Twinkling lights and nested loops: distributed problem solving and spreadsheet development. *International Journal of Man-Machine Studies*, 34:161–184, 1991.

[109] Microsoft Developer Network. Excel primary interop assembly reference. Class ApplicationClass. Website. At http://msdn.microsoft.com/en-us/library/microsoft.office.interop.excel.applicationclass.aspx on 9 June 2013.

[110] Microsoft Developer Network. XL97: How to obtain the Excel 97 auto recalculation patch. Website, January 2007. At http://support.microsoft.com/kb/q174868/ on 15 June 2013.

[111] Gregory Neverov and Paul Roe. Cross-stage persistence in Metaphor. In *First MetaOCaml Workshop, Vancouver, Canada*, pages 168–185, October 2004.

[112] H.R. Nielson and F. Nielson. *Semantics with Applications. An Appetizer*. Springer-Verlag, 2007.

[113] Fabian Nuñez. An extended spreadsheet paradigm for data visualisation systems, and its implementation. Master's thesis, University of Cape Town, November 2000.

[114] European Patent Office. Espacenet. Website. At http://worldwide.espacenet.com/ on 9 June 2013.

[115] OpenOffice. Calc – the all-purpose spreadsheet. Website. At http://www.openoffice.org/product/calc.html on 9 June 2013.

[116] Niek Otten. Re: Ctrl+Alt+F9 not performing full recalculation on some PCs. Excel Forum posting, 8 October 2006, 2006. At http://www.excelforum.com/excel-worksheet-functions/570413-ctrl-alt-f9-not-performing-full-recalculation-on-some-pcs.html on 9 June 2013.

[117] Jocelyn Paine. Defining Excel functions without Visual Basic: a compiler that converts Excel function definition sheets to VBA. Website. At http://www.j-paine.org/dobbs/udfs.html on 5 January 2014.

[118] Ray Panko. Spreadsheet research. Website. At http://panko.shidler.hawaii.edu/SSR/ on 5 January 2014.

[119] Einar Pehrson. Cleansheets. Website. At http://freecode.com/projects/csheets.

[120] Simon Peyton Jones, Alan Blackwell, and Margaret Burnett. A user-centred approach to functions in Excel. In *ICFP '03: Proceedings of the Eighth ACM SIGPLAN International Conference on Functional Programming*, pages 165–176. ACM, 2003.

[121] Kurt W. Piersol. Object-oriented spreadsheets: the analytic spreadsheet package. In *Conference Proceedings on Object-Oriented Programming Systems, Languages and Applications (OOPSLA'86), Portland, Oregon*, pages 385–390. ACM Press, 1986.

[122] Morten Poulsen and Poul Serek. Optimized recalculation for spreadsheets with the use of support graph. Master's thesis, IT University of Copenhagen, Denmark, 2007.

[123] Jonas Druedahl Rask and Simon Eikeland Timmermann. Funsheet. Integration of sheet-defined functions in Excel using C#. Master's thesis, IT University of Copenhagen, June 2014.

[124] ReportingEngines. Formula One for Java. Website. At http://www.mit.edu/~mbarker/formula1/ on 9 June 2013.

[125] Jeffrey Richter. *CLR via C#*. Microsoft Press, fourth edition, 2012.

[126] Boaz Ronen, Michael A. Palley, and Henry C. Lucas. Spreadsheet analysis and design. *Communications of the ACM*, 32(1):84–93, 1989.

[127] Gregg Rothermel et al. A methodology for testing spreadsheets. *ACM Transactions on Software Engineering Methodology*, 10(1):110–147, 2001.

[128] Gregg Rothermel, Lixin Li, and Margaret Burnett. Testing strategies for form-based visual programs. In *Eighth International Symposium on Software Reliability Engineering*, pages 96–107. IEEE Computer Society, 1997.

[129] Gregg Rothermel, Lixin Li, C. DuPuis, and Margaret Burnett. What you see is what you test: a methodology for testing form-based visual programs. In *20th International Conference on Software Engineering*, pages 198–207. IEEE Computer Society, 1998.

[130] Erik Ruf. *Topics in Online Partial Evaluation*. PhD thesis, Stanford University, California, February 1993. Published as technical report CSL-TR-93-563.

[131] Erik Ruf and Daniel Weise. Opportunities for online partial evaluation. Technical Report CSL-TR-92-516, Computer Systems Laboratory, Stanford University, Stanford, CA, April 1992.

[132] Jonathan Sachs. Recollections: Developing Lotus 1-2-3. *IEEE Annals of the History of Computing*, 29(3):41–48, July-September 2007.

[133] Jorma Sajaniemi. Modeling spreadsheet audit: a rigorous approach to automatic visualization. *Journal of Visual Languages and Computing*, 11(1):49–82, 2000.

[134] Nader Salas. Collaborative spreadsheet with traceability. Master's thesis, IT University of Copenhagen, August 2011.

[135] Chris Scaffidi, Mary Shaw, and Brad Myers. Estimating the numbers of end users and end user programmers. In *IEEE Symposium on Visual Languages and Human-Centric Computing*, pages 207–214, 2005.

[136] Russell Schulz. comp.apps.spreadsheet FAQ. Newsgroup, June 2002. At http://www.faqs.org/faqs/spreadsheets/faq/ on 9 June 2013.

[137] Peter Sestoft. A Spreadsheet Core Implementation in C#. Technical Report ITU-TR-2006-91, IT University of Copenhagen, September 2006. 135 pages.

[138] Peter Sestoft. Numeric performance in C, C# and Java. Technical report, IT University of Copenhagen, February 2009. 14 pages. At http://www.itu.dk/people/sestoft/papers/numericperformance.pdf on 9 June 2013.

[139] Peter Sestoft. Online partial evaluation of sheet-defined functions. In A. Banerjee, O. Danvy, K. Doh, and J. Hatcliff, editors, *Semantics, Abstract Interpretation, and Reasoning about Programs*, volume 129 of *Electronic Proceedings in Theoretical Computer Science*, pages 136–160, 2013.

[140] Peter Sestoft. Spreadsheet patents. Technical Report ITU-TR-2014-178, IT University of Copenhagen, 2014. ISBN 978-87-7949-317-9. (To appear).

[141] Peter Sestoft and Jens Zeilund Sørensen. Sheet-defined functions: implementation and initial evaluation. In Y. Dittrich et al., editors, *International Symposium on End-User Development, June 2013*, volume 7897 of *Lecture Notes in Computer Science*, pages 88–103, 2013.

[142] Charles Severance. An interview with William Kahan. *IEEE Computer*, 31(3):114–115, March 1998.

[143] Bradford L. Smith. Abykus. An object-oriented spreadsheet for windows. Website. At http://www.abykus.com/ on 9 June 2013.

[144] EUSES: End Users Shaping Effective Software. Wysiwyt: What you see is what you test. Website. At http://eusesconsortium.org/wysiwyt.php on 9 June 2013.

[145] Michael Sperber et al., editors. *Revised [6] Report on the Algorithmic Language Scheme*. Cambridge University Press, 2010.

[146] SpreadsheetGear LLC. SpreadsheetGear for .NET. Website. At http://www.spreadsheetgear.com/ on 9 June 2013.

[147] Marc Stadelmann. A spreadsheet based on constraints. In *UIST '93: Proceedings of the 6th Annual ACM Symposium on User Interface Software and Technology*, pages 217–224. ACM Press, 1993.

[148] Statfactory Ltd.. FCell add-in. Webpage. At http://www.statfactory.co.uk/fcell-add-in/ on 12 January 2014.

[149] Jørgen Staunstrup. *A Formal Approach to Program Design*. Kluwer, 1994.

[150] Microsoft Support. How formula calculations are performed in Excel. Website, September 2011. At http://support.microsoft.com/kb/825012 on 5 January 2014.

[151] Jens Zeilund Sørensen. An evaluation of sheet-defined financial functions in Funcalc. Master's thesis, IT University of Copenhagen, March 2012.

[152] S. Tanimoto. Viva: A visual language for image processing. *Journal of Visual Languages & Computing*, 1(2):127–139, June 1990.

[153] United States Court of Appeals for the Federal Circuit. Refac versus Lotus. Opinion 95-1350, April 1996. At http://caselaw.findlaw.com/us-federal-circuit/1339862.html on 9 June 2013.

[154] United States Patent and Trademark Office. Patent full-text and full-page image databases. Website. At http://patft.uspto.gov/ on 9 June 2013.

[155] Usenet. comp.apps.spreadsheet. Newsgroup.

[156] Johannes G. van der Corput. Verteilungsfunktionen. *Proc. Ned. Akad. v. Wet.*, 38:813–821, 1935.

[157] Michael van Schothorst et al. Relating microbiological criteria to food safety objectives and performance objectives. *Food Control*, 20:967–979, 2009.

[158] Noah Vawter. DFT multiply demo spreadsheet. Website, 2002. At http://www.gweep.net/~shifty/portfolio/fftmulspreadsheet/ on 9 June 2013.

[159] Andrew P. Wack. *Partitioning dependency graphs for concurrent execution: a parallel spreadsheet on a realistically modelled message passing environment*. PhD thesis, University of Delaware, 1995.

[160] David Wakeling. Spreadsheet functional programming. *Journal of Functional Programming*, 17(1):131–143, 2007.

[161] Guijun Wang and Allen Ambler. Solving display-based problems. In *IEEE Symposium on Visual Languages, Boulder, Colorado*, pages 122–129. IEEE Computer Society, 1996.

[162] Daniel Weise, Roland Conybeare, Erik Ruf, and Scott Seligman. Automatic online partial evaluation. In J. Hughes, editor, *Functional Programming Languages and Computer Architecture, Cambridge, Massachusetts, August 1991 (Lecture Notes in Computer Science, vol. 523)*, pages 165–191. Springer-Verlag, 1991.

[163] Wikipedia. Spreadsheet. Website. At http://en.wikipedia.org/wiki/Spreadsheet on 9 June 2013.

[164] Wikipedia. Visicalc. Website. At http://en.wikipedia.org/wiki/VisiCalc on 9 June 2013.

[165] Charles Williams. Excel and UDF performance stuff. Website. At http://fastexcel.wordpress.com/ on 5 January 2014.

[166] Stephen Wolfram. *The Mathematica Book*. Cambridge University Press, 1999.

[167] Alan G. Yoder and David L. Cohn. Architectural issues in spreadsheet languages. In *1994 Conference on Programming Languages and System Architectures. Lecture Notes in Computer Science, vol. 782*. Springer-Verlag, 1994. Also at http://www3.nd.edu/~csesoft/tech_reports/1993.html on 9 June 2013.

[168] Alan G. Yoder and David L. Cohn. Observations on spreadsheet languages, intension and dataflow. Technical Report TR-94-22, Computer Science and Engineering, University of Notre Dame, 1994. At http://www3.nd.edu/~csesoft/tech_reports/1994.html on 9 June 2013.

[169] Alan G. Yoder and David L. Cohn. Real spreadsheets for real programmers. In *Proceedings of the IEEE Computer Society 1994 International Conference on Computer Languages, May 16-19, 1994, Toulouse, France*, pages 20–30, 1994. At http://www3.nd.edu/~csesoft/tech_reports/1994.html on 9 June 2013.

[170] Alan G. Yoder and David L. Cohn. Domain-specific and general-purpose aspects of spreadsheet languages. In Sam Kamin, editor, *DSL '97 - First ACM SIGPLAN Workshop on Domain-Specific Languages, Paris, France*, University of Illinois Computer Science Report, pages 37–47, 1997.

Index